Praise

"A must-read resource for anyone who is serious about embracing the opportunity of big data."

— *Craig Vaughan*
Global Vice President at SAP

"This timely book says out loud what has finally become apparent: in the modern world, Data is Business, and you can no longer think business without *thinking data*. Read this book and you will understand the Science behind thinking data."

— *Ron Bekkerman*
Chief Data Officer at Carmel Ventures

"A great book for business managers who lead or interact with data scientists, who wish to better understand the principles and algorithms available without the technical details of single-disciplinary books."

— *Ronny Kohavi*
Partner Architect at Microsoft Online Services Division

"Provost and Fawcett have distilled their mastery of both the art and science of real-world data analysis into an unrivalled introduction to the field."

— *Geoff Webb*
Editor-in-Chief of *Data Mining and Knowledge Discovery* Journal

"I would love it if everyone I had to work with had read this book."

— *Claudia Perlich*
Chief Scientist of Dstillery and Advertising Research Foundation Innovation Award Grand Winner (2013)

Data Science for Business

Foster Provost and Tom Fawcett

Beijing · Cambridge · Farnham · Köln · Sebastopol · Tokyo

Data Science for Business

by Foster Provost and Tom Fawcett

Printed in the United States of America.

Published by O'Reilly Media, Inc., 1005 Gravenstein Highway North, Sebastopol, CA 95472.

O'Reilly books may be purchased for educational, business, or sales promotional use. Online editions are also available for most titles (*http://my.safaribooksonline.com*). For more information, contact our corporate/institutional sales department: 800-998-9938 or *corporate@oreilly.com*.

Editors: Mike Loukides and Meghan Blanchette	**Cover Designer:** Mark Paglietti
Production Editor: Christopher Hearse	**Interior Designer:** David Futato
Proofreader: Kiel Van Horn	**Illustrator:** Rebecca Demarest
Indexer: WordCo Indexing Services, Inc.	

July 2013:   First Edition

Revision History for the First Edition:

2013-07-25:   First release

2013-12-19:   Second release

See *http://oreilly.com/catalog/errata.csp?isbn=9781449361327* for release details.

ISBN: 978-1-449-36132-7

[LSI]

For our fathers.

Table of Contents

Fundamental concepts: Identifying informative attributes; Segmenting data by progressive attribute selection.

Exemplary techniques: Finding correlations; Attribute/variable selection; Tree induction.

Fundamental concepts: Finding "optimal" model parameters based on data; Choosing the goal for data mining; Objective functions; Loss functions.

Exemplary techniques: Linear regression; Logistic regression; Support-vector machines.

7. Decision Analytic Thinking I: What Is a Good Model?. 187

Fundamental concepts: Careful consideration of what is desired from data science results; Expected value as a key evaluation framework; Consideration of appropriate comparative baselines.

Exemplary techniques: Various evaluation metrics; Estimating costs and benefits; Calculating expected profit; Creating baseline methods for comparison.

8. Visualizing Model Performance. 209

Fundamental concepts: Visualization of model performance under various kinds of uncertainty; Further consideration of what is desired from data mining results.

Exemplary techniques: Profit curves; Cumulative response curves; Lift curves; ROC curves.

9. Evidence and Probabilities. 233

Fundamental concepts: Explicit evidence combination with Bayes' Rule; Probabilistic reasoning via assumptions of conditional independence.

Exemplary techniques: Naive Bayes classification; Evidence lift.

Fundamental concepts: The importance of constructing mining-friendly data representations; Representation of text for data mining.

Exemplary techniques: Bag of words representation; TFIDF calculation; N-grams; Stemming; Named entity extraction; Topic models.

Fundamental concept: Solving business problems with data science starts with analytical engineering: designing an analytical solution, based on the data, tools, and techniques available.

Exemplary technique: Expected value as a framework for data science solution design.

Fundamental concepts: Our fundamental concepts as the basis of many common data science techniques; The importance of familiarity with the building blocks of data science.

Exemplary techniques: Association and co-occurrences; Behavior profiling; Link prediction; Data reduction; Latent information mining; Movie recommendation; Bias-variance decomposition of error; Ensembles of models; Causal reasoning from data.

Fundamental concepts: Our principles as the basis of success for a data-driven business; Acquiring and sustaining competitive advantage via data science; The importance of careful curation of data science capability.

Preface

Data Science for Business is intended for several sorts of readers:

- Business people who will be working with data scientists, managing data science–oriented projects, or investing in data science ventures,
- Developers who will be implementing data science solutions, and
- Aspiring data scientists.

This is not a book about algorithms, nor is it a replacement for a book about algorithms. We deliberately avoided an algorithm-centered approach. We believe there is a relatively small set of fundamental concepts or principles that underlie techniques for extracting useful knowledge from data. These concepts serve as the *foundation* for many well-known algorithms of data mining. Moreover, these concepts underlie the analysis of data-centered business problems, the creation and evaluation of data science solutions, and the evaluation of general data science strategies and proposals. Accordingly, we organized the exposition around these general principles rather than around specific algorithms. Where necessary to describe procedural details, we use a combination of text and diagrams, which we think are more accessible than a listing of detailed algorithmic steps.

The book does not presume a sophisticated mathematical background. However, by its very nature the material is somewhat technical—the goal is to impart a significant understanding of data science, not just to give a high-level overview. In general, we have tried to minimize the mathematics and make the exposition as "conceptual" as possible.

Colleagues in industry comment that the book is invaluable for helping to align the understanding of the business, technical/development, and data science teams. That observation is based on a small sample, so we are curious to see how general it truly is (see Chapter 5!). Ideally, we envision a book that any data scientist would give to his collaborators from the development or business teams, effectively saying: if you really want to design/implement top-notch data science solutions to business problems, we all need to have a common understanding of this material.

Colleagues also tell us that the book has been quite useful in an unforeseen way: for preparing to interview data science job candidates. The demand from business for hiring data scientists is strong and increasing. In response, more and more job seekers are presenting themselves as data scientists. Every data science job candidate should understand the fundamentals presented in this book. (Our industry colleagues tell us that they are surprised how many do not. We have half-seriously discussed a follow-up pamphlet "Cliff's Notes to Interviewing for Data Science Jobs.")

Our Conceptual Approach to Data Science

In this book we introduce a collection of the most important fundamental concepts of data science. Some of these concepts are "headliners" for chapters, and others are introduced more naturally through the discussions (and thus they are not necessarily labeled as fundamental concepts). The concepts span the process from envisioning the problem, to applying data science techniques, to deploying the results to improve decision-making. The concepts also undergird a large array of business analytics methods and techniques.

The concepts fit into three general types:

1. Concepts about how data science fits in the organization and the competitive landscape, including ways to attract, structure, and nurture data science teams; ways for thinking about how data science leads to competitive advantage; and tactical concepts for doing well with data science projects.

2. General ways of thinking data-analytically. These help in identifying appropriate data and consider appropriate methods. The concepts include the *data mining process* as well as the collection of different *high-level data mining tasks*.

3. General concepts for actually extracting knowledge from data, which undergird the vast array of data science tasks and their algorithms.

For example, one fundamental concept is that of determining the similarity of two entities described by data. This ability forms the basis for various specific tasks. It may be used directly to *find* customers similar to a given customer. It forms the core of several *prediction* algorithms that estimate a target value such as the expected resource usage of a client or the probability of a customer to respond to an offer. It is also the basis for *clustering* techniques, which group entities by their shared features without a focused objective. Similarity forms the basis of *information retrieval*, in which documents or webpages relevant to a search query are retrieved. Finally, it underlies several common algorithms for *recommendation*. A traditional algorithm-oriented book might present each of these tasks in a different chapter, under different names, with common aspects buried in algorithm details or mathematical propositions. In this book we instead focus on the unifying concepts, presenting specific tasks and algorithms as natural manifestations of them.

As another example, in evaluating the utility of a pattern, we see a notion of *lift* — how much more prevalent a pattern is than would be expected by chance—recurring broadly across data science. It is used to evaluate very different sorts of patterns in different contexts. Algorithms for targeting advertisements are evaluated by computing the lift one gets for the targeted population. Lift is used to judge the weight of evidence for or against a conclusion. Lift helps determine whether a co-occurrence (an association) in data is interesting, as opposed to simply being a natural consequence of popularity.

We believe that explaining data science around such fundamental concepts not only aids the reader, it also facilitates communication between business stakeholders and data scientists. It provides a shared vocabulary and enables both parties to understand each other better. The shared concepts lead to deeper discussions that may uncover critical issues otherwise missed.

To the Instructor

This book has been used successfully as a textbook for a very wide variety of data science courses. Historically, the book arose from the development of Foster's multidisciplinary Data Science classes at the Stern School at NYU, starting in the fall of 2005.[1] The original class was nominally for MBA students and MSIS students, but drew students from schools across the university. The most interesting aspect of the class was not that it appealed to MBA and MSIS students, for whom it was designed. More interesting, it also was found to be very valuable by students with strong backgrounds in machine learning and other technical disciplines. Part of the reason seemed to be that the focus on fundamental principles and other issues besides algorithms was missing from their curricula.

At NYU we now use the book in support of a variety of data science–related programs: the original MBA and MSIS programs, undergraduate business analytics, NYU/Stern's new MS in Business Analytics program, and as the Introduction to Data Science for NYU's new MS in Data Science. In addition, (prior to publication) the book has been adopted by more than twenty other universities for programs in nine countries (and counting), in business schools, in computer science programs, and for more general introductions to data science.

Stay tuned to the books' websites (see below) for information on how to obtain helpful instructional material, including lecture slides, sample homework questions and prob-

---

1. Of course, each author has the distinct impression that he did the majority of the work on the book.

lems, example project instructions based on the frameworks from the book, exam questions, and more to come.

 We keep an up-to-date list of known adoptees on the book's website (*http://www.data-science-for-biz.com/*). Click *Who's Using It* at the top.

Other Skills and Concepts

There are many other concepts and skills that a practical data scientist needs to know besides the fundamental principles of data science. These skills and concepts will be discussed in Chapter 1 and Chapter 2. The interested reader is encouraged to visit the book's website for pointers to material for learning these additional skills and concepts (for example, scripting in Python, Unix command-line processing, datafiles, common data formats, databases and querying, big data architectures and systems like MapReduce and Hadoop, data visualization, and other related topics).

Sections and Notation

In addition to occasional footnotes, the book contains boxed "sidebars." These are essentially extended footnotes. We reserve these for material that we consider interesting and worthwhile, but too long for a footnote and too much of a digression for the main text.

 Technical Details Ahead — A note on the starred sections
The occasional mathematical details are relegated to optional "starred" sections. These section titles will have asterisk prefixes, and they will be preceeded by a paragraph rendered like this one. Such "starred" sections contain more detailed mathematics and/or more technical details than elsewhere, and these introductory paragraph explains its purpose. The book is written so that these sections may be skipped without loss of continuity, although in a few places we remind readers that details appear there.

Constructions in the text like (Smith and Jones, 2003) indicate a reference to an entry in the bibliography (in this case, the 2003 article or book by Smith and Jones); "Smith and Jones (2003)" is a similar reference. A single bibliography for the entire book appears in the endmatter.

In this book we try to keep math to a minimum, and what math there is we have simplified as much as possible without introducing confusion. For our readers with technical backgrounds, a few comments may be in order regarding our simplifying choices.

1. We avoid Sigma (Σ) and Pi (Π) notation, commonly used in textbooks to indicate sums and products, respectively. Instead we simply use equations with ellipses like this:

$$f(x) = w_1 x_1 + w_2 x_2 + \cdots + w_n x_n$$

   In the technical, "starred" sections we sometimes adopt Sigma and Pi notation when this ellipsis approach is just too cumbersome. We assume people reading these sections are somewhat more comfortable with math notation and will not be confused.

2. Statistics books are usually careful to distinguish between a value and its estimate by putting a "hat" on variables that are estimates, so in such books you'll typically see a true probability denoted p and its estimate denoted $\hat{p}$. In this book we are almost always talking about estimates from data, and putting hats on everything makes equations verbose and ugly. Everything should be assumed to be an estimate from data unless we say otherwise.

3. We simplify notation and remove extraneous variables where we believe they are clear from context. For example, when we discuss classifiers mathematically, we are technically dealing with decision predicates over feature vectors. Expressing this formally would lead to equations like:

$$\hat{f}_R(\mathbf{x}) = x_{Age} \times -1 + 0.7 \times x_{Balance} + 60$$

   Instead we opt for the more readable:

$$f(\mathbf{x}) = Age \times -1 + 0.7 \times Balance + 60$$

   with the understanding that $\mathbf{x}$ is a vector and *Age* and *Balance* are components of it.

We have tried to be consistent with typography, reserving fixed-width typewriter fonts like `sepal_width` to indicate attributes or keywords in data. For example, in the text-mining chapter, a word like *'discussing'* designates a word in a document while `dis cuss` might be the resulting token in the data.

The following typographical conventions are used in this book:

Italic
> Indicates new terms, URLs, email addresses, filenames, and file extensions.

`Constant width`
> Used for program listings, as well as within paragraphs to refer to program elements such as variable or function names, databases, data types, environment variables, statements, and keywords.

`Constant width italic`
> Shows text that should be replaced with user-supplied values or by values determined by context.

Throughout the book we have placed special inline tips and warnings relevant to the material. They will be rendered differently depending on whether you're reading paper, PDF, or an ebook, as follows:

A sentence or paragraph typeset like this signifies a tip or a suggestion.

This text and element signifies a general note.

Text rendered like this signifies a warning or caution. These are more important than tips and are used sparingly.

Using Examples

In addition to being an introduction to data science, this book is intended to be useful in discussions of and day-to-day work in the field. Answering a question by citing this book and quoting examples does not require permission. We appreciate, but do not require, attribution. Formal attribution usually includes the title, author, publisher, and ISBN. For example: "*Data Science for Business* by Foster Provost and Tom Fawcett (O'Reilly). Copyright 2013 Foster Provost and Tom Fawcett, 978-1-449-36132-7."

If you feel your use of examples falls outside fair use or the permission given above, feel free to contact us at *permissions@oreilly.com*.

Safari® Books Online

Safari Books Online is an on-demand digital library that delivers expert content in both book and video form from the world's leading authors in technology and business.

Technology professionals, software developers, web designers, and business and creative professionals use Safari Books Online as their primary resource for research, problem solving, learning, and certification training.

Safari Books Online offers a range of product mixes and pricing programs for organizations, government agencies, and individuals. Subscribers have access to thousands of books, training videos, and prepublication manuscripts in one fully searchable database from publishers like O'Reilly Media, Prentice Hall Professional, Addison-Wesley Professional, Microsoft Press, Sams, Que, Peachpit Press, Focal Press, Cisco Press, John Wiley & Sons, Syngress, Morgan Kaufmann, IBM Redbooks, Packt, Adobe Press, FT Press, Apress, Manning, New Riders, McGraw-Hill, Jones & Bartlett, Course Technology, and dozens more. For more information about Safari Books Online, please visit us online.

How to Contact Us

Please address comments and questions concerning this book to the publisher:

O'Reilly Media, Inc.
1005 Gravenstein Highway North
Sebastopol, CA 95472
800-998-9938 (in the United States or Canada)
707-829-0515 (international or local)
707-829-0104 (fax)

We have two web pages for this book, where we list errata, examples, and any additional information. You can access the publisher's page at *http://oreil.ly/data-science* and the authors' page at *http://www.data-science-for-biz.com*.

To comment or ask technical questions about this book, send email to *bookquestions@oreilly.com*.

For more information about O'Reilly Media's books, courses, conferences, and news, see their website at *http://www.oreilly.com*.

Find us on Facebook: *http://facebook.com/oreilly*

Follow us on Twitter: *http://twitter.com/oreillymedia*

Watch us on YouTube: *http://www.youtube.com/oreillymedia*

Acknowledgments

Thanks to all the many colleagues and others who have provided invaluable ideas, feedback, criticism, suggestions, and encouragement based on discussions and many prior draft manuscripts. At the risk of missing someone, let us thank in particular: Panos Adamopoulos, Manuel Arriaga, Josh Attenberg, Solon Barocas, Ron Bekkerman, Josh Blumenstock, Ohad Brazilay, Aaron Brick, Jessica Clark, Nitesh Chawla, Peter Devito, Vasant Dhar, Jan Ehmke, Theos Evgeniou, Justin Gapper, Tomer Geva, Daniel Gillick, Shawndra Hill, Nidhi Kathuria, Ronny Kohavi, Marios Kokkodis, Tom Lee, Philipp Marek, David Martens, Sophie Mohin, Lauren Moores, Alan Murray, Nick Nishimura, Balaji Padmanabhan, Jason Pan, Claudia Perlich, Gregory Piatetsky-Shapiro, Tom Phillips, Kevin Reilly, Maytal Saar-Tsechansky, Evan Sadler, Galit Shmueli, Roger Stein, Nick Street, Kiril Tsemekhman, Craig Vaughan, Chris Volinsky, Wally Wang, Geoff Webb, Debbie Yuster, and Rong Zheng. We would also like to thank more generally the students from Foster's classes, Data Mining for Business Analytics, Practical Data Science, Introduction to Data Science, and the Data Science Research Seminar. Questions and issues that arose when using prior drafts of this book provided substantive feedback for improving it.

Thanks to all the colleagues who have taught us about data science and about how to teach data science over the years. Thanks especially to Maytal Saar-Tsechansky and Claudia Perlich. Maytal graciously shared with Foster her notes for her data mining class many years ago. The classification tree example in Chapter 3 (thanks especially for the "bodies" visualization) is based mostly on her idea and example; her ideas and example were the genesis for the visualization comparing the partitioning of the instance space with trees and linear discriminant functions in Chapter 4, the "Will David Respond" example in Chapter 6 is based on her example, and probably other things long forgotten. Claudia has taught companion sections of Data Mining for Business Analytics/Introduction to Data Science along with Foster for the past few years, and has taught him much about data science in the process (and beyond).

Thanks to David Stillwell, Thore Graepel, and Michal Kosinski for providing the Facebook Like data for some of the examples. Thanks to Nick Street for providing the cell nuclei data and for letting us use the cell nuclei image in Chapter 4. Thanks to David Martens for his help with the mobile locations visualization. Thanks to Chris Volinsky for providing data from his work on the Netflix Challenge. Thanks to Sonny Tambe for early access to his results on big data technologies and productivity. Thanks to Patrick Perry for pointing us to the bank call center example used in Chapter 12. Thanks to Geoff Webb for the use of the Magnum Opus association mining system.

Most of all we thank our families for their love, patience and encouragement.

A great deal of open source software was used in the preparation of this book and its examples. The authors wish to thank the developers and contributors of:

- Python and Perl
- Scipy, Numpy, Matplotlib, and Scikit-Learn
- Weka
- The Machine Learning Repository at the University of California at Irvine (Bache & Lichman, 2013)

Finally, we encourage readers to check our website (*http://www.data-science-for-biz.com*) for updates to this material, new chapters, errata, addenda, and accompanying slide sets.

—Foster Provost and Tom Fawcett

CHAPTER 1

Introduction: Data-Analytic Thinking

Dream no small dreams for they have no power to
move the hearts of men.

—Johann Wolfgang von Goethe

The past fifteen years have seen extensive investments in business infrastructure, which have improved the ability to collect data throughout the enterprise. Virtually every aspect of business is now open to data collection and often even instrumented for data collection: operations, manufacturing, supply-chain management, customer behavior, marketing campaign performance, workflow procedures, and so on. At the same time, information is now widely available on external events such as market trends, industry news, and competitors' movements. This broad availability of data has led to increasing interest in methods for extracting useful information and knowledge from data—the realm of data science.

The Ubiquity of Data Opportunities

With vast amounts of data now available, companies in almost every industry are focused on exploiting data for competitive advantage. In the past, firms could employ teams of statisticians, modelers, and analysts to explore datasets manually, but the volume and variety of data have far outstripped the capacity of manual analysis. At the same time, computers have become far more powerful, networking has become ubiquitous, and algorithms have been developed that can connect datasets to enable broader and deeper analyses than previously possible. The convergence of these phenomena has given rise to the increasingly widespread business application of data science principles and data-mining techniques.

Probably the widest applications of data-mining techniques are in marketing for tasks such as targeted marketing, online advertising, and recommendations for cross-selling.

Data mining is used for general customer relationship management to analyze customer behavior in order to manage attrition and maximize expected customer value. The finance industry uses data mining for credit scoring and trading, and in operations via fraud detection and workforce management. Major retailers from Walmart to Amazon apply data mining throughout their businesses, from marketing to supply-chain management. Many firms have differentiated themselves strategically with data science, sometimes to the point of evolving into data mining companies.

The primary goals of this book are to help you view business problems from a data perspective and understand principles of extracting useful knowledge from data. There is a fundamental structure to data-analytic thinking, and basic principles that should be understood. There are also particular areas where intuition, creativity, common sense, and domain knowledge must be brought to bear. A data perspective will provide you with structure and principles, and this will give you a framework to systematically analyze such problems. As you get better at data-analytic thinking you will develop intuition as to how and where to apply creativity and domain knowledge.

Throughout the first two chapters of this book, we will discuss in detail various topics and techniques related to data science and data mining. The terms "data science" and "data mining" often are used interchangeably, and the former has taken a life of its own as various individuals and organizations try to capitalize on the current hype surrounding it. At a high level, *data science* is a set of fundamental principles that guide the extraction of knowledge from data. Data mining is the extraction of knowledge from data, via technologies that incorporate these principles. As a term, "data science" often is applied more broadly than the traditional use of "data mining," but data mining techniques provide some of the clearest illustrations of the principles of data science.

It is important to understand data science even if you never intend to apply it yourself. Data-analytic thinking enables you to evaluate proposals for data mining projects. For example, if an employee, a consultant, or a potential investment target proposes to improve a particular business application by extracting knowledge from data, you should be able to assess the proposal systematically and decide whether it is sound or flawed. This does not mean that you will be able to tell whether it will actually succeed—for data mining projects, that often requires trying—but you should be able to spot obvious flaws, unrealistic assumptions, and missing pieces.

Throughout the book we will describe a number of fundamental data science principles, and will illustrate each with at least one data mining technique that embodies the principle. For each principle there are usually many specific techniques that embody it, so in this book we have chosen to emphasize the basic principles in preference to specific techniques. That said, we will not make a big deal about the difference between data science and data mining, except where it will have a substantial effect on understanding the actual concepts.

Let's examine two brief case studies of analyzing data to extract predictive patterns.

Example: Hurricane Frances

Consider an example from a *New York Times* story from 2004:

> Hurricane Frances was on its way, barreling across the Caribbean, threatening a direct hit on Florida's Atlantic coast. Residents made for higher ground, but far away, in Bentonville, Ark., executives at Wal-Mart Stores decided that the situation offered a great opportunity for one of their newest data-driven weapons … predictive technology.
>
> A week ahead of the storm's landfall, Linda M. Dillman, Wal-Mart's chief information officer, pressed her staff to come up with forecasts based on what had happened when Hurricane Charley struck several weeks earlier. Backed by the trillions of bytes' worth of shopper history that is stored in Wal-Mart's data warehouse, she felt that the company could 'start predicting what's going to happen, instead of waiting for it to happen,' as she put it. (Hays, 2004)

Consider *why* data-driven prediction might be useful in this scenario. It might be useful to predict that people in the path of the hurricane would buy more bottled water. Maybe, but this point seems a bit obvious, and why would we need data science to discover it? It might be useful to project the *amount of increase* in sales due to the hurricane, to ensure that local Wal-Marts are properly stocked. Perhaps mining the data could reveal that a particular DVD sold out in the hurricane's path—but maybe it sold out that week at Wal-Marts across the country, not just where the hurricane landing was imminent. The prediction could be somewhat useful, but is probably more general than Ms. Dillman was intending.

It would be more valuable to discover patterns due to the hurricane that were not obvious. To do this, analysts might examine the huge volume of Wal-Mart data from prior, similar situations (such as Hurricane Charley) to identify *unusual* local demand for products. From such patterns, the company might be able to anticipate unusual demand for products and rush stock to the stores ahead of the hurricane's landfall.

Indeed, that is what happened. *The New York Times* (Hays, 2004) reported that: "… the experts mined the data and found that the stores would indeed need certain products —and not just the usual flashlights. 'We didn't know in the past that strawberry Pop-Tarts increase in sales, like seven times their normal sales rate, ahead of a hurricane,' Ms. Dillman said in a recent interview. 'And the pre-hurricane top-selling item was beer.'"[1]

---

1. Of course! What goes better with strawberry Pop-Tarts than a nice cold beer?

Example: Predicting Customer Churn

How are such data analyses performed? Consider a second, more typical business scenario and how it might be treated from a data perspective. This problem will serve as a running example that will illuminate many of the issues raised in this book and provide a common frame of reference.

Assume you just landed a great analytical job with MegaTelCo, one of the largest telecommunication firms in the United States. They are having a major problem with customer retention in their wireless business. In the mid-Atlantic region, 20% of cell phone customers leave when their contracts expire, and it is getting increasingly difficult to acquire new customers. Since the cell phone market is now saturated, the huge growth in the wireless market has tapered off. Communications companies are now engaged in battles to attract each other's customers while retaining their own. Customers switching from one company to another is called *churn*, and it is expensive all around: one company must spend on incentives to attract a customer while another company loses revenue when the customer departs.

You have been called in to help understand the problem and to devise a solution. Attracting new customers is much more expensive than retaining existing ones, so a good deal of marketing budget is allocated to prevent churn. Marketing has already designed a special retention offer. Your task is to devise a precise, step-by-step plan for how the data science team should use MegaTelCo's vast data resources to decide which customers should be offered the special retention deal prior to the expiration of their contracts.

Think carefully about what data you might use and how they would be used. Specifically, how should MegaTelCo choose a set of customers to receive their offer in order to best reduce churn for a particular incentive budget? Answering this question is much more complicated than it may seem initially. We will return to this problem repeatedly through the book, adding sophistication to our solution as we develop an understanding of the fundamental data science concepts.

 In reality, customer retention has been a major use of data mining technologies—especially in telecommunications and finance businesses. These more generally were some of the earliest and widest adopters of data mining technologies, for reasons discussed later.

Data Science, Engineering, and Data-Driven Decision Making

Data science involves principles, processes, and techniques for understanding phenomena via the (automated) analysis of data. In this book, we will view the ultimate goal

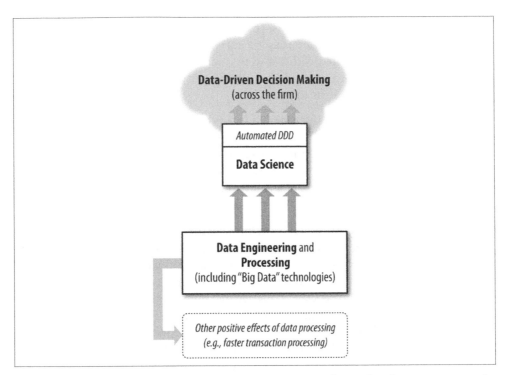

Figure 1-1. Data science in the context of various data-related processes in the organization.

of data science as improving decision making, as this generally is of direct interest to business.

Figure 1-1 places data science in the context of various other closely related and data-related processes in the organization. It distinguishes data science from other aspects of data processing that are gaining increasing attention in business. Let's start at the top.

Data-driven decision-making (DDD) refers to the practice of basing decisions on the analysis of data, rather than purely on intuition. For example, a marketer could select advertisements based purely on her long experience in the field and her eye for what will work. Or, she could base her selection on the analysis of data regarding how consumers react to different ads. She could also use a combination of these approaches. DDD is not an all-or-nothing practice, and different firms engage in DDD to greater or lesser degrees.

The benefits of data-driven decision-making have been demonstrated conclusively. Economist Erik Brynjolfsson and his colleagues from MIT and Penn's Wharton School conducted a study of how DDD affects firm performance (Brynjolfsson, Hitt, & Kim, 2011). They developed a measure of DDD that rates firms as to how strongly they use data to make decisions across the company. They show that statistically, the more data-driven a firm is, the more productive it is—even controlling for a wide range of possible confounding factors. And the differences are not small. One standard deviation higher on the DDD scale is associated with a 4%–6% increase in productivity. DDD also is correlated with higher return on assets, return on equity, asset utilization, and market value, and the relationship seems to be causal.

The sort of decisions we will be interested in in this book mainly fall into two types: (1) decisions for which "discoveries" need to be made within data, and (2) decisions that repeat, especially at massive scale, and so decision-making can benefit from even small increases in decision-making accuracy based on data analysis. The Walmart example above illustrates a type 1 problem: Linda Dillman would like to discover knowledge that will help Walmart prepare for Hurricane Frances's imminent arrival.

In 2012, Walmart's competitor Target was in the news for a data-driven decision-making case of its own, also a type 1 problem (Duhigg, 2012). Like most retailers, Target cares about consumers' shopping habits, what drives them, and what can influence them. Consumers tend to have inertia in their habits and getting them to change is very difficult. Decision makers at Target knew, however, that the arrival of a new baby in a family is one point where people do change their shopping habits significantly. In the Target analyst's words, "As soon as we get them buying diapers from us, they're going to start buying everything else too." Most retailers know this and so they compete with each other trying to sell baby-related products to new parents. Since most birth records are public, retailers obtain information on births and send out special offers to the new parents.

However, Target wanted to get a jump on their competition. They were interested in whether they could *predict* that people *are expecting* a baby. If they could, they would gain an advantage by making offers before their competitors. Using techniques of data science, Target analyzed historical data on customers who *later* were revealed to have been pregnant, and were able to extract information that could predict which consumers were pregnant. For example, pregnant mothers often change their diets, their wardrobes, their vitamin regimens, and so on. These indicators could be extracted from historical data, assembled into predictive models, and then deployed in marketing campaigns. We will discuss predictive models in much detail as we go through the book. For the time being, it is sufficient to understand that a predictive model abstracts away most of the complexity of the world, focusing in on a particular set of indicators that correlate in some way with a quantity of interest (who will churn, or who will purchase, who is pregnant, etc.). Importantly, in both the Walmart and the Target examples, the data analysis was not testing a simple hypothesis. Instead, the data were explored with the hope that something useful would be discovered.[2]

Our churn example illustrates a type 2 DDD problem. MegaTelCo has hundreds of millions of customers, each a candidate for defection. Tens of millions of customers have contracts expiring each month, so each one of them has an increased likelihood of defection in the near future. If we can improve our ability to estimate, for a given customer, how profitable it would be for us to focus on her, we can potentially reap large benefits by applying this ability to the millions of customers in the population. This same logic applies to many of the areas where we have seen the most intense application of data science and data mining: direct marketing, online advertising, credit scoring, financial trading, help-desk management, fraud detection, search ranking, product recommendation, and so on.

The diagram in Figure 1-1 shows data science supporting data-driven decision-making, but also overlapping with data-driven decision-making. This highlights the often overlooked fact that, increasingly, business decisions are being made *automatically* by computer systems. Different industries have adopted automatic decision-making at different rates. The finance and telecommunications industries were early adopters, largely because of their precocious development of data networks and implementation of massive-scale computing, which allowed the aggregation and modeling of data at a large scale, as well as the application of the resultant models to decision-making.

In the 1990s, automated decision-making changed the banking and consumer credit industries dramatically. In the 1990s, banks and telecommunications companies also implemented massive-scale systems for managing data-driven fraud control decisions. As retail systems were increasingly computerized, merchandising decisions were automated. Famous examples include Harrah's casinos' reward programs and the automated recommendations of Amazon and Netflix. Currently we are seeing a revolution in advertising, due in large part to a huge increase in the amount of time consumers are spending online, and the ability online to make (literally) split-second advertising decisions.

Data Processing and "Big Data"

It is important to digress here to address another point. There is a lot to data processing that is not data science—despite the impression one might get from the media. Data engineering and processing are critical to support data science, but they are more general. For example, these days many data processing skills, systems, and technologies often are mistakenly cast as data science. To understand data science and data-driven

---

2. Target was successful enough that this case raised ethical questions on the deployment of such techniques. Concerns of ethics and privacy are interesting and very important, but we leave their discussion for another time and place.

businesses it is important to understand the differences. Data science needs access to data and it often benefits from sophisticated data engineering that data processing technologies may facilitate, but these technologies are not data science technologies per se. They support data science, as shown in Figure 1-1, but they are useful for much more. Data processing technologies are very important for many data-oriented business tasks that do not involve extracting knowledge or data-driven decision-making, such as efficient transaction processing, modern web system processing, and online advertising campaign management.

"Big data" technologies (such as Hadoop, HBase, and MongoDB) have received considerable media attention recently. *Big data* essentially means datasets that are too large for traditional data processing systems, and therefore require new processing technologies. As with the traditional technologies, big data technologies are used for many tasks, including data engineering. Occasionally, big data technologies are actually used for *implementing* data mining techniques. However, much more often the well-known big data technologies are used for data processing *in support of* the data mining techniques and other data science activities, as represented in Figure 1-1.

Previously, we discussed Brynjolfsson's study demonstrating the benefits of data-driven decision-making. A separate study, conducted by economist Prasanna Tambe of NYU's Stern School, examined the extent to which *big data* technologies seem to help firms (Tambe, 2012). He finds that, after controlling for various possible confounding factors, using big data technologies is associated with significant additional productivity growth. Specifically, one standard deviation higher utilization of big data technologies is associated with 1%–3% higher productivity than the average firm; one standard deviation lower in terms of big data utilization is associated with 1%–3% lower productivity. This leads to potentially very large productivity differences between the firms at the extremes.

From Big Data 1.0 to Big Data 2.0

One way to think about the state of big data technologies is to draw an analogy with the business adoption of Internet technologies. In Web 1.0, businesses busied themselves with getting the basic internet technologies in place, so that they could establish a web presence, build electronic commerce capability, and improve the efficiency of their operations. We can think of ourselves as being in the era of Big Data 1.0. Firms are busying themselves with building the capabilities to process large data, largely in support of their current operations—for example, to improve efficiency.

Once firms had incorporated Web 1.0 technologies thoroughly (and in the process had driven down prices of the underlying technology) they started to look further. They began to ask what the Web could do for them, and how it could improve things they'd always done—and we entered the era of Web 2.0, where new systems and companies began taking advantage of the interactive nature of the Web. The changes brought on by this shift in thinking are pervasive; the most obvious are the incorporation of social-networking components, and the rise of the "voice" of the individual consumer (and citizen).

We should expect a Big Data 2.0 phase to follow Big Data 1.0. Once firms have become capable of processing massive data in a flexible fashion, they should begin asking: *"What can I now do that I couldn't do before, or do better than I could do before?"* This is likely to be the golden era of data science. The principles and techniques we introduce in this book will be applied far more broadly and deeply than they are today.

 It is important to note that in the Web 1.0 era some precocious companies began applying Web 2.0 ideas far ahead of the mainstream. Amazon is a prime example, incorporating the consumer's "voice" early on, in the rating of products, in product reviews (and deeper, in the rating of product reviews). Similarly, we see some companies already applying Big Data 2.0. Amazon again is a company at the forefront, providing data-driven recommendations from massive data. There are other examples as well. Online advertisers must process extremely large volumes of data (billions of ad impressions per day is not unusual) and maintain a very high throughput (real-time bidding systems make decisions in tens of milliseconds). We should look to these and similar industries for hints at advances in big data and data science that subsequently will be adopted by other industries.

Data and Data Science Capability as a Strategic Asset

The prior sections suggest one of the fundamental principles of data science: *data, and the capability to extract useful knowledge from data, should be regarded as key strategic assets.* Too many businesses regard data analytics as pertaining mainly to realizing value from some existing data, and often without careful regard to whether the business has the appropriate analytical talent. Viewing these as assets allows us to think explicitly about the extent to which one should invest in them. Often, we don't have exactly the right data to best make decisions and/or the right talent to best support making decisions from the data. Further, thinking of these as assets should lead us to the realization that they are *complementary*. The best data science team can yield little value without the appropriate data; the right data often cannot substantially improve decisions without suitable data science talent. As with all assets, it is often necessary to make investments. Building a top-notch data science team is a nontrivial undertaking, but can make a huge difference for decision-making. We will discuss strategic considerations involving data science in detail in Chapter 13. Our next case study will introduce the idea that thinking explicitly about how to invest in data assets very often pays off handsomely.

The classic story of little Signet Bank from the 1990s provides a case in point. Previously, in the 1980s, data science had transformed the business of consumer credit. Modeling the probability of default had changed the industry from personal assessment of the likelihood of default to strategies of massive scale and market share, which brought along concomitant economies of scale. It may seem strange now, but at the time, credit cards essentially had uniform pricing, for two reasons: (1) the companies did not have adequate information systems to deal with differential pricing at massive scale, and (2) bank management believed customers would not stand for price discrimination. Around 1990, two strategic visionaries (Richard Fairbanks and Nigel Morris) realized that information technology was powerful enough that they could do more sophisticated predictive modeling—using the sort of techniques that we discuss throughout this book—and offer different terms (nowadays: pricing, credit limits, low-initial-rate balance transfers, cash back, loyalty points, and so on). These two men had no success persuading the big banks to take them on as consultants and let them try. Finally, after running out of big banks, they succeeded in garnering the interest of a small regional Virginia bank: Signet Bank. Signet Bank's management was convinced that modeling profitability, not just default probability, was the right strategy. They knew that a small proportion of customers actually account for *more than* 100% of a bank's profit from credit card operations (because the rest are break-even or money-losing). If they could model profitability, they could make better offers to the best customers and "skim the cream" of the big banks' clientele.

But Signet Bank had one really big problem in implementing this strategy. They did not have the appropriate data to model profitability with the goal of offering different terms to different customers. No one did. Since banks were offering credit with a specific set of terms and a specific default model, they had the data to model profitability (1) for the terms they actually have offered in the past, and (2) for the sort of customer who was actually offered credit (that is, those who were deemed worthy of credit by the existing model).

What could Signet Bank do? They brought into play a fundamental strategy of data science: acquire the necessary data at a cost. Once we view data as a business asset, we should think about whether and how much we are willing to invest. In Signet's case, data could be generated on the profitability of customers given different credit terms by conducting experiments. Different terms were offered at random to different customers. This may seem foolish outside the context of data-analytic thinking: you're likely to lose money! This is true. In this case, losses are the cost of data acquisition. The data-analytic thinker needs to consider whether she expects the data to have sufficient value to justify the investment.

So what happened with Signet Bank? As you might expect, when Signet began randomly offering terms to customers for data acquisition, the number of bad accounts soared. Signet went from an industry-leading "charge-off" rate (2.9% of balances went unpaid) to almost 6% charge-offs. Losses continued for a few years while the data scientists worked to build predictive models from the data, evaluate them, and deploy them to improve profit. Because the firm viewed these losses as investments in data, they persisted despite complaints from stakeholders. Eventually, Signet's credit card operation turned around and became so profitable that it was spun off to separate it from the bank's other operations, which now were overshadowing the consumer credit success.

Fairbanks and Morris became Chairman and CEO and President and COO, and proceeded to apply data science principles throughout the business—not just customer acquisition but retention as well. When a customer calls looking for a better offer, data-driven models calculate the potential profitability of various possible actions (different offers, including sticking with the status quo), and the customer service representative's computer presents the best offers to make.

You may not have heard of little Signet Bank, but if you're reading this book you've probably heard of the spin-off: Capital One. Fairbanks and Morris's new company grew to be one of the largest credit card issuers in the industry with one of the lowest charge-off rates. In 2000, the bank was reported to be carrying out 45,000 of these "scientific tests" as they called them.[3]

Studies giving clear quantitative demonstrations of the value of a data asset are hard to find, primarily because firms are hesitant to divulge results of strategic value. One exception is a study by Martens and Provost (2011) assessing whether data on the specific transactions of a bank's consumers can improve models for deciding what product offers to make. The bank built models from data to decide whom to target with offers for different products. The investigation examined a number of different types of data and their effects on predictive performance. Sociodemographic data provide a substantial ability to model the sort of consumers that are more likely to purchase one product or another. However, sociodemographic data only go so far; after a certain volume of data, no additional advantage is conferred. In contrast, detailed data on customers' individual (anonymized) transactions improve performance substantially over just using socio-demographic data. The relationship is clear and striking and—significantly, for the point here—the predictive performance continues to improve as more data are used, increasing throughout the range investigated by Martens and Provost with no sign of abating. This has an important implication: banks with bigger data assets may have an important strategic advantage over their smaller competitors. If these trends generalize, and the banks are able to apply sophisticated analytics, banks with bigger data assets should be better able to identify the best customers for individual products. The net result will be either increased adoption of the bank's products, decreased cost of customer acquisition, or both.

The idea of data as a strategic asset is certainly not limited to Capital One, nor even to the banking industry. Amazon was able to gather data early on online customers, which has created significant switching costs: consumers find value in the rankings and recommendations that Amazon provides. Amazon therefore can retain customers more easily, and can even charge a premium (Brynjolfsson & Smith, 2000). Harrah's casinos

---

3. You can read more about Capital One's story (Clemons & Thatcher, 1998; McNamee 2001).

famously invested in gathering and mining data on gamblers, and moved itself from a small player in the casino business in the mid-1990s to the acquisition of Caesar's Entertainment in 2005 to become the world's largest gambling company. The huge valuation of Facebook has been credited to its vast and unique data assets (Sengupta, 2012), including both information about individuals and their likes, as well as information about the structure of the social network. Information about network structure has been shown to be important to predicting and has been shown to be remarkably helpful in building models of who will buy certain products (Hill, Provost, & Volinsky, 2006). It is clear that Facebook has a remarkable data asset; whether they have the right data science strategies to take full advantage of it is an open question.

In the book we will discuss in more detail many of the fundamental concepts behind these success stories, in exploring the principles of data mining and data-analytic thinking.

Data-Analytic Thinking

Analyzing case studies such as the churn problem improves our ability to approach problems "data-analytically." Promoting such a perspective is a primary goal of this book. When faced with a business problem, you should be able to assess whether and how data can improve performance. We will discuss a set of fundamental concepts and principles that facilitate careful thinking. We will develop frameworks to structure the analysis so that it can be done systematically.

As mentioned above, it is important to understand data science even if you never intend to do it yourself, because data analysis is now so critical to business strategy. Businesses increasingly are driven by data analytics, so there is great professional advantage in being able to interact competently with and within such businesses. Understanding the fundamental concepts, and having frameworks for organizing data-analytic thinking not only will allow one to interact competently, but will help to envision opportunities for improving data-driven decision-making, or to see data-oriented competitive threats.

Firms in many traditional industries are exploiting new and existing data resources for competitive advantage. They employ data science teams to bring advanced technologies to bear to increase revenue and to decrease costs. In addition, many new companies are being developed with data mining as a key strategic component. Facebook and Twitter, along with many other "Digital 100" companies (*Business Insider*, 2012), have high valuations due primarily to data assets they are committed to capturing or creating.[4] Increasingly, managers need to oversee analytics teams and analysis projects, marketers have to organize and understand data-driven campaigns, venture capitalists must be

---

4. Of course, this is not a new phenomenon. Amazon and Google are well-established companies that get tremendous value from their data assets.

able to invest wisely in businesses with substantial data assets, and business strategists must be able to devise plans that exploit data.

As a few examples, if a consultant presents a proposal to mine a data asset to improve your business, you should be able to assess whether the proposal makes sense. If a competitor announces a new data partnership, you should recognize when it may put you at a strategic disadvantage. Or, let's say you take a position with a venture firm and your first project is to assess the potential for investing in an advertising company. The founders present a convincing argument that they will realize significant value from a unique body of data they will collect, and on that basis are arguing for a substantially higher valuation. Is this reasonable? With an understanding of the fundamentals of data science you should be able to devise a few probing questions to determine whether their valuation arguments are plausible.

On a scale less grand, but probably more common, data analytics projects reach into all business units. Employees throughout these units must interact with the data science team. If these employees do not have a fundamental grounding in the principles of data-analytic thinking, they will not really understand what is happening in the business. This lack of understanding is much more damaging in data science projects than in other technical projects, because the data science is supporting improved decision-making. As we will describe in the next chapter, this requires a close interaction between the data scientists and the business people responsible for the decision-making. Firms where the business people do not understand what the data scientists are doing are at a substantial disadvantage, because they waste time and effort or, worse, because they ultimately make wrong decisions.

The need for managers with data-analytic skills

The consulting firm McKinsey and Company estimates that "there will be a shortage of talent necessary for organizations to take advantage of big data. By 2018, the United States alone could face a shortage of 140,000 to 190,000 people with deep analytical skills as well as 1.5 million managers and analysts with the know-how to use the analysis of big data to make effective decisions." (Manyika, 2011). Why 10 times as many managers and analysts than those with deep analytical skills? Surely data scientists aren't so difficult to manage that they need 10 managers! The reason is that a business can get leverage from a data science team for making better decisions in multiple areas of the business. However, as McKinsey is pointing out, the managers in those areas need to understand the fundamentals of data science to effectively get that leverage.

This Book

This book concentrates on the fundamentals of data science and data mining. These are a set of principles, concepts, and techniques that structure thinking and analysis. They allow us to understand data science processes and methods surprisingly deeply, without needing to focus in depth on the large number of specific data mining algorithms.

There are many good books covering data mining algorithms and techniques, from practical guides to mathematical and statistical treatments. This book instead focuses on the fundamental concepts and how they help us to think about problems where data mining may be brought to bear. That doesn't mean that we will ignore the data mining techniques; many algorithms are exactly the embodiment of the basic concepts. But with only a few exceptions we will not concentrate on the deep technical details of how the techniques actually work; we will try to provide just enough detail so that you will understand what the techniques do, and how they are based on the fundamental principles.

Data Mining and Data Science, Revisited

This book devotes a good deal of attention to the extraction of useful (nontrivial, hope-fully actionable) patterns or models from large bodies of data (Fayyad, Piatetsky-Shapiro, & Smyth, 1996), and to the fundamental data science principles underlying such data mining. In our churn-prediction example, we would like to *take the data* on prior churn and *extract patterns*, for example patterns of behavior, *that are useful*—that can help us to predict those customers who are more likely to leave in the future, or that can help us to design better services.

The fundamental concepts of data science are drawn from many fields that study data analytics. We introduce these concepts throughout the book, but let's briefly discuss a few now to get the basic flavor. We will elaborate on all of these and more in later chapters.

Fundamental concept: *Extracting useful knowledge from data to solve business problems can be treated systematically by following a process with reasonably well-defined stages.* The Cross Industry Standard Process for Data Mining, abbreviated CRISP-DM (CRISP-DM Project, 2000), is one codification of this process. Keeping such a process in mind provides a framework to structure our thinking about data analytics problems. For example, in actual practice one repeatedly sees analytical "solutions" that are not based on careful analysis of the problem or are not carefully evaluated. Structured thinking about analytics emphasizes these often under-appreciated aspects of supporting decision-making with data. Such structured thinking also contrasts critical points where human creativity is necessary versus points where high-powered analytical tools can be brought to bear.

Fundamental concept: *From a large mass of data, information technology can be used to find informative descriptive attributes of entities of interest.* In our churn example, a customer would be an entity of interest, and each customer might be described by a large number of attributes, such as usage, customer service history, and many other factors. Which of these actually gives us information on the customer's likelihood of leaving the company when her contract expires? How much information? Sometimes this process is referred to roughly as finding variables that "correlate" with churn (we will discuss this notion precisely). A business analyst may be able to hypothesize some and test them, and there are tools to help facilitate this experimentation (see "Other Analytics Techniques and Technologies" on page 35). Alternatively, the analyst could apply information technology to automatically discover informative attributes—essentially doing large-scale automated experimentation. Further, as we will see, this concept can be applied recursively to build models to predict churn based on multiple attributes.

Fundamental concept: *If you look too hard at a set of data, you will find something—but it might not generalize beyond the data you're looking at.* This is referred to as *overfitting* a dataset. Data mining techniques can be very powerful, and the need to detect and avoid overfitting is one of the most important concepts to grasp when applying data mining to real problems. The concept of overfitting and its avoidance permeates data science processes, algorithms, and evaluation methods.

Fundamental concept: *Formulating data mining solutions and evaluating the results involves thinking carefully about the context in which they will be used.* If our goal is the extraction of potentially *useful* knowledge, how can we formulate what is useful? It depends critically on the application in question. For our churn-management example, how exactly are we going to use the patterns extracted from historical data? Should the value of the customer be taken into account in addition to the likelihood of leaving? More generally, does the pattern lead to better decisions than some reasonable alternative? How well would one have done by chance? How well would one do with a smart "default" alternative?

These are just four of the fundamental concepts of data science that we will explore. By the end of the book, we will have discussed a dozen such fundamental concepts in detail, and will have illustrated how they help us to structure data-analytic thinking and to understand data mining techniques and algorithms, as well as data science applications, quite generally.

Chemistry Is Not About Test Tubes: Data Science Versus the Work of the Data Scientist

Before proceeding, we should briefly revisit the engineering side of data science. At the time of this writing, discussions of data science commonly mention not just analytical skills and techniques for understanding data but popular tools used. Definitions of data scientists (and advertisements for positions) specify not just areas of expertise but also specific programming languages and tools. It is common to see job advertisements mentioning data mining techniques (e.g., random forests, support vector machines), specific application areas (recommendation systems, ad placement optimization), alongside popular software tools for processing big data (Hadoop, MongoDB). There is often little distinction between the science and the technology for dealing with large datasets.

We must point out that data science, like computer science, is a young field. The particular concerns of data science are fairly new and general principles are just beginning to emerge. The state of data science may be likened to that of chemistry in the mid-19th century, when theories and general principles were being formulated and the field was largely experimental. Every good chemist had to be a competent lab technician. Similarly, it is hard to imagine a working data scientist who is not proficient with certain sorts of software tools.

Having said this, this book focuses on the science and not on the technology. You will not find instructions here on how best to run massive data mining jobs on Hadoop clusters, or even what Hadoop is or why you might want to learn about it.[5] We focus here on the general principles of data science that have emerged. In 10 years' time the predominant technologies will likely have changed or advanced enough that a discussion here would be obsolete, while the general principles are the same as they were 20 years ago, and likely will change little over the coming decades.

Summary

This book is about the extraction of useful information and knowledge from large volumes of data, in order to improve business decision-making. As the massive collection of data has spread through just about every industry sector and business unit, so have the opportunities for mining the data. Underlying the extensive body of techniques for mining data is a much smaller set of fundamental concepts comprising *data science*. These concepts are general and encapsulate much of the essence of data mining and business analytics.

Success in today's data-oriented business environment requires being able to think about how these fundamental concepts apply to particular business problems—to think data-analytically. For example, in this chapter we discussed the principle that data should be thought of as a business asset, and once we are thinking in this direction we start to ask whether (and how much) we should invest in data. Thus, an understanding of these fundamental concepts is important not only for data scientists themselves, but for any-

---

5. OK: Hadoop is a widely used open source architecture for doing highly parallelizable computations. It is one of the current "big data" technologies for processing massive datasets that exceed the capacity of relational database systems. Hadoop is based on the MapReduce parallel processing framework introduced by Google.

one working with data scientists, employing data scientists, investing in data-heavy ventures, or directing the application of analytics in an organization.

Thinking data-analytically is aided by conceptual frameworks discussed throughout the book. For example, the automated extraction of patterns from data is a process with well-defined stages, which are the subject of the next chapter. Understanding the process and the stages helps to structure our data-analytic thinking, and to make it more systematic and therefore less prone to errors and omissions.

There is convincing evidence that data-driven decision-making and big data technologies substantially improve business performance. Data science supports data-driven decision-making—and sometimes conducts such decision-making automatically—and depends upon technologies for "big data" storage and engineering, but its principles are separate. The data science principles we discuss in this book also differ from, and are complementary to, other important technologies, such as statistical hypothesis testing and database querying (which have their own books and classes). The next chapter describes some of these differences in more detail.

CHAPTER 2

Business Problems and Data Science Solutions

Fundamental concepts: *A set of canonical data mining tasks; The data mining process; Supervised versus unsupervised data mining.*

An important principle of data science is that data mining is a *process* with fairly well-understood stages. Some involve the application of information technology, such as the automated discovery and evaluation of patterns from data, while others mostly require an analyst's creativity, business knowledge, and common sense. Understanding the whole process helps to structure data mining projects, so they are closer to systematic analyses rather than heroic endeavors driven by chance and individual acumen.

Since the data mining process breaks up the overall task of finding patterns from data into a set of well-defined subtasks, it is also useful for structuring discussions about data science. In this book, we will use the process as an overarching framework for our discussion. This chapter introduces the data mining process, but first we provide additional context by discussing common types of data mining tasks. Introducing these allows us to be more concrete when presenting the overall process, as well as when introducing other concepts in subsequent chapters.

We close the chapter by discussing a set of important business analytics subjects that are not the focus of this book (but for which there are many other helpful books), such as databases, data warehousing, and basic statistics.

From Business Problems to Data Mining Tasks

Each data-driven business decision-making problem is unique, comprising its own combination of goals, desires, constraints, and even personalities. As with much engineering, though, there are sets of common tasks that underlie the business problems. In collaboration with business stakeholders, data scientists decompose a business problem into subtasks. The solutions to the subtasks can then be composed to solve the overall problem. Some of these subtasks are unique to the particular business problem, but others are common data mining tasks. For example, our telecommunications churn problem is unique to MegaTelCo: there are specifics of the problem that are different from churn problems of any other telecommunications firm. However, a subtask that will likely be part of the solution to any churn problem is to estimate from historical data the probability of a customer terminating her contract shortly after it has expired. Once the idiosyncratic MegaTelCo data have been assembled into a particular format (described in the next chapter), this probability estimation fits the mold of one very common data mining task. We know a lot about solving the common data mining tasks, both scientifically and practically. In later chapters, we also will provide data science frameworks to help with the decomposition of business problems and with the re-composition of the solutions to the subtasks.

 A critical skill in data science is the ability to decompose a data-analytics problem into pieces such that each piece matches a known task for which tools are available. Recognizing familiar problems and their solutions avoids wasting time and resources reinventing the wheel. It also allows people to focus attention on more interesting parts of the process that require human involvement—parts that have not been automated, so human creativity and intelligence must come into play.

Despite the large number of specific data mining algorithms developed over the years, there are only a handful of fundamentally different types of tasks these algorithms address. It is worth defining these tasks clearly. The next several chapters will use the first two (classification and regression) to illustrate several fundamental concepts. In what follows, the term "an individual" will refer to an entity about which we have data, such as a customer or a consumer, or it could be an inanimate entity such as a business. We will make this notion more precise in Chapter 3. In many business analytics projects, we want to find "correlations" between a particular variable describing an individual and other variables. For example, in historical data we may know which customers left the company after their contracts expired. We may want to find out which other variables correlate with a customer leaving in the near future. Finding such correlations are the most basic examples of classification and regression tasks.

1. *Classification* and class *probability estimation* attempt to predict, for each individual in a population, which of a (small) set of classes this individual belongs to. Usually the classes are mutually exclusive. An example classification question would be: "Among all the customers of MegaTelCo, which are likely to respond to a given offer?" In this example the two classes could be called `will respond` and `will not respond`.

For a classification task, a data mining procedure produces a model that, given a new individual, determines which class that individual belongs to. A closely related task is *scoring* or class *probability estimation*. A scoring model applied to an individual produces, instead of a class prediction, a score representing the probability (or some other quantification of likelihood) that that individual belongs to each class. In our customer response scenario, a scoring model would be able to evaluate each individual customer and produce a score of how likely each is to respond to the offer. Classification and scoring are very closely related; as we shall see, a model that can do one can usually be modified to do the other.

2. *Regression* ("value estimation") attempts to estimate or predict, for each individual, the numerical value of some variable for that individual. An example regression question would be: "How much will a given customer use the service?" The property (variable) to be predicted here is *service usage*, and a model could be generated by looking at other, similar individuals in the population and their historical usage. A regression procedure produces a model that, given an individual, estimates the value of the particular variable specific to that individual.

   Regression is related to classification, but the two are different. Informally, classification predicts *whether* something will happen, whereas regression predicts *how much* something will happen. The difference will become clearer as the book progresses.

3. *Similarity matching* attempts to *identify* similar individuals based on data known about them. Similarity matching can be used directly to find similar entities. For example, IBM is interested in finding companies similar to their best business customers, in order to focus their sales force on the best opportunities. They use similarity matching based on "firmographic" data describing characteristics of the companies. Similarity matching is the basis for one of the most popular methods for making product recommendations (finding people who are similar to you in terms of the products they have liked or have purchased). Similarity measures underlie certain solutions to other data mining tasks, such as classification, regression, and clustering. We discuss similarity and its uses at length in Chapter 6.

4. *Clustering* attempts to *group* individuals in a population together by their similarity, but not driven by any specific purpose. An example clustering question would be: "Do our customers form natural groups or segments?" Clustering is useful in preliminary domain exploration to see which natural groups exist because these groups in turn may suggest other data mining tasks or approaches. Clustering also is used as input to decision-making processes focusing on questions such as: *What products should we offer or develop? How should our customer care teams (or sales teams) be structured?* We discuss clustering in depth in Chapter 6.

5. *Co-occurrence grouping* (also known as frequent itemset mining, association rule discovery, and market-basket analysis) attempts to find *associations* between entities based on transactions involving them. An example co-occurrence question

would be: *What items are commonly purchased together*? While clustering looks at similarity between objects based on the objects' attributes, co-occurrence grouping considers similarity of objects based on their appearing together in transactions. For example, analyzing purchase records from a supermarket may uncover that ground meat is purchased together with hot sauce much more frequently than we might expect. Deciding how to act upon this discovery might require some creativity, but it could suggest a special promotion, product display, or combination offer. Co-occurrence of products in purchases is a common type of grouping known as market-basket analysis. Some *recommendation* systems also perform a type of affinity grouping by finding, for example, pairs of books that are purchased frequently by the same people ("people who bought X also bought Y").

The result of co-occurrence grouping is a description of items that occur together. These descriptions usually include statistics on the frequency of the co-occurrence and an estimate of how surprising it is.

6. *Profiling* (also known as behavior description) attempts to characterize the typical behavior of an individual, group, or population. An example profiling question would be: "What is the typical cell phone usage of this customer segment?" Behavior may not have a simple description; profiling cell phone usage might require a complex description of night and weekend airtime averages, international usage, roaming charges, text minutes, and so on. Behavior can be described generally over an entire population, or down to the level of small groups or even individuals.

Profiling is often used to establish behavioral norms for anomaly detection applications such as fraud detection and monitoring for intrusions to computer systems (such as someone breaking into your iTunes account). For example, if we know what kind of purchases a person typically makes on a credit card, we can determine whether a new charge on the card fits that profile or not. We can use the degree of mismatch as a suspicion score and issue an alarm if it is too high.

7. *Link prediction* attempts to predict connections between data items, usually by suggesting that a link should exist, and possibly also estimating the strength of the link. Link prediction is common in social networking systems: "Since you and Karen share 10 friends, maybe you'd like to be Karen's friend?" Link prediction can also estimate the strength of a link. For example, for recommending movies to customers one can think of a graph between customers and the movies they've watched or rated. Within the graph, we search for links that do *not* exist between customers and movies, but that we predict should exist and should be strong. These links form the basis for recommendations.

8. *Data reduction* attempts to take a large set of data and replace it with a smaller set of data that contains much of the important information in the larger set. The smaller dataset may be easier to deal with or to process. Moreover, the smaller dataset may better reveal the information. For example, a massive dataset on consumer movie-viewing preferences may be reduced to a much smaller dataset re-

vealing the consumer taste preferences that are latent in the viewing data (for example, viewer genre preferences). Data reduction usually involves loss of information. What is important is the trade-off for improved insight.

9. *Causal modeling* attempts to help us understand what events or actions actually *influence* others. For example, consider that we use predictive modeling to target advertisements to consumers, and we observe that indeed the targeted consumers purchase at a higher rate subsequent to having been targeted. Was this because the advertisements influenced the consumers to purchase? Or did the predictive models simply do a good job of identifying those consumers who would have purchased anyway? Techniques for causal modeling include those involving a substantial investment in data, such as randomized controlled experiments (e.g., so-called "A/B tests"), as well as sophisticated methods for drawing causal conclusions from observational data. Both experimental and observational methods for causal modeling generally can be viewed as "counterfactual" analysis: they attempt to understand what would be the difference between the situations—which cannot both happen —where the "treatment" event (e.g., showing an advertisement to a particular individual) were to happen, and were not to happen.

In all cases, a careful data scientist should always include with a causal conclusion the exact assumptions that must be made in order for the causal conclusion to hold (there *always* are such assumptions—always ask). When undertaking causal modeling, a business needs to weigh the trade-off of increasing investment to reduce the assumptions made, versus deciding that the conclusions are good enough given the assumptions. Even in the most careful randomized, controlled experimentation, assumptions are made that could render the causal conclusions invalid. The discovery of the "placebo effect" in medicine illustrates a notorious situation where an assumption was overlooked in carefully designed randomized experimentation.

Discussing all of these tasks in detail would fill multiple books. In this book, we present a collection of the most fundamental data science principles—principles that together underlie all of these types of tasks. We will illustrate the principles mainly using classification, regression, similarity matching, and clustering, and will discuss others when they provide important illustrations of the fundamental principles (toward the end of the book).

Consider which of these types of tasks might fit our churn-prediction problem. Often, practitioners formulate churn prediction as a problem of finding *segments* of customers who are more or less likely to leave. This segmentation problem sounds like a classification problem, or possibly clustering, or even regression. To decide the best formulation, we first need to introduce some important distinctions.

Supervised Versus Unsupervised Methods

Consider two similar questions we might ask about a customer population. The first is: "Do our customers naturally fall into different groups?" Here no specific purpose or *target* has been specified for the grouping. When there is no such target, the data mining problem is referred to as *unsupervised*. Contrast this with a slightly different question: "Can we find groups of customers who have particularly high likelihoods of canceling their service soon after their contracts expire?" Here there is a specific target defined: will a customer leave when her contract expires? In this case, segmentation is being done for a specific reason: to take action based on likelihood of churn. This is called a *supervised* data mining problem.

 A note on the terms: Supervised and unsupervised learning
The terms *supervised* and *unsupervised* were inherited from the field of machine learning. Metaphorically, a teacher "supervises" the learner by carefully providing target information along with a set of examples. An unsupervised learning task might involve the same set of examples but would not include the target information. The learner would be given no information about the purpose of the learning, but would be left to form its own conclusions about what the examples have in common.

The difference between these questions is subtle but important. If a specific target can be provided, the problem can be phrased as a supervised one. Supervised tasks require different techniques than unsupervised tasks do, and the results often are much more useful. A supervised technique is given a specific purpose for the grouping—predicting the target. Clustering, an unsupervised task, produces groupings based on similarities, but there is no guarantee that these similarities are meaningful or will be useful for any particular purpose.

Technically, another condition must be met for supervised data mining: there must be *data* on the target. It is not enough that the target information exist in principle; it must also exist in the data. For example, it might be useful to know whether a given customer will stay for at least six months, but if in historical data this retention information is missing or incomplete (if, say, the data are only retained for two months) the target values cannot be provided. Acquiring data on the target often is a key data science investment. The value for the target variable for an individual is often called the individual's *label*, emphasizing that often (not always) one must incur expense to actively label the data.

Classification, regression, and causal modeling generally are solved with supervised methods. Similarity matching, link prediction, and data reduction could be either. Clustering, co-occurrence grouping, and profiling generally are unsupervised. The fundamental principles of data mining that we will present underlie all these types of technique.

Two main subclasses of *supervised* data mining, classification and regression, are distinguished by the type of target. Regression involves a numeric target while classification involves a categorical (often binary) target. Consider these similar questions we might address with supervised data mining:

"Will this customer purchase service S1 if given incentive I?"
> This is a classification problem because it has a binary target (the customer either purchases or does not).

"Which service package (S1, S2, or none) will a customer likely purchase if given incentive I?"
> This is also a classification problem, with a three-valued target.

"How much will this customer use the service?"
> This is a regression problem because it has a numeric target. The target variable is the amount of usage (actual or predicted) per customer.

There are subtleties among these questions that should be brought out. For business applications we often want a numerical *prediction* over a categorical target. In the churn example, a basic yes/no prediction of whether a customer is likely to continue to subscribe to the service may not be sufficient; we want to model the *probability* that the customer will continue. This is still considered classification modeling rather than regression because the underlying target is categorical. Where necessary for clarity, this is called "class probability estimation."

A vital part in the early stages of the data mining process is (i) to decide whether the line of attack will be supervised or unsupervised, and (ii) if supervised, to produce a precise definition of a target variable. This variable must be a specific quantity that will be the focus of the data mining (and for which we can obtain values for some example data). We will return to this in Chapter 3.

Data Mining and Its Results

There is another important distinction pertaining to mining data: the difference between (1) mining the data to find patterns and build models, and (2) *using* the results of data mining. Students often confuse these two processes when studying data science, and managers sometimes confuse them when discussing business analytics. The use of data mining results should influence and inform the data mining process itself, but the two should be kept distinct.

In our churn example, consider the deployment scenario in which the results will be used. We want to use the model to predict which of our customers will leave. Specifically, assume that data mining has created a class probability estimation model M. Given each

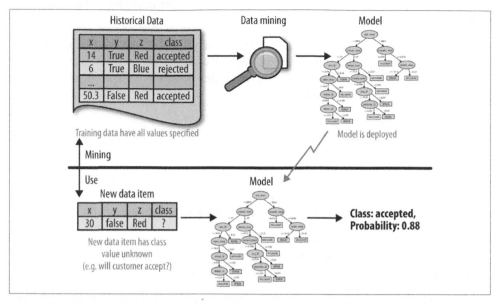

Figure 2-1. Data mining versus the use of data mining results. The upper half of the figure illustrates the mining of historical data to produce a model. Importantly, the historical data have the target ("class") value specified. The bottom half shows the result of the data mining in use, where the model is applied to new data for which we do not know the class value. The model predicts both the class value and the probability that the class variable will take on that value.

existing customer, described using a set of characteristics, M takes these characteristics as input and produces a score or probability estimate of attrition. This is the *use* of the results of data mining. The data mining produces the model M from some other, often historical, data.

Figure 2-1 illustrates these two phases. Data mining produces the probability estimation model, as shown in the top half of the figure. In the use phase (bottom half), the model is applied to a new, unseen case and it generates a probability estimate for it.

The Data Mining Process

Data mining is a craft. It involves the application of a substantial amount of science and technology, but the proper application still involves art as well. But as with many mature crafts, there is a well-understood process that places a structure on the problem, allowing reasonable consistency, repeatability, and objectiveness. A useful codification of the data mining process is given by the Cross Industry Standard Process for Data Mining (CRISP-DM; Shearer, 2000), illustrated in Figure 2-2.[1]

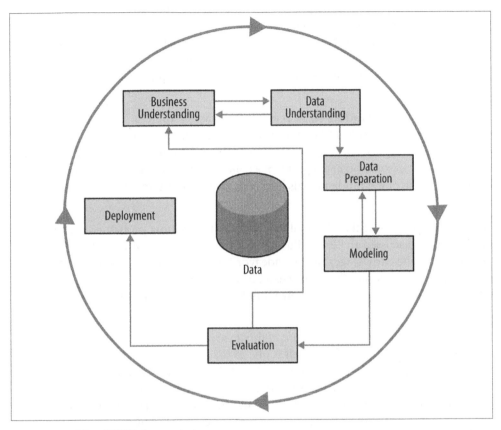

Figure 2-2. The CRISP data mining process.

This process diagram makes explicit the fact that iteration is the rule rather than the exception. Going through the process once without having solved the problem is, generally speaking, not a failure. Often the entire process is an exploration of the data, and after the first iteration the data science team knows much more. The next iteration can be much more well-informed. Let's now discuss the steps in detail.

---

1. See also the Wikipedia page on the CRISP-DM process model (*http://wikipedia.org/wiki/Cross_Indus try_Standard_Process_for_Data_Mining*).

Business Understanding

Initially, it is vital to understand the problem to be solved. This may seem obvious, but business projects seldom come pre-packaged as clear and unambiguous data mining problems. Often recasting the problem and designing a solution is an iterative process of discovery. The diagram shown in Figure 2-2 represents this as cycles within a cycle, rather than as a simple linear process. The initial formulation may not be complete or optimal so multiple iterations may be necessary for an acceptable solution formulation to appear.

The Business Understanding stage represents a part of the craft where the analysts' creativity plays a large role. Data science has some things to say, as we will describe, but often the key to a great success is a creative problem formulation by some analyst regarding how to cast the business problem as one or more data science problems. High-level knowledge of the fundamentals helps creative business analysts see novel formulations.

We have a set of powerful tools to solve particular data mining problems: the basic data mining tasks discussed in "From Business Problems to Data Mining Tasks" on page 19. Typically, the early stages of the endeavor involve designing a solution that takes advantage of these tools. This can mean structuring (engineering) the problem such that one or more subproblems involve building models for classification, regression, probability estimation, and so on.

In this first stage, *the design team should think carefully about the problem to be solved and about the use scenario*. This itself is one of the most important fundamental principles of data science, to which we have devoted two entire chapters (Chapter 7 and Chapter 11). What exactly do we want to do? How exactly would we do it? What parts of this use scenario constitute possible data mining models? In discussing this in more detail, we will begin with a simplified view of the use scenario, but as we go forward we will loop back and realize that often the use scenario must be adjusted to better reflect the actual business need. We will present conceptual tools to help our thinking here, for example framing a business problem in terms of expected value can allow us to systematically decompose it into data mining tasks.

Data Understanding

If solving the business problem is the goal, the data comprise the available raw material from which the solution will be built. It is important to understand the strengths and limitations of the data because rarely is there an exact match with the problem. Historical data often are collected for purposes unrelated to the current business problem, or for no explicit purpose at all. A customer database, a transaction database, and a marketing response database contain different information, may cover different intersecting populations, and may have varying degrees of reliability.

It is also common for the *costs* of data to vary. Some data will be available virtually for free while others will require effort to obtain. Some data may be purchased. Still other data simply won't exist and will require entire ancillary projects to arrange their collection. A critical part of the data understanding phase is estimating the costs and benefits of each data source and deciding whether further investment is merited. Even after all datasets are acquired, collating them may require additional effort. For example, customer records and product identifiers are notoriously variable and noisy. Cleaning and matching customer records to ensure only one record per customer is itself a complicated analytics problem (Hernández & Stolfo, 1995; Elmagarmid, Ipeirotis, & Verykios, 2007).

As data understanding progresses, solution paths may change direction in response, and team efforts may even fork. Fraud detection provides an illustration of this. Data mining has been used extensively for fraud detection, and many fraud detection problems involve classic supervised data mining tasks. Consider the task of catching credit card fraud. Charges show up on each customer's account, so fraudulent charges are usually caught—if not initially by the company, then later by the customer when account activity is reviewed. We can assume that nearly all fraud is identified and reliably labeled, since the legitimate customer and the person perpetrating the fraud are different people and have opposite goals. Thus credit card transactions have reliable labels (*fraud* and *legitimate*) that may serve as targets for a supervised technique.

Now consider the related problem of catching Medicare fraud. This is a huge problem in the United States costing billions of dollars annually. Though this may seem like a conventional fraud detection problem, as we consider the relationship of the business problem to the data, we realize that the problem is significantly different. The perpetrators of fraud—medical providers who submit false claims, and sometimes their patients—are also legitimate service providers and users of the billing system. Those who commit fraud are a subset of the legitimate users; there is no separate disinterested party who will declare exactly what the "correct" charges should be. Consequently the Medicare billing data have no reliable target variable indicating fraud, and a supervised learning approach that could work for credit card fraud is not applicable. Such a problem usually requires unsupervised approaches such as profiling, clustering, anomaly detection, and co-occurrence grouping.

The fact that both of these are fraud detection problems is a superficial similarity that is actually misleading. In data understanding we need to dig beneath the surface to uncover the structure of the business problem and the data that are available, and then match them to one or more data mining tasks for which we may have substantial science and technology to apply. It is not unusual for a business problem to contain several data mining tasks, often of different types, and combining their solutions will be necessary (see Chapter 11).

Data Preparation

The analytic technologies that we can bring to bear are powerful but they impose certain requirements on the data they use. They often require data to be in a form different from how the data are provided naturally, and some conversion will be necessary. Therefore a data preparation phase often proceeds along with data understanding, in which the data are manipulated and converted into forms that yield better results.

Typical examples of data preparation are converting data to tabular format, removing or inferring missing values, and converting data to different types. Some data mining techniques are designed for symbolic and categorical data, while others handle only numeric values. In addition, numerical values must often be normalized or scaled so that they are comparable. Standard techniques and rules of thumb are available for doing such conversions. Chapter 3 discusses the most typical format for mining data in some detail.

In general, though, this book will not focus on data preparation techniques, which could be the topic of a book by themselves (Pyle, 1999). We will define basic data formats in following chapters, and will only be concerned with data preparation details when they shed light on some fundamental principle of data science or are necessary to present a concrete example.

 More generally, data scientists may spend considerable time early in the process defining the variables used later in the process. This is one of the main points at which human creativity, common sense, and business knowledge come into play. Often the quality of the data mining solution rests on how well the analysts structure the problems and craft the variables (and sometimes it can be surprisingly hard for them to admit it).

One very general and important concern during data preparation is to beware of "leaks" (Kaufman et al. 2012). A leak is a situation where a variable collected in historical data gives information on the target variable—information that appears in historical data but is not actually available when the decision has to be made. As an example, when predicting whether at a particular point in time a website visitor would end her session or continue surfing to another page, the variable "total number of webpages visited in the session" is predictive. However, the total number of webpages visited in the session would not be known until after the session was over (Kohavi et al., 2000)—at which point one would know the value for the target variable! As another illustrative example, consider predicting whether a customer *will be* a "big spender"; knowing the categories of the items purchased (or worse, the amount of tax paid) are very predictive, but are not known at decision-making time (Kohavi & Parekh, 2003). Leakage must be considered carefully during data preparation, because data preparation typically is performed after the fact—from historical data. We present a more detailed example of a real leak that was challenging to find in Chapter 14.

Modeling

Modeling is the subject of the next several chapters and we will not dwell on it here, except to say that the output of modeling is some sort of model or pattern capturing regularities in the data.

The modeling stage is the primary place where data mining techniques are applied to the data. It is important to have some understanding of the fundamental ideas of data mining, including the sorts of techniques and algorithms that exist, because this is the part of the craft where the most science and technology can be brought to bear.

Evaluation

The purpose of the evaluation stage is to assess the data mining results rigorously and to gain confidence that they are valid and reliable before moving on. If we look hard enough at any dataset we will find patterns, but they may not survive careful scrutiny. We would like to have confidence that the models and patterns extracted from the data are true regularities and not just idiosyncrasies or sample anomalies. It is possible to deploy results immediately after data mining but this is inadvisable; it is usually far easier, cheaper, quicker, and safer to test a model first in a controlled laboratory setting.

Equally important, the evaluation stage also serves to help ensure that the model satisfies the original business goals. Recall that the primary goal of data science for business is to support decision making, and that we started the process by focusing on the business problem we would like to solve. Usually a data mining solution is only a piece of the larger solution, and it needs to be evaluated as such. Further, even if a model passes strict evaluation tests in "in the lab," there may be external considerations that make it impractical. For example, a common flaw with detection solutions (such as fraud detection, spam detection, and intrusion monitoring) is that they produce too many false alarms. A model may be extremely accurate (> 99%) by laboratory standards, but evaluation in the actual business context may reveal that it still produces too many false alarms to be economically feasible. (How much would it cost to provide the staff to deal with all those false alarms? What would be the cost in customer dissatisfaction?)

Evaluating the results of data mining includes both quantitative and qualitative assessments. Various stakeholders have interests in the business decision-making that will be accomplished or supported by the resultant models. In many cases, these stakeholders need to "sign off" on the deployment of the models, and in order to do so need to be satisfied by the quality of the model's decisions. What that means varies from application to application, but often stakeholders are looking to see whether the model is going to do more good than harm, and especially that the model is unlikely to make catastrophic mistakes.[2] To facilitate such qualitative assessment, the data scientist must think about the *comprehensibility* of the model to stakeholders (not just to the data scientists). And if the model itself is not comprehensible (e.g., maybe the model is a very complex mathematical formula), how can the data scientists work to make the behavior of the model be comprehensible.

Finally, a comprehensive evaluation framework is important because getting detailed information on the performance of a deployed model may be difficult or impossible. Often there is only limited access to the deployment environment so making a comprehensive evaluation "in production" is difficult. Deployed systems typically contain many "moving parts," and assessing the contribution of a single part is difficult. Firms with sophisticated data science teams wisely build testbed environments that mirror production data as closely as possible, in order to get the most realistic evaluations before taking the risk of deployment.

Nonetheless, in some cases we may want to extend evaluation into the development environment, for example by instrumenting a live system to be able to conduct randomized experiments. In our churn example, if we have decided from laboratory tests that a data mined model will give us better churn reduction, we may want to move on to an "in vivo" evaluation, in which a live system randomly applies the model to some customers while keeping other customers as a control group (recall our discussion of causal modeling from Chapter 1). Such experiments must be designed carefully, and the technical details are beyond the scope of this book. The interested reader could start with the lessons-learned articles by Ron Kohavi and his coauthors (Kohavi et al., 2007, 2009, 2012). We may also want to instrument deployed systems for evaluations to make sure that the world is not changing to the detriment of the model's decision-making. For example, behavior can change—in some cases, like fraud or spam, in direct response to the deployment of models. Additionally, the output of the model is critically dependent on the input data; input data can change in format and in substance, often without any alerting of the data science team. Raeder et al. (2012) present a detailed discussion of system design to help deal with these and other related evaluation-in-deployment issues.

Deployment

In deployment the results of data mining—and increasingly the data mining techniques themselves—are put into real use in order to realize some return on investment. The clearest cases of deployment involve implementing a predictive model in some information system or business process. In our churn example, a model for predicting the likelihood of churn could be integrated with the business process for churn management

---

2. For example, in one data mining project a model was created to diagnose problems in local phone networks, and to dispatch technicians to the likely site of the problem. Before deployment, a team of phone company stakeholders requested that the model be tweaked so that exceptions were made for hospitals.

—for example, by sending special offers to customers who are predicted to be particularly at risk. (We will discuss this in increasing detail as the book proceeds.) A new fraud detection model may be built into a workforce management information system, to monitor accounts and create "cases" for fraud analysts to examine.

Increasingly, the data mining techniques themselves are deployed. For example, for targeting online advertisements, systems are deployed that automatically build (and test) models in production when a new advertising campaign is presented. Two main reasons for deploying the data mining system itself rather than the models produced by a data mining system are (i) the world may change faster than the data science team can adapt, as with fraud and intrusion detection, and (ii) a business has too many modeling tasks for their data science team to manually curate each model individually. In these cases, it may be best to deploy the data mining phase into production. In doing so, it is critical to instrument the process to alert the data science team of any seeming anomalies and to provide fail-safe operation (Raeder et al., 2012).

 Deployment can also be much less "technical." In a celebrated case, data mining discovered a set of rules that could help to quickly diagnose and fix a common error in industrial printing. The deployment succeeded simply by taping a sheet of paper containing the rules to the side of the printers (Evans & Fisher, 2002). Deployment can also be much more subtle, such as a change to data acquisition procedures, or a change to strategy, marketing, or operations resulting from insight gained from mining the data.

Deploying a model into a production system typically requires that the model be recoded for the production environment, usually for greater speed or compatibility with an existing system. This may incur substantial expense and investment. In many cases, the data science team is responsible for producing a working prototype, along with its evaluation. These are passed to a development team.

 Practically speaking, there are risks with "over the wall" transfers from data science to development. It may be helpful to remember the maxim: "Your model is not what the data scientists design, it's what the engineers build." From a management perspective, it is advisable to have members of the development team involved early on in the data science project. They can begin as advisors, providing critical insight to the data science team. Increasingly in practice, these particular developers are "data science engineers"—software engineers who have particular expertise both in the production systems and in data science. These developers gradually assume more responsibility as the project matures. At some point the developers will take the lead and assume ownership of the product. Generally, the data scientists should still remain involved in the project into final deployment, as advisors or as developers depending on their skills.

Regardless of whether deployment is successful, the process often returns to the Business Understanding phase. The process of mining data produces a great deal of insight into the business problem and the difficulties of its solution. A second iteration can yield an improved solution. Just the experience of thinking about the business, the data, and the performance goals often leads to new ideas for improving business performance, and even new lines of business or new ventures.

Note that it is not necessary to fail in deployment to start the cycle again. The Evaluation stage may reveal that results are not good enough to deploy, and we need to adjust the problem definition or get different data. This is represented by the "shortcut" link from Evaluation back to Business Understanding in the process diagram. In practice, there should be shortcuts back from each stage to each prior one because the process always retains some exploratory aspects, and a project should be flexible enough to revisit prior steps based on discoveries made.[3]

Implications for Managing the Data Science Team

It is tempting—but usually a mistake—to view the data mining process as a software development cycle. Indeed, data mining projects are often treated and managed as engineering projects, which is understandable when they are initiated by software departments, with data generated by a large software system and analytics results fed back into it. Managers are usually familiar with software technologies and are comfortable managing software projects. Milestones can be agreed upon and success is usually unambiguous. Software managers might look at the CRISP data mining cycle (Figure 2-2) and think it looks comfortably similar to a software development cycle, so they should be right at home managing an analytics project the same way.

This can be a mistake because data mining is an exploratory undertaking closer to research and development than it is to engineering. The CRISP cycle is based around exploration; it iterates on *approaches* and *strategy* rather than on software designs. Outcomes are far less certain, and the results of a given step may change the fundamental understanding of the problem. Engineering a data mining solution directly for deployment can be an expensive premature commitment. Instead, analytics projects should prepare to invest in information to reduce uncertainty in various ways. Small investments can be made via pilot studies and throwaway prototypes. Data scientists should

---

3. Software professionals may recognize the similarity to the philosophy of "Fail faster to succeed sooner" (Muoio, 1997).

review the literature to see what else has been done and how it has worked. On a larger scale, a team can invest substantially in building experimental testbeds to allow extensive agile experimentation. If you're a software manager, this will look more like research and exploration than you're used to, and maybe more than you're comfortable with.

Software skills versus analytics skills

Although data mining involves software, it also requires skills that may not be common among programmers. In software engineering, the ability to write efficient, high-quality code from requirements may be paramount. Team members may be evaluated using software metrics such as the amount of code written or number of bug tickets closed. In analytics, it's more important for individuals to be able to formulate problems well, to prototype solutions quickly, to make reasonable assumptions in the face of ill-structured problems, to design experiments that represent good investments, and to analyze results. In building a data science team, these qualities, rather than traditional software engineering expertise, are skills that should be sought.

Other Analytics Techniques and Technologies

Business analytics involves the application of various technologies to the analysis of data. Many of these go beyond this book's focus on data-analytic thinking and the principles of extracting useful patterns from data. Nonetheless, it is important to be acquainted with these related techniques, to understand what their goals are, what role they play, and when it may be beneficial to consult experts in them.

To this end, we present six groups of related analytic techniques. Where appropriate we draw comparisons and contrasts with data mining. The main difference is that data mining focuses on the *automated* search for *knowledge*, *patterns*, or *regularities* from data.[4] An important skill for a business analyst is to be able to recognize what sort of analytic technique is appropriate for addressing a particular problem.

Statistics

The term "statistics" has two different uses in business analytics. First, it is used as a catchall term for the computation of particular numeric values of interest from data (e.g., "We need to gather some statistics on our customers' usage to determine what's going wrong here.") These values often include sums, averages, rates, and so on. Let's

---

4. It is important to keep in mind that it is rare for the discovery to be completely automated. The important factor is that data mining automates at least partially the search and discovery process, rather than providing technical support for manual search and discovery.

call these "summary statistics." Often we want to dig deeper, and calculate summary statistics *conditionally* on one or more subsets of the population (e.g., "Does the churn rate differ between male and female customers?" and "What about high-income customers in the Northeast (denotes a region of the USA)?") Summary statistics are the basic building blocks of much data science theory and practice.

Summary statistics should be chosen with close attention to the business problem to be solved (one of the fundamental principles we will present later), and also with attention to the *distribution* of the data they are summarizing. For example, the average (mean) income in the United States according to the 2004 Census Bureau Economic Survey was over $60,000. If we were to use that as a measure of the average income in order to make policy decisions, we would be misleading ourselves. The distribution of incomes in the U.S. is highly skewed, with many people making relatively little and some people making fantastically much. In such cases, the arithmetic mean tells us relatively little about how much people are making. Instead, we should use a different measure of "average" income, such as the median. The median income—that amount where half the population makes more and half makes less—in the U.S. in the 2004 Census study was only $44,389 —considerably less than the mean. This example may seem obvious because we are so accustomed to hearing about the "median income," but the same reasoning applies to any computation of summary statistics: have you thought about the problem you would like to solve or the question you would like to answer? Have you considered the distribution of the data, and whether the chosen statistic is appropriate?

The other use of the term "statistics" is to denote the field of study that goes by that name, for which we might differentiate by using the proper name, Statistics. The field of Statistics provides us with a huge amount of knowledge that underlies analytics, and can be thought of as a component of the larger field of Data Science. For example, Statistics helps us to understand different data distributions and what statistics are appropriate to summarize each. Statistics helps us understand how to use data to test hypotheses and to estimate the uncertainty of conclusions. In relation to data mining, hypothesis testing can help determine whether an observed pattern is likely to be a valid, general regularity as opposed to a chance occurrence in some particular dataset. Most relevant to this book, many of the techniques for extracting models or patterns from data have their roots in Statistics.

For example, a preliminary study may suggest that customers in the Northeast have a churn rate of 22.5%, whereas the nationwide average churn rate is only 15%. This may be just a chance fluctuation since the churn rate is not constant; it varies over regions and over time, so differences are to be expected. But the Northeast rate is one and a half times the U.S. average, which seems unusually high. What is the chance that this is due to random variation? Statistical hypothesis testing is used to answer such questions.

Closely related is the quantification of uncertainty into confidence intervals. The overall churn rate is 15%, but there is some variation; traditional statistical analysis may reveal that 95% of the time the churn rate is expected to fall between 13% and 17%.

This contrasts with the (complementary) process of data mining, which may be seen as hypothesis *generation*. Can we find patterns in data in the first place? Hypothesis generation should then be followed by careful hypothesis testing (generally on different data; see Chapter 5). In addition, data mining procedures may produce numerical estimates, and we often also want to provide confidence intervals on these estimates. We will return to this when we discuss the evaluation of the results of data mining.

In this book we are not going to spend more time discussing these basic statistical concepts. There are plenty of introductory books on statistics and statistics for business, and any treatment we would try to squeeze in would be either very narrow or superficial.

That said, one statistical term that is often heard in the context of business analytics is "correlation." For example, "Are there any indicators that correlate with a customer's later defection?" As with the term statistics, "correlation" has both a general-purpose meaning (variations in one quantity tell us something about variations in the other), and a specific technical meaning (e.g., linear correlation based on a particular mathematical formula). The notion of correlation will be the jumping off point for the rest of our discussion of data science for business, starting in the next chapter.

Database Querying

A *query* is a specific request for a subset of data or for statistics about data, formulated in a technical language and posed to a database system. Many tools are available to answer one-off or repeating queries about data posed by an analyst. These tools are usually frontends to database systems, based on Structured Query Language (SQL) or a tool with a graphical user interface (GUI) to help formulate queries (e.g., query-by-example, or QBE). For example, if the analyst can define "profitable" in operational terms computable from items in the database, then a query tool could answer: "Who are the most profitable customers in the Northeast?" The analyst may then run the query to retrieve a list of the most profitable customers, possibly ranked by profitability. This activity differs fundamentally from data mining in that there is no discovery of patterns or models.

Database queries are appropriate when an analyst already has an idea of what might be an interesting subpopulation of the data, and wants to investigate this population or confirm a hypothesis about it. For example, if an analyst suspects that middle-aged men living in the Northeast have some particularly interesting churning behavior, she could compose a SQL query:

```
SELECT * FROM CUSTOMERS WHERE AGE > 45 and SEX='M' and DOMICILE = 'NE'
```

If those are the people to be targeted with an offer, a query tool can be used to retrieve all of the information about them ("*") from the CUSTOMERS table in the database.

In contrast, data mining could be used to come up with this query in the first place—as a pattern or regularity in the data. A data mining procedure might examine prior customers who did and did not defect, and determine that this segment (characterized as "AGE is greater than 45 and SEX is male and DOMICILE is Northeast-USA") is predictive with respect to churn rate. After translating this into a SQL query, a query tool could then be used to find the matching records in the database.

Query tools generally have the ability to execute sophisticated logic, including computing summary statistics over subpopulations, sorting, joining together multiple tables with related data, and more. Data scientists often become quite adept at writing queries to extract the data they need.

On-line Analytical Processing (OLAP) provides an easy-to-use GUI to query large data collections, for the purpose of facilitating data exploration. The idea of "on-line" processing is that it is done in realtime, so analysts and decision makers can find answers to their queries quickly and efficiently. Unlike the "ad hoc" querying enabled by tools like SQL, for OLAP the dimensions of analysis must be pre-programmed into the OLAP system. If we've foreseen that we would want to explore sales volume by region and time, we could have these three dimensions programmed into the system, and drill down into populations, often simply by clicking and dragging and manipulating dynamic charts.

OLAP systems are designed to facilitate manual or visual exploration of the data by analysts. OLAP performs no modeling or automatic pattern finding. As an additional contrast, unlike with OLAP, data mining tools generally can incorporate new dimensions of analysis easily as part of the exploration. OLAP tools can be a useful complement to data mining tools for discovery from business data.

Data Warehousing

Data warehouses collect and coalesce data from across an enterprise, often from multiple transaction-processing systems, each with its own database. Analytical systems can access data warehouses. Data warehousing may be seen as a facilitating technology of data mining. It is not always necessary, as most data mining does not access a data warehouse, but firms that decide to invest in data warehouses often can apply data mining more broadly and more deeply in the organization. For example, if a data warehouse integrates records from sales and billing as well as from human resources, it can be used to find characteristic patterns of effective salespeople.

Regression Analysis

Some of the same methods we discuss in this book are at the core of a different set of analytic methods, which often are collected under the rubric *regression analysis*, and are widely applied in the field of statistics and also in other fields founded on econometric analysis. This book will focus on different issues than usually encountered in a regression analysis book or class. Here we are less interested in explaining a particular dataset as we are in extracting patterns that will generalize to other data, and for the purpose of improving some business process. Typically, this will involve estimating or predicting values for cases that are not in the analyzed data set. So, as an example, in this book we are less interested in digging into the reasons for churn (important as they may be) in a particular historical set of data, and more interested in predicting which customers who have not yet left would be the best to target to reduce future churn. Therefore, we will spend some time talking about testing patterns on new data to evaluate their generality, and about techniques for reducing the tendency to find patterns specific to a particular set of data, but that do not generalize to the population from which the data come.

The topic of explanatory modeling versus predictive modeling can elicit deep-felt debate,[5] which goes well beyond our focus. What is important is to realize that there is considerable overlap in the *techniques* used, but that the lessons learned from explanatory modeling do not all apply to predictive modeling. So a reader with some background in regression analysis may encounter new and even seemingly contradictory lessons.[6]

Machine Learning and Data Mining

The collection of methods for extracting (predictive) models from data, now known as machine learning methods, were developed in several fields contemporaneously, most notably Machine Learning, Applied Statistics, and Pattern Recognition. Machine Learning as a field of study arose as a subfield of Artificial Intelligence, which was concerned with methods for improving the knowledge or performance of an intelligent agent over time, in response to the agent's experience in the world. Such improvement often involves analyzing data from the environment and making predictions about unknown quantities, and over the years this data analysis aspect of machine learning has come to play a very large role in the field. As machine learning methods were deployed broadly, the scientific disciplines of Machine Learning, Applied Statistics, and Pattern Recognition developed close ties, and the separation between the fields has blurred.

---

5. The interested reader is urged to read the discussion by Shmueli (2010).

6. Those who pursue the study in depth will have the seeming contradictions worked out. Such deep study is not necessary to understand the fundamental principles.

The field of Data Mining (or KDD: Knowledge Discovery and Data Mining) started as an offshoot of Machine Learning, and they remain closely linked. Both fields are concerned with the analysis of data to find useful or informative patterns. Techniques and algorithms are shared between the two; indeed, the areas are so closely related that researchers commonly participate in both communities and transition between them seamlessly. Nevertheless, it is worth pointing out some of the differences to give perspective.

Speaking generally, because Machine Learning is concerned with many types of performance improvement, it includes subfields such as robotics and computer vision that are not part of KDD. It also is concerned with issues of *agency* and *cognition*—how will an intelligent agent use learned knowledge to reason and act in its environment—which are not concerns of Data Mining.

Historically, KDD spun off from Machine Learning as a research field focused on concerns raised by examining real-world applications, and a decade and a half later the KDD community remains more concerned with applications than Machine Learning is. As such, research focused on commercial applications and business issues of data analysis tends to gravitate toward the KDD community rather than to Machine Learning. KDD also tends to be more concerned with the entire process of data analytics: data preparation, model learning, evaluation, and so on.

Answering Business Questions with These Techniques

To illustrate how these techniques apply to business analytics, consider a set of questions that may arise and the technologies that would be appropriate for answering them. These questions are all related but each is subtly different. It is important to understand these differences in order to understand what technologies one needs to employ and what people may be necessary to consult.

1. *Who are the most profitable customers?*

   If "profitable" can be defined clearly based on existing data, this is a straightforward database query. A standard query tool could be used to retrieve a set of customer records from a database. The results could be sorted by cumulative transaction amount, or some other operational indicator of profitability.

2. *Is there really a difference between the profitable customers and the average customer?*

   This is a question about a conjecture or hypothesis (in this case, "There is a difference in value to the company between the profitable customers and the average customer"), and statistical hypothesis testing would be used to confirm or disconfirm it. Statistical analysis could also derive a probability or confidence bound that the difference was real. Typically, the result would be like: "The value of these profitable customers is significantly different from that of the average customer, with probability < 5% that this is due to random chance."

3. *But who really are these customers? Can I characterize them?*

   We often would like to do more than just list out the profitable customers. We would like to describe common characteristics of profitable customers. The characteristics of individual customers can be extracted from a database using techniques such as database querying, which also can be used to generate summary statistics. A deeper analysis should involve determining what characteristics *differentiate* profitable customers from unprofitable ones. This is the realm of data science, using data mining techniques for automated pattern finding—which we discuss in depth in the subsequent chapters.

4. *Will some particular new customer be profitable? How much revenue should I expect this customer to generate?*

   These questions could be addressed by data mining techniques that examine historical customer records and produce predictive models of profitability. Such techniques would generate models from historical data that could then be applied to new customers to generate predictions. Again, this is the subject of the following chapters.

Note that this last pair of questions are subtly different data mining questions. The first, a classification question, may be phrased as a prediction of whether a given new customer will be profitable (yes/no or the probability thereof). The second may be phrased as a prediction of the value (numerical) that the customer will bring to the company. More on that as we proceed.

Summary

Data mining is a craft. As with many crafts, there is a well-defined process that can help to increase the likelihood of a successful result. This process is a crucial conceptual tool for thinking about data science projects. We will refer back to the data mining process repeatedly throughout the book, showing how each fundamental concept fits in. In turn, understanding the fundamentals of data science substantially improves the chances of success as an enterprise invokes the data mining process.

The various fields of study related to data science have developed a set of canonical task types, such as classification, regression, and clustering. Each task type serves a different purpose and has an associated set of solution techniques. A data scientist typically attacks a new project by decomposing it such that one or more of these canonical tasks is revealed, choosing a solution technique for each, then composing the solutions. Doing this expertly may take considerable experience and skill. A successful data mining project involves an intelligent compromise between what the data can do (i.e., what they can predict, and how well) and the project goals. For this reason it is important to keep in mind how data mining results will be used, and use this to inform the data mining process itself.

Data mining differs from, and is complementary to, important supporting technologies such as statistical hypothesis testing and database querying (which have their own books and classes). Though the boundaries between data mining and related techniques are not always sharp, it is important to know about other techniques' capabilities and strengths to know when they should be used.

To a business manager, the data mining process is useful as a framework for analyzing a data mining project or proposal. The process provides a systematic organization, including a set of questions that can be asked about a project or a proposed project to help understand whether the project is well conceived or is fundamentally flawed. We will return to this after we have discussed in detail some more of the fundamental principles themselves—to which we turn now.

CHAPTER 3

Introduction to Predictive Modeling: From Correlation to Supervised Segmentation

Fundamental concepts: *Identifying informative attributes; Segmenting data by progressive attribute selection.*

Exemplary techniques: *Finding correlations; Attribute/variable selection; Tree induction.*

The previous chapters discussed models and modeling at a high level. This chapter delves into one of the main topics of data mining: predictive modeling. Following our example of data mining for churn prediction from the first section, we will begin by thinking of predictive modeling as *supervised* segmentation—how can we segment the population into groups that differ from each other with respect to some quantity of interest. In particular, how can we segment the population with respect to something that we would like to predict or estimate. The target of this prediction can be something we would like to avoid, such as which customers are likely to leave the company when their contracts expire, which accounts have been defrauded, which potential customers are likely not to pay off their account balances (*write-offs*, such as defaulting on one's phone bill or credit card balance), or which web pages contain objectionable content. The target might instead be cast in a positive light, such as which consumers are most likely to respond to an advertisement or special offer, or which web pages are most appropriate for a search query.

In the process of discussing supervised segmentation, we introduce one of the fundamental ideas of data mining: finding or selecting important, informative variables or "attributes" of the entities described by the data. What exactly it means to be "informative" varies among applications, but generally, *information is a quantity that reduces uncertainty about something.* So, if an old pirate gives me information about where his treasure is hidden that does not mean that I know for certain where it is, it only means that my uncertainty about where the treasure is hidden is reduced. The better the information, the more my uncertainty is reduced.

Now, recall the notion of "supervised" data mining from the previous chapter. A key to supervised data mining is that we have some target quantity we would like to predict or to otherwise understand better. Often this quantity is unknown or unknowable at the time we would like to make a business decision, such as whether a customer will churn soon after her contract expires, or which accounts have been defrauded. Having a target variable crystalizes our notion of finding informative attributes: is there one or more other variables that reduces our uncertainty about the value of the target? This also gives a common analytics application of the general notion of correlation discussed above: we would like to find knowable attributes that correlate with the target of interest —that reduce our uncertainty in it. Just finding these correlated variables may provide important insight into the business problem.

Finding informative attributes also is useful to help us deal with increasingly larger databases and data streams. Datasets that are too large pose computational problems for analytic techniques, especially when the analyst does not have access to high-performance computers. One tried-and-true method for analyzing very large datasets is first to select a subset of the data to analyze. Selecting informative attributes provides an "intelligent" method for selecting an informative subset of the data. In addition, attribute selection prior to data-driven modeling can increase the accuracy of the modeling, for reasons we will discuss in Chapter 5.

Finding informative attributes also is the basis for a widely used predictive modeling technique called *tree induction*, which we will introduce toward the end of this chapter as an application of this fundamental concept. Tree induction incorporates the idea of supervised segmentation in an elegant manner, repeatedly selecting informative attributes. By the end of this chapter we will have achieved an understanding of: the basic concepts of predictive modeling; the fundamental notion of finding informative attributes, along with one particular, illustrative technique for doing so; the notion of tree-structured models; and a basic understanding of the process for extracting tree-structured models from a dataset—performing supervised segmentation.

Models, Induction, and Prediction

Generally speaking, a model is a simplified representation of reality created to serve a purpose. It is simplified based on some assumptions about what is and is not important for the specific purpose, or sometimes based on constraints on information or tractability. For example, a map is a model of the physical world. It abstracts away a tremendous amount of information that the mapmaker deemed irrelevant for its purpose. It preserves, and sometimes further simplifies, the relevant information. For example, a road map keeps and highlights the roads, their basic topology, their relationships to places one would want to travel, and other relevant information. Various professions have well-known model types: an architectural blueprint, an engineering prototype, the

Figure 3-1 table:

Name	Balance	Age	Employed	Write-off
Mike	$200,000	42	no	yes
Mary	$35,000	33	yes	no
Claudio	$115,000	40	no	no
Robert	$29,000	23	yes	yes
Dora	$72,000	31	no	no

Attributes — Target attribute

This is one row (example).
Feature vector is: **<Claudio,115000,40,no>**
Class label (value of Target attribute) is **no**

Figure 3-1. Data mining terminology for a supervised classification problem. The problem is supervised because it has a target attribute and some "training" data where we know the value for the target attribute. It is a classification (rather than regression) problem because the target is a category (yes or no) rather than a number.

Black-Scholes model of option pricing, and so on. Each of these abstracts away details that are not relevant to their main purpose and keeps those that are.

In data science, a predictive model is a formula for estimating the unknown value of interest: the target. The formula could be mathematical, or it could be a logical statement such as a rule. Often it is a hybrid of the two. Given our division of supervised data mining into classification and regression, we will consider classification models (and class-probability estimation models) and regression models.

Terminology: Prediction

In common usage, prediction means to forecast a future event. In data science, prediction more generally means *to estimate an unknown value*. This value could be something in the future (in common usage, true prediction), but it could also be something in the present or in the past. Indeed, since data mining usually deals with historical data, models very often are built and tested using events from the past. Predictive models for credit scoring estimate the likelihood that a potential customer will default (become a write-off). Predictive models for spam filtering estimate whether a given piece of email is spam. Predictive models for fraud detection judge whether an account has been defrauded. The key is that the model is intended to be used to estimate an unknown value.

This is in contrast to *descriptive* modeling, where the primary purpose of the model is not to estimate a value but instead to gain insight into the underlying phenomenon or process. A descriptive model of churn behavior would tell us what customers who churn typically look like.[1] A descriptive model must be judged in part on its intelligibility, and a less accurate model may be preferred if it is easier to understand. A predictive model may be judged solely on its predictive performance, although we will discuss why intelligibility is nonetheless important. The difference between these model types is not as strict as this may imply; some of the same techniques can be used for both, and usually one model can serve both purposes (though sometimes poorly). Sometimes much of the value of a predictive model is in the understanding gained from looking at it rather than in the predictions it makes.

Before we discuss predictive modeling further, we must introduce some terminology. Supervised learning is model creation where the model describes a relationship between a set of selected variables (*attributes* or *features*) and a predefined variable called the *target* variable. The model estimates the value of the target variable as a function (possibly a probabilistic function) of the features. So, for our churn-prediction problem we would like to build a model of the propensity to churn as a function of customer account attributes, such as age, income, length with the company, number of calls to customer service, overage charges, customer demographics, data usage, and others.

Figure 3-1 illustrates some of the terminology we introduce here, in an oversimplified example problem of credit write-off prediction. An *instance* or *example* represents a fact or a data point—in this case a historical customer who had been given credit. This is also called a *row* in database or spreadsheet terminology. An instance is described by a set of *attributes* (fields, columns, variables, or features). An instance is also sometimes called a *feature vector*, because it can be represented as a fixed-length ordered collection (vector) of feature values. Unless stated otherwise, we will assume that the values of all the attributes (but not the target) are present in the data.

---

1. Descriptive modeling often is used to work toward a causal understanding of the data generating process (*why do people churn?*).

Many Names for the Same Things

The principles and techniques of data science historically have been studied in several different fields, including machine learning, pattern recognition, statistics, databases, and others. As a result there often are several different names for the same things. We typically will refer to a *dataset*, whose form usually is the same as a *table* of a database or a *worksheet* of a spreadsheet. A dataset contains a set of *examples* or *instances*. An instance also is referred to as a *row* of a database table or sometimes a *case* in statistics.

The features (table columns) have many different names as well. Statisticians speak of *independent variables* or *predictors* as the attributes supplied as input. In operations research you may also hear *explanatory variable*. The target variable, whose values are to be predicted, is commonly called the *dependent variable* in statistics. This terminology may be somewhat confusing; the independent variables may not be independent of each other (or anything else), and the dependent variable doesn't always depend on all the independent variables. For this reason we have avoided the dependent/independent terminology in this book. Some experts consider the target variable to be included in the set of features, some do not. The important thing is rather obvious: the target variable is not used to predict itself. However, it may be that prior values for the target variable are quite helpful to predict future values—so such prior values may be included as features.

The creation of models from data is known as model induction. Induction is a term from philosophy that refers to generalizing from specific cases to general rules (or laws, or truths). Our models are general rules in a statistical sense (they usually do not hold 100% of the time; often not nearly), and the procedure that creates the model from the data is called the induction algorithm or learner. Most inductive procedures have variants that induce models both for classification and for regression. We will discuss mainly classification models because they tend to receive less attention in other treatments of statistics, and because they are relevant to many business problems (and thus much work in data science focuses on classification).

Terminology: Induction and deduction

Induction can be contrasted with *deduction*. Deduction starts with general rules and specific facts, and creates other specific facts from them. The *use* of our models can be considered a procedure of (probabilistic) deduction. We will get to this shortly.

The input data for the induction algorithm, used for inducing the model, are called the *training* data. As mentioned in Chapter 2, they are called *labeled* data because the value for the target variable (the label) is known.

Let's return to our example churn problem. Based on what we learned in Chapter 1 and Chapter 2, we might decide that in the modeling stage we should build a "supervised segmentation" model, which divides the sample into segments having (on average) higher or lower tendency to leave the company after contract expiration. To think about how this might be done, let's now turn to one of our fundamental concepts: How can we select one or more attributes/features/variables that will best divide the sample *with respect to our target variable of interest*?

Supervised Segmentation

Recall that a predictive model focuses on estimating the value of some particular target variable of interest. An intuitive way of thinking about extracting patterns from data in a supervised manner is to try to segment the population into subgroups that have different values for the target variable (and within the subgroup the instances have similar values for the target variable). If the segmentation is done using values of variables that will be known when the target is not, then these segments can be used to predict the value of the target variable. Moreover, the segmentation may at the same time provide a human-understandable set of segmentation patterns. One such segment expressed in English might be: "Middle-aged professionals who reside in New York City on average have a churn rate of 5%." Specifically, the term "middle-aged professionals who reside in New York City" is the definition of the segment (which references some particular attributes) and "a churn rate of 5%" describes the predicted value of the target variable for the segment.[2]

Often we are interested in applying data mining when we have many attributes, and are not sure exactly what the segments should be. In our churn-prediction problem, who is to say what are the best segments for predicting the propensity to churn? If there exist in the data segments with significantly different (average) values for the target variable, we would like to be able to extract them automatically.

This brings us to our fundamental concept: how can we judge whether a variable contains important information about the target variable? How much? We would like automatically to get a selection of the more informative variables with respect to the particular task at hand (namely, predicting the value of the target variable). Even better, we might like to rank the variables by how good they are at predicting the value of the target.

Consider just the selection of the single most informative attribute. Solving this problem will introduce our first concrete data mining technique—simple, but easily extendable to be very useful. In our example, what variable gives us the most information about

---

2. The predicted value can be estimated from the data in different ways, which we will get to. At this point we can think of it roughly as an average of some sort from the training data that fall into the segment.

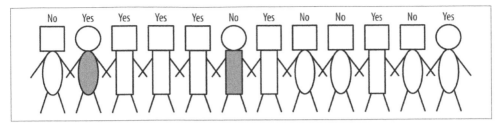

Figure 3-2. A set of people to be classified. The label over each head represents the value of the target variable (write-off or not). Colors and shapes represent different predictor attributes.

the future churn rate of the population? Being a professional? Age? Place of residence? Income? Number of complaints to customer service? Amount of overage charges?

We now will look carefully into one useful way to select informative variables, and then later will show how this technique can be used repeatedly to build a supervised segmentation. While very useful and illustrative, please keep in mind that direct, multivariate supervised segmentation is just one application of this fundamental idea of selecting informative variables. This notion should become one of your conceptual tools when thinking about data science problems more generally. For example, as we go forward we will delve into other modeling approaches, ones that do not incorporate variable selection directly. When the world presents you with very large sets of attributes, it may be (extremely) useful to harken back to this early idea and to select a subset of informative attributes. Doing so can substantially reduce the size of an unwieldy dataset, and as we will see, often will improve the accuracy of the resultant model.

Selecting Informative Attributes

Given a large set of examples, how do we select an attribute to partition them in an informative way? Let's consider a binary (two class) classification problem, and think about what we would like to get out of it. To be concrete, Figure 3-2 shows a simple segmentation problem: twelve people represented as stick figures. There are two types of heads: square and circular; and two types of bodies: rectangular and oval; and two of the people have gray bodies while the rest are white.

These are the attributes we will use to describe the people. Above each person is the binary target label, *Yes* or *No*, indicating (for example) whether the person becomes a loan write-off. We could describe the data on these people as:

- Attributes:
  — head-shape: square, circular
  — body-shape: rectangular, oval
  — body-color: gray, white
- Target variable:
  — write-off: Yes, No

So let's ask ourselves: which of the attributes would be best to segment these people into groups, in a way that will distinguish write-offs from non-write-offs? Technically, we would like the resulting groups to be as *pure* as possible. By pure we mean *homogeneous with respect to the target variable*. If every member of a group has the same value for the target, then the group is pure. If there is at least one member of the group that has a different value for the target variable than the rest of the group, then the group is impure.

Unfortunately, in real data we seldom expect to find a variable that will make the segments pure. However, if we can reduce the impurity substantially, then we can both learn something about the data (and the corresponding population), and importantly for this chapter, we can use the attribute in a predictive model—in our example, predicting that members of one segment will have higher or lower write-off rates than those in another segment. If we can do that, then we can for example offer credit to those with the lower predicted write-off rates, or can offer different credit terms based on the different predicted write-off rates.

Technically, there are several complications:

1. Attributes rarely split a group perfectly. Even if one subgroup happens to be pure, the other may not. For example, in Figure 3-2, consider if the second person were not there. Then *body-color=gray* would create a pure segment (*write-off=no*). However, the other associated segment, *body-color=white*, still is not pure.

2. In the prior example, the condition *body-color=gray* only splits off one single data point into the pure subset. Is this better than another split that does not produce any pure subset, but reduces the impurity more broadly?

3. Not all attributes are binary; many attributes have three or more distinct values. We must take into account that one attribute can split into two groups while another might split into three groups, or seven. How do we compare these?

4. Some attributes take on numeric values (continuous or integer). Does it make sense to make a segment for every numeric value? (No.) How should we think about creating supervised segmentations using numeric attributes?

Fortunately, for classification problems we can address all the issues by creating a formula that evaluates how well each attribute splits a set of examples into segments, with respect to a chosen target variable. Such a formula is based on a *purity measure*.

The most common splitting criterion is called *information gain*, and it is based on a purity measure called *entropy*. Both concepts were invented by one of the pioneers of information theory, Claude Shannon, in his seminal work in the field (Shannon, 1948).

Entropy is a measure of disorder that can be applied to a set, such as one of our individual segments. Consider that we have a set of *properties* of members of the set, and each member has one and only one of the properties. In supervised segmentation, the member properties will correspond to the values of the target variable. Disorder corresponds to how mixed (impure) the segment is with respect to these properties of interest. So, for example, a mixed up segment with lots of write-offs and lots of non-write-offs would have high entropy.

More technically, entropy is defined as:

Equation 3-1. Entropy

$$entropy = -p_1 \log (p_1) - p_2 \log (p_2) - \cdots$$

Each p_i is the probability (the relative percentage) of property i within the set, ranging from $p_i = 1$ when all members of the set have property i, and $p_i = 0$ when no members of the set have property i. The ... simply indicates that there may be more than just two properties (and for the technically minded, the logarithm is generally taken as base 2).

Since the entropy equation might not lend itself to intuitive understanding, Figure 3-3 shows a plot of the entropy of a set containing 10 instances of two classes, + and –. We can see then that entropy measures the general disorder of the set, ranging from zero at minimum disorder (the set has members all with the same, single property) to one at maximal disorder (the properties are equally mixed). Since there are only two classes, $p_+ = 1-p_-$. Starting with all negative instances at the lower left, $p_+ = 0$, the set has minimal disorder (it is pure) and the entropy is zero. If we start to switch class labels of elements of the set from – to +, the entropy increases. Entropy is maximized at 1 when the instance classes are balanced (five of each), and $p_+ = p_- = 0.5$. As more class labels are switched, the + class starts to predominate and the entropy lowers again. When all instances are positive, $p_+ = 1$ and entropy is minimal again at zero.

As a concrete example, consider a set S of 10 people with seven of the *non-write-off* class and three of the *write-off* class. So:

$p(\text{non-write-off}) = 7 / 10 = 0.7$
$p(\text{write-off}) = 3 / 10 = 0.3$

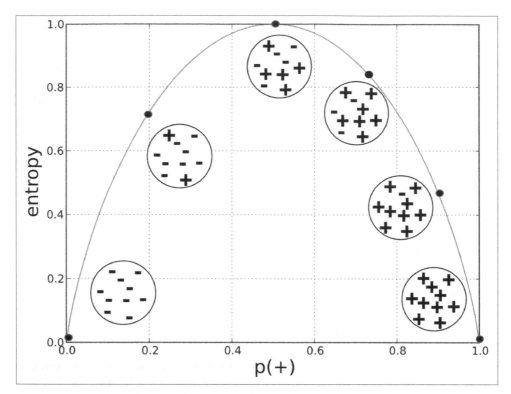

Figure 3-3. Entropy of a two-class set as a function of p(+).

$$entropy(S) \quad = \quad -[0.7 \times \log_2 (0.7) + 0.3 \times \log_2 (0.3)]$$

$$\approx \quad -[0.7 \times -0.51 + 0.3 \times -1.74]$$

$$\approx \quad 0.88$$

Entropy is only part of the story. We would like to measure how *informative* an attribute is with respect to our target: how much gain in information it gives us about the value of the target variable. An attribute segments a set of instances into several subsets. Entropy only tells us how impure one individual subset is. Fortunately, with entropy to measure how disordered any set is, we can define *information gain* (IG) to measure how much an attribute improves (decreases) entropy over the whole segmentation it creates. Strictly speaking, information gain measures the *change* in entropy due to any amount of new information being added; here, in the context of supervised segmentation, we consider the information gained by splitting the set on all values of a single attribute. Let's say the attribute we split on has *k* different values. Let's call the original set of examples the *parent* set, and the result of splitting on the attribute values the *k children* sets. Thus, information gain is a function of both a parent set and of the children resulting from some partitioning of the parent set—how much information has this attribute provided? That depends on how much purer the children are than the parent. Stated in the context of predictive modeling, if we were to know the value of this attribute, how much would it increase our knowledge of the value of the target variable?

Specifically, the definition of information gain (IG) is:

Equation 3-2. Information gain

$$IG(parent, children) = entropy(parent) -$$
$$[p(c_1) \times entropy(c_1) + p(c_2) \times entropy(c_2) + \cdots]$$

Notably, the entropy for each child (c_i) is weighted by the proportion of instances belonging to that child, $p(c_i)$. This addresses directly our concern from above that splitting off a single example, and noticing that that set is pure, may not be as good as splitting the parent set into two nice large, relatively pure subsets, even if neither is pure.

As an example, consider the split in Figure 3-4. This is a two-class problem (• and ★). Examining the figure, the children sets certainly seem "purer" than the parent set. The parent set has 30 instances consisting of 16 dots and 14 stars, so:

$$entropy(parent) = -[p(•) \times \log_2 p(•) + p(★) \times \log_2 p(★)]$$
$$\approx -[0.53 \times -0.9 + 0.47 \times -1.1]$$
$$\approx 0.99 \quad (\text{very impure})$$

The entropy of the *left* child is:

$$entropy(Balance < 50K) = -[p(•) \times \log_2 p(•) + p(★) \times \log_2 p(★)]$$
$$\approx -[0.92 \times (-0.12) + 0.08 \times (-3.7)]$$
$$\approx 0.39$$

The entropy of the *right* child is:

$$entropy(Balance \geq 50K) = -[p(•) \times \log_2 p(•) + p(★) \times \log_2 p(★)]$$
$$\approx -[0.24 \times (-2.1) + 0.76 \times (-0.39)]$$
$$\approx 0.79$$

Using Equation 3-2, the information gain of this split is:

$$IG \quad = \quad entropy(parent) - [\, p(\text{Balance} < 50K) \times entropy(\text{Balance} < 50K)$$
$$+ p(\text{Balance} \geq 50K) \times entropy(\text{Balance} \geq 50K)]$$
$$\approx \quad 0.99 - [0.43 \times 0.39 + 0.57 \times 0.79]$$
$$\approx \quad 0.37$$

So this split reduces entropy substantially. In predictive modeling terms, the attribute provides a lot of information on the value of the target.

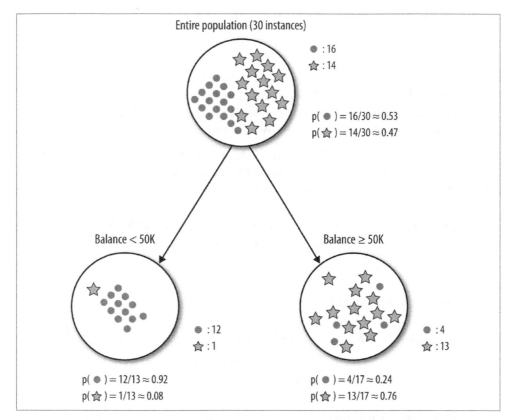

Figure 3-4. Splitting the "write-off" sample into two segments, based on splitting the Balance attribute (account balance) at 50K.

As a second example, consider another candidate split shown in Figure 3-5. This is the same parent set as in Figure 3-4, but instead we consider splitting on the attribute *Residence* with three values: OWN, RENT, and OTHER. Without showing the detailed calculations:

$$entropy(parent) \approx 0.99$$
$$entropy(\text{Residence=OWN}) \approx 0.54$$
$$entropy(\text{Residence=RENT}) \approx 0.97$$
$$entropy(\text{Residence=OTHER}) \approx 0.98$$
$$IG \approx 0.13$$

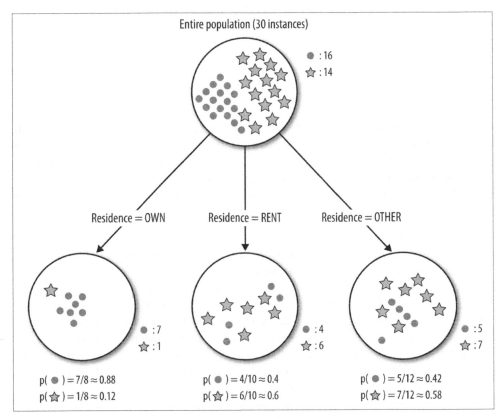

Figure 3-5. A classification tree split on the three-valued Residence attribute.

The Residence variable does have a positive information gain, but it is lower than that of Balance. Intuitively, this is because, while the one child Residence=OWN has considerably reduced entropy, the other values RENT and OTHER produce children that are no more pure than the parent. Thus, based on these data, the Residence variable is less informative than Balance.

Looking back at our concerns from above about creating supervised segmentation for classification problems, information gain addresses them all. It does not require absolute purity. It can be applied to any number of child subsets. It takes into account the relative sizes of the children, giving more weight to larger subsets.[3]

Numeric variables

We have not discussed what exactly to do if the attribute is numeric. Numeric variables can be "discretized" by choosing a split point (or many split points) and then treating the result as a categorical attribute. For example, Income could be divided into two or more ranges. Information gain can be applied to evaluate the segmentation created by this discretization of the numeric attribute. We still are left with the question of how to choose the split point(s) for the numeric attribute. Conceptually, we can try all reasonable split points, and choose the one that gives the highest information gain.

Finally, what about supervised segmentations for regression problems—problems with a numeric target variable? Looking at reducing the impurity of the child subsets still makes intuitive sense, but information gain is not the right measure, because entropy-based information gain is based on the distribution of the *properties* in the segmentation. Instead, we would want a measure of the purity of the numeric (target) values in the subsets.

We will not go through a derivation here, but the fundamental idea is important: a natural measure of impurity for numeric values is *variance*. If the set has all the same values for the numeric target variable, then the set is pure and the variance is zero. If the numeric target values in the set are very different, then the set will have high variance. We can create a similar notion to information gain by looking at reductions in variance between parent and children. The process proceeds in direct analogy to the derivation for information gain above. To create the best segmentation given a numeric target, we might choose the one that produces the best weighted average variance reduction. In essence, we again would be finding variables that have the best correlation with the target, or alternatively, are most predictive of the target.

Example: Attribute Selection with Information Gain

Now we are ready to apply our first concrete data mining technique. For a dataset with instances described by attributes and a target variable, we can determine which attribute is the most informative with respect to estimating the value of the target variable. (We will delve into this more deeply below.) We also can rank a set of attributes by their informativeness, in particular by their information gain. This can be used simply to understand the data better. It can be used to help predict the target. Or it can be used

---

3. Technically, there remains a concern with attributes with very many values, as splitting on them may result in large information gain, but not be predictive. This problem ("overfitting") is the subject of Chapter 5.

to reduce the size of the data to be analyzed, by selecting a subset of attributes in cases where we can not or do not want to process the entire dataset.

To illustrate the use of information gain, we introduce a simple but realistic dataset taken from the machine learning dataset repository at the University of California at Irvine.[4] It is a dataset describing edible and poisonous mushrooms taken from The Audubon Society Field Guide to North American Mushrooms. From the description:

> This dataset includes descriptions of hypothetical samples corresponding to 23 species of gilled mushrooms in the Agaricus and Lepiota Family (pp. 500–525). Each species is identified as definitely edible, definitely poisonous, or of unknown edibility and not recommended. This latter class was combined with the poisonous one. The Guide clearly states that there is no simple rule for determining the edibility of a mushroom; no rule like "leaflets three, let it be" for Poisonous Oak and Ivy.

Each data example (instance) is one mushroom sample, described in terms of its observable attributes (the features). The twenty-odd attributes and the values for each are listed in Table 3-1. For a given example, each attribute takes on a single discrete value (e.g., *gill-color=black*). We use 5,644 examples from the dataset, comprising 2,156 poisonous and 3,488 edible mushrooms.

This is a classification problem because we have a target variable, called *edible?*, with two values *yes* (edible) and *no* (poisonous), specifying our two classes. Each of the rows in the training set has a value for this target variable. We will use information gain to answer the question: "Which single attribute is the most useful for distinguishing edible (edible?=Yes) mushrooms from poisonous (edible?=No) ones?" This is a basic attribute selection problem. In much larger problems we could imagine selecting the best ten or fifty attributes out of several hundred or thousand, and often you want do this if you suspect there are far too many attributes for your mining problem, or that many are not useful. Here, for simplicity, we will find the single best attribute instead of the top ten.

Table 3-1. The attributes of the Mushroom dataset

Attribute name	Possible values
CAP-SHAPE	bell, conical, convex, flat, knobbed, sunken
CAP-SURFACE	fibrous, grooves, scaly, smooth
CAP-COLOR	brown, buff, cinnamon, gray, green, pink, purple, red, white, yellow
BRUISES?	yes, no
ODOR	almond, anise, creosote, fishy, foul, musty, none, pungent, spicy
GILL-ATTACHMENT	attached, descending, free, notched
GILL-SPACING	close, crowded, distant

---

4. See this UC Irvine Machine Learning Repository page (*http://archive.ics.uci.edu/ml/datasets/Mushroom*).

Attribute name	Possible values
GILL-SIZE	broad, narrow
GILL-COLOR	black, brown, buff, chocolate, gray, green, orange, pink, purple, red, white, yellow
STALK-SHAPE	enlarging, tapering
STALK-ROOT	bulbous, club, cup, equal, rhizomorphs, rooted, missing
STALK-SURFACE-ABOVE-RING	fibrous, scaly, silky, smooth
STALK-SURFACE-BELOW-RING	fibrous, scaly, silky, smooth
STALK-COLOR-ABOVE-RING	brown, buff, cinnamon, gray, orange, pink, red, white, yellow
STALK-COLOR-BELOW-RING	brown, buff, cinnamon, gray, orange, pink, red, white, yellow
VEIL-TYPE	partial, universal
VEIL-COLOR	brown, orange, white, yellow
RING-NUMBER	none, one, two
RING-TYPE	cobwebby, evanescent, flaring, large, none, pendant, sheathing, zone
SPORE-PRINT-COLOR	black, brown, buff, chocolate, green, orange, purple, white, yellow
POPULATION	abundant, clustered, numerous, scattered, several, solitary
HABITAT	grasses, leaves, meadows, paths, urban, waste, woods
EDIBLE? *(Target variable)*	yes, no

Since we now have a way to measure information gain this is straightforward: we are asking for the single attribute that gives the highest information gain.

To do this, we calculate the information gain achieved by splitting on each attribute. The information gain from Equation 3-2 is defined on a parent and a set of children. The parent in each case is the whole dataset. First we need *entropy(parent)*, the entropy of the whole dataset. If the two classes were perfectly balanced in the dataset it would have an entropy of 1. This dataset is slightly unbalanced (more edible than poisonous mushrooms are represented) and its entropy is 0.96.

To illustrate entropy reduction graphically, we'll show a number of *entropy graphs* for the mushroom domain (Figure 3-6 through Figure 3-8). Each graph is a two-dimensional description of the entire dataset's entropy as it is divided in various ways by different attributes. On the *x* axis is the proportion of the dataset (0 to 1), and on the *y* axis is the entropy (also 0 to 1) of a given piece of the data. The amount of shaded area in each graph represents the amount of entropy in the dataset when it is divided by some chosen attribute (or not divided, in the case of Figure 3-6). Our goal of having the lowest entropy corresponds to having as *little* shaded area as possible.

The first chart, Figure 3-6, shows the entropy of the entire dataset. In such a chart, the highest possible entropy corresponds to the entire area being shaded; the lowest possible entropy corresponds to the entire area being white. Such a chart is useful for visualizing information gain from different partitions of a dataset, because any partition can be shown simply as slices of the graph (with widths corresponding to the proportion of the dataset), each with its own entropy. The weighted sum of entropies in the information gain calculation will be depicted simply by the total amount of shaded area.

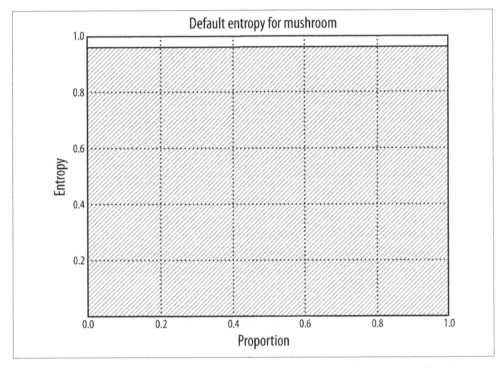

Figure 3-6. Entropy chart for the entire Mushroom dataset. The entropy for the entire dataset is 0.96, so 96% of the area is shaded.

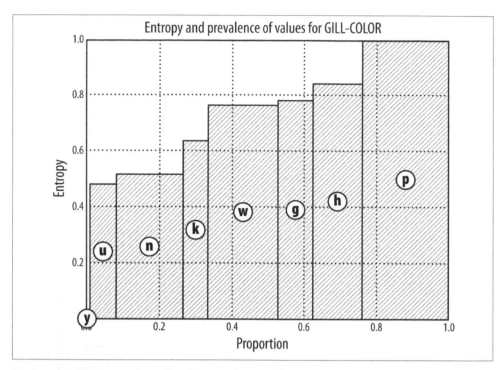

Figure 3-7. Entropy chart for the Mushroom dataset as split by GILL-COLOR. The amount of shading corresponds to the total (weighted sum) entropy, with each bar corresponding to the entropy of one of the attribute's values, and the width of the bar corresponding to the prevalence of that value in the data.

For our entire dataset, the global entropy is 0.96, so Figure 3-6 shows a large shaded area below the line $y = 0.96$. We can think of this as our starting entropy—any informative attribute should produce a new graph with less shaded area. Now we show the entropy charts of three sample attributes. Each value of an attribute occurs in the dataset with a different frequency, so each attribute splits the set in a different way.

Figure 3-7 shows the dataset split apart by the attribute GILL-COLOR, whose values are coded as y (yellow), u (purple), n (brown), and so on. The width of each attribute represents what proportion of the dataset has that value, and the height is its entropy. We can see that GILL-COLOR reduces the entropy somewhat; the shaded area in Figure 3-7 is considerably less than the area in Figure 3-6.

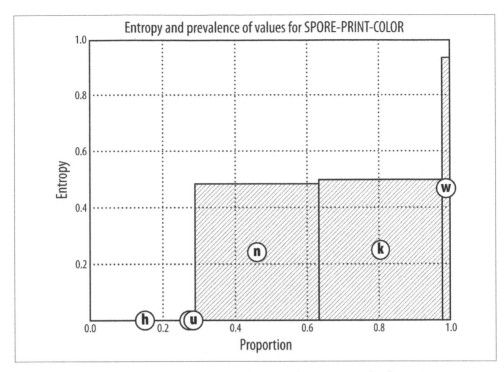

Figure 3-8. Entropy chart for the Mushroom dataset as split by SPORE-PRINT-COLOR. The amount of shading corresponds to the total (weighted sum) entropy, with each bar corresponding to the entropy of one of the attribute's values, and the width of the bar corresponding to the prevalence of that value in the data.

Similarly, Figure 3-8 shows how SPORE-PRINT-COLOR decreases uncertainty (entropy). A few of the values, such as h (`chocolate`), specify the target value perfectly and thus produce zero-entropy bars. But notice that they don't account for very much of the population, only about 30%.

Figure 3-9 shows the graph produced by ODOR. Many of the values, such as a (`almond`), c (`creosote`), and m (`musty`) produce zero-entropy partitions; only n (`no odor`) has a considerable entropy (about 20%). In fact, ODOR has the highest information gain of any attribute in the Mushroom dataset. It can reduce the dataset's total entropy to about 0.1, which gives it an information gain of 0.96 – 0.1 = 0.86. What is this saying? Many odors are completely characteristic of poisonous or edible mushrooms, so odor is a very informative attribute to check when considering mushroom edibility.[5] If you're

---

5. This assumes odor can be measured accurately, of course. If your sense of smell is poor you may not want to bet your life on it. Frankly, you probably wouldn't want to bet your life on the results of mining data from a field guide. Nevertheless, it makes a nice example.

going to build a model to determine the mushroom edibility using only a *single* feature, you should choose its odor. If you were going to build a more complex model you might start with the attribute ODOR before considering adding others. In fact, this is exactly the topic of the next section.

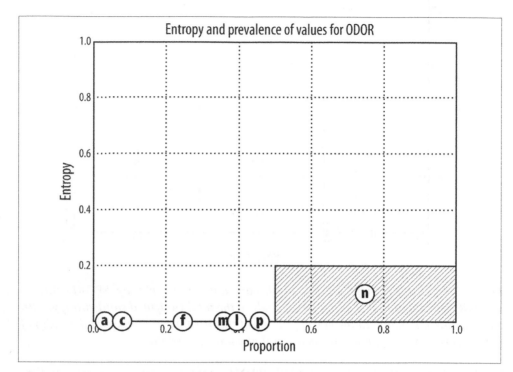

Figure 3-9. Entropy chart for the Mushroom dataset as split by ODOR. The amount of shading corresponds to the total (weighted sum) entropy, with each bar corresponding to the entropy of one of the attribute's values, and the width of the bar corresponding to the prevalence of that value in the data.

Supervised Segmentation with Tree-Structured Models

We have now introduced one of the fundamental ideas of data mining: finding informative attributes from the data. Let's continue on the topic of creating a supervised segmentation, because as important as it is, attribute selection alone does not seem to be sufficient. If we select the single variable that gives the most information gain, we create a very simple segmentation. If we select multiple attributes each giving some information gain, it's not clear how to put them together. Recall from earlier that we would like to create segments that use multiple attributes, such as "Middle-aged professionals who reside in New York City on average have a churn rate of 5%." We now introduce an elegant application of the ideas we've developed for selecting important attributes, to produce a multivariate (multiple attribute) supervised segmentation.

Consider a segmentation of the data to take the form of a "tree," such as that shown in Figure 3-10. In the figure, the tree is upside down with the root at the top. The tree is made up of *nodes*, interior nodes and terminal nodes, and branches emanating from the interior nodes. Each interior node in the tree contains a test of an attribute, with each branch from the node representing a distinct value, or range of values, of the attribute. Following the branches from the root node down (in the direction of the arrows), each path eventually terminates at a terminal node, or *leaf*. The tree creates a segmentation of the data: every data point will correspond to one and only one path in the tree, and thereby to one and only one leaf. In other words, each leaf corresponds to a segment, and the attributes and values along the path give the characteristics of the segment. So the rightmost path in the tree in Figure 3-10 corresponds to the segment "Older, unemployed people with high balances." The tree is a *supervised* segmentation, because each leaf contains a value for the target variable. Since we are talking about classification, here each leaf contains a classification for its segment. Such a tree is called a *classification tree* or more loosely a *decision tree*.

Classification trees often are used as predictive models—"tree structured models." In use, when presented with an example for which we do not know its classification, we can predict its classification by finding the corresponding segment and using the class value at the leaf. Mechanically, one would start at the root node and descend through the interior nodes, choosing branches based on the specific attribute values in the example. The nonleaf nodes are often referred to as "decision nodes," because when descending through the tree, at each node one uses the values of the attribute to make a decision about which branch to follow. Following these branches ultimately leads to a final decision about what class to predict: eventually a terminal node is reached, which gives a class prediction. In a tree, no two parents share descendants and there are no cycles; the branches always "point downwards" so that every example always ends up at a leaf node with some specific class determination.

Consider how we would use the classification tree in Figure 3-10 to classify an example of the person named Claudio from Figure 3-1. The values of Claudio's attributes are *Balance=115K, Employed=No*, and *Age=40*. We begin at the root node that tests *Employed*. Since the value is *No* we take the right branch. The next test is *Balance*. The value of *Balance* is 115K, which is greater than 50K so we take a right branch again to a node that tests *Age*. The value is 40 so we take the left branch. This brings us to a leaf node specifying *class=Not Write-off*, representing a prediction that Claudio will not default. Another way of saying this is that we have classified Claudio into a segment defined by *(Employed=No, Balance=115K, Age<45)* whose classification is *Not Write -off*.

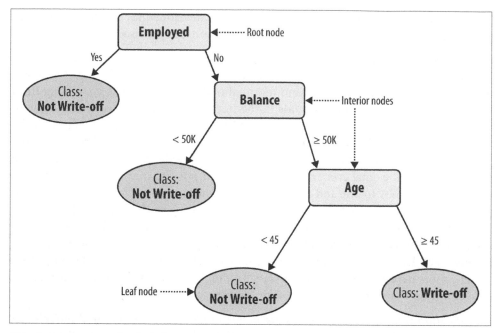

Figure 3-10. A simple classification tree.

Classification trees are one sort of tree-structured model. As we will see later, in business applications often we want to predict the probability of membership in the class (e.g., the probability of churn or the probability of write-off), rather than the class itself. In this case, the leaves of the *probability estimation tree* would contain these probabilities rather than a simple value. If the target variable is numeric, the leaves of the *regression tree* contain numeric values. However, the basic idea is the same for all.

Trees provide a model that can represent exactly the sort of supervised segmentation we often want, and we know how to use such a model to predict values for new cases (in "use"). However, we still have not addressed how to create such a model from the data. We turn to that now.

There are many techniques to induce a supervised segmentation from a dataset. One of the most popular is to create a tree-structured model (*tree induction*). These techniques are popular because tree models are easy to understand, and because the induction procedures are elegant (simple to describe) and easy to use. They are robust to many common data problems and are relatively efficient. Most data mining packages include some type of tree induction technique.

How do we create a classification tree from data? Combining the ideas introduced above, the goal of the tree is to provide a supervised segmentation—more specifically, to partition the instances, based on their attributes, into subgroups that have similar values

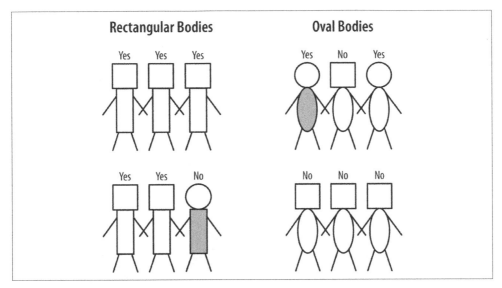

Figure 3-11. First partitioning: splitting on body shape (rectangular versus oval).

for their target variables. We would like for each "leaf" segment to contain instances that tend to belong to the same class.

To illustrate the process of classification tree induction, consider the very simple example set shown previously in Figure 3-2.

Tree induction takes a divide-and-conquer approach, starting with the whole dataset and applying variable selection to try to create the "purest" subgroups possible using the attributes. In the example, one way is to separate people based on their body type: rectangular versus oval. This creates the two groups shown in Figure 3-11. How good is this partitioning? The rectangular-body people on the left are mostly *Yes*, with a single *No* person, so it is mostly pure. The oval-body group on the right has mostly *No* people, but two *Yes* people. This step is simply a direct application of the attribute selection ideas presented above. Let's consider this "split" to be the one that yields the largest information gain.

Looking at Figure 3-11, we can now see the elegance of tree induction, and why it resonates well with so many people. The left and right subgroups are simply smaller versions of the problem with which we initially were faced! We can simply take each data subset and *recursively* apply attribute selection to find the best attribute to partition it. So in our example, we recursively consider the oval-body group (Figure 3-12). To split this group again we now consider another attribute: head shape. This splits the group in two on the right side of the figure. How good is this partitioning? Each new group has a single target label: four (square heads) of *No*, and two (round heads) of

Yes. These groups are "maximally pure" with respect to class labels and there is no need to split them further.

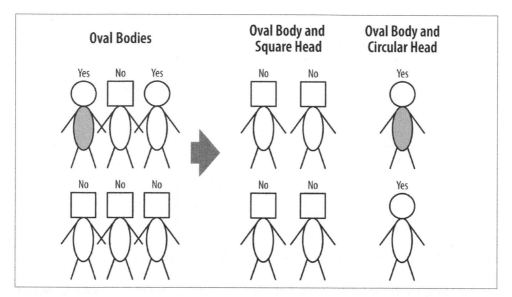

Figure 3-12. Second partitioning: the oval body people sub-grouped by head type.

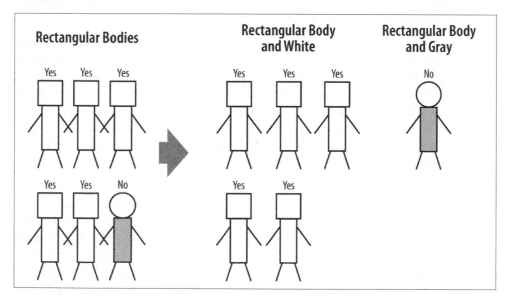

Figure 3-13. Third partitioning: the rectangular body people subgrouped by body color.

We still have not done anything with the rectangular body group on the left side of Figure 3-11, so let's consider how to split them. There are five *Yes* people and one *No* person. There are two attributes we could split upon: head shape (square or round), and body color (white or gray). Either of these would work, so we arbitrarily choose body color. This produces the groupings in Figure 3-13. These are pure groups (all of one type) so we are finished. The classification tree corresponding to these groupings is shown in Figure 3-14.

In summary, the procedure of classification tree induction is a recursive process of divide and conquer, where the goal at each step is to select an attribute to partition the current group into subgroups that are as pure as possible with respect to the target variable. We perform this partitioning recursively, splitting further and further until we are done. We choose the attributes to split upon by testing all of them and selecting whichever yields the purest subgroups. When are we done? (In other words, when do we stop recursing?) It should be clear that we would stop when the nodes are pure, or when we run out of variables to split on. But we may want to stop earlier; we will return to this question in Chapter 5.

Visualizing Segmentations

Continuing with the metaphor of predictive model building as supervised segmentation, it is instructive to visualize exactly how a classification tree partitions the instance space. The instance space is simply the space described by the data features. A common form of instance space visualization is a scatterplot on some pair of features, used to compare one variable against another to detect correlations and relationships.

Though data may contain dozens or hundreds of variables, it is only really possible to visualize segmentations in two or three dimensions at once. Still, visualizing models in instance space in a few dimensions is useful for understanding the different *types* of models because it provides insights that apply to higher dimensional spaces as well. It may be difficult to compare very different families of models just by examining their form (e.g., a mathematical formula versus a set of rules) or the algorithms that generate them. Often it is easier to compare them based on how they partition the instance space.

For example, Figure 3-15 shows a simple classification tree next to a two-dimensional graph of the instance space: Balance on the *x* axis and Age on the *y* axis. The root node of the classification tree tests Balance against a threshold of 50K. In the graph, this corresponds to a vertical line at 50K on the *x* axis splitting the plane into Balance<50K and Balance≥50K. At the left of this line lie the instances whose Balance values are less than 50K; there are 13 examples of class Write-off (black dot) and 2 examples of class non-Write-off (plus sign) in this region.

On the right branch out of the root node are instances with Balance≥50K. The next node in the classification tree tests the Age attribute against the threshold 45. In the

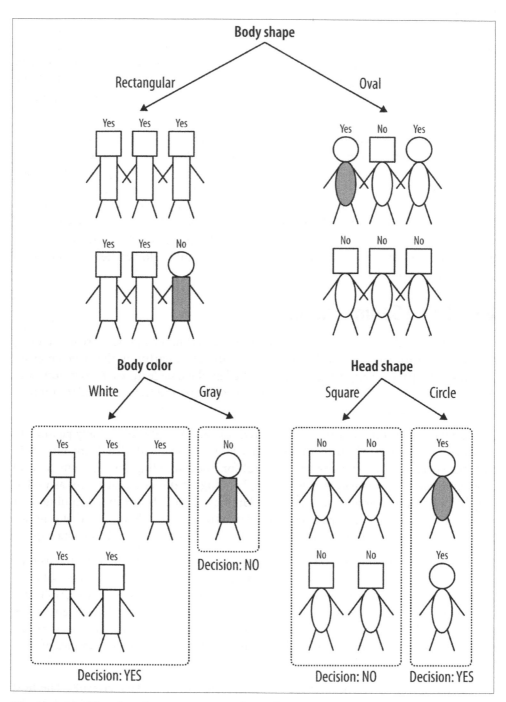

Figure 3-14. The classification tree resulting from the splits done in Figure 3-11 to Figure 3-13.

graph this corresponds to the horizontal dotted line at Age=45. It appears only on the right side of the graph because this partition only applies to examples with Balance≥50. The Age decision node assigns to its left branch instances with Age<45, corresponding to the lower right segment of the graph, representing: (Balance≥50K AND Age<45).

Notice that each internal (decision) node corresponds to a split of the instance space. Each leaf node corresponds to an unsplit region of the space (a segment of the population). Whenever we follow a path in the tree out of a decision node we are restricting attention to one of the two (or more) subregions defined by the split. As we descend through a classification tree we consider progressively more focused subregions of the instance space.

Decision lines and hyperplanes

The lines separating the regions are known as *decision lines* (in two dimensions) or more generally *decision surfaces* or *decision boundaries*. Each node of a classification tree tests a single variable against a fixed value so the decision boundary corresponding to it will always be perpendicular to the axis representing this variable. In two dimensions, the line will be either horizontal or vertical. If the data had three variables the instance space would be three-dimensional and each boundary surface imposed by a classification tree would be a two-dimensional plane. In higher dimensions, since each node of a classification tree tests one variable it may be thought of as "fixing" that one dimension of a decision boundary; therefore, for a problem of *n* variables, each node of a classification tree imposes an *(n–1)*-dimensional "hyperplane" decision boundary on the instance space.

You will often see the term *hyperplane* used in data mining literature to refer to the general separating surface, whatever it may be. Don't be intimidated by this terminology. You can always just think of it as a generalization of a line or a plane.

Other decision surfaces are possible, as we shall see later.

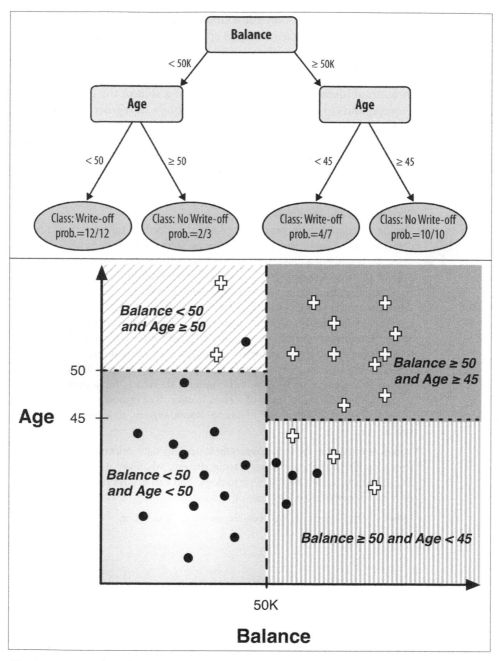

Figure 3-15. A classification tree and the partitions it imposes in instance space. The black dots correspond to instances of the class Write-off, the plus signs correspond to instances of class non-Write-off. The shading shows how the tree leaves correspond to segments of the population in instance space.

Trees as Sets of Rules

Before moving on from the interpretation of classification trees, we should mention their interpretation as logical statements. Consider again the tree shown at the top of Figure 3-15. You classify a new unseen instance by starting at the root node and following the attribute tests downward until you reach a leaf node, which specifies the instance's predicted class. If we trace down a single path from the root node to a leaf, collecting the conditions as we go, we generate a rule. Each rule consists of the attribute tests along the path connected with AND. Starting at the root node and choosing the left branches of the tree, we get the rule:

```
IF (Balance < 50K) AND (Age < 50) THEN Class=Write-off
```

We can do this for every possible path to a leaf node. From this tree we get three more rules:

```
IF (Balance < 50K) AND (Age ≥ 50) THEN Class=No Write-off
IF (Balance ≥ 50K) AND (Age < 45) THEN Class=Write-off
IF (Balance ≥ 50K) AND (Age ≥ 45) THEN Class=No Write-off
```

The classification tree is equivalent to this rule set. If these rules look repetitive, that's because they are: the tree gathers common rule prefixes together toward the top of the tree. Every classification tree can be expressed as a set of rules this way. Whether the tree or the rule set is more intelligible is a matter of opinion; in this simple example, both are fairly easy to understand. As the model becomes larger, some people will prefer the tree or the rule set.

Probability Estimation

In many decision-making problems, we would like a more informative prediction than just a classification. For example, in our churn-prediction problem, rather than simply predicting whether a person will leave the company within 90 days of contract expiration, we would much rather have an estimate of the probability that he will leave the company within that time. Such estimates can be used for many purposes. We will discuss some of these in detail in later chapters, but briefly: you might then rank prospects by their probability of leaving, and then allocate a limited incentive budget to the highest probability instances. Alternatively, you may want to allocate your incentive budget to the instances with the highest expected loss, for which you'll need (an estimate of) the probability of churn. Once you have such probability estimates you can use them in a more sophisticated decision-making process than these simple examples, as we'll describe in later chapters.

There is another, even more insidious problem with models that give simple classifica-tions, rather than estimates of class membership probability. Consider the problem of estimating credit default. Under normal circumstances, for just about any segment of the population to which we would be considering giving credit, the probability of write-off will be very small—far less than 0.5. In this case, when we build a model to estimate the classification (write-off or not), we'd have to say that for each segment, the members are likely not to default—and they will all get the same classification (not write-off). For example, in a naively built tree model every leaf will be labeled "not write-off." This turns out to be a frustrating experience for new data miners: after all that work, the model really just says that no one is likely to default? This does *not* mean that the model is useless. It may be that the different segments indeed have very different probabilities of write-off, they just all are less than 0.5. If instead we use these probabilities for assigning credit, we may be able reduce our risk substantially.

So, in the context of supervised segmentation, we would like each segment (leaf of a tree model) to be assigned an estimate of the probability of membership in the different classes. Figure 3-15 more generally shows a "probability estimation tree" model for our simple write-off prediction example, giving not only a prediction of the class but also the estimate of the probability of membership in the class.[6]

Fortunately, the tree induction ideas we have discussed so far can easily produce prob-ability estimation trees instead of simple classification trees.[7] Recall that the tree induc-tion procedure subdivides the instance space into regions of class purity (low entropy). If we are satisfied to assign the same class probability to every member of the segment corresponding to a tree leaf, we can use instance counts at each leaf to compute a class probability estimate. For example, if a leaf contains n positive instances and m negative instances, the probability of any new instance being positive may be estimated as $n/(n +m)$. This is called a *frequency-based* estimate of class membership probability.

At this point you may spot a problem with estimating class membership probabilities this way: we may be overly optimistic about the probability of class membership for segments with very small numbers of instances. At the extreme, if a leaf happens to have only a single instance, should we be willing to say that there is a 100% probability that members of that segment will have the class that this one instance happens to have?

---

6. We often deal with binary classification problems, such as write-off or not, or churn or not. In these cases it is typical just to report the probability of membership in one chosen class $p(c)$, because the other is just $1 - p(c)$.

7. Often these are still called classification trees, even if the decision maker intends to use the probability esti-mates rather than the simple classifications.

This phenomenon is one example of a fundamental issue in data science ("overfitting"), to which we devote a chapter later in the book. For completeness, let's quickly discuss one easy way to address this problem of small samples for tree-based class probability estimation. Instead of simply computing the frequency, we would often use a "smoothed" version of the frequency-based estimate, known as the Laplace correction, the purpose of which is to moderate the influence of leaves with only a few instances. The equation for binary class probability estimation becomes:

$$p(c) = \frac{n + 1}{n + m + 2}$$

where n is the number of examples in the leaf belonging to class c, and m is the number of examples not belonging to class c.

Let's walk through an example with and without the Laplace correction. A leaf node with two positive instances and no negative instances would produce the same frequency-based estimate ($p = 1$) as a leaf node with 20 positive instances and no negatives. However, the first leaf node has much less evidence and may be extreme only due to there being so few instances. Its estimate should be tempered by this consideration. The Laplace equation smooths its estimate down to $p = 0.75$ to reflect this uncertainty; the Laplace correction has much less effect on the leaf with 20 instances ($p \approx 0.95$). As the number of instances increases, the Laplace equation converges to the frequency-based estimate. Figure 3-16 shows the effect of Laplace correction on several class ratios as the number of instances increases (2/3, 4/5, and 1/1). For each ratio the solid horizontal line shows the uncorrected (constant) estimate, while the corresponding dashed line shows the estimate with the Laplace correction applied. The uncorrected line is the asymptote of the Laplace correction as the number of instances goes to infinity.

Example: Addressing the Churn Problem with Tree Induction

Now that we have a basic data mining technique for predictive modeling, let's consider the churn problem again. How could we use tree induction to help solve it?

For this example, we have a historical data set of 20,000 customers. At the point of collecting the data, each customer either had stayed with the company or had left (churned). Each customer is described by the variables listed in Table 3-2.

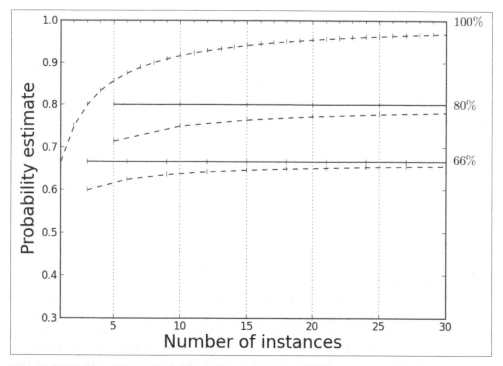

Figure 3-16. The effect of Laplace smoothing on probability estimation for several instance ratios.

Table 3-2. Attributes for the cellular phone churn-prediction problem

Variable	Explanation
COLLEGE	Is the customer college educated?
INCOME	Annual income
OVERAGE	Average overcharges per month
LEFTOVER	Average number of leftover minutes per month
HOUSE	Estimated value of dwelling (from census tract)
HANDSET_PRICE	Cost of phone
LONG_CALLS_PER_MONTH	Average number of long calls (15 mins or over) per month
AVERAGE_CALL_DURATION	Average duration of a call
REPORTED_SATISFACTION	Reported level of satisfaction
REPORTED_USAGE_LEVEL	Self-reported usage level
LEAVE *(Target variable)*	Did the customer stay or leave (churn)?

These variables comprise basic demographic and usage information available from the customer's application and account. We want to use these data with our tree induction technique to predict which new customers are going to churn.

Before starting to build a classification tree with these variables, it is worth asking, *How good are each of these variables individually?* For this we measure the information gain of each attribute, as discussed earlier. Specifically, we apply Equation 3-2 to each variable independently over the entire set of instances, to see what each gains us.

The results are in Figure 3-17, with a table listing the exact values. As you can see, the first three variables—the house value, the number of leftover minutes, and the number of long calls per month—have a higher information gain than the rest.[8] Perhaps surprisingly, neither the amount the phone is used nor the reported degree of satisfaction seems, in and of itself, to be very predictive of churning.

Applying a classification tree algorithm to the data, we get the tree shown in Figure 3-18. The highest information gain feature (HOUSE) according to Figure 3-17 is at the root of the tree. This is to be expected since it will always be chosen first. The second best feature, OVERAGE, also appears high in the tree. However, the order in which features are chosen for the tree doesn't exactly correspond to their ranking in Figure 3-17. Why is this?

The answer is that the table ranks each feature by how good it is *independently*, evaluated separately on the entire population of instances. Nodes in a classification tree depend on the instances above them in the tree. Therefore, except for the root node, features in a classification tree are not evaluated on the entire set of instances. The information gain of a feature depends on the set of instances against which it is evaluated, so the ranking of features for some internal node may not be the same as the global ranking.

We have not yet discussed how we decide to stop building the tree. The dataset has 20,000 examples yet the tree clearly doesn't have 20,000 leaf nodes. Can't we just keep selecting more attributes to split upon, building the tree downwards until we've exhausted the data? The answer is yes, we can, but we should stop long before the model becomes that complex. This issue ties in closely with model generality and overfitting, whose discussion we defer to Chapter 5.

8. Note that the information gains for the attributes in this churn data set are much smaller than those shown previously for the mushroom data set.

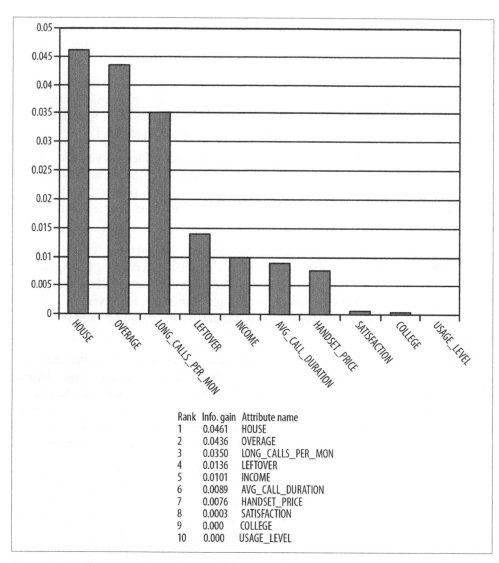

Figure 3-17. Churn attributes from Table 3-2 ranked by information gain.

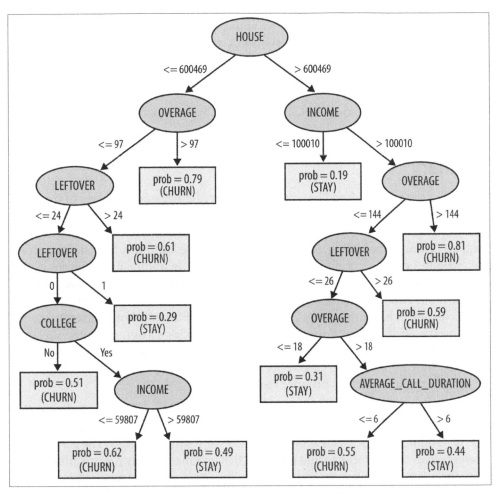

Figure 3-18. Classification tree learned from the cellular phone churn data. Rectangular leaves correspond to segments of the population, defined by the path from the root at the top. Probabilities at the leaves are the estimated probabilities of churning for the corresponding segment; in parentheses are shown the classifications resulting from applying a decision threshold of 0.5 to the probabilities (i.e., are the individuals in the segment more likely to CHURN or to STAY?).

Consider a final issue with this dataset. After building a tree model from the data, we measured its accuracy against the data to see how good of a model it is. Specifically, we used a training set consisting half of people who churned and the other half who did not; after learning a classification tree from this, we applied the tree to the dataset to see how many of the examples it could classify correctly. The tree achieved 73% accuracy on its decisions. This raises two questions:

1. First, do you trust this number? If we applied the tree to another sample of 20,000 people from the same dataset, do you think we'd still get about 73% accuracy?

2. If you *do* trust the number, does it mean this model is good? In other words, is a model with 73% accuracy worth using?

We will revisit these questions in Chapter 7 and Chapter 8, which delve into issues of model evaluation.

Summary

In this chapter, we introduced basic concepts of predictive modeling, one of the main tasks of data science, in which a model is built that can estimate the value of a target variable for a new unseen example. In the process, we introduced one of data science's fundamental notions: finding and selecting informative attributes. Selecting informative attributes can be a useful data mining procedure in and of itself. Given a large collection of data, we now can find those variables that correlate with or give us information about another variable of interest. For example, if we gather historical data on which customers have or have not left the company (churned) shortly after their contracts expire, attribute selection can find demographic or account-oriented variables that provide information about the likelihood of customers churning. One basic measure of attribute information is called *information gain*, which is based on a purity measure called *entropy*; another is variance reduction.

Selecting informative attributes forms the basis of a common modeling technique called tree induction. Tree induction recursively finds informative attributes for subsets of the data. In so doing it segments the space of instances into similar regions. The partitioning is "supervised" in that it tries to find segments that give increasingly precise information about the quantity to be predicted, the target. The resulting tree-structured model partitions the space of all possible instances into a set of segments with different predicted values for the target. For example, when the target is a binary "class" variable such as churn versus not churn, or write-off versus not write-off, each leaf of the tree corresponds to a population segment with a different estimated probability of class membership.

 As an exercise, think about what would be different in building a tree-structured model for regression rather than for classification. What would need to be changed from what you've learned about classification tree induction?

Historically, tree induction has been a very popular data mining procedure because it is easy to understand, easy to implement, and computationally inexpensive. Research on tree induction goes back at least to the 1950s and 1960s. Some of the earliest popular tree induction systems include CHAID (Chi-squared Automatic Interaction Detection) (Kass, 1980) and CART (Classification and Regression Trees) (Breiman, Friedman, Olshen, & Stone, 1984), which are still widely used. C4.5 and C5.0 are also very popular tree induction algorithms, which have a notable lineage (Quinlan, 1986, 1993). J48 is a reimplementation of C4.5 in the Weka package (Witten & Frank, 2000; Hall et al., 2001).

In practice, tree-structured models work remarkably well, though they may not be the most accurate model one can produce from a particular data set. In many cases, especially early in the application of data mining, it is important that models be understood and explained easily. This can be useful not just for the data science team but for communicating results to stakeholders not knowledgeable about data mining.

CHAPTER 4

Fitting a Model to Data

Fundamental concepts: *Finding "optimal" model parameters based on data; Choosing the goal for data mining; Objective functions; Loss functions.*

Exemplary techniques: *Linear regression; Logistic regression; Support-vector machines.*

As we have seen, predictive modeling involves finding a model of the target variable in terms of other descriptive attributes. In Chapter 3, we constructed a supervised segmentation model by recursively finding informative attributes on ever-more-precise subsets of the set of all instances, or from the geometric perspective, ever-more-precise subregions of the instance space. From the data we produced both the structure of the model (the particular tree model that resulted from the tree induction) and the numeric "parameters" of the model (the probability estimates at the leaf nodes).

An alternative method for learning a predictive model from a dataset is to start by specifying the structure of the model with certain numeric parameters left unspecified. Then the data mining calculates the best parameter values given a particular set of training data. A very common case is where the structure of the model is a parameterized mathematical function or equation of a set of numeric attributes. The attributes used in the model could be chosen based on domain knowledge regarding which attributes ought to be informative in predicting the target variable, or they could be chosen based on other data mining techniques, such as the attribute selection procedures introduced in Chapter 3. The data miner specifies the form of the model and the attributes; the goal of the data mining is to tune the parameters so that the model fits the data as well as possible. This general approach is called *parameter learning* or *parametric modeling*.

In certain fields of statistics and econometrics, the bare model with unspecified parameters is called "the model." We will clarify that this is the structure of the model, which still needs to have its parameters specified to be useful.

Many data mining procedures fall within this general framework. We will illustrate with some of the most common, all of which are based on *linear* models. If you've taken a statistics course, you're probably already familiar with one linear modeling technique: linear regression. We will see the same differences in models that we've seen already, such as the differences in task between classification, class probability estimation, and regression. As examples we will present some common techniques used for predicting (estimating) unknown numeric values, unknown binary values (such as whether a document or web page is relevant to a query), as well as likelihoods of events, such as default on credit, response to an offer, fraud on an account, and so on.

We also will explicitly discuss something that we skirted in Chapter 3: what exactly do we mean when we say a model fits the data well? This is the crux of the fundamental concept of this chapter—fitting a model to data by finding "optimal" model parameters —and is a notion that will resurface in later chapters. Because of its fundamental concepts, this chapter is more mathematically focused than the rest. We will keep the math to a minimum, and encourage the less mathematical reader to proceed boldly.

Sidebar: Simplifying Assumptions in This Chapter

The point of this chapter is to introduce and explain parametric modeling. To keep the discussion focused, and to avoid excessive footnotes, we've made some simplifying assumptions:

- First, for classification and class probability estimation we will consider only binary classes: the models predict events that either take place or do not, such as responding to an offer, leaving the company, being defrauded, etc. The methods here can all be generalized to work with multiple (nonbinary) classes, but the generalization complicates the description unnecessarily.

- Second, because we're dealing with equations, this chapter assumes all attributes are numeric. There are techniques for converting categorical (symbolic) attributes into numerical values for use with these equations.

- Finally, we ignore the need to normalize numeric measurements to a common scale. Attributes such as Age and Income have vastly different ranges and they are usually normalized to a common scale to help with model interpretability, as well as other things (to be discussed later).

We ignore these complications in this chapter. However, dealing with them is ultimately important and often necessary regardless of the data mining technique.

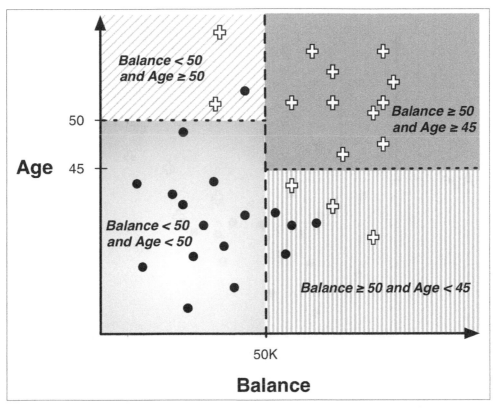

Figure 4-1. *A dataset split by a classification tree with four leaf nodes.*

Classification via Mathematical Functions

Recall the instance-space view of tree models from Chapter 3. One such diagram is replicated in Figure 4-1. It shows the space broken up into regions by horizontal and vertical *decision boundaries* that partition the instance space into similar regions. Examples in each region should have similar values for the target variable. In the last chapter we saw how the entropy measure gives us a way of measuring homogeneity so we can choose such boundaries.

A main purpose of creating homogeneous regions is so that we can predict the target variable of a new, unseen instance by determining which segment it falls into. For example, in Figure 4-1, if a new customer falls into the lower-left segment, we can conclude that the target value is very likely to be "•". Similarly, if it falls into the upper-right segment, we can predict its value as "+".

The instance-space view is helpful because if we take away the axis-parallel boundaries (see Figure 4-2) we can see that there clearly are other, possibly better, ways to partition

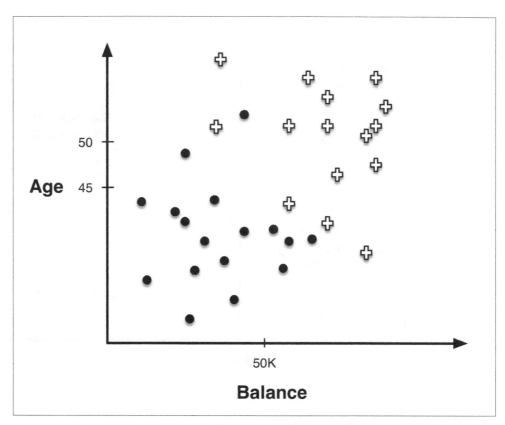

Figure 4-2. The raw data points of Figure 4-1, without decision lines.

the space. For example, we can separate the instances almost perfectly (by class) if we are allowed to introduce a boundary that is still a straight line, but is not perpendicular to the axes (Figure 4-3).

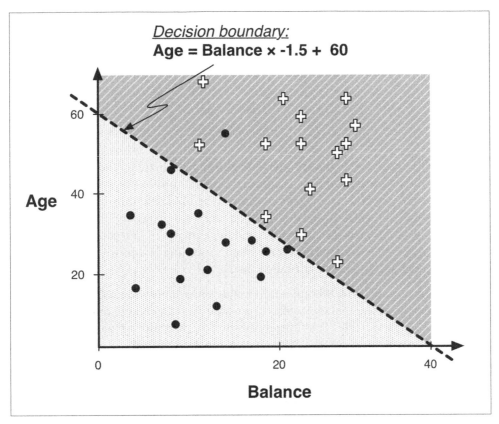

Figure 4-3. The dataset of Figure 4-2 with a single linear split.

This is called a *linear* classifier and is essentially a weighted sum of the values for the various attributes, as we will describe next.

Linear Discriminant Functions

Our goal is going to be to fit our model to the data, and to do so it is quite helpful to represent the model mathematically. You may recall that the equation of a line in two dimensions is $y = mx + b$, where m is the slope of the line and b is the y intercept (the y value when $x = 0$). The line in Figure 4-3 can be expressed in this form (with Balance in thousands) as:

$$Age = (-1.5) \times Balance + 60$$

We would classify an instance **x** as a + if it is above the line, and as a • if it is below the line. Rearranging this mathematically leads to the function that is the basis of all the techniques discussed in this chapter. For this example decision boundary, the classification solution is shown in Equation 4-1.

Equation 4-1. Classification function

$$class(\mathbf{x}) = \begin{cases} + \text{ if } - 1.0 \times Age - 1.5 \times Balance + 60 > 0 \\ \bullet \text{ if } - 1.0 \times Age - 1.5 \times Balance + 60 \leq 0 \end{cases}$$

This is called a *linear discriminant* because it discriminates between the classes, and the function of the decision boundary is a linear combination—a weighted sum—of the attributes. In the two dimensions of our example, the linear combination corresponds to a line. In three dimensions, the decision boundary is a plane, and in higher dimensions it is a *hyperplane* (see Decision lines and hyperplanes in "Visualizing Segmentations" on page 67). For our purposes, the important thing is that we can express the model as a weighted sum of the attribute values.

Thus, this linear model is a different sort of multivariate supervised segmentation. Our goal with supervised segmentation still is to separate the data into regions with different values of the target variable. The difference is that the method for taking multiple attributes into account is to create a mathematical function of them.

In "Trees as Sets of Rules" on page 71 we showed how a classification tree corresponds to a rule set—a logical classification model of the data. A linear discriminant function is a numeric classification model. For example, consider our feature vector $\mathbf{x}$, with the individual component features being x_i. A linear model then can be written as follows in Equation 4-2.

Equation 4-2. A general linear model

$$f(\mathbf{x}) = w_0 + w_1 x_1 + w_2 x_2 + \cdots$$

The concrete example from Equation 4-1 can be written in this form:

$$f(\mathbf{x}) = 60 - 1.0 \times Age - 1.5 \times Balance$$

To use this model as a linear discriminant, for a given instance represented by a feature vector $\mathbf{x}$, we check whether $f(\mathbf{x})$ is positive or negative. As discussed above, in the two-dimensional case, this corresponds to seeing whether the instance $\mathbf{x}$ falls above or below the line.

Linear functions are one of the workhorses of data science; now we finally come to the data mining. We now have a *parameterized* model: the weights of the linear function

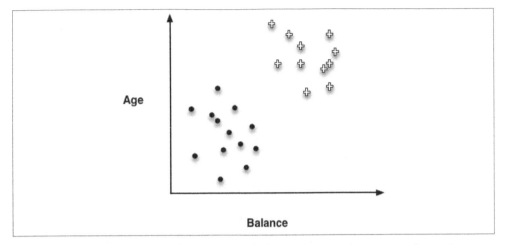

Figure 4-4. A basic instance space in two dimensions containing points of two classes.

(w_i) are the parameters.[1] The data mining is going to "fit" this parameterized model to a particular dataset—meaning specifically, to find a good set of weights on the features.

After learning, these weights are often loosely interpreted as importance indicators of the features. Roughly, the larger the magnitude of a feature's weight, the more important that feature is for classifying the target—assuming all feature values have been normalized to the same range, as mentioned in "Sidebar: Simplifying Assumptions in This Chapter" on page 82. By the same token, if a feature's weight is near zero the corresponding feature can usually be ignored or discarded. For now, we are interested in a set of weights that discriminate the training data well and predict as accurately as possible the value of the target variable for cases where we don't know it.

---

1. In order that the line need not go through the origin, it is typical to include the weight w_0, which is the intercept.

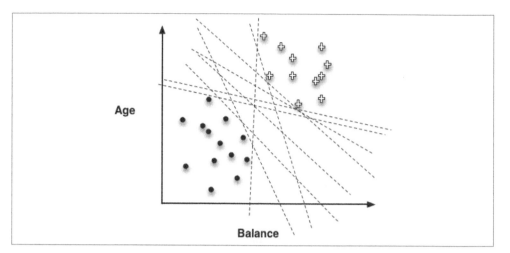

Figure 4-5. Many different possible linear boundaries can separate the two groups of points of Figure 4-4.

Unfortunately, it's not trivial to choose the "best" line to separate the classes. Let's consider a simple case, illustrated in Figure 4-4. Here the training data can indeed be separated by class using a linear discriminant. However, as shown in Figure 4-5, there actually are many different linear discriminants that can separate the classes perfectly. They have very different slopes and intercepts, and each represents a different model of the data. In fact, there are infinitely many lines (models) that classify this training set perfectly. Which should we pick?

Optimizing an Objective Function

This brings us to one of the most important fundamental ideas in data mining—one that surprisingly is often overlooked even by data scientists themselves: we need to ask, what should be our goal or *objective* in choosing the parameters? In our case, this would allow us to answer the question: what weights should we choose? Our general procedure will be to define an *objective function* that represents our goal, and can be calculated for a particular set of weights and a particular set of data. We will then find the optimal value for the weights by maximizing or minimizing the objective function. What can easily be overlooked is that these weights are "best" only if we believe that the objective function truly represents what we want to achieve, or practically speaking, is the best proxy we can come up with. We will return to this later in the book.

Unfortunately, creating an objective function that matches the true goal of the data mining is usually impossible, so data scientists often choose based on faith[2] and expe-

---

2. And sometimes it can be surprisingly hard for them to admit it.

rience. Several choices have been shown to be remarkably effective. One of these choices creates the so-called "support vector machine," about which we will say a few words after presenting a concrete example with a simpler objective function. After that, we will briefly discuss linear models for regression, rather than classification, and end with one of the most useful data mining techniques of all: *logistic regression*. Its name is something of a misnomer—logistic regression doesn't really do what we call regression, which is the estimation of a numeric target value. Logistic regression applies linear models to class probability estimation, which is particularly useful for many applications.

Linear regression, logistic regression, and support vector machines are all very similar instances of our basic fundamental technique: fitting a (linear) model to data. The key difference is that each uses a different objective function.

An Example of Mining a Linear Discriminant from Data

To illustrate linear discriminant functions, we use an adaptation of the Iris dataset (*http://archive.ics.uci.edu/ml/datasets/Iris*) taken from the UCI Dataset Repository (*http://archive.ics.uci.edu/ml/*) (Bache & Lichman, 2013). This is an old and fairly simple dataset representing various types of iris, a genus of flowering plant. The original dataset includes three species of irises represented with four attributes, and the data mining problem is to classify each instance as belonging to one of the three species based on the attributes.

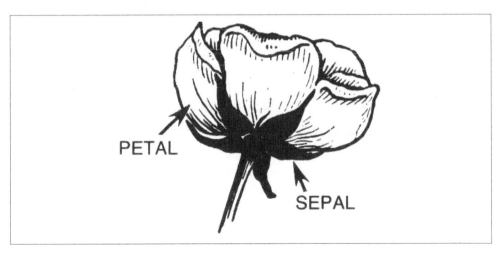

Figure 4-6. Two parts of a flower. Width measurements of these are used in the Iris dataset.

For this illustration we'll use just two species of irises, *Iris Setosa* and *Iris Versicolor*. The dataset describes a collection of flowers of these two species, each described with two measurements: the Petal width and the Sepal width (Figure 4-6). The flower dataset is plotted in Figure 4-7, with these two attributes on the *x* and *y* axis, respectively. Each instance is one flower and corresponds to one dot on the graph. The filled dots are of the species *Iris Setosa* and the circles are instances of the species *Iris Versicolor*.

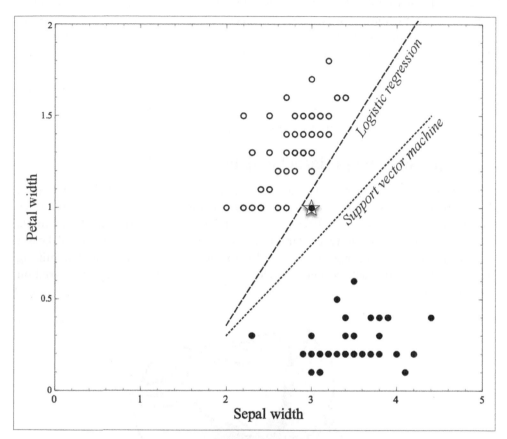

Figure 4-7. A dataset and two learned linear classifiers.

Two different separation lines are shown in the figure, one generated by logistic regression and the second by another linear method, a support vector machine (which will be described shortly). Note that the data comprise two fairly distinct clumps, with a few outliers. Logistic regression separates the two classes completely: all the *Iris Versicolor* examples are to the left of its line and all the *Iris Setosa* to the right. The Support vector machine line is almost midway between the clumps, though it misclassifies the starred point at (3, 1).[3] Which separator do you think is better? In Chapter 5, we will get into

---

3. We added the starred point to the original dataset to emphasize the difference in the discriminating lines produced by the two procedures.

details of why these separators are different and why one might be preferable to the other. For now it's enough just to notice that the methods produce different boundaries because they're optimizing different functions.

Linear Discriminant Functions for Scoring and Ranking Instances

In many applications, we don't simply want a *yes* or *no* prediction of whether an instance belongs to the class, but we want some notion of which examples are more or less likely to belong to the class. For example, which consumers are most likely to respond to this offer? Which customers are most likely to leave when their contracts expire? One option is to build a model that produces an estimate of class membership probability, as we did with tree induction for class probability estimation in Chapter 3. We can do this with linear models as well, and will treat this in detail below when we introduce logistic regression.

In other applications, we do not need a precise probability estimate. We simply need a score that will rank cases by the likelihood of belonging to one class or the other. For example, for targeted marketing we may have a limited budget for targeting prospective customers. We would like to have a list of consumers ranked by their predicted likelihood of responding positively to our offer. We don't necessarily need to be able to estimate the exact probability of response accurately, as long as the list is ranked reasonably well, and the consumers at the top of the list are the ones most likely to respond.

Linear discriminant functions can give us such a ranking for free. Look at Figure 4-4, and consider the + instances to be responders and • instances to be nonresponders. Assume we are presented with a new instance $\mathbf{x}$ for which we do not yet know the class (i.e., we have not yet made an offer to $\mathbf{x}$). In which portion of the instance space would we like $\mathbf{x}$ to fall in order to expect the highest likelihood of response? Where would we be most certain that $\mathbf{x}$ would *not* respond? Where would we be most *un*certain?

Many people suspect that right near the decision boundary we would be most uncertain about a class (and see the discussion below on the "margin"). Far away from the decision boundary, on the + side, would be where we would expect the highest likelihood of response. In the equation of the separating boundary, given above in Equation 4-2, $f(\mathbf{x})$ will be zero when $\mathbf{x}$ is sitting on the decision boundary (technically, $\mathbf{x}$ in that case is one of the points of the line or hyperplane). $f(\mathbf{x})$ will be relatively small when $\mathbf{x}$ is near the boundary. And $f(\mathbf{x})$ will be large (and positive) when $\mathbf{x}$ is far from the boundary in the + direction. Thus $f(\mathbf{x})$ itself—the output of the linear discriminant function—gives an intuitively satisfying ranking of the instances by their (estimated) likelihood of belonging to the class of interest.

Support Vector Machines, Briefly

If you're even on the periphery of the world of data science these days, you eventually will run into the *support vector machine* or "SVM." This is a notion that can strike fear into the hearts even of people quite knowledgeable in data science. Not only is the name itself opaque, but the method often is imbued with the sort of magic that derives from perceived effectiveness without understanding.

Fortunately, we now have the concepts necessary to understand support vector machines. In short, support vector machines are linear discriminants. For many business users interacting with data scientists, that will be sufficient. Nevertheless, let's look at SVMs a little more carefully; if we can get through some minor details, the procedure for fitting the linear discriminant is intuitively satisfying.

As with linear discriminants generally, SVMs classify instances based on a linear function of the features, described above in Equation 4-2.

 You may also hear of *nonlinear* support vector machines. Oversimplifying slightly, a nonlinear SVM uses different features (that are functions of the original features), so that the linear discriminant with the new features is a nonlinear discriminant with the original features.

So, as we've discussed, the crucial question becomes: what is the objective function that is used to fit an SVM to data? For now we will skip the mathematical details in order to gain an intuitive understanding. There are two main ideas.

Recall Figure 4-5 showing the infinitude of different possible linear discriminants that would separate the classes, and recall that choosing an objective function for fitting the data amounts to choosing which of these lines is the best. SVMs choose based on a simple, elegant idea: instead of thinking about separating with a line, first fit the fattest bar between the classes. This is shown by the parallel dashed lines in Figure 4-8.

The SVM's objective function incorporates the idea that a wider bar is better. Then once the widest bar is found, the linear discriminant will be the center line through the bar (the solid middle line in Figure 4-8). The distance between the dashed parallel lines is called the *margin* around the linear discriminant, and thus the objective is to maximize the margin.

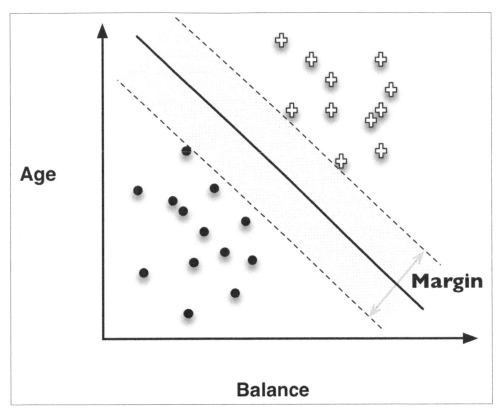

Figure 4-8. The points of Figure 4-2 and the maximal margin classifier.

The idea of maximizing the margin is intuitively satisfying for the following reason. The training dataset is just a sample from some population. In predictive modeling, we are interested in predicting the target for instances that we have not yet seen. These instances will be scattered about. Hopefully they will be distributed similarly to the training data, but they will in fact be different points. In particular, some of the positive examples will likely fall closer to the discriminant boundary than any positive example we have yet seen. All else being equal, the same applies to the negative examples. In other words, they may fall in the margin. The margin-maximizing boundary gives the maximal leeway for classifying such points. Specifically, by choosing the SVM decision boundary, in order for a new instance to be misclassified, one would have to place it further into the margin than with any other linear discriminant. (Or, of course, completely on the wrong side of the margin bar altogether.)

The second important idea of SVMs lies in how they handle points falling on the wrong side of the discrimination boundary. The original example of Figure 4-2 shows a situation in which a single line cannot perfectly separate the data into classes. This is true of most data from complex real-world applications—some data points will inevitably be misclassified by the model. This does not pose a problem for the general notion of linear discriminants, as their classifications don't necessarily have to be correct for all points. However, when fitting the linear function to the data we cannot simply ask which of all the lines that separate the data perfectly should we choose. There may be no such perfect separating line!

Once again, the support-vector machine's solution is intuitively satisfying. Skipping the math, the idea is as follows. In the objective function that measures how well a particular model fits the training points, we will simply penalize a training point for being on the wrong side of the decision boundary. In the case where the data indeed are linearly separable, we incur no penalty and simply maximize the margin. If the data are *not* linearly separable, the best fit is some balance between a fat margin and a low total error penalty. The penalty for a misclassified point is proportional to the distance from the margin boundary, so if possible the SVM will make only "small" errors. Technically, this error function is known as *hinge loss* (see "Sidebar: Loss functions" on page 95 and Figure 4-9).

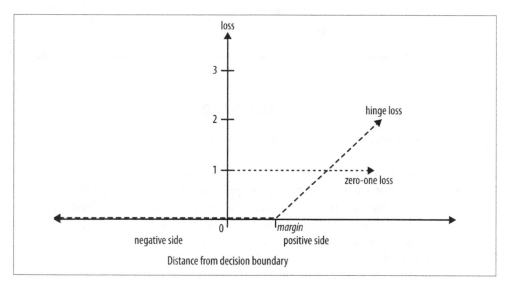

Figure 4-9. Two loss functions illustrated. The x axis shows the distance from the decision boundary. The y axis shows the loss incurred by a negative instance as a function of its distance from the decision boundary. (The case of a positive instance is symmetric.) If the negative instance is on the negative side of the boundary, there is no loss. If it is on the positive (wrong) side of the boundary, the different loss functions penalize it differently. (See "Sidebar: Loss functions" on page 95.)

Regression via Mathematical Functions

The previous chapter introduced the fundamental notion of selecting informative variables. We showed that this notion applies to classification, to regression, and to class probability estimation. Here too, this chapter's basic notion of fitting linear functions to data applies to classification, regression, and to class probability estimation. Let's now discuss regression briefly.[4]

Sidebar: Loss functions

The term "loss" is used across data science as a general term for error penalty. A loss function determines how much penalty should be assigned to an instance based on the error in the model's predicted value—in our present context, based on its distance from the separation boundary. Several loss functions are commonly used (two are shown in Figure 4-9). In the figure, the horizontal axis is the distance from the separating boundary. Errors have positive distances from the separator in Figure 4-9, while correct classifications have negative distances (the choice is arbitrary in this diagram).

Support vector machines use *hinge loss*, so called because the loss graph looks like a hinge. Hinge loss incurs no penalty for an example that is not on the wrong side of the margin. The hinge loss only becomes positive when an example is on the wrong side of the boundary and beyond the margin. Loss then increases linearly with the example's distance from the margin, thereby penalizing points more the farther they are from the separating boundary.

Zero-one loss, as its name implies, assigns a loss of zero for a correct decision and one for an incorrect decision.

For contrast, consider a different sort of loss function. *Squared error* specifies a loss proportional to the square of the distance from the boundary. Squared error loss usually is used for numeric value prediction (regression), rather than classification. The squaring of the error has the effect of greatly penalizing predictions that are grossly wrong. For classification, this would apply large penalties to points far over on the "wrong side" of the separating boundary. Unfortunately, using squared error for classification also penalizes points far on the *correct* side of the decision boundary. For most business problems, choosing squared-error loss for classification or class-probability estimation thus would violate our principle of thinking carefully about whether the loss function

---

4. There is an immense literature on linear regression for descriptive analysis of data, and we encourage the reader to delve into it. In this book, we treat linear regression simply as one of many modeling techniques. Our treatment does differ from what you are likely to have learned about regression analysis, because we focus on linear regression for making predictions. Other authors have discussed in detail the differences between descriptive modeling and predictive modeling (Shmueli, 2010).

is aligned with the business goal. (Hinge-like versions of squared error have been created because of this misalignment [Rosset & Zhu, 2007].)

We have already discussed most of what we need for linear regression. The linear regression model structure is exactly the same as for the linear discriminant function Equation 4-2:

$$f(\mathbf{x}) = w_0 + w_1 x_1 + w_2 x_2 + \cdots$$

So, following our general framework for thinking about parametric modeling, we need to decide on the objective function we will use to optimize the model's fit to the data. There are many possibilities. Each different linear regression modeling procedure uses one particular choice (and the data scientist should think carefully about whether it is appropriate for the problem).

The most common ("standard") linear regression procedure makes a powerful and convenient choice. Recall that for regression problems the target variable is numeric. The linear function estimates this numeric target value using Equation 4-2, and of course the *training* data have the actual target value. Therefore, an intuitive notion of the fit of the model is: how far away are the estimated values from the true values on the training data? In other words, how big is the error of the fitted model? Presumably we'd like to minimize this error. For a particular training dataset, we could compute this error for each individual data point and sum up the results. Then the model that fits the data best would be the model with the minimum sum of errors on the training data. And that is exactly what regression procedures do.

You might notice that we really have not actually specified the objective function, because there are many ways to compute the error between an estimated value and an actual value. The method that is most natural is to simply subtract one from the other (and take the absolute value). So if I predict 10 and the actual value is 12 or 8, I make an error of 2. This is called *absolute error*, and we could then minimize the sum of absolute errors or equivalently the mean of the absolute errors across the training data. This makes a lot of sense, but it is not what standard linear regression procedures do.

Standard linear regression procedures instead minimize the sum or mean of the *squares* of these errors—which gives the procedure its common name "least squares" regression. So why do so many people use least squares regression without much thought to alternatives? The short answer is convenience. It is the technique we learn in basic statistics classes (and beyond). It is available to us to use in various software packages. Originally, the least squared error function was introduced by the famous 18th century mathematician Carl Friedrich Gauss, and there are certain theoretical arguments for its use (relating to the normal or "Gaussian" distribution). Often, more importantly, it turns out that squared error is particularly convenient mathematically.[5] This was helpful in the days before computers. From a data science perspective, the convenience extends to theoretical analyses, including a clean decomposition of model error into different sources. More pragmatically, analysts often claim to prefer squared error because it strongly penalizes very large errors. Whether the quadratic penalty is actually appropriate is specific to each application. (Why not take the fourth power of the errors, and penalize large errors even more strongly?)

Importantly, any choice for the objective function has both advantages and drawbacks. For least squares regression a serious drawback is that it is very sensitive to the data: erroneous or otherwise outlying data points can severely skew the resultant linear function. For some business applications, we may not have the resources to spend as much time on manual massaging of the data as we would in other applications. At the extreme, for systems that build and apply models totally automatically, the modeling needs to be much more robust than when doing a detailed regression analysis "by hand." Therefore, for the former application we may want to use a more robust modeling procedure (e.g., use as the objective function absolute error instead of squared error). An important thing to remember is that once we see linear regression simply as an instance of fitting a (linear) model to data, we see that we have to choose the objective function to optimize —and we should do so with the ultimate business application in mind.

Class Probability Estimation and Logistic "Regression"

As mentioned earlier, for many applications we would like to estimate the probability that a new instance belongs to the class of interest. In many cases, we would like to use the estimated probability in a decision-making context that includes other factors such as costs and benefits. For example, predictive modeling from large consumer data is used widely in fraud detection across many industries, especially banking, telecommunications, and online commerce. A linear discriminant could be used to identify accounts or transactions as likely to have been defrauded. The director of the fraud control operation may want the analysts to focus not simply on the cases most likely to be fraud, but on the cases where the most money is at stake—that is, accounts where the company's monetary loss is expected to be the highest. For this we need to estimate the actual probability of fraud. (Chapter 7 will discuss in detail the use of expected value to frame business problems.)

Fortunately, within this same framework for fitting linear models to data, by choosing a different objective function we can produce a model designed to give accurate estimates of class probability. The most common procedure by which we do this is called logistic regression.

---

5. Gauss agreed with objections to the arbitrariness of this choice.

What exactly is an accurate estimate of class membership probability is a subject of debate beyond the scope of this book. Roughly, we would like (i) the probability estimates to be well calibrated, meaning that if you take 100 cases whose class membership probability is estimated to be 0.2, then about 20 of them will actually belong to the class. We would also like (ii) the probability estimates to be discriminative, in that if possible they give meaningfully different probability estimates to different examples. The latter condition keeps us from simply giving the "base rate" (the overall prevalence in the population) as the prediction for every example. Say 0.5% of accounts overall are fraudulent. Without condition (ii) we could simply predict the same 0.5% probability for each account; those estimates would be well calibrated—but not discriminative at all.

To understand logistic regression, it is instructive to first consider: exactly what is the problem with simply using our basic linear model (Equation 4-2) to estimate the class probability? As we discussed, an instance being further from the separating boundary intuitively ought to lead to a higher probability of being in one class or the other, and the output of the linear function, $f(\mathbf{x})$, gives the distance from the separating boundary. However, this also shows the problem: $f(x)$ ranges from $-\infty$ to ∞, and a probability should range from zero to one.

So let's take a brief stroll down a garden path and ask how else we might cast our distance from the separator, $f(x)$, in terms of the likelihood of class membership. Is there another representation of the likelihood of an event that we use in everyday life? If we could come up with one that ranges from $-\infty$ to ∞, then we might model this other notion of likelihood with our linear equation.

One very useful notion of the likelihood of an event is the odds. The odds of an event is the ratio of the probability of the event occurring to the probability of the event not occurring. So, for example, if the event has an 80% probability of occurrence, the odds are 80:20 or 4:1. And if the linear function were to give us the odds, a little algebra would tell us the probability of occurrence. Let's look at a more detailed example. Table 4-1 shows the odds corresponding to various probabilities.

Table 4-1. Probabilities and the corresponding odds.

Probability	Corresponding odds
0.5	50:50 or 1
0.9	90:10 or 9
0.999	999:1 or 999
0.01	1:99 or 0.0101
0.001	1:999 or 0.001001

Looking at the range of the odds in Table 4-1, we can see that it still is not quite right as an interpretation of the distance from the separating boundary. Again, the distance from the boundary is between $-\infty$ and ∞, but as we can see from the example, the odds range from 0 to ∞. Nonetheless, we can solve our garden-path problem simply by taking the logarithm of the odds (called the "log-odds"), since for any number in the range 0 to ∞ its log will be between $-\infty$ to ∞. These are shown in Table 4-2.

Table 4-2. Probabilities, odds, and the corresponding log-odds.

Probability	Odds	Log-odds
0.5	50:50 or 1	0
0.9	90:10 or 9	2.19
0.999	999:1 or 999	6.9
0.01	1:99 or 0.0101	−4.6
0.001	1:999 or 0.001001	−6.9

So if we only cared about modeling *some* notion of likelihood, rather than the class membership probability specifically, we could model the *log-odds* with *f(x)*.

Lo and behold, our garden path has taken us directly back to our main topic. This is exactly a logistic regression model: the same linear function *f(x)* that we've examined throughout the chapter is used as a measure of the log-odds of the "event" of interest. More specifically, *f(x)* is the model's estimation of the log-odds that **x** belongs to the positive class. For example, the model might estimate the log-odds that a customer described by feature vector **x** will leave the company when her contract expires. Moreover, with a little algebra we can translate these log-odds into the probability of class membership. This is a little more technical than most of the book, so we've relegated it to a special "technical details" subsection (next), which also discusses what exactly is the objective function that is optimized to fit a logistic regression to the data. You can read that section in detail or just skim it. The most important points are:

- For probability estimation, logistic regression uses the same linear model as do our linear discriminants for classification and linear regression for estimating numeric target values.

- The output of the logistic regression model is interpreted as the log-odds of class membership.

- These log-odds can be translated directly into the probability of class membership. Therefore, logistic regression often is thought of simply as a model for the probability of class membership. You have undoubtedly dealt with logistic regression models many times without even knowing it. They are used widely to estimate quantities like the probability of default on credit, the probability of response to an offer, the probability of fraud on an account, the probability that a document is relevant to a topic, and so on.

After the technical details section, we will compare the linear models we've developed in this chapter with the tree-structured models we developed in Chapter 3.

Note: Logistic regression is a misnomer

Above we mentioned that the name logistic *regression* is a misnomer under the modern use of data science terminology. Recall that the distinction between classification and regression is whether the value for the target variable is categorical or numeric. For logistic regression, the model produces a numeric estimate (the estimation of the log-odds). However, the values of the target variable in the data are categorical. Debating this point is rather academic. What is important to understand is what logistic regression is doing. It is estimating the log-odds or, more loosely, the probability of class membership (a numeric quantity) over a categorical class. So we consider it to be a class probability estimation model and *not* a regression model, despite its name.

* Logistic Regression: Some Technical Details

Technical Details Ahead

Since logistic regression is used so widely, and is not as intuitive as linear regression, let's examine a few of the technical details. You may skip this subsection without it affecting your understanding of the rest of the book.

So, technically, what is the bottom line for the logistic regression model?

Let's use $(p_+(\mathbf{x}))$ to represent the model's estimate of the probability of class membership of a data item represented by feature vector $\mathbf{x}$.[6] Recall that the class + is whatever is the (binary) event that we are modeling: responding to an offer, leaving the company after contract expiration, being defrauded, etc. The estimated probability of the event not occurring is therefore $(1 - p_+(\mathbf{x}))$.

---

6. Often technical treatments use the "hat" notation, $\hat{p}$, to differentiate the model's *estimate* of the probability of class membership from the actual probability of class membership. We will not use the hat, but the technically savvy reader should keep that in mind.

Equation 4-3. Log-odds linear function

$$\log\left(\frac{p_+(\mathbf{x})}{1 - p_+(\mathbf{x})}\right) = f(\mathbf{x}) = w_0 + w_1 x_1 + w_2 x_2 + \cdots$$

Thus, Equation 4-3 specifies that for a particular data item, described by feature-vector **x**, the log-odds of the class is equal to our linear function, $f(\mathbf{x})$. Since often we actually want the estimated probability of class membership, not the log-odds, we can solve for $(p_+(\mathbf{x}))$ in Equation 4-3. This yields the not-so-pretty quantity in Equation 4-4.

Equation 4-4. The logistic function

$$p_+(\mathbf{x}) = \frac{1}{1 + e^{-f(\mathbf{x})}}$$

Although the quantity in Equation 4-4 is not very pretty, by plotting it in a particular way we can see that it matches exactly our intuitive notion that we would like there to be relative certainty in the estimations of class membership far from the decision boundary, and uncertainty near the decision boundary.

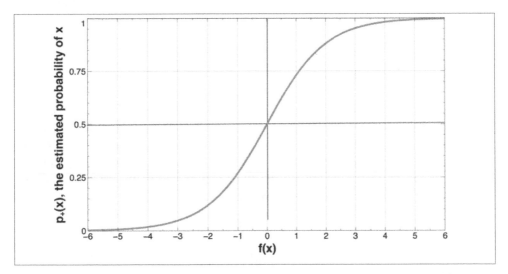

Figure 4-10. Logistic regression's estimate of class probability as a function of f(x), (i.e., the distance from the separating boundary). This curve is called a "sigmoid" curve because of its "S" shape, which squeezes the probabilities into their correct range (between zero and one).

Figure 4-10 plots the estimated probability $(p_+(\mathbf{x}))$ (vertical axis) as a function of the distance from the decision boundary (horizontal axis). The figure shows that at the decision boundary (at distance $x = 0$), the probability is 0.5 (a coin toss). The probability varies approximately linearly near to the decision boundary, but then approaches certainty farther away. Part of the "fitting" of the model to the data includes determining the slope of the almost-linear part, and thereby how quickly we are certain of the class as we move away from the boundary.

The other main technical point that we omitted in our main discussion above is: what then is the objective function we use to fit the logistic regression model to the data? Recall that the training data have binary values of the target variable. The model can be applied to the training data to produce estimates that each of the training data points belongs to the target class. What would we want? Ideally, any positive example $\mathbf{x}_+$ would have $(p_+(\mathbf{x}_+) = 1)$ and any negative example $\mathbf{x}_-$ would have $(p_+(\mathbf{x}_-) = 0)$. Unfortunately, with real-world data it is unlikely that we will be able to estimate these probabilities perfectly (consider the task of estimating that a consumer described by demographic variables would respond to a particular offer). Nevertheless, we still would like $(p_+(\mathbf{x}_+))$ to be as close as possible to one and $(p_+(\mathbf{x}_-))$ to be as close as possible to zero.

This leads us to the standard objective function for fitting a logistic regression model to data. Consider the following function computing the "likelihood" that a particular labeled example belongs to the correct class, given a set of parameters $\mathbf{w}$ that produces class probability estimates $(p_+(\mathbf{x}))$:

$$g(\mathbf{x},\mathbf{w}) = \begin{cases} p_+(\mathbf{x}) & \text{if } \mathbf{x} \text{ is a } + \\ 1 - p_+(\mathbf{x}) & \text{if } \mathbf{x} \text{ is a } \bullet \end{cases}$$

The g function gives the model's estimated probability of seeing $\mathbf{x}$'s actual class given $\mathbf{x}$'s features. Now consider summing the g values across all the examples in a labeled dataset. And do that for different parameterized models—in our case, different sets of weights ($\mathbf{w}$) for the logistic regression. The model (set of weights) that gives the highest sum is the model that gives the highest "likelihood" to the data—the "maximum likelihood" model. The maximum likelihood model "on average" gives the highest probabilities to the positive examples and the lowest probabilities to the negative examples.

Class Labels and Probabilities

One may be tempted to think that the target variable *is* a representation of the probability of class membership, and the observed values of the target variable in the training data simply report probabilities of $p(x) = 1$ for cases that are observed to be in the class and $p(x) = 0$ for instances that are observed not to be in the class. However, this is not generally consistent with how logistic regression models are used. Take an application to targeted marketing for example. For a consumer c, our model may estimate the probability of responding to the offer to be $p(c\ responds) = 0.02$. In the data, we see that the person indeed does respond. That does not mean that this consumer's probability of responding actually was 1.0, nor that the model incurred a large error on this example. The consumer's probability may indeed have been around $p(c\ responds) = 0.02$, which actually is a high probability of response for many campaigns, and the consumer just happened to respond this time.

A more satisfying way to think about it is that the training data comprise a set of statistical "draws" from the underlying probabilities, rather than representing the underlying probabilities themselves. The logistic regression procedure then tries to estimate the probabilities (the probability distribution over the instance space) with a linear-log-odds model, based on the observed data on the result of the draws from the distribution.

Example: Logistic Regression versus Tree Induction

Though classification trees and linear classifiers both use linear decision boundaries, there are two important differences between them:

1. A classification tree uses decision boundaries that are *perpendicular* to the instance-space axes (see Figure 4-1), whereas the linear classifier can use decision boundaries of any direction or orientation (see Figure 4-3). This is a direct consequence of the fact that classification trees select a single attribute at a time whereas linear classifiers use a weighted combination of all attributes.

2. A classification tree is a "piecewise" classifier that segments the instance space recursively when it has to, using a divide-and-conquer approach. In principle, a classification tree can cut up the instance space arbitrarily finely into very small regions (though we will see reasons to avoid that in Chapter 5). A linear classifier places a *single* decision surface through the entire space. It has great freedom in the orientation of the surface, but it is limited to a single division into two segments. This is a direct consequence of there being a single (linear) equation that uses all of the variables, and must fit the entire data space.

It is usually not easy to determine in advance which of these characteristics are a better match to a given dataset. You likely will not know what the best decision boundary will look like. So practically speaking, what are the consequences of these differences?

When applied to a business problem, there is a difference in the comprehensibility of the models to stakeholders with different backgrounds. For example, what exactly a logistic regression model is doing can be quite understandable to people with a strong background in statistics, and very difficult to understand for those who do not. A decision tree, if it is not too large, may be considerably more understandable to someone without a strong statistics or mathematics background.

Why is this important? For many business problems, the data science team does not have the ultimate say in which models are used or implemented. Often there is at least one manager who must "sign off" on the use of a model in practice, and in many cases a set of stakeholders need to be satisfied with the model. For example, to put in place a new model to dispatch technicians to repair problems after customer calls to the telephone company, managers from operations support, customer service, and technical development all need to be satisfied that the new model will do more good than harm —since for this problem no model is perfect.

Let's try logistic regression on a simple but realistic dataset, the Wisconsin Breast Cancer Dataset (*http://archive.ics.uci.edu/ml/datasets/Breast+Cancer+Wisconsin+(Diagnostic)*). As with the Iris data set from a few sections back and the Mushroom dataset from the previous chapter, this is another popular dataset from the the machine learning dataset repository at the University of California at Irvine.

Each example describes characteristics of a cell nuclei image, which has been labeled as either *benign* or *malignant* (cancerous), based on an expert's diagnosis of the cells. A sample cell image is shown in Figure 4-11.

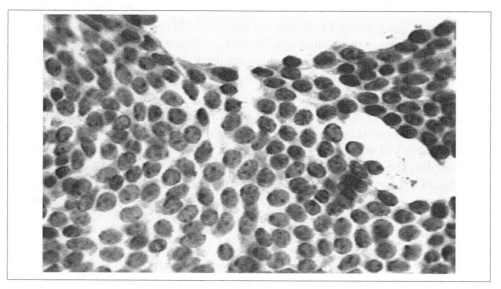

Figure 4-11. One of the cell images from which the Wisconsin Breast Cancer dataset was derived. (Image courtesy of Nick Street and Bill Wolberg.)

From each image 10 fundamental characteristics were extracted, listed in Table 4-3.

Table 4-3. The attributes of the Wisconsin Breast Cancer dataset.

Attribute name	Description
RADIUS	Mean of distances from center to points on the perimeter
TEXTURE	Standard deviation of grayscale values
PERIMETER	Perimeter of the mass
AREA	Area of the mass
SMOOTHNESS	Local variation in radius lengths
COMPACTNESS	Computed as: $perimeter^2/area - 1.0$
CONCAVITY	Severity of concave portions of the contour
CONCAVE POINTS	Number of concave portions of the contour
SYMMETRY	A measure of the symmetry of the nucleii
FRACTAL DIMENSION	'Coastline approximation' - 1.0
DIAGNOSIS (Target)	Diagnosis of cell sample: malignant or benign

These were "computed from a digitized image of a fine needle aspirate (FNA) of a breast mass. They describe characteristics of the cell nuclei present in the image." From each of these basic characteristics, three values were computed: the mean (_mean), standard error (_SE), and "worst" or largest (mean of the three largest values, _worst). This resulted in 30 measured attributes in the dataset. There are 357 benign images and 212 malignant images.

Table 4-4. Linear equation learned by logistic regression on the Wisconsin Breast Cancer dataset (see text and Table 4-3 for a description of the attributes).

Attribute	Weight (learned parameter)
SMOOTHNESS_worst	22.3
CONCAVE_mean	19.47
CONCAVE_worst	11.68
SYMMETRY_worst	4.99
CONCAVITY_worst	2.86
CONCAVITY_mean	2.34
RADIUS_worst	0.25
TEXTURE_worst	0.13
AREA_SE	0.06
TEXTURE_mean	0.03
TEXTURE_SE	−0.29
COMPACTNESS_mean	−7.1
COMPACTNESS_SE	−27.87
w_0 (intercept)	−17.7

Table 4-4 shows the linear model learned by logistic regression to predict benign versus malignant for this dataset. Specifically, it shows the nonzero weights ordered from highest to lowest.

The performance of this model is quite good—it makes only six mistakes on the entire dataset, yielding an accuracy of about 98.9% (the percentage of the instances that the model classifies correctly). For comparison, a classification tree was learned from the same dataset (using Weka's J48 implementation). The resulting tree is shown in Figure 4-12. The tree has 25 nodes altogether, with 13 leaf nodes. Recall that this means that the tree model partitions the instances into 13 segments. The classification tree's accuracy is 99.1%, slightly higher than that of logistic regression.

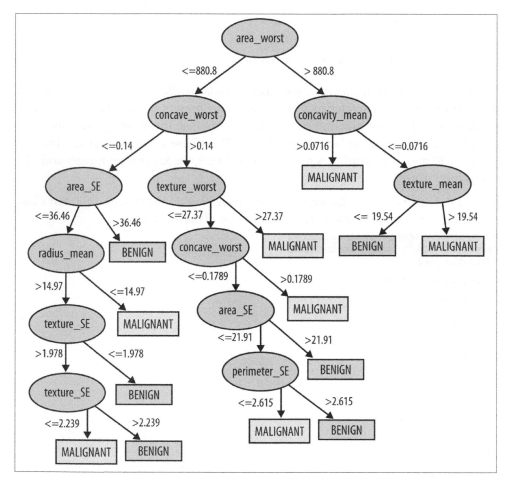

Figure 4-12. Decision tree learned from the Wisconsin Breast Cancer dataset.

The intent of this experiment is only to illustrate the results of two different methods on a dataset, but it is worth digressing briefly to think about these performance results. First, an accuracy figure like 98.9% sounds like a very good result. Is it? We see many such accuracy numbers thrown around in the data mining literature, but evaluating classifiers on real-world problems like cancer diagnosis is often difficult and complex. We discuss evaluation in detail in Chapter 7 and Chapter 8.

Second, consider the two performance results here: 98.9% versus 99.1%. Since the classification tree gives slightly higher accuracy, we might be tempted to conclude that it's the better model. Should we believe this? This difference is caused by only a *single* additional error out of the 569 examples. Furthermore, the accuracy numbers were derived by evaluating each model on the same set of examples it was built from. How confident should we be in this evaluation? Chapter 5, Chapter 7, and Chapter 8 discuss guidelines and pitfalls of model evaluation.

Nonlinear Functions, Support Vector Machines, and Neural Networks

So far this chapter has focused on the numeric functions most commonly used in data science: linear models. This set of models includes a wide variety of different techniques. In addition, in Figure 4-13 we show that such linear functions can actually represent nonlinear models, *if we include more complex features in the functions*. In this example, we used the Iris dataset from "An Example of Mining a Linear Discriminant from Data" on page 89 and added a squared term to the input data: **Sepal width^2**. The resulting model is a curved line (a parabola) in the original feature space. We also added a single data point to the original dataset, an Iris Versicolor example added at (4, 0.7), shown starred.

Our fundamental concept is much more general than just the application of fitting linear functions. Of course, we could specify arbitrarily complex numeric functions and fit their parameters to the data. The two most common families of techniques that are based on fitting the parameters of complex, nonlinear functions are *nonlinear support-vector machines* and *neural networks*.

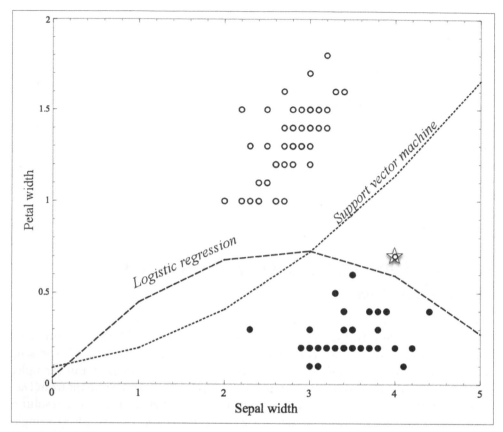

Figure 4-13. The Iris dataset with a nonlinear feature. In this figure, logistic regression and support vector machine—both linear models—are provided an additional feature, **Sepal width²**, *which allows both the freedom to create more complex, nonlinear models (boundaries), as shown.*

One can think of nonlinear support vector machines as essentially a systematic way of implementing the "trick" we just discussed of adding more complex terms and fitting a linear function to them. Support vector machines have a so-called "kernel function" that maps the original features to some other feature space. Then a linear model is fit to this new feature space, just as in our simple example in Figure 4-13. Generalizing this, one could implement a nonlinear support vector machine with a "polynomial kernel," which essentially means it would consider "higher-order" combinations of the original features (e.g., squared features, products of features). A data scientist would become familiar with the different alternatives for kernel functions (linear, polynomial, and others).

Neural networks also implement complex nonlinear numeric functions, based on the fundamental concepts of this chapter. Neural networks offer an intriguing twist. One can think of a neural network as a "stack" of models. On the bottom of the stack are the original features. From these features are learned a variety of relatively simple models. Let's say these are logistic regressions. Then, each subsequent layer in the stack applies a simple model (let's say, another logistic regression) to the outputs of the next layer down. So in a two-layer stack, we would learn a set of logistic regressions from the original features, and then learn a logistic regression using as features the outputs of the first set of logistic regressions. We could think of this very roughly as first creating a set of "experts" in different facets of the problem (the first-layer models), and then learning how to weight the opinions of these different experts (the second-layer model).[7]

The idea of neural networks gets even more intriguing. We might ask: if we are learning those lower-layer logistic regressions—the different experts—what would be the *target* variable for each? While some practitioners build stacked models where the lower-layer experts are built to represent specific things using specific target variables (e.g., Perlich et al., 2013), more generally with neural networks target labels for training are provided only for the final layer (the actual target variable). So how are the lower-layer logistic regressions trained? We can understand by returning to the fundamental concept of this chapter. The stack of models can be represented by one big parameterized numeric function. The parameters now are the coefficients of all the models, taken together. So once we have decided on an objective function representing what we want to optimize (e.g., the fit to the training data, based on some fitting function), we can then apply an optimization procedure to find the best parameters to this very complex numeric function. When we're done, we have the parameters to all the models, and thereby have learned the "best" set of lower-level experts and also the best way to combine them, all simultaneously.

Note: Neural networks are useful for many tasks

This section describes neural networks for classification and regression. The field of neural networks is broad and deep, with a long history. Neural networks have found wide application throughout data mining. They are commonly used for many other tasks mentioned in Chapter 2, such as clustering, time series analysis, profiling, and so on.

So, given how cool that sounds, why wouldn't we want to do that all the time? The tradeoff is that as we increase the amount of flexibility we have to fit the data, we increase the chance that we fit the data *too* well. The model can fit details of its particular training set rather than finding patterns or models that apply more generally. Specifically, we really want models that apply to other data drawn from the same population or appli-

---

7. Compare this with the notion of *ensemble methods* described in Chapter 12.

cation. This concern is not specific to neural networks, but is very general. It is one of the most important concepts in data science—and it is the subject of the next chapter.

Summary

This chapter introduced a second type of predictive modeling technique called function fitting or parametric modeling. In this case the model is a partially specified equation: a numeric function of the data attributes, with some unspecified numeric parameters. The task of the data mining procedure is to "fit" the model to the data by finding the best set of parameters, in some sense of "best."

There are many varieties of function fitting techniques, but most use the same linear model structure: a simple weighted sum of the attribute values. The parameters to be fit by the data mining are the weights on the attributes. Linear modeling techniques include traditional linear regression, logistic regression, and linear discriminants such as support-vector machines. Conceptually the key difference between these techniques is their answer to a key issue, *What exactly do we mean by best fitting the data?* The goodness of fit is described by an "objective function," and each technique uses a different function. The resulting techniques may be quite different.

We now have seen two very different sorts of data modeling, tree induction and function fitting, and have compared them (in "Example: Logistic Regression versus Tree Induction" on page 103). We have also introduced two criteria by which models can be evaluated: the predictive performance of a model and its intelligibility. It is often advantageous to build different sorts of models from a dataset to gain insight.

This chapter focused on the fundamental concept of optimizing a model's fit to data. However, doing this leads to the most important fundamental *problem* with data mining —if you look hard enough, you will find structure in a dataset, even if it's just there by chance. This tendency is known as *overfitting*. Recognizing and avoiding overfitting is an important general topic in data science; and we devote the entire next chapter to it.

CHAPTER 5

Overfitting and Its Avoidance

Fundamental concepts: *Generalization; Fitting and overfitting; Complexity control.*

Exemplary techniques: *Cross-validation; Attribute selection; Tree pruning; Regularization.*

One of the most important fundamental notions of data science is that of overfitting and generalization. If we allow ourselves enough flexibility in searching for patterns in a particular dataset, we will find patterns. Unfortunately, these "patterns" may be just chance occurrences in the data. As discussed previously, we are interested in patterns that generalize—that predict well for instances that we have not yet observed. Finding chance occurrences in data that look like interesting patterns, but which do not generalize, is called *overfitting* the data.

Generalization

Consider the following (extreme) example. You're a manager at MegaTelCo, responsible for reducing customer churn. I run a data mining consulting group. You give my data science team a set of historical data on customers who have stayed with the company and customers who have departed within six months of contract expiration. My job is to build a model to distinguish customers who are likely to churn based on some features, as we've discussed previously. I mine the data and build a model. I give you back the code for the model, to implement in your company's churn-reduction system.

Of course you are interested in whether my model is any good, so you ask your technical team to check the performance of the model on the historical data. You understand that historical performance is no guarantee of future success, but your experience tells you that churn patterns remain relatively stable, except for major changes to the industry (such as the introduction of the iPhone), and you know of no such major changes since these data were collected. So, the tech team runs the historical dataset through the model. Your technical lead reports back that this data science team is amazing. The model is

100% accurate. It does not make a single mistake, identifying correctly all the churners as well as the nonchurners.

You're experienced enough not to be comfortable with that answer. You've had experts looking at churn behavior for a long time, and if there really were 100% accurate indicators, you figure you would be doing better than you currently are. Maybe this is just a lucky fluke?

It was not a lucky fluke. Our data science team can do that every time. Here is how we built the model. We stored the feature vector for each customer who has churned in a database table. Let's call that T_c. Then, in use, when the model is presented with a customer to determine the likelihood of churning, it takes the customer's feature vector, looks her up in T_c, and reports "100% likelihood of churning" if she is in T_c and "0% likelihood of churning" if she is not in T_c. So, when the tech team applies our model to the historical dataset, the model predicts perfectly.[1]

Call this simple approach a *table model*. It memorizes the training data and performs no generalization. What is the problem with this? Consider how we'll use the model in practice. When a *previously unseen* customer's contract is about to expire, we'll want to apply the model. Of course, this customer was not part of the historical dataset, so the lookup will fail since there will be no exact match, and the model will predict "0% likelihood of churning" for this customer. In fact, the model will predict this for every customer (not in the training data). A model that looked perfect would be completely useless in practice!

This may seem like an absurd scenario. In reality, no one would throw raw customer data into a table and claim it was a "predictive model" of anything. But it is important to think about why this is a bad idea, because it fails for the same reason other, more realistic data mining efforts may fail. It is an extreme example of two related fundamental concepts of data science: *generalization* and *overfitting*. Generalization is the property of a model or modeling process, whereby the model applies to data that were not used to build the model. In this example, the model does not generalize at all beyond the data that were used to build it. It is tailored, or "fit," perfectly to the training data. In fact, it is "overfit."

This is the important point. Every dataset is a finite sample of a population—in this case, the population of phone customers. We want models to apply not just to the exact training set but to the general population from which the training data came. We may worry that the training data were not representative of the true population, but that is not the problem here. The data were representative, but the data mining did not create a model that generalized beyond the training data.

---

1. Technically, this is not necessarily true: there may be two customers with the same feature vector description, one of whom churns and the other does not. We can ignore that possibility for the sake of this example. For example, we can assume that the unique customer ID is one of the features.

Overfitting

Overfitting is the tendency of data mining procedures to tailor models to the training data, at the expense of generalization to previously unseen data points. The example from the previous section was contrived; the data mining built a model using pure memorization, the most extreme overfitting procedure possible. However, all data mining procedures have the tendency to overfit to some extent—some more than others. The idea is that if we look hard enough we will find patterns in a dataset. As the Nobel Laureate Ronald Coase said, "If you torture the data long enough, it will confess."

Unfortunately, the problem is insidious. The answer is not to use a data mining procedure that doesn't overfit because all of them do. Nor is the answer to simply use models that produce less overfitting, because there is a fundamental trade-off between model complexity and the possibility of overfitting. Sometimes we may simply want more complex models, because they will better capture the real complexities of the application and thereby be more accurate. There is no single choice or procedure that will eliminate overfitting. The best strategy is to recognize overfitting and to manage complexity in a principled way.

The rest of this chapter discusses overfitting in more detail, methods for assessing the degree of overfitting at modeling time, as well as methods for avoiding overfitting as much as possible.

Overfitting Examined

Before discussing what to do about overfitting, we need to know how to recognize it.

Holdout Data and Fitting Graphs

Let's now introduce a simple analytic tool: the *fitting graph*. A fitting graph shows the accuracy of a model as a function of complexity. To examine *over*fitting, we need to introduce a concept that is fundamental to evaluation in data science: *holdout* data.

The problem in the prior section was that the model was evaluated on the training data —exactly the same data that were used to build it. Evaluation on training data provides no assessment of how well the model generalizes to unseen cases. What we need to do is to "hold out" some data for which we know the value of the target variable, but which will not be used to build the model. These are not the actual *use* data, for which we ultimately would like to predict the value of the target variable. Instead, creating holdout data is like creating a "lab test" of generalization performance. We will simulate the use scenario on these holdout data: we will hide from the model (and possibly the modelers) the actual values for the target on the holdout data. The model will predict the values. Then we estimate the *generalization performance* by comparing the predicted values with the hidden true values. There is likely to be a difference between the model's ac-

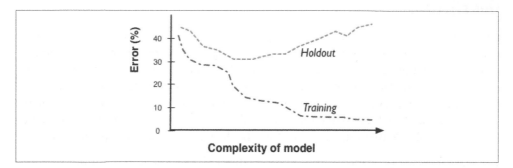

Figure 5-1. A typical fitting graph. Each point on a curve represents an accuracy estimation of a model with a specified complexity (as indicated on the horizontal axis). Accuracy estimates on training data and testing data vary differently based on how complex we allow a model to be. When the model is not allowed to be complex enough, it is not very accurate. As the models get too complex, they look very accurate on the training data, but in fact are overfitting—the training accuracy diverges from the holdout (generalization) accuracy.

curacy on the training set (sometimes called the "in-sample" accuracy) and the model's generalization accuracy, as estimated on the holdout data. Thus, when the holdout data are used in this manner, they often are called the "test set."

The accuracy of a model depends on how complex we allow it to be. A model can be complex in different ways, as we will discuss in this chapter. First let us use this distinction between training data and holdout data to define the fitting graph more precisely. The fitting graph (see Figure 5-1) shows the difference between a modeling procedure's accuracy on the training data and the accuracy on holdout data as model complexity changes. Generally, there will be more overfitting as one allows the model to be more complex. (Technically, the chance of overfitting increases as one allows the modeling procedure more flexibility in the models it can produce; we will ignore that distinction in this book).

Figure 5-2 shows a fitting graph for the customer churn "table model" described earlier. Since this was an extreme example the fitting graph will be peculiar. Again, the x axis measures the complexity of the model; in this case, the number of rows allowed in the table. The y axis measures the error. As we allow the table to increase in size, we can memorize more and more of the training set, and with each new row the training set error decreases. Eventually the table is large enough to contain the entire training set (marked N on the x axis) and the error goes to zero and remains there. However, the testing (holdout) set error starts at some value (let's call it b) and never decreases, because there is never an overlap between the training and holdout sets. The large gap between the two is a strong indication of memorization.

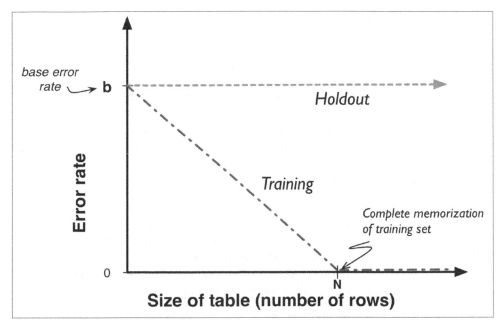

Figure 5-2. A fitting graph for the customer churn (table) model.

Note: Base rate

What would *b* be? Since the table model always predicts no churn for every new case with which it is presented, it will get every no churn case right and every churn case wrong. Thus the error rate will be the percentage of churn cases in the population. This is known as the *base rate*, and a classifier that always selects the majority class is called a base rate classifier.

A corresponding baseline for a regression model is a simple model that always predicts the mean or median value of the target variable.

You will occasionally hear reference to "base rate performance," and this is what it refers to. We will revisit the base rate again in the next chapter.

We've discussed in the previous chapters two very different sorts of modeling procedures: recursive partitioning of the data as done for tree induction, and fitting a numeric model by finding an optimal set of parameters, for example the weights in a linear model. We can now examine overfitting for each of these procedures.

Overfitting in Tree Induction

Recall how we built tree-structured models for classification. We applied a fundamental ability to find important, predictive individual attributes repeatedly (recursively) to smaller and smaller data subsets. Let's assume for illustration that the dataset does not have two instances with exactly the same feature vector but different target values. If we continue to split the data, eventually the subsets will be pure—all instances in any chosen subset will have the same value for the target variable. These will be the leaves of our tree. There might be multiple instances at a leaf, all with the same value for the target variable. If we have to, we can keep splitting on attributes, and subdividing our data until we're left with a single instance at each leaf node, which is pure by definition.

What have we just done? We've essentially built a version of the lookup table discussed in the prior section as an extreme example of overfitting! Any training instance given to the tree for classification will make its way down, eventually landing at the appropriate leaf—the leaf corresponding to the subset of the data that includes this particular training instance. What will be the accuracy of this tree on the training set? It will be perfectly accurate, predicting correctly the class for every training instance.

Will it generalize? Possibly. This tree should be slightly better than the lookup table because every previously unseen instance will arrive at *some* classification, rather than just failing to match; the tree will give a nontrivial classification even for instances it has not seen before. Therefore, it is useful to examine empirically how well the accuracy on the training data tends to correspond to the accuracy on test data.

A procedure that grows trees until the leaves are pure tends to overfit. Tree-structured models are very flexible in what they can represent. Indeed, they can represent any function of the features, and if allowed to grow without bound they can fit it to arbitrary precision. But the trees may need to be huge in order to do so. The complexity of the tree lies in the number of nodes.

Figure 5-3 shows a typical fitting graph for tree induction. Here we artificially limit the maximum size of each tree, as measured by the number of nodes it's allowed to have, indicated on the x axis (which is log scale for convenience). For each tree size we create a new tree from scratch, using the training data. We measure two values: its accuracy on the training set and its accuracy on the holdout (test) set. If the data subsets at the leaves are not pure, we will predict the target variable based on some average over the target values in the subset, as we discussed in Chapter 3.

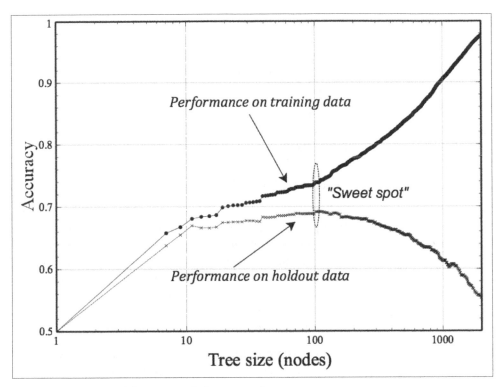

Figure 5-3. A typical fitting graph for tree induction.

Beginning at the left, the tree is very small and has poor performance. As it is allowed more and more nodes it improves rapidly, and both training-set accuracy and holdout-set accuracy improve. Also we see that training-set accuracy always is at least a little better than holdout-set accuracy, since we did get to look at the training data when building the model. But at some point the tree starts to overfit: it acquires details of the training set that are not characteristic of the population in general, as represented by the holdout set. In this example overfitting starts to happen at around $x = 100$ nodes, denoted the "sweet spot" in the graph. As the trees are allowed to get larger, the training-set accuracy continues to increase—in fact, it is capable of memorizing the entire training set if we let it, leading to an accuracy of 1.0 (not shown). But the holdout accuracy declines as the tree grows past its "sweet spot"; the data subsets at the leaves get smaller and smaller, and the model generalizes from fewer and fewer data. Such inferences will be increasingly error-prone and the performance on the holdout data suffers.

In summary, from this fitting graph we may infer that overfitting on this dataset starts to dominate at around 100 nodes, so we should restrict tree size to this value.[2] This represents the best trade-off between the extremes of (i) not splitting the data at all and simply using the average target value in the entire dataset, and (ii) building a complete tree out until the leaves are pure.

Unfortunately, no one has come up with a procedure to determine this exact sweet spot theoretically, so we have to rely on empirically based techniques. Before discussing those, let's examine overfitting in our second sort of modeling procedure.

Overfitting in Mathematical Functions

There are different ways to allow more or less complexity in mathematical functions. There are entire books on the topic. This section discusses one very important way, and "*Avoiding Overfitting for Parameter Optimization" on page 136 discusses a second one. We urge you to at least skim that advanced (starred) section because it introduces concepts and vocabulary in common use by data scientists these days, that can make a non-data scientist's head swim. Here we will summarize and give you enough to understand such discussions at a conceptual level.[3] But first, let's discuss a much more straightforward way in which functions can become too complex.

One way mathematical functions can become more complex is by adding more variables (more attributes). For example, say that we have a linear model as described in Equation 4-2:

$$f(\mathbf{x}) = w_0 + w_1 x_1 + w_2 x_2 + w_3 x_3$$

As we add more x_i's, the function becomes more and more complicated. Each x_i has a corresponding w_i, which is a learned parameter of the model.

Modelers sometimes even change the function from being truly linear in the original attributes by adding new attributes that are nonlinear versions of original attributes. For example, I might add a fourth attribute $x_4 = x_1^2$. Also, we might expect that the ratio of x_2 and x_3 is important, so we add a new attribute $x_5 = x_2/x_3$. Now we're trying to find the parameters (weights) of:

$$f(\mathbf{x}) = w_0 + w_1 x_1 + w_2 x_2 + w_3 x_3 + w_4 x_4 + w_5 x_5$$

---

2. Note that 100 nodes is not some special universal value. It is specific to this particular dataset. If we changed the data significantly, or even just used a different tree-building algorithm, we'd probably want to make another fitting graph to find the new sweet spot.

3. We also will have enough of a conceptual toolkit by that point to understand support vector machines a little better—as being almost equivalent to logistic regression with complexity (overfitting) control.

Either way, a dataset may end up with a very large number of attributes, and using all of them gives the modeling procedure much leeway to fit the training set. You might recall from geometry that in two dimensions you can fit a line to any two points and in three dimensions you can fit a plane to any three points. This concept generalizes: as you increase the dimensionality, you can perfectly fit larger and larger sets of arbitrary points. And even if you cannot fit the dataset perfectly, you can fit it better and better with more dimensions—that is, with more attributes.

Often, modelers carefully prune the attributes in order to avoid overfitting. Modelers will use a sort of holdout technique introduced above to assess the information in the individual attributes. Careful manual attribute selection is a wise practice in cases where considerable human effort can be spent on modeling, and where there are reasonably few attributes. In many modern applications, where large numbers of models are built automatically, and/or where there are very large sets of attributes, manual selection may not be feasible. For example, companies that do data science-driven targeting of online display advertisements can build thousands of models each week, sometimes with millions of possible features. In such cases there is no choice but to employ automatic feature selection (or to ignore feature selection all together).

Example: Overfitting Linear Functions

In "An Example of Mining a Linear Discriminant from Data" on page 89, we introduced a simple dataset called iris, comprising data describing two species of Iris flowers. Now let's revisit that to see the effects of overfitting in action.

Figure 5-4 shows the original Iris dataset graphed with its two attributes, Petal width and Sepal width. Recall that each instance is one flower and corresponds to one dot on the graph. The filled dots are of the species *Iris Setosa* and the circles are instances of the species *Iris Versicolor*. Note several things here: first, the two classes of iris are very distinct and separable. In fact, there is a wide gap between the two "clumps" of instances. Both logistic regression and support vector machines place separating boundaries (lines) in the middle. In fact, the two separating lines are so similiar that they're indistinguishable in the graph.

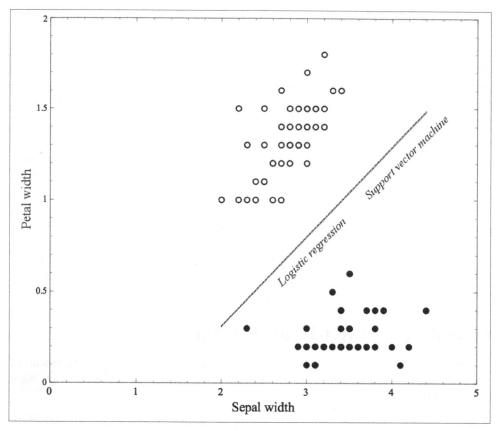

Figure 5-4. The original Iris dataset and the models (boundary lines) that two linear methods learn. In this case, both linear regression and a support vector machine learn the same model (the decision boundary, shown as a line).

In Figure 5-5, we've added a single new example: an *Iris Setosa* point at (3,1). Realistically, we might consider this example to be an outlier or an error since it's much closer to the *Versicolor* examples than the *Setosas*. Notice how the logistic regression line moves in response: it separates the two groups perfectly, while the SVM line barely moves at all.

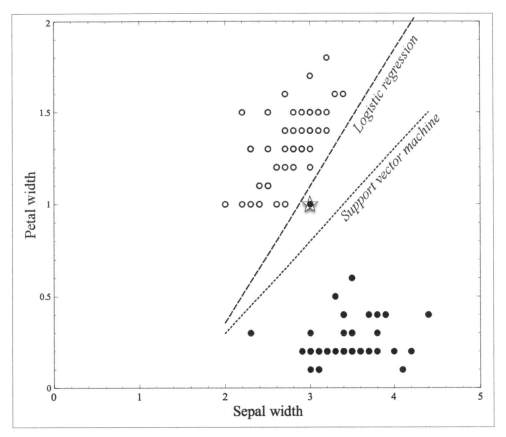

Figure 5-5. The Iris dataset from Figure 5-4 with a single new Iris Setosa example added (shown by star). Note how logistic regression has changed its model considerably.

In Figure 5-6 we've added a different outlier at (4,0.7), this time a *Versicolor* example down in the *Setosa* region. Again, the support vector machine line moves very little in response, but the logistic regression line moves considerably.

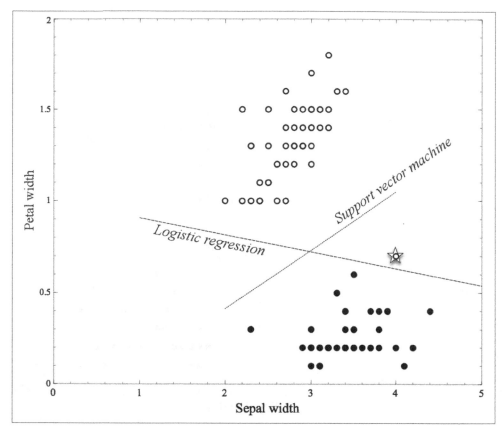

Figure 5-6. The Iris dataset from Figure 5-4 with a single new Iris Versicolor example added (shown by star). Note how logistic regression again changes its model considerably.

In Figure 5-5 and Figure 5-6, Logistic regression appears to be overfitting. Arguably, the examples introduced in each are outliers that should not have a strong influence on the model—they contribute little to the "mass" of the species examples. Yet in the case of logistic regression they clearly do. If a linear boundary exists, logistic regression will find it,[4] even if this means moving the boundary to accommodate outliers. The SVM tends to be less sensitive to individual examples. The SVM training procedure incorporates complexity control, which we will describe technically later.

---

4. Technically, only *some* logistic regression algorithms are guaranteed to find it. Some do not have this guarantee. However, this fact is not germane to the overfitting point we're making here.

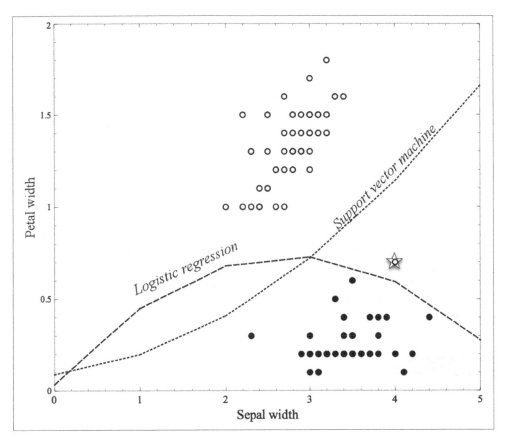

*Figure 5-7. The Iris dataset from Figure 5-6 with its Iris Versicolor example added (shown by star). In this figure, both logistic regression and support vector machine are given an additional feature, **Sepal width²**, which allows both the freedom to create more complex, nonlinear models (boundaries).*

As we said earlier, another way mathematical functions can become more complex is by adding more variables. In Figure 5-7, we have done just this: we used the same dataset as in Figure 5-6 but we added a single extra attribute, the square of the Sepal width. Providing this attribute gives each method more flexibility in fitting the data because it may assign weights to the squared term. Geometrically, this means the separating boundary can be not just a line but a *parabola*. This additional freedom allows both methods to create curved surfaces that can fit the regions more closely. In cases where curved surfaces may be necessary, this freedom may be necessary, but it also gives the methods far more opportunity to overfit. Note however that the SVM, even though its boundary now is curved, the training procedure still has opted for the larger margin around the boundary, rather than the perfect separation of the positive different classes.

* Example: Why Is Overfitting Bad?

 Technical Details Ahead

At the beginning of the chapter, we said that a model that only memorizes is useless because it always overfits and is incapable of generalizing. But technically this only demonstrates that overfitting hinders us from improving a model after a certain complexity. It does not explain why overfitting often causes models to become *worse*, as Figure 5-3 shows. This section goes into a detailed example showing how this happens and why. It may be skipped without loss of continuity.

Why does performance degrade? The short answer is that as a model gets more complex it is allowed to pick up harmful spurious correlations. These correlations are idiosyncracies of the specific training set used and do not represent characteristics of the population in general. The harm occurs when these spurious correlations produce *incorrect* generalizations in the model. This is what causes performance to decline when overfitting occurs. In this section we go through an example in detail to show how this can happen.

Table 5-1. A small set of training examples

Instance	x	y	Class
1	p	r	c_1
2	p	r	c_1
3	p	r	c_1
4	q	s	c_1
5	p	s	c_2
6	q	r	c_2
7	q	s	c_2
8	q	r	c_2

Consider a simple two-class problem with classes c_1 and c_2 and attributes x and y. We have a population of examples, evenly balanced between the classes. Attribute x has two values, p and q, and y has two values, r and s. In the general population, $x = p$ occurs 75% of the time in class c_1 examples and in 25% of the c_2 examples, so x provides some prediction of the class. By design, y has no predictive power at all, and indeed we see that in the data sample both of y's values occur in both classes equally. In short, the instances in this domain are difficult to separate, with only x providing some predictive power. The best we can achieve is 75% accuracy by looking at x.

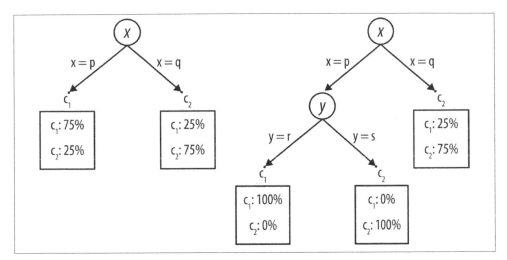

Figure 5-8. Classification trees for the overfitting example. (a) The optimal tree has on-ly three nodes. (b) An overfit tree, which fits the training data better, has worse general-ization accuracy because the extraneous structure makes suboptimal predictions.

Table 5-1 shows a very small training set of examples from this domain. What would a classification tree learner do with these? We won't go into the entropy calculations, but attribute x provides some leverage so a tree learner would split on it and create the tree shown in Figure 5-8. Since x provides the only leverage, this should be the optimal tree. Its error rate is 25%—equal to the theoretical minimum error rate.

However, observe from Table 5-1 that *in this particular* dataset y's values of r and s are not evenly split between the classes, so y does seem to provide some predictiveness. Specifically, once we choose x=p (instances 1-4), we see that y=r predicts c_1 perfectly (instances 1-3). Hence, from this dataset, tree induction would achieve information gain by splitting on y's values and create two new leaf nodes, shown in Figure 5-8.

Based on our training set, the tree in (b) performs well, better than (a). It classifies seven of the eight training examples correctly, whereas the tree in (a) classifies only six out of eight correct. But this is due to the fact that y=r purely by chance correlates with class c_1 in this data sample; in the general population there is no such correlation. We have been misled, and the extra branch in (b) is not simply extraneous, it is harmful. Recall that we defined the general population to have x=p occuring in 75% of the class c_1 examples and 25% of the c_2 examples. But the spurious y=s branch predicts c_2, which is wrong in the general population. In fact, we expect this spurious branch to contribute one in eight errors made by the tree. Overall, the (b) tree will have a total expected error rate of 30%, while (a) will have an error rate of 25%.

We conclude this example by emphasizing several points. First, this phenomenon is not particular to classification trees. Trees are convenient for this example because it is easy to point to a portion of a tree and declare it to be spurious, but all model types are susceptible to overfitting effects. Second, this phenomenon is not due to the training data in Table 5-1 being atypical or biased. Every dataset is a finite sample of a larger population, and every sample will have variations even when there is no bias in the sampling. Finally, as we have said before, there is no general analytic way to determine in advance whether a model has overfit or not. In this example we defined what the population looked like so we could declare that a given model had overfit. In practice, you will not have such knowledge and it will be necessary to use a holdout set to detect overfitting.

From Holdout Evaluation to Cross-Validation

Later we will present a general technique in broad use to try to avoid overfitting, which applies to attribute selection as well as tree complexity, and beyond. But first, we need to discuss holdout evaluation in more detail. Before we can work to avoid overfitting, we need to be able to avoid being fooled by overfitting. At the beginning of this chapter we introduced the idea that in order to have a fair evaluation of the generalization performance of a model, we should estimate its accuracy on holdout data—data not used in building the model, but for which we do know the actual value of the target variable. Holdout testing is similar to other sorts of evaluation in a "laboratory" setting.

While a holdout set will indeed give us an estimate of generalization performance, it is just a single estimate. Should we have any confidence in a single estimate of model accuracy? It might have just been a single particularly lucky (or unlucky) choice of training and test data. We will not go into the details of computing confidence intervals on such quantities, but it is important to discuss a general testing procedure that will end up helping in several ways.

Cross-validation is a more sophisticated holdout training and testing procedure. We would like not only a simple estimate of the generalization performance, but also some statistics on the estimated performance, such as the mean and variance, so that we can understand how the performance is expected to vary across datasets. This variance is critical for assessing confidence in the performance estimate, as you might have learned in a statistics class.

Cross-validation also makes better use of a limited dataset. Unlike splitting the data into one training and one holdout set, cross-validation computes its estimates over *all* the data by performing multiple splits and systematically swapping out samples for testing.

Sidebar: Building a modeling "laboratory"

Building the infrastructure for a modeling lab may be costly and time consuming, but after this investment many aspects of model performance can be evaluated quickly in a controlled environment. However, holdout testing cannot capture all the complexities of the real world where the model will be used. Data scientists should work to understand the actual use scenario so as to make the lab setting as much like it as possible, to avoid surprises when the two do not match. For example, consider a company that wants to use data science to improve its targeting of costly personally targeted advertisements. As a campaign progresses, more and more data arrive on people who make purchases after having seen the ad versus those who do not. These data can be used to build models to discriminate between those to whom we should and should not advertise. Examples can be put aside to evaluate how accurate the models are in predicting whether consumers will respond to the ad.

When the resultant models are put into production, targeting consumers "in the wild," the company is surprised that the models do not work as well as they did in the lab. Why not? There could be many reasons, but notice one in particular: the training and holdout data do not really match the data to which the model will be applied in the field. Specifically, the training data all are consumers who had been targeted in the campaign. Otherwise, we would not know the value of the target variable (whether they responded). Even before the data mining, the company did not simply target randomly; they had some criteria for targeting people they believed would respond. In the field, the model is applied to consumers more broadly—not just to consumers who meet these criteria. The fact that the training and deployment populations are different is a likely source of performance degradation.

This phenomenon is not limited to advertisement targeting. Consider credit scoring, where we would like to build models to predict the likelihood of a consumer defaulting on credit. Again, the data we have on write-offs versus non-write-offs are based on those to whom we previously extended credit, who presumably were those thought to be low risk.

In both of these cases, think about what you might do as a business to gather a more appropriate dataset from which to build predictive models. Remember to apply the fundamental concept introduced in Chapter 1: think of data as an asset in which you may want to *invest*.

Cross-validation begins by splitting a labeled dataset into *k* partitions called *folds*. Typically, *k* will be five or ten. The top pane of Figure 5-9 shows a labeled dataset (the original dataset) split into five folds. Cross-validation then iterates training and testing *k* times, in a particular way. As depicted in the bottom pane of Figure 5-9, in each iteration of the cross-validation, a different fold is chosen as the test data. In this iteration, the other

k–1 folds are combined to form the training data. So, in each iteration we have (k–1)/k of the data used for training and 1/k used for testing.

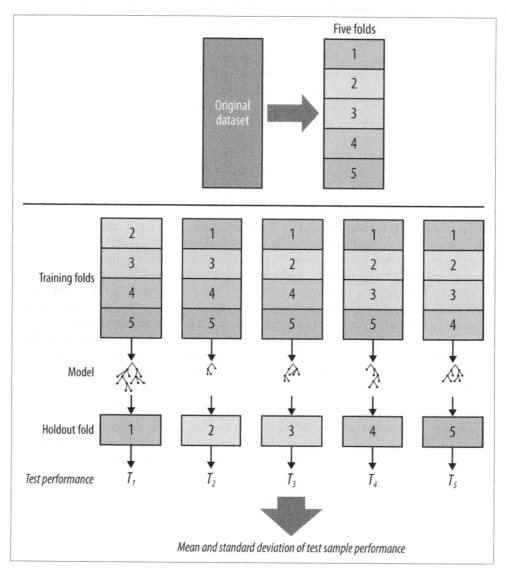

Figure 5-9. An illustration of cross-validation. The purpose of cross-validation is to use the original labeled data efficiently to estimate the performance of a modeling procedure. Here we show five-fold cross-validation: the original dataset is split randomly into five equal-sized pieces. Then, each piece is used in turn as the test set, with the other four used to train a model. The result is five different accuracy results, which then can be used to compute the average accuracy and its variance.

Each iteration produces one model, and thereby one estimate of generalization performance, for example, one estimate of accuracy. When cross-validation is finished, every
example will have been used only once for testing but $k-1$ times for training. At this
point we have performance estimates from all the k folds and we can compute the
average and standard deviation.

The Churn Dataset Revisited

Consider again the churn dataset introduced in "Example: Addressing the Churn Problem with Tree Induction" on page 73. In that section we used the entire dataset both for
training and testing, and we reported an accuracy of 73%. We ended that section by
asking a question, *Do you trust this number?* By this point you should know enough to
mistrust any performance measurement done on the training set, because overfitting is
a very real possibility. Now that we have introduced cross-validation we can redo the
evaluation more carefully.

Figure 5-10 shows the results of ten-fold cross-validation. In fact, two model types are
shown. The top graph shows results with logistic regression, and the bottom graph
shows results with classification trees. To be precise: the dataset was first shuffled, then
divided into ten partitions. Each partition in turn served as a single holdout set while
the other nine were collectively used for training. The horizontal line in each graph is
the average of accuracies of the ten models of that type.

There are several things to observe here. First, the average accuracy of the folds with
classification trees is 68.6%—significantly lower than our previous measurement of
73%. This means there was some overfitting occurring with the classification trees, and
this new (lower) number is a more realistic measure of what we can expect. Second,
there is variation in the performances in the different folds (the standard deviation of
the fold accuracies is 1.1), and thus it is a good idea to average them to get a notion of
the performance as well as the variation we can expect from inducing classification trees
on this dataset.

Finally, compare the fold accuracies between logistic regression and classification trees.
There are certain commonalities in both graphs—for example, neither model type did
very well on Fold Three and both performed well on Fold Ten. But there are definite
differences between the two. An important thing to notice is that logistic regression
models show slightly lower average accuracy (64.1%) and with higher variation (standard deviation of 1.3) than the classification trees do. On this particular dataset, trees
may be preferable to logistic regression because of their greater stability and performance. But this is not absolute; other datasets will produce different results, as we shall
see.

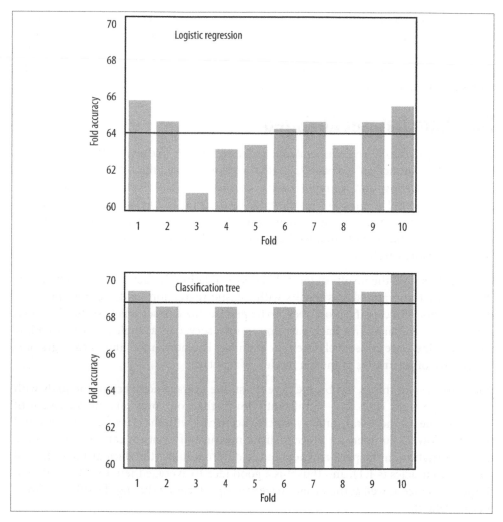

Figure 5-10. Fold accuracies for cross-validation on the churn problem. At the top are accuracies of logistic regression models trained on a dataset of 20,000 instances divided into ten folds. At the bottom are accuracies of classification trees on the same folds. In each graph the horizontal line shows the average accuracy of the folds. (Note the selection of the range of the y axis, which emphasizes the differences in accuracy.)

Learning Curves

If the training set size changes, you may also expect different generalization performance from the resultant model. All else being equal, the generalization performance of data-driven modeling generally improves as more training data become available, up to a point. A plot of the generalization performance against the amount of training data is called a *learning curve*. The learning curve is another important analytical tool.

Learning curves for tree induction and logistic regression are shown in Figure 5-11 for the telecommunications churn problem.[5] Learning curves usually have a characteristic shape. They are steep initially as the modeling procedure finds the most apparent regularities in the dataset. Then as the modeling procedure is allowed to train on larger and larger datasets, it finds more accurate models. However, the marginal advantage of having more data decreases, so the learning curve becomes less steep. In some cases, the curve flattens out completely because the procedure can no longer improve accuracy even with more training data.

It is important to understand the difference between learning curves and fitting graphs (or fitting curves). A learning curve shows the generalization performance—the performance only on testing data, plotted against the *amount of training data* used. A fitting graph shows the generalization performance as well as the performance on the training data, but plotted against model *complexity*. Fitting graphs generally are shown for a fixed amount of training data.

Even on the same data, different modeling procedures can produce very different learning curves. In Figure 5-11, observe that for smaller training-set sizes, logistic regression yields better generalization accuracy than tree induction. However, as the training sets get larger, the learning curve for logistic regression levels off faster, the curves cross, and tree induction soon is more accurate. This performance relates back to the fact that with more flexibility comes more overfitting. Given the same set of features, classification trees are a more flexible model representation than linear logistic regression. This means two things: for smaller data, tree induction will tend to overfit more. Often, as we see for the data in Figure 5-11, this leads logistic regression to perform better for smaller datasets (not always, though). On the other hand, the figure also shows that the flexibility of tree induction can be an advantage with larger training sets: the tree can represent substantially nonlinear relationships between the features and the target. Whether the tree induction can actually capture those relationships needs to be evaluated empirically—using an analytical tool such as learning curves.

5. Perlich et al. (2003) show learning curves for tree induction and logistic regression for dozens of classification problems.

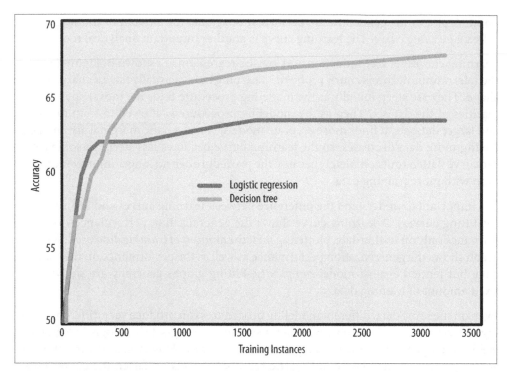

Figure 5-11. Learning curves for tree induction and logistic regression for the churn problem. As the training size grows (x axis), generalization performance (y axis) improves. Importantly, the improvement rates are different for the two induction techniques and change differently with the amount of training data. Logistic regression has less flexibility, allowing it to overfit less with small data, but keeping it from modeling the full complexity of the data. Tree induction is much more flexible, leading it to overfit more with small data, but to model more complex regularities with larger training sets.

The learning curve has additional analytical uses. For example, we've made the point that data can be an asset. The learning curve may show that generalization performance has leveled off so investing in more training data is probably not worthwhile; instead, one should accept the current performance or look for another way to improve the model, such as by devising better features. Alternatively, the learning curve might show generalization accuracy continuing to improve, so obtaining more training data could be a good investment.

Overfitting Avoidance and Complexity Control

To avoid overfitting, we control the complexity of the models induced from the data. Let's start by examining complexity control in tree induction, since tree induction has much flexibility and therefore will tend to overfit a good deal without some mechanism to avoid it. This discussion in the context of trees will lead us to a very general mechanism that will be applicable to other models.

Avoiding Overfitting with Tree Induction

The main problem with tree induction is that it will keep growing the tree to fit the training data until it creates pure leaf nodes. This will likely result in large, overly complex trees that overfit the data. We have seen how this can be detrimental. Tree induction commonly uses two techniques to avoid overfitting. These strategies are (i) to stop growing the tree before it gets too complex, and (ii) to grow the tree until it is too large, then "prune" it back, reducing its size (and thereby its complexity).

There are various methods for accomplishing both. The simplest method to limit tree size is to specify a minimum number of instances that must be present in a leaf. The idea behind this minimum-instance stopping criterion is that for predictive modeling, we essentially are using the data at the leaf to make a statistical estimate of the value of the target variable for future cases that would fall to that leaf. If we make predictions of the target based on a very small subset of data, we might expect them to be inaccurate —especially when we built the tree specifically to try to get pure leaves. A nice property of controlling complexity in this way is that tree induction will automatically grow the tree branches that have a lot of data and cut short branches that have fewer data—thereby automatically adapting the model based on the data distribution.

A key question becomes what threshold we should use. How few instances are we willing to tolerate at a leaf? Five instances? Thirty? One hundred? There is no fixed number, although practitioners tend to have their own preferences based on experience. However, researchers have developed techniques to decide the stopping point statistically. Statistics provides the notion of a "hypothesis test," which you might recall from a basic statistics class. Roughly, a hypothesis test tries to assess whether a difference in some statistic is not due simply to chance. In most cases, the hypothesis test is based on a "p-value," which gives a limit on the probability that the difference in statistic is due to chance. If this value is below a threshold (often 5%, but problem specific), then the hypothesis test concludes that the difference is likely not due to chance. So, for stopping tree growth, an alternative to setting a fixed size for the leaves is to conduct a hypothesis test at every leaf to determine whether the observed difference in (say) information gain could have been due to chance. If the hypothesis test concludes that it was likely not due to chance, then the split is accepted and the tree growing continues. (See "Sidebar: Beware of "multiple comparisons"" on page 139.)

The second strategy for reducing overfitting is to "prune" an overly large tree. Pruning means to cut off leaves and branches, replacing them with leaves. There are many ways to do this, and the interested reader can look into the data mining literature for details. One general idea is to estimate whether replacing a set of leaves or a branch with a leaf would reduce accuracy. If not, then go ahead and prune. The process can be iterated on progressive subtrees until any removal or replacement would reduce accuracy.

We conclude our example of avoiding overfitting in tree induction with the method that will generalize to many different data modeling techniques. Consider the following idea: what if we built trees with all sorts of different complexities? For example, say we stop building the tree after only one node. Then build a tree with two nodes. Then three nodes, etc. We have a set of trees of different complexities. Now, if only there were a way to estimate their generalization performance, we could pick the one that is (estimated to be) the best!

A General Method for Avoiding Overfitting

More generally, if we have a collection of models with different complexities, we could choose the best simply by estimating the generalization performance of each. But how could we estimate their generalization performance? On the (labeled) test data? There's one big problem with that: test data should be strictly *independent* of model building so that we can get an independent estimate of model accuracy. For example, we might want to estimate the ultimate business performance or to compare the best model we can build from one family (say, classification trees) against the best model from another family (say, logistic regression). If we don't care about comparing models or getting an independent estimate of the model accuracy and/or variance, then we could pick the best model based on the testing data.

However, even if we do want these things, we still can proceed. The key is to realize that there was nothing special about the first training/test split we made. Let's say we are saving the test set for a final assessment. We can take the training set and split it again into a training subset and a testing subset. Then we can build models on this training subset and pick the best model based on this testing subset. Let's call the former the *sub-training set* and the latter the *validation set* for clarity. The validation set is separate from the final test set, on which we are never going to make any modeling decisions. This procedure is often called *nested* holdout testing.

Returning to our classification tree example, we can induce trees of many complexities from the subtraining set, then we can estimate the generalization performance for each from the validation set. This would correspond to choosing the top of the inverted-U-shaped holdout curve in Figure 5-3. Say the best model by this assessment has a complexity of 122 nodes (the "sweet spot"). Then we could use this model as our best choice, possibly estimating the actual generalization performance on the final holdout test set. We also could add one more twist. This model was built on a subset of our training data, since we had to hold out the validation set in order to choose the complexity. But once we've chosen the complexity, why not induce a *new* tree with 122 nodes from the whole, original training set? Then we might get the best of both worlds: using the subtraining/validation split to pick the best complexity without tainting the test set, *and* building a model of this best complexity on the entire training set (subtraining plus validation).

This approach is used in many sorts of modeling algorithms to control complexity. The general method is to choose the value for some complexity parameter by using some sort of nested holdout procedure. Again, it is nested because a second holdout procedure is performed on the training set selected by the first holdout procedure.

Often, nested cross-validation is used. Nested cross-validation is more complicated, but it works as you might suspect. Say we would like to do cross-validation to assess the generalization accuracy of a new modeling technique, which has an adjustable complexity parameter C, but we do not know how to set it. So, we run cross-validation as described above. However, before building the model for each fold, we take the training set (refer to Figure 5-9) and first run an experiment: we run another entire cross-validation on just that training set to find the value of C estimated to give the best accuracy. The result of that experiment is used only to set the value of C to build the actual model for that fold of the cross-validation. Then we build another model using the entire training fold, using that value for C, and test on the corresponding test fold. The only difference from regular cross-validation is that for each fold we first run this experiment to find C, using another, smaller, cross-validation.

If you understood all that, you would realize that if we used 5-fold cross-validation in both cases, we actually have built 30 total models in the process (yes, *thirty*). This sort of experimental complexity-controlled modeling only gained broad practical application over the last decade or so, because of the obvious computational burden involved.

This idea of using the data to choose the complexity experimentally, as well as to build the resulting model, applies across different induction algorithms and different sorts of complexity. For example, we mentioned that complexity increases with the size of the feature set, so it is usually desirable to cull the feature set. A common method for doing this is to run with many different feature sets, using this sort of nested holdout procedure to pick the best.

For example, *sequential forward selection* (SFS) of features uses a nested holdout procedure to first pick the best individual feature, by looking at all models built using just one feature. After choosing a first feature, SFS tests all models that add a second feature to this first chosen feature. The best pair is then selected. Next the same procedure is done for three, then four, and so on. When adding a feature does not improve classification accuracy on the validation data, the SFS process stops. (There is a similar procedure called *sequential backward elimination* of features. As you might guess, it works by starting with all features and discarding features one at a time. It continues to discard features as long as there is no performance loss.)

This is a common approach. In modern environments with plentiful data and computational power, the data scientist routinely sets modeling parameters by experimenting using some tactical, nested holdout testing (often nested cross-validation).

The next section shows a different way that this method applies to controlling overfitting when learning numerical functions (as described in Chapter 4). We urge you to at least skim the following section because it introduces concepts and vocabulary in common use by data scientists these days.

* Avoiding Overfitting for Parameter Optimization

As just described, avoiding overfitting involves complexity control: finding the "right" balance between the fit to the data and the complexity of the model. In trees we saw various ways for trying to keep the tree from getting too big (too complex) when fitting the data. For equations, such as logistic regression, that unlike trees do not automatically select what attributes to include, complexity can be controlled by choosing a "right" set of attributes.

Chapter 4 introduced the popular family of methods that builds models by explicitly optimizing the fit to the data via a set of numerical parameters. We discussed various linear members of this family, including linear discriminant learners, linear regression, and logistic regression. Many nonlinear models are fit to the data in exactly the same way.

As might be expected given our discussion so far in this chapter and the figures in "Example: Overfitting Linear Functions" on page 119, these procedures also can overfit the data. However, their explicit optimization framework provides an elegant, if technical, method for complexity control. The general strategy is that instead of just optimizing the fit to the data, we optimize some combination of fit and simplicity. Models will be better if they fit the data better, but they also will be better if they are simpler. This general methodology is called *regularization*, a term that is heard often in data science discussions.

Technical Details Ahead

The rest of this section discusses briefly (and slightly technically) how regularization is done. Don't worry if you don't really understand the technical details. Do remember that regularization is trying to optimize not just the fit to the data, but a combination of fit to the data and simplicity of the model.

Recall from Chapter 4 that to fit a model involving numeric parameters w to the data we find the set of parameters that maximizes some "objective function" indicating how well it fits the data:

$$\underset{\mathbf{w}}{\arg\max} \ \ \text{fit}(\mathbf{x}, \mathbf{w})$$

(The arg max$_\mathbf{w}$ just means that you want to maximize the fit over all possible arguments $\mathbf{w}$, and are interested in the particular argument $\mathbf{w}$ that gives the maximum. These would be the parameters of the final model.)

Complexity control via regularization works by adding to this objective function a penalty for complexity:

$$\underset{\mathbf{w}}{\arg\max} \ \ \left[\text{fit}(\mathbf{x}, \mathbf{w}) - \lambda \cdot \text{penalty}(\mathbf{w})\right]$$

The λ term is simply a weight that determines how much importance the optimization procedure should place on the penalty, compared to the data fit. At this point, the modeler has to choose λ and the penalty function.

So, as a concrete example, recall from "* Logistic Regression: Some Technical Details" on page 100 that to learn a standard logistic regression model, from data, we find the numeric parameters $\mathbf{w}$ that yield the linear model most likely to have generated the observed data—the "maximum likelihood" model. Let' represent that as:

$$\underset{\mathbf{w}}{\arg\max} \ \ g_{\text{likelihood}}(\mathbf{x}, \mathbf{w})$$

To learn a "regularized" logistic regression model we would instead compute:

$$\underset{\mathbf{w}}{\arg\max} \ \ \left[g_{\text{likelihood}}(\mathbf{x}, \mathbf{w}) - \lambda \cdot \text{penalty}(\mathbf{w})\right]$$

There are different penalties that can be applied, with different properties.[6] The most commonly used penalty is the sum of the squares of the weights, sometimes called the "L2-norm" of w. The reason is technical, but basically functions can fit data better if they are allowed to have very large positive and negative weights. The sum of the squares of the weights gives a large penalty when weights have large absolute values.

---

6. The book *The Elements of Statistical Learning* (Hastie, Tibshirani, & Friedman, 2009) contains an excellent technical discussion of these.

If we incorporate the L2-norm penalty into standard least-squares linear regression, we get the statistical procedure called *ridge regression*. If instead we use the sum of the absolute values (rather than the squares), known as the L1-norm, we get a procedure known as the *lasso* (Hastie et al., 2009). More generally, this is called L1-regularization. For reasons that are quite technical, L1-regularization ends up zeroing out many coefficients. Since these coefficients are the multiplicative weights on the features, L1-regularization effectively performs an automatic form of feature selection.

Now we have the machinery to describe in more detail the linear support vector machine, introduced in "Support Vector Machines, Briefly" on page 92. There we waved our hands and told you that the support vector machine "maximizes the margin" between the classes by fitting the "fattest bar" between the classes. Separately we discussed that it uses hinge loss (see "Sidebar: Loss functions" on page 95) to penalize errors. We now can connect these together, and directly to logistic regression. Specifically, linear support vector machine learning is almost equivalent to the L2-regularized logistic regression just discussed; the only difference is that a support vector machine uses hinge loss instead of likelihood in its optimization. The support vector machine optimizes this equation:

$$\arg \max_{\mathbf{w}} \left[-g_{\text{hinge}}(\mathbf{x}, \mathbf{w}) - \lambda \cdot \text{penalty}(\mathbf{w}) \right]$$

where g_{hinge}, the hinge loss term, is negated because lower hinge loss is better.

Finally, you may be saying to yourself: all this is well and good, but a lot of magic seems to be hidden in this λ parameter, which the modeler has to choose. How in the world would the modeler choose that for some real domain like churn prediction, or online ad targeting, or fraud detection?

It turns out that we already have a straightforward way to choose λ. We've discussed how a good tree size and a good feature set can be chosen via nested cross-validation on the training data. We can choose λ the same way. This cross-validation would essentially conduct automated experiments on subsets of the training data and find a good λ value. Then this λ would be used to learn a regularized model on all the training data. This has become the standard procedure for building numerical models that give a good balance between data fit and model complexity. This general approach to optimizing the parameter values of a data mining procedure is known as grid search.

Sidebar: Beware of "multiple comparisons"

Consider the following scenario. You run an investment firm. Five years ago, you wanted to have some marketable small-cap mutual fund products to sell, but your analysts had been awful at picking small-cap stocks. So you undertook the following procedure. You started 1,000 different mutual funds, each including a small set of stocks randomly chosen from those that make up the Russell 2000 index (the main index for small-cap stocks). Your firm invested in all 1,000 of these funds, but told no one about them. Now, five years later, you look at their performance. Since they have different stocks in them, they will have had different returns. Some will be about the same as the index, some will be worse, and some will be better. The best one might be a lot better. Now, you liquidate all the funds but the best few, and you present these to the public. You can "honestly" claim that their 5-year return is substantially better than the return of the Russell 2000 index.

So, what's the problem? The problem is that you randomly chose the stocks! You have no idea whether the stocks in these "best" funds performed better because they indeed are fundamentally better, or because you cherry-picked the best from a large set that simply varied in performance. If you flip 1,000 fair coins many times each, one of them will have come up heads much more than 50% of the time. However, choosing that coin as the "best" of the coins for later flipping obviously is silly. These are instances of "the problem of multiple comparisons," a very important statistical phenomenon that business analysts and data scientists should always keep in mind. Beware whenever someone does many tests and then picks the results that look good. Statistics books will warn against running multiple statistical hypothesis tests, and then looking at the ones that give "significant" results. These usually violate the assumptions behind the statistical tests, and the actual significance of the results is dubious.

The underlying reasons for overfitting when building models from data are essentially problems of multiple comparisons (Jensen & Cohen, 2000). Note that even the procedures for avoiding overfitting themselves undertake multiple comparisons (e.g., choosing the best complexity for a model by comparing many complexities). There is no silver bullet or magic formula to truly get "the optimal" model to fit the data. Nonetheless, care can be taken to reduce overfitting as much as possible, by using the holdout procedures described in this chapter and if possible by looking carefully at the results before declaring victory. For example, if the fitting graph truly has an inverted-U-shape, one can be much more confident that the top represents a "good" complexity than if the curve jumps around randomly.

Summary

Data mining involves a fundamental trade-off between model complexity and the possibility of overfitting. A complex model may be necessary if the phenomenon producing the data is itself complex, but complex models run the risk of overfitting training data (i.e., modeling details of the data that are not found in the general population). An overfit model will not generalize to other data well, even if they are from the same population.

All model types can be overfit. There is no single choice or technique to eliminate overfitting. The best strategy is to recognize overfitting by testing with a holdout set. Several types of curves can help detect and measure overfitting. A *fitting graph* has two curves showing the model performance on the training and testing data as a function of model complexity. A fitting curve on testing data usually has an approximate U or inverted-U-shape (depending on whether error or accuracy is plotted). The accuracy starts off low when the model is simple, increases as complexity increases, flattens out, then starts to decrease again as overfitting sets in. A *learning curve* shows model performance on testing data plotted against the *amount of training data* used. Usually model performance increases with the amount of data, but the rate of increase and the final asymptotic performance can be quite different between models.

A common experimental methodology called *cross-validation* specifies a systematic way of splitting up a single dataset such that it generates multiple performance measures. These values tell the data scientist what average behavior the model yields as well as the variation to expect.

The general method for reining in model complexity to avoid overfitting is called model *regularization*. Techniques include tree pruning (cutting a classification tree back when it has become too large), feature selection, and employing explicit complexity penalties into the objective function used for modeling.

CHAPTER 6

Similarity, Neighbors, and Clusters

Fundamental concepts: *Calculating similarity of objects described by data; Using similarity for prediction; Clustering as similarity-based segmentation.*

Exemplary techniques: *Searching for similar entities; Nearest neighbor methods; Clustering methods; Distance metrics for calculating similarity.*

Similarity underlies many data science methods and solutions to business problems. If two things (people, companies, products) are similar in some ways they often share other characteristics as well. Data mining procedures often are based on grouping things by similarity or searching for the "right" sort of similarity. We saw this implicitly in previous chapters where modeling procedures create boundaries for grouping instances together that have similar values for their target variables. In this chapter we will look at similarity directly, and show how it applies to a variety of different tasks. We include sections with some technical details, in order that the more mathematical reader can understand similarity in more depth; these sections can be skipped.

Different sorts of business tasks involve reasoning from similar examples:

- We may want to *retrieve* similar things directly. For example, IBM wants to find companies that are similar to their best business customers, in order to have the sales staff look at them as prospects. Hewlett-Packard maintains many high-performance servers for clients; this maintenance is aided by a tool that, given a server configuration, retrieves information on other similarly configured servers. Advertisers often want to serve online ads to consumers who are similar to their current good customers.

- Similarity can be used for doing *classification* and *regression*. Since we now know a good bit about classification, we will illustrate the use of similarity with a classification example below.

- We may want to group similar items together into *clusters*, for example to see whether our customer base contains groups of similar customers and what these groups have in common. Previously we discussed supervised segmentation; this is unsupervised segmentation. After discussing the use of similarity for classification, we will discuss its use for clustering.

- Modern retailers such as Amazon and Netflix use similarity to provide *recommendations* of similar products or from similar people. Whenever you see statements like "People who like X also like Y" or "Customers with your browsing history have also looked at …" similarity is being applied. In Chapter 12, we will discuss how a customer can be similar to a movie, if the two are described by the same "taste dimensions." In this case, to make recommendations we can find the movies that are most similar to the customer (and which the customer has not already seen).

- Reasoning from similar cases of course extends beyond business applications; it is natural to fields such as medicine and law. A doctor may reason about a new difficult case by recalling a similar case (either treated personally or documented in a journal) and its diagnosis. A lawyer often argues cases by citing legal precedents, which are similar historical cases whose dispositions were previously judged and entered into the legal casebook. The field of Artificial Intelligence has a long history of building systems to help doctors and lawyers with such case-based reasoning. Similarity judgments are a key component.

In order to discuss these applications further, we need to take a minute to formalize similarity and its cousin, distance.

Similarity and Distance

Once an object can be represented as data, we can begin to talk more precisely about the similarity between objects, or alternatively the distance between objects. For example, let's consider the data representation we have used throughout the book so far: represent each object as a feature vector. Then, the closer two objects are in the space defined by the features, the more similar they are.

Recall that when we build and apply predictive models, the goal is to determine the value of a target characteristic. In doing so, we've used the implicit similarity of objects already. "Visualizing Segmentations" on page 67 discussed the geometric interpretation of some classification models and "Classification via Mathematical Functions" on page 83 discussed how two different model types divide up an instance space into regions based on closeness of instances with similar class labels. Many methods in data science may be seen in this light: as methods for organizing the space of data instances (representations of important objects) so that instances near each other are treated similarly for some purpose. Both classification trees and linear classifiers establish boundaries between regions of differing classifications. They have in common the view that instances sharing a common region in space should be similar; what differs between the methods is how the regions are represented and discovered.

So why not reason about the similarity or distance between objects directly? To do so, we need a basic method for measuring similarity or distance. What does it mean that two companies or two consumers are similar? Let's examine this carefully. Consider two instances from our simplified credit application domain:

Attribute	Person A	Person B
Age	23	40
Years at current address	2	10
Residential status (1=Owner, 2=Renter, 3=Other)	2	1

These data items have multiple attributes, and there's no single best method for reducing them to a single similarity or distance measurement. There are many different ways to measure the similarity or distance between Person A and Person B. A good place to begin is with measurements of distance from basic geometry.

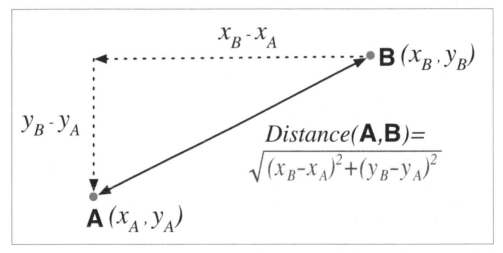

Figure 6-1. Euclidean distance.

Recall from our prior discussions of the geometric interpretation that if we have two (numeric) features, then each object is a point in a two-dimensional space. Figure 6-1 shows two data items, A and B, located on a two-dimensional plane. Object A is at coordinates (x_A, y_A) and B is at (x_B, y_B). At the risk of too much repetition, note that these coordinates are just the values of the two features of the objects. We can draw a right triangle between the two objects, as shown, whose base is the difference in the x's: $(x_A - x_B)$ and whose height is the difference in the y's: $(y_A - y_B)$. The Pythagorean theorem tells us that the distance between A and B is given by the length of the hypotenuse, and is equal to the square root of the summed squares of the lengths of the other two sides of the triangle, which in this case is $\sqrt{(x_A - x_B)^2 + (y_A - y_B)^2}$. Essentially, we can compute the overall distance by computing the distances of the individual dimensions—the individual features in our setting. This is called the *Euclidean distance* [1] between two points, and it's probably the most common geometric distance measure.

Euclidean distance is not limited to two dimensions. If A and B were objects described by three features, they could be represented by points in three-dimensional space and their positions would then be represented as (x_A, y_A, z_A) and (x_B, y_B, z_B). The distance between A and B would then include the term $(z_A - z_B)^2$. We can add arbitrarily many features, each a new dimension. When an object is described by n features, n dimensions $(d_1, d_2, ..., d_n)$, the general equation for Euclidean distance in n dimensions is shown in Equation 6-1:

Equation 6-1. General Euclidean distance

$$\sqrt{(d_{1,A} - d_{1,B})^2 + (d_{2,A} - d_{2,B})^2 + ... + (d_{n,A} - d_{n,B})^2}$$

We now have a metric for measuring the distance between any two objects described by vectors of numeric features—a simple formula based on the distances of the objects' individual features. Recalling persons A and B, above, their Euclidean distance is:

$$d(A, B) = \sqrt{(23 - 40)^2 + (2 - 10)^2 + (2 - 1)^2}$$
$$\approx 18.8$$

So the distance between these examples is about 19. This distance is just a number—it has no units, and no meaningful interpretation. It is only really useful for comparing the similarity of one pair of instances to that of another pair. It turns out that comparing similarities is extremely useful.

Nearest-Neighbor Reasoning

Now that we have a way to measure distance, we can use it for many different data-analysis tasks. Recalling examples from the beginning of the chapter, we could use this measure to find the companies most similar to our best corporate customers, or the online consumers most similar to our best retail customers. Once we have found these, we can take whatever action is appropriate in the business context. For corporate customers, IBM does this to help direct its sales force. Online advertisers do this to target ads. These most-similar instances are called *nearest neighbors*.

---

1. After Euclid, the 4th century B.C. Greek mathematician known as the Father of Geometry.

Example: Whiskey Analytics

Let's talk about a fresh example. One of us (Foster) likes single malt Scotch whiskey. If you've had more than one or two, you realize that there is a lot of variation among the hundreds of different single malts. When Foster finds a single malt he really likes, he wants to find other similar ones—both because he likes to explore the "space" of single malts, but also because any given liquor store or restaurant only has a limited selection. He wants to be able to pick one he'll really like. For example, the other evening a dining companion recommended trying the single malt "Bunnahabhain."[2] It was unusual and very good. Out of all the many single malts, how could Foster find other ones like that?

Let's take a data science approach. Recall from Chapter 2 that we first should think about the exact question we would like to answer, and what are the appropriate data to answer it. How can we describe single malt Scotch whiskeys as feature vectors, in such a way that we think similar whiskeys will have similar taste? This is exactly the project undertaken by François-Joseph Lapointe and Pierre Legendre (1994) of the University of Montréal. They were interested in several classification and organizational questions about Scotch whiskeys. We'll adopt some of their approach here.[3]

It turns out that tasting notes are published for many whiskeys. For example, Michael Jackson is a well-known whiskey and beer connoisseur who has written *Michael Jackson's Malt Whisky Companion: A Connoisseur's Guide to the Malt Whiskies of Scotland* (Jackson, 1989), which describes 109 different single malt Scotches of Scotland. The descriptions are in the form of tasting notes on each Scotch, such as: *"Appetizing aroma of peat smoke, almost incense-like, heather honey with a fruity softness."*

As data scientists, we are making progress. We have found a potentially useful source of data. However, we do not yet have whiskeys described by feature vectors, only by tasting notes. We need to press on with our data formulation. Following Lapointe and Legendre (1994), let's create some numeric features that, for any whiskey, will summarize the information in the tasting notes. Define five general whiskey attributes, each with many possible values:

1. **Color:** *yellow, very pale, pale, pale gold, gold, old gold, full gold, amber,* etc.   (14 values)

2. **Nose:** *aromatic, peaty, sweet, light, fresh, dry, grassy,* etc.   (12 values)

3. **Body:** *soft, medium, full, round, smooth, light, firm, oily.*   (8 values)

4. **Palate:** *full, dry, sherry, big, fruity, grassy, smoky, salty,* etc.   (15 values)

5. **Finish:** *full, dry, warm, light, smooth, clean, fruity, grassy, smoky,* etc.   (19 values)

---

2. No, he can't pronounce it properly either.

3. For a real business based on whiskey analytics, see: the website WhiskyClassified.com (*http://www.whisky classified.com/*)

It is important to note that these category values are *not* mutually exclusive (e.g., Aberlour's palate is described as medium, full, soft, round and smooth). In general, any of the values can co-occur (though some of them, like Color being both light and smoky, never do) but because they can co-occur, each value of each variable was coded as a separate feature by Lapointe and Legendre. Consequently there are 68 binary features of each whiskey.

Foster likes Bunnahabhain, so we can use Lapointe and Legendre's representation of whiskeys with Euclidean distance to find similar ones for him. For reference, here is their description of Bunnahabhain:

- *Color:* gold
- *Nose:* fresh and sea
- *Body:* firm, medium, and light
- *Palate:* sweet, fruity, and clean
- *Finish:* full

Here is Bunnahabhain's description and the five single-malt Scotches most similar to Bunnahabhain, by increasing distance:

Whiskey	Distance	Descriptors
Bunnahabhain	—	*gold; firm,med,light; sweet,fruit,clean; fresh,sea; full*
Glenglassaugh	0.643	gold; firm,light,smooth; sweet,grass; fresh,grass
Tullibardine	0.647	gold; firm,med,smooth; sweet,fruit,full,grass,clean; sweet; big,arome,sweet
Ardbeg	0.667	sherry; firm,med,full,light; sweet; dry,peat,sea;salt
Bruichladdich	0.667	pale; firm,light,smooth; dry,sweet,smoke,clean; light; full
Glenmorangie	0.667	p.gold; med,oily,light; sweet,grass,spice; sweet,spicy,grass,sea,fresh; full,long

Using this list we could find a Scotch similar to Bunnahabhain. At any particular shop we might have to go down the list a bit to find one they stock, but since the Scotches are ordered by similarity we can easily find the most similar Scotch (and also have a vague idea as to how similar the closest available Scotch is as compared to the alternatives that are not available).

 If you're interested in playing with the Scotch Whiskey dataset, Lapointe and Legendre have made their data and paper available at: *http://adn.biol.umontreal.ca/~numericalecology/data/scotch.html* .

This is an example of the direct application of similarity to solve a problem. Once we understand this fundamental notion, we have a powerful conceptual tool for approaching a variety of problems, such as those laid out above (finding similar companies, similar consumers, etc.). As we see in the whiskey example, the data scientist often still has work to do to actually define the data so that the similarity will be with respect to a useful set of characteristics. Later we will present some other notions of similarity and distance. Now, let's move on to another very common use of similarity in data science.

Nearest Neighbors for Predictive Modeling

We also can use the idea of nearest neighbors to do predictive modeling in a different way. Take a minute to recall everything you now know about predictive modeling from prior chapters. To use similarity for predictive modeling, the basic procedure is beautifully simple: given a new example whose target variable we want to predict, we scan through all the training examples and choose several that are the most similar to the new example. Then we predict the new example's target value, based on the nearest neighbors' (known) target values. How to do that last step needs to be defined; for now, let's just say that we have some *combining function* (like voting or averaging) operating on the neighbors' known target values. The combining function will give us a prediction.

Classification

Since we have focused a great deal on classification tasks so far in the book, let's begin by seeing how neighbors can be used to classify a new instance in a super-simple setting. Figure 6-2 shows a new example whose label we want to predict, indicated by a "?." Following the basic procedure introduced above, the nearest neighbors (in this example, three of them) are retrieved and their known target variables (classes) are consulted. In this case, two examples are positive and one is negative. What should be our combining function? A simple combining function in this case would be majority vote, so the predicted class would be positive.

Adding just a little more complexity, consider a credit card marketing problem. The goal is to predict whether a new customer will respond to a credit card offer based on how other, similar customers have responded. The data (still oversimplified of course) are shown in Table 6-1.

Table 6-1. Nearest neighbor example: Will David respond or not?

Customer	Age	Income (1000s)	Cards	Response (target)	Distance from David
David	37	50	2	?	0
John	35	35	3	Yes	$\sqrt{(35 - 37)^2 + (35 - 50)^2 + (3 - 2)^2} = 15.16$
Rachael	22	50	2	No	$\sqrt{(22 - 37)^2 + (50 - 50)^2 + (2 - 2)^2} = 15$
Ruth	63	200	1	No	$\sqrt{(63 - 37)^2 + (200 - 50)^2 + (1 - 2)^2} = 152.23$
Jefferson	59	170	1	No	$\sqrt{(59 - 37)^2 + (170 - 50)^2 + (1 - 2)^2} = 122$
Norah	25	40	4	Yes	$\sqrt{(25 - 37)^2 + (40 - 50)^2 + (4 - 2)^2} = 15.74$

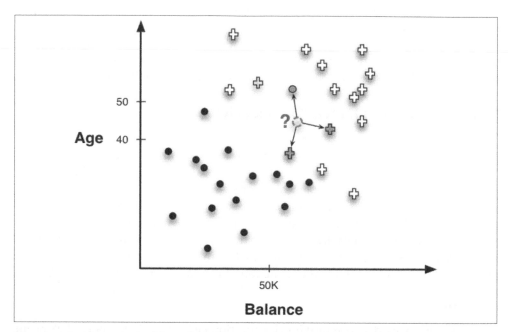

Figure 6-2. Nearest neighbor classification. The point to be classified, labeled with a question mark, would be classified + because the majority of its nearest (three) neighbors are +.

In this example data, there are five existing customers we previously have contacted with a credit card offer. For each of them we have their name, age, income, the number of cards they already have, and whether they responded to the offer. For a new person, David, we want to predict whether he will respond to the offer or not.

The last column in Table 6-1 shows a distance calculation, using Equation 6-1, of how far each instance is from David. Three customers (John, Rachael, and Norah) are fairly similar to David, with a distance of about 15. The other two customers (Ruth and Jefferson) are much farther away. Therefore, David's three nearest neighbors are Rachael, then John, then Norah. Their responses are No, Yes, and Yes, respectively. If we take a majority vote of these values, we predict Yes (David will respond). This touches upon some important issues with nearest-neighbor methods: how many neighbors should we use? Should they have equal weights in the combining function? We discuss these later in the chapter.

Probability Estimation

We've made the point that it's usually important not just to classify a new example but to estimate its probability—to assign a score to it, because a score gives more information than just a Yes/No decision. Nearest neighbor classification can be used to do this fairly easily. Consider again the classification task of deciding whether David will be a responder or not. His nearest neighbors (Rachael, John, and Norah) have classes of No, Yes, and Yes, respectively. If we score for the Yes class, so that Yes=1 and No=0, we can average these into a score of *2/3* for David. If we were to do this in practice, we might want to use more than just three nearest neighbors to compute the probability estimates (and recall the discussion of estimating probabilities from small samples in "Probability Estimation" on page 71).

Regression

Once we can retrieve nearest neighbors, we can use them for any predictive mining task by combining them in different ways. We just saw how to do classification by taking a majority vote of a target. We can do regression in a similar way.

Assume we had the same dataset as in Table 6-1, but this time we want to predict David's Income. We won't redo the distance calculation, but assume that David's three nearest neighbors were again Rachael, John, and Norah. Their respective incomes are 50, 35, and 40 (in thousands). We then use these values to generate a prediction for David's income. We could use the average (about 42) or the median (40).

 It is important to note that in retrieving neighbors we do not use the target variable because we're trying to predict it. Thus Income would not enter into the distance calculation as it does in Table 6-1. However, we're free to use any other variables whose values are available to determine distance.

How Many Neighbors and How Much Influence?

In the course of explaining how classification, regression, and scoring may be done, we have used an example with only three neighbors. Several questions may have occurred to you. First, why *three* neighbors, instead of just one, or five, or one hundred? Second, should we treat all neighbors the same? Though all are called "nearest" neighbors, some are nearer than others, and shouldn't this influence how they're used?

There is no simple answer to how many neighbors should be used. Odd numbers are convenient for breaking ties for majority vote classification with two-class problems. Nearest neighbor algorithms are often referred to by the shorthand k-NN, where the k refers to the number of neighbors used, such as 3-NN.

In general, the greater k is the more the estimates are smoothed out among neighbors. If you have understood everything so far, with a little thought you should realize that if we increase k to the maximum possible (so that $k = n$) the entire dataset would be used for every prediction. Elegantly, this simply predicts the average over the entire dataset for any example. For classification, this would predict the majority class in the entire dataset; for regression, the average of all the target values; for class probability estimation, the "base rate" probability (see Note: Base rate in "Holdout Data and Fitting Graphs" in Chapter 5).

Even if we're confident about the number of neighbor examples we should use, we may realize that neighbors have different similarity to the example we're trying to predict. Shouldn't this influence how they're used?

For classification we started with a simple strategy of *majority* voting, retrieving an odd number of neighbors to break ties. However, this ignores an important piece of information: how close each neighbor is to the instance. For example, consider what would happen if we used $k = 4$ neighbors to classify David. We would retrieve the responses (Yes, No, Yes, No), causing the responses to be evenly mixed. But the first three are very close to David (distance ≈ 15) while the fourth is much further away (distance ≈ 122). Intuitively, this fourth instance shouldn't contribute as much to the vote as the first three. To incorporate this concern, nearest-neighbor methods often use *weighted voting* or *similarity moderated voting* such that each neighbor's contribution is scaled by its similarity.

Consider again the data in Table 6-1, involving predicting whether David will respond to a credit card offer. We showed that if we predict David's class by majority vote it depends greatly on the number of neighbors we choose. Let's redo the calculations, this time using *all* neighbors but scaling each by its similarity to David, using as the scaling weight the reciprocal of the square of the distance. Here are the neighbors ordered by their distance from David:

Name	Distance	Similarity weight	Contribution	Class
Rachael	15.0	0.004444	0.344	No
John	15.2	0.004348	0.336	Yes
Norah	15.7	0.004032	0.312	Yes
Jefferson	122.0	0.000067	0.005	No
Ruth	152.2	0.000043	0.003	No

The Contribution column is the amount that each neighbor contributes to the final calculation of the target probability prediction (the contributions are proportional to the weights, but adding up to one). We see that distances greatly effect contributions: Rachael, John and Norah are most similar to David and effectively determine our prediction of his response, while Jefferson and Ruth are so far away that they contribute virtually nothing. Summing the contributions for the positive and negative classes, the final probability estimates for David are 0.65 for Yes and 0.35 for No.

This concept generalizes to other sorts of prediction tasks, for example regression and class probability estimation. Generally, we can think of the procedure as weighted *scoring*. Weighted scoring has a nice consequence in that it reduces the importance of deciding how many neighbors to use. Because the contribution of each neighbor is moderated by its distance, the influence of neighbors naturally drops off the farther they are from the instance. Consequently, when using weighted scoring the exact value of k is much less critical than with majority voting or unweighted averaging. Some methods avoiding committing to a k by retrieving a very large number of instances (e.g., all instances, $k = n$) and depend upon distance weighting to moderate the influences.

Sidebar: Many names for nearest-neighbor reasoning

As with many things in data mining, different terms exist for nearest-neighbor classifiers, in part because similar ideas were pursued independently. Nearest-neighbor classifiers were established long ago in statistics and pattern recognition (Cover & Hart, 1967). The idea of classifying new instances directly by consulting a database (a "memory") of instances has been termed *instance-based learning* (Aha, Kibler, & Albert, 1991) and *memory-based learning* (Lin & Vitter, 1994). Because no model is built during "training" and most effort is deferred until instances are retrieved, this general idea is known as *lazy learning* (Aha, 1997).

A related technique in artificial intelligence is *Case-Based Reasoning* (Kolodner, 1993; Aamodt & Plaza, 1994), abbreviated CBR. Past cases are commonly used by doctors and lawyers to reason about new cases, so case-based reasoning has a well-established history in these fields.

However, there are also significant differences between case-based reasoning and nearest-neighbor methods. Cases in CBR are typically not simple feature vector instances but instead are very detailed summaries of an episode, including items such as a patient's symptoms, medical history, diagnosis, treatment, and outcome; or the details of a legal case including plaintiff and defendant arguments, precedents cited, and judgement. Because cases are so detailed, in CBR they are used not just to provide a class label but to provide diagnostic and planning information that can be used to deal with the case after it is retrieved. Adapting historical cases to be used in a new situation is usually a complex process that requires significant effort.

Geometric Interpretation, Overfitting, and Complexity Control

As with other models we've seen, it is instructive to visualize the classification regions created by a nearest-neighbor method. Although no explicit boundary is created, there are implicit regions created by instance neighborhoods. These regions can be calculated by systematically probing points in the instance space, determining each point's classification, and constructing the boundary where classifications change.

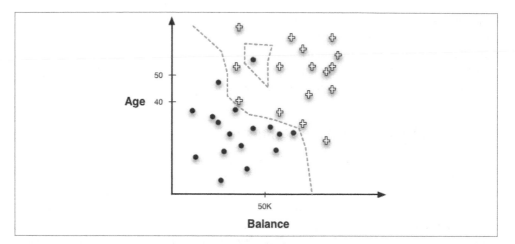

Figure 6-3. Boundaries created by a 1-NN classifier.

Figure 6-3 illustrates such a region created by a 1-NN classifier around the instances of our "Write-off" domain. Compare this with the classification tree regions from Figure 3-15 and the regions created by the linear boundary in Figure 4-3.

Notice that the boundaries are not lines, nor are they even any recognizable geometric shape; they are erratic and follow the frontiers between training instances of different classes. The nearest-neighbor classifier follows very specific boundaries around the training instances. Note also the one negative instance isolated inside the positive instances creates a "negative island" around itself. This point might be considered noise or an outlier, and another model type might smooth over it.

Some of this sensitivity to outliers is due to the use of a 1-NN classifier, which retrieves only single instances, and so has a more erratic boundary than one that averages multiple neighbors. We will return to that in a minute. More generally, irregular concept boundaries are characteristic of all nearest-neighbor classifiers, because they do not impose any particular geometric form on the classifier. Instead, they form boundaries in instance space tailored to the specific data used for training.

This should recall our discussions of overfitting and complexity control from Chapter 5. If you're thinking that 1-NN must overfit very strongly, then you are correct. In fact, think about what would happen if you evaluated a 1-NN classifier on the training data. When classifying each training data point, any reasonable distance metric would lead to the retrieval of that training point itself as its own nearest neighbor! Then its own value for the target variable would be used to predict itself, and voilà, perfect classification. The same goes for regression. The 1-NN memorizes the training data. It does a little better than our strawman lookup table from the beginning of Chapter 5, though. Since the lookup table did not have any notion of similarity, it simply predicted perfectly for exact training examples, and gave some default prediction for all others. The 1-NN classifier predicts perfectly for training examples, but it also can make an often reasonable prediction on other examples: it uses the most similar training example.

Thus, in terms of overfitting and its avoidance, the k in a k-NN classifier is a complexity parameter. At one extreme, we can set $k = n$ and we do not allow much complexity at all in our model. As described previously, the n-NN model (ignoring similarity weighting) simply predicts the average value in the dataset for each case. At the other extreme, we can set $k = 1$, and we will get an extremely complex model, which places complicated boundaries such that every training example will be in a region labeled by its own class.

Now let's return to an earlier question: how should one choose k? We can use the same procedure discussed in "A General Method for Avoiding Overfitting" on page 134 for setting other complexity parameters: we can conduct cross-validation or other nested holdout testing on the training set, for a variety of different values of k, searching for one that gives the best performance on the training data. Then when we have chosen a value of k, we build a k-NN model from the entire training set. As discussed in detail in Chapter 5, since this procedure only uses the training data, we can still evaluate it on the test data and get an unbiased estimate of its generalization performance. Data mining tools usually have the ability to do such nested cross-validation to set k automatically.

Figure 6-4 and Figure 6-5 show different boundaries created by nearest-neighbor classifiers. Here a simple three-class problem is classified using different numbers of neighbors. In Figure 6-4, only a single neighbor is used, and the boundaries are erratic and very specific to the training examples in the dataset. In Figure 6-5, 30 nearest neighbors are averaged to form a classification. The boundaries are obviously different from Figure 6-4 and are much less jagged. Note, however, that in neither case are the boundaries smooth curves or regular piecewise geometric regions that we would expect to see with a linear model or a tree-structured model. The boundaries for k-NN are more strongly defined by the data.

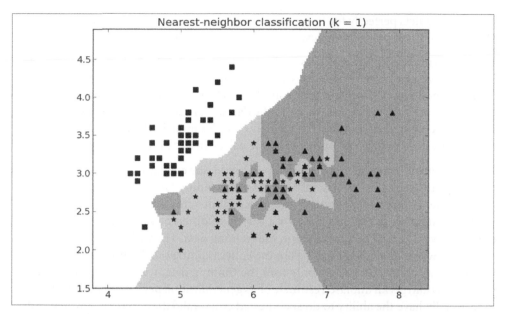

Figure 6-4. Classification boundaries created on a three-class problem created by 1-NN (single nearest neighbor).

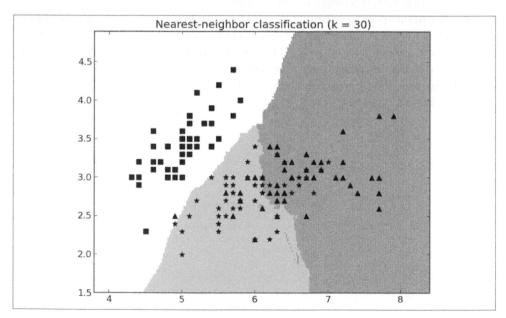

Figure 6-5. Classification boundaries created on a three-class problem created by 30-NN (averaging 30 nearest neighbors).

Issues with Nearest-Neighbor Methods

Before concluding a discussion of nearest-neighbor methods as predictive models, we should mention several issues regarding their use. These often come into play in real-world applications.

Intelligibility

Intelligibility of nearest-neighbor classifiers is a complex issue. As mentioned, in some fields such as medicine and law, reasoning about similar historical cases is a natural way of coming to a decision about a new case. In such fields, a nearest-neighbor method may be a good fit. In other areas, the lack of an explicit, interpretable model may pose a problem.

There are really two aspects to this issue of intelligibility: the justification of a specific *decision* and the intelligibility of an entire *model*.

With *k*-NN, it usually is easy to describe how a single instance is decided: the set of neighbors participating in the decision can be presented, along with their contributions. This was done for the example involving the prediction of whether David would respond, earlier in Table 6-1. Some careful phrasing and judicious presentation of nearest neighbors are useful. For example, Netflix uses a form of nearest-neighbor classification for their recommendations, and explains their movie recommendations with sentences like:

> "The movie *Billy Elliot* was recommended based on your interest in *Amadeus*, *The Constant Gardener* and *Little Miss Sunshine*"

Amazon presents recommendations with phrases like: "Customers with similar searches purchased…" and "Related to Items You've Viewed."

Whether such justifications are adequate depends on the application. An Amazon customer may be satisfied with such an explanation for why she got a recommendation. On the other hand, a mortgage applicant may not be satisfied with the explanation, "We declined your mortgage application because you remind us of the Smiths and the Mitchells, who both defaulted." Indeed, some legal regulations restrict the sorts of models that can be used for credit scoring to models for which very simple explanations can be given based on specific, important variables. For example, with a linear model, one may be able to say: "all else being equal, if your income had been $20,000 higher you would have been granted this particular mortgage."

It also is easy to explain how the entire nearest-neighbor model generally decides new cases. The idea of finding the most similar cases and looking at how they were classified, or what value they had, is intuitive to many.

What is difficult is to explain more deeply what "knowledge" has been mined from the data. If a stakeholder asks "What did your system learn from the data about my customers? On what basis does it make its decisions?" there may be no easy answer because there is no explicit model. Strictly speaking, the nearest-neighbor "model" consists of the entire case set (the database), the distance function, and the combining function. In two dimensions we can visualize this directly as we did in the prior figures. However, this is not possible when there are many dimensions. The knowledge embedded in this model is not usually understandable, so if model intelligibility and justification are critical, nearest-neighbor methods should be avoided.

Dimensionality and domain knowledge

Nearest-neighbor methods typically take into account all features when calculating the distance between two instances. "Heterogeneous Attributes" on page 157 below discusses one of the difficulties with attributes: numeric attributes may have vastly different ranges, and unless they are scaled appropriately the effect of one attribute with a wide range can swamp the effect of another with a much smaller range. But apart from this, there is a problem with having too many attributes, or many that are irrelevant to the similarity judgment.

For example, in the credit card offer domain, a customer database could contain much incidental information such as number of children, length of time at job, house size, median income, make and model of car, average education level, and so on. Conceivably some of these could be relevant to whether the customer would accept the credit card offer, but probably most would be irrelevant. Such problems are said to be high-dimensional—they suffer from the so-called *curse of dimensionality*—and this poses problems for nearest neighbor methods. Much of the reason and effects are quite technical,[4] but roughly, since all of the attributes (dimensions) contribute to the distance calculations, instance similarity can be confused and misled by the presence of too many irrelevant attributes.

There are several ways to fix the problem of many, possibly irrelevant attributes. One is *feature selection*, the judicious determination of features that should be included in the data mining model. Feature selection can be done manually by the data miner, using background knowledge as what attributes are relevant. This is one of the main ways in which a data mining team injects domain knowledge into the data mining process. As discussed in Chapter 3 and Chapter 5 there are also automated feature selection methods that can process the data and make judgments about which attributes give information about the target.

Another way of injecting domain knowledge into similarity calculations is to tune the similarity/distance function manually. We may know, for example, that the attribute

---

4. For example, it turns out that for technical reasons, with large numbers of features, certain particular instances appear extremely frequently in other instances' sets of k nearest neighbors. These particular instances thereby have a very large influence on many classifications.

Number of Credit Cards should have a strong influence on whether a customer accepts an offer for another one. A data scientist can tune the distance function by assigning different weights to the different attributes (e.g., giving a larger weight to *Number of Credit Cards*). Domain knowledge can be added not only because we believe we know what will be more predictive, but more generally because we know something about the similar entities we want to find. When looking for similar whiskeys, I may know that "peatiness" is important to my judging a single malt as tasting similar, so I could give *peaty* a higher weight in the similarity calculation. If another taste variable is unimportant, I could remove it or simply give it a low weight.

Computational efficiency

One benefit of nearest-neighbor methods is that training is very fast because it usually involves only storing the instances. No effort is expended in creating a model. The main computational cost of a nearest neighbor method is borne by the prediction/classification step, when the database must be queried to find nearest neighbors of a new instance. This can be very expensive, and the classification expense should be a consideration. Some applications require extremely fast predictions; for example, in online advertisement targeting, decisions may need to be made in a few tens of milliseconds. For such applications, a nearest neighbor method may be impractical.

There are techniques for speeding up neighbor retrievals. Specialized data structures like kd-trees and hashing methods (Shakhnarovich, Darrell, & Indyk, 2005; Papadopoulos & Manolopoulos, 2005) are employed in some commerical database and data mining systems to make nearest neighbor queries more efficient. However, be aware that many small-scale and research data mining tools usually do not employ such techniques, and still rely on naive brute-force retrieval.

Some Important Technical Details Relating to Similarities and Neighbors

Heterogeneous Attributes

Up to this point we have been using Euclidean distance, showing that it was easy to calculate. If attributes are numeric and are directly comparable, the distance calculation is indeed straightforward. When examples contain complex, heterogeneous attributes things become more complicated. Consider another example in the same domain but with a few more attributes:

Attribute	Person A	Person B
Sex	Male	Female

Attribute	Person A	Person B
Age	23	40
Years at current address	2	10
Residential status (1=Owner, 2=Renter, 3=Other)	2	1
Income	50,000	90,000

Several complications now arise. First, the equation for Euclidean distance is numeric, and Sex is a categorical (symbolic) attribute. It must be encoded numerically. For binary variables, a simple encoding like M=0, F=1 may be sufficient, but if there are multiple values for a categorical attribute this will not be good enough.

Also important, we have variables that, though numeric, have very different scales and ranges. Age might have a range from 18 to 100, while Income might have a range from $10 to $10,000,000. Without scaling, our distance metric would consider ten dollars of income difference to be as significant as ten years of age difference, and this is clearly wrong. For this reason nearest-neighbor-based systems often have variable-scaling front ends. They measure the ranges of variables and scale values accordingly, or they apportion values to a fixed number of bins. The general principle at work is that care must be taken that the similarity/distance computation is meaningful for the application.

* Other Distance Functions

Technical Details Ahead

For simplicity, up to this point we have used only a single metric, Euclidean distance. Here we include more details about distance functions and some alternatives.

It is important to note that the similarity measures presented here represent only a tiny fraction of all the similarity measures that have been used. These ones are particularly popular, but both the data scientist and the business analyst should keep in mind that it is important to use a meaningful similarity metric with respect to the business problem at hand. This section may be skipped without loss of continuity.

As noted previously, Euclidean distance is probably the most widely used distance metric in data science. It is general, intuitive and computationally very fast. Because it employs the *squares* of the distances along each individual dimension, it is sometimes called the *L2 norm* and sometimes represented by $|| \cdot ||_2$. Equation 6-2 shows how it looks formally.

Equation 6-2. Euclidean distance (L2 norm)

$$d_{\text{Euclidean}}(\mathbf{X,Y}) = \|\mathbf{X} - \mathbf{Y}\|_2 = \sqrt{(x_1 - y_1)^2 + (x_2 - y_2)^2 + \cdots}$$

Though Euclidean distance is widely used, there are many other distance calculations. The *Dictionary of Distances* by Deza & Deza (Elsevier Science, 2006) lists several hundred, of which maybe a dozen or so are used regularly for mining data. The reason there are so many is that in a nearest-neighbor method the distance function is critical. It basically reduces a comparison of two (potentially complex) examples into a single number. The data types and specifics of the domain of application greatly influence how the differences in individual attributes should combine.

The *Manhattan distance* or *L1-norm* is the sum of the (*unsquared*) pairwise distances, as shown in Equation 6-3.

Equation 6-3. Manhattan distance (L1 norm)

$$d_{\text{Manhattan}}(\mathbf{X,Y}) = \|\mathbf{X} - \mathbf{Y}\|_1 = |x_1 - y_1| + |x_2 - y_2| + \cdots$$

This simply sums the differences along the different dimensions between X and Y. It is called Manhattan (or taxicab) distance because it represents the total street distance you would have to travel in a place like midtown Manhattan (which is arranged in a grid) to get between two points—the total east-west distance traveled plus the total north-south distance traveled.

Researchers studying the whiskey analytics problem introduced above used another common distance metric.[5] Specifically, they used *Jaccard distance*. Jaccard distance treats the two objects as *sets* of characteristics. Thinking about the objects as sets allows one to think about the size of the union of all the characteristics of two objects X and Y, $|X \cup Y|$, and the size of the set of characteristics shared by the two objects (the intersection), $|X \cap Y|$. Given two objects, X and Y, the Jaccard distance is the proportion of all the characteristics (that either has) that are shared by the two. This is appropriate for problems where the possession of a common characteristic between two items is important, but the common *absence* of a characteristic is not. For example, in finding similar whiskeys it is significant if two whiskeys are both peaty, but it may not be significant that they are both not *salty*. In set notation, the Jaccard distance metric is shown in Equation 6-4.

---

5. See Lapointe and Legendre (1994), Section 3 ("Classification of Pure Malt Scotch Whiskies"), for a detailed discussion of how they engineered their problem formulation. Available online (*http://www.dcs.ed.ac.uk/home/jhb/whisky/lapointe/text.html*).

Equation 6-4. Jaccard distance

$$d_{\text{Jaccard}}(X, Y) = 1 - \frac{|X \cap Y|}{|X \cup Y|}$$

Cosine distance is often used in text classification to measure the similarity of two documents. It is defined in Equation 6-5.

Equation 6-5. Cosine distance

$$d_{cosine}(\mathbf{X,Y}) = 1 - \frac{\mathbf{X} \cdot \mathbf{Y}}{\|\mathbf{X}\|_2 \cdot \|\mathbf{Y}\|_2}$$

where $\|\cdot\|_2$ again represents the L2 norm, or Euclidean length, of each feature vector (for a vector this is simply the distance from the origin).

 The information retrieval literature more commonly talks about *cosine similarity*, which is simply the fraction in Equation 6-5. Alternatively, it is 1 − cosine distance.

In text classification, each word or token corresponds to a dimension, and the location of a document along each dimension is the number of occurrences of the word in that document. For example, suppose document A contains seven occurrences of the word *performance*, three occurrences of *transition*, and two occurrences of *monetary*. Document B contains two occurrences of *performance*, three occurrences of *transition*, and no occurrences of *monetary*. The two documents would be represented as vectors of counts of these three words: A = <7,3,2> and B = <2,3,0>. The cosine distance of the two documents is:

$$
\begin{aligned}
d_{cosine}(A, B) &= 1 - \frac{\langle 7, 3, 2 \rangle \cdot \langle 2, 3, 0 \rangle}{\|\langle 7, 3, 2 \rangle\|_2 \cdot \|\langle 2, 3, 0 \rangle\|_2} \\
&= 1 - \frac{7 \cdot 2 + 3 \cdot 3 + 2 \cdot 0}{\sqrt{49 + 9 + 4} \cdot \sqrt{4 + 9}} \\
&= 1 - \frac{23}{28.4} \approx 0.19
\end{aligned}
$$

Cosine distance is particularly useful when you want to ignore differences in scale across instances—technically, when you want to ignore the magnitude of the vectors. As a concrete example, in text classification you may want to ignore whether one document is much longer than another, and just concentrate on the textual content. So in our example above, suppose we have a third document, C, which has seventy occurrences of the word *performance*, thirty occurrences of *transition*, and twenty occurrences of *monetary*. The vector representing C would be C = <70, 30, 20>. If you work through the math you'll find that the cosine distance between A and C is zero—because C is simply A multiplied by 10.

As a final example illustrating the variety of distance metrics, let's again consider text but in a very different way. Sometimes you may want to measure the distance between two strings of characters. For example, often a business application needs to be able to judge when two data records correspond to the same person. Of course, there may be misspellings. We would want to be able to say how similar two text fields are. Let's say we have two strings:

1. `1113 Bleaker St.`
2. `113 Bleecker St.`

We want to determine how similar these are. For this purpose, another type of distance function is useful, called *edit distance* or the *Levenshtein metric*. This metric counts the minimum number of edit operations required to convert one string into the other, where an edit operation consists of either inserting, deleting, or replacing a character (one could choose other edit operators). In the case of our two strings, the first could be transformed into the second with this sequence of operations:

1. Delete a `1`,
2. Insert a c, and
3. Replace an a with an e.

So these two strings have an edit distance of three. We might compute a similar edit distance calculation for other fields, such as name (thereby dealing with missing middle initials, for example), and then calculate a higher-level similarity that combines the various edit-distance similarities.

 Edit distance is also used commonly in biology where it is applied to measure the genetic distance between strings of alleles. In general, edit distance is a common choice when data items consist of strings or sequences where order is very important.

* Combining Functions: Calculating Scores from Neighbors

Technical Details Ahead

For completeness, let us also briefly discuss "combining functions"—the formulas used for calculating the prediction of an instance from a set of the instance's nearest neighbors.

We began with majority voting, a simple strategy. This decision rule can be seen in Equation 6-6:

Equation 6-6. Majority vote classification

$$c(\mathbf{x}) = \underset{c \in \text{classes}}{\arg\max} \ \text{score}(c, \text{neighbors}_k(\mathbf{x}))$$

Here *neighbors$_k$*($\mathbf{x}$) returns the k nearest neighbors of instance $\mathbf{x}$, *arg max* returns the argument (c in this case) that maximizes the quantity that follows it, and the score function is defined as shown in Equation 6-7.

Equation 6-7. Majority scoring function

$$\text{score}(c, N) = \sum_{\mathbf{y} \in N} [class(\mathbf{y}) = c]$$

Here the expression *[class(y)=c]* has the value one if *class*($\mathbf{y}$) = c and zero otherwise.

Similarity-moderated voting, discussed in "How Many Neighbors and How Much Influence?" on page 149, can be accomplished by modifying Equation 6-6 to incorporate a weight, as shown in Equation 6-8.

Equation 6-8. Similarity-moderated classification

$$\text{score}(c, N) = \sum_{\mathbf{y} \in N} w(\mathbf{x},\mathbf{y}) \times [class(\mathbf{y}) = c]$$

where w is a weighting function based on the similarity between examples $\mathbf{x}$ and $\mathbf{y}$. The inverse of the square of the distance is commonly used:

$$w(\mathbf{x},\mathbf{y}) = \frac{1}{dist^2(\mathbf{x},\mathbf{y})}$$

where *dist* is whatever distance function is being used in the domain.

It is straightforward to alter Equation 6-6 and Equation 6-8 to produce a score that can be used as a probability estimate. Equation 6-8 already produces a score so we just have to scale it by the total scores contributed by all neighbors so that it is between zero and one, as shown in Equation 6-9.

Equation 6-9. Similarity-moderated scoring

$$p(c \mid \mathbf{x}) = \frac{\sum\limits_{\mathbf{y} \in \text{neighbors}(\mathbf{x})} w(\mathbf{x},\mathbf{y}) \times [\text{class}(\mathbf{y}) = c]}{\sum\limits_{\mathbf{y} \in \text{neighbors}(\mathbf{x})} w(\mathbf{x},\mathbf{y})}$$

Finally, with one more step we can generalize this equation to do regression. Recall that in a regression problem, instead of trying to estimate the class of a new instance *x* we are trying to estimate some value *f(x)* given the *f* values of the neighbors of **x**. We can simply replace the bracketed class-specific part of Equation 6-9 with numeric values. This will estimate the regression value as the weighted average of the neighbors' target values (although depending on the application, alternative combining functions might be sensible, such as the median).

Equation 6-10. Similarity-moderated regression

$$f(\mathbf{x}) = \frac{\sum\limits_{\mathbf{y} \in \text{neighbors}(\mathbf{x})} w(\mathbf{x},\mathbf{y}) \times t(\mathbf{y})}{\sum\limits_{\mathbf{y} \in \text{neighbors}(\mathbf{x})} w(\mathbf{x},\mathbf{y})}$$

where *t(y)* is the target value for example **y**.

So, for example, for estimating the expected spending of a prospective customer with a particular set of characteristics, Equation 6-10 would estimate this amount as the distance-weighted average of the neighbors' historical spending amounts.

Clustering

As noted at the beginning of the chapter, the notions of similarity and distance underpin much of data science. To increase our appreciation of this, let's look at a very different sort of task. Recall the first application of data science that we looked at deeply: supervised segmentation—finding groups of objects that differ with respect to some target characteristic of interest. For example, find groups of customers that differ with respect to their propensity to leave the company when their contracts expire. Why, in talking about supervised segmentation, do we always use the modifier "supervised"?

In other applications we may want to find groups of objects, for example groups of customers, but not driven by some prespecified target characteristic. Do our customers naturally fall into different groups? This may be useful for many reasons. For example, we may want to step back and consider our marketing efforts more broadly. Do we understand who our customers are? Can we develop better products, better marketing campaigns, better sales methods, or better customer service by understanding the natural subgroups? This idea of finding natural groupings in the data may be called unsupervised segmentation, or more simply *clustering*.

Clustering is another application of our fundamental notion of similarity. The basic idea is that we want to find groups of objects (consumers, businesses, whiskeys, etc.), where the objects within groups are similar, but the objects in different groups are not so similar.

 Supervised modeling involves discovering patterns to predict the value of a specified target variable, based on data where we know the values of the target variable. Unsupervised modeling does not focus on a target variable. Instead it looks for other sorts of regularities in a set of data.

Example: Whiskey Analytics Revisited

Before getting into details, let's revisit our example problem of whiskey analytics. We discussed using similarity measures to find similar single malt scotch whiskeys. Why might we want to take a step further and find clusters of similar whiskeys?

One reason we might want to find clusters of whiskeys is simply to understand the problem better. This is an example of exploratory data analysis, to which data-rich businesses should continually devote some energy and resources, as such exploration can lead to useful and profitable discoveries. In our example, if we are interested in Scotch whiskeys, we may simply want to understand the natural groupings by taste—because we want to understand our "business," which might lead to a better product or service. Let's say that we run a small shop in a well-to-do neighborhood, and as part of our business strategy we want to be known as the place to go for single-malt scotch whiskeys. We may not be able to have the largest selection, given our limited space and ability to invest in inventory, but we might choose a strategy of having a broad and eclectic collection. If we understood how the single malts grouped by taste, we could (for example) choose from each taste group a popular member and a lesser-known member. Or an expensive member and a more affordable member. Each of these is based on having a good understanding of how the whiskeys group by taste.

Let's now talk about clustering more generally. We will present the two main sorts of clustering, illustrating the concept of similarity in action. In the process, we can examine actual clusters of whiskeys.

Hierarchical Clustering

Let's start with a very simple example. At the top of Figure 6-6 we see six points, A-F, arranged on a plane (i.e., a two-dimensional instance space). Using Euclidean distance renders points more similar to each other if they are closer to each other in the plane. Circles labeled 1-5 are placed over the points to indicate *clusters*. This diagram shows the key aspects of what is called "hierarchical" clustering. It is a *clustering* because it groups the points by their similarity. Notice that the only overlap between clusters is when one cluster contains other clusters. Because of this structure, the circles actually represent a hierarchy of clusterings. The most general (highest-level) clustering is just the single cluster that contains everything—cluster 5 in the example. The lowest-level clustering is when we remove all the circles, and the points themselves are six (trivial) clusters. Removing circles in decreasing order of their numbers in the figure produces a collection of different clusterings, each with a larger number of clusters.

The graph on the bottom of the figure is called a *dendrogram*, and it shows explicitly the hierarchy of the clusters. Along the x axis are arranged (in no particular order except to avoid line crossings) the individual data points. The y axis represents the distance between the clusters (we'll talk more about that presently). At the bottom ($y = 0$) each point is in a separate cluster. As y increases, different groupings of clusters fall within the distance constraint: first A and C are clustered together, then B and E are merged, then the BE cluster is merged with D, and so on, until all clusters are merged at the top. The numbers at the joins of the dendrograms correspond to the numbered circles in the top diagram.

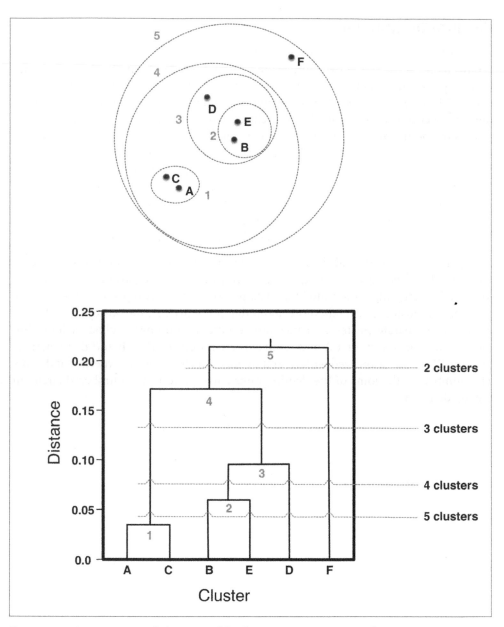

Figure 6-6. Six points and their possible clusterings. At top are shown six points, A-F, with circles 1-5 showing different distance-based groupings that could be imposed. These groups form an implicit hierarchy. At the bottom is a dendrogram corresponding to the groupings, which makes the hierarchy explicit.

Both parts of Figure 6-6 show that hierarchical clustering doesn't just create "a clustering," or a single set of groups of objects. It creates a collection of ways to group the points. To see this clearly, consider "clipping" the dendrogram with a horizontal line, ignoring everything above the line. As the line moves downward, we get different clusterings with increasing numbers of clusters, as shown in the figure. Clip the dendrogram at the line labeled "2 clusters," and below that we see two different groups; here, the singleton point F and the group containing all the other points. Referring back to the top part of the figure, we see that indeed F stands apart from the rest. Clipping the dendrogram at the 2-cluster point corresponds to removing circle 5. If we move down to the horizontal line labeled "3 clusters," and clip the dendrogram there, we see that the dendrogram is left with three groups below the line (AC, BED, F), which corresponds in the plot to removing circles 5 and 4, and we then see the same three clusters. Intuitively, the clusters make sense. F is still off by itself. A and C form a close group. B, E, and D form a close group.

An advantage of hierarchical clustering is that it allows the data analyst to see the groupings—the "landscape" of data similarity—before deciding on the number of clusters to extract. As shown by the horizontal dashed lines, the diagram can be cut across at any point to give any desired number of clusters. Note also that once two clusters are joined at one level, they remain joined in all higher levels of the hierarchy.

Hierarchical clusterings generally are formed by starting with each node as its own cluster. Then clusters are merged iteratively until only a single cluster remains. The clusters are merged based on the similarity or distance function that is chosen. So far we have discussed distance between instances. For hierarchical clustering, we need a distance function between clusters, considering individual instances to be the smallest clusters. This is sometimes called the *linkage* function. So, for example, the linkage function could be "the Euclidean distance between the closest points in each of the clusters," which would apply to any two clusters.

Note: Dendrograms

Two things can usually be noticed in a dendrogram. Because the y axis represents the distance between clusters, the dendrogram can give an idea of where natural clusters may occur. Notice in the dendrogram of Figure 6-6 there is a relatively long distance between cluster 3 (at about 0.10) and cluster 4 (at about 0.17). This suggests that this segmentation of the data, yielding three clusters, might be a good division. Also notice point F in the dendrogram. Whenever a single point merges high up in a dendrogram, this is an indication that it seems different from the rest, which we might call an "outlier," and want to investigate it.

One of the best known uses of hierarchical clustering is in the "Tree of Life" (Sugden et al., 2003; Pennisi, 2003), a hierarchical phylogenetic chart of all life on earth. This chart is based on a hierarchical clustering of RNA sequences. A portion of a tree from the Interactive Tree of Life (*http://itol.embl.de/index.shtml*) is shown in Figure 6-7 (Letunic & Bork, 2006). Large hierarchical trees are often displayed radially to conserve space, as is done here. This diagram shows a global phylogeny (taxonomy) of fully sequenced genomes, automatically reconstructed by Francesca Ciccarelli and colleagues (2006). The center is the "last universal ancestor" of all life on earth, from which branch the three domains of life (eukaryota, bacteria, and archaea). Figure 6-8 shows a magnified portion of this tree containing the particular bacterium Helicobacter pylori, which causes ulcers.

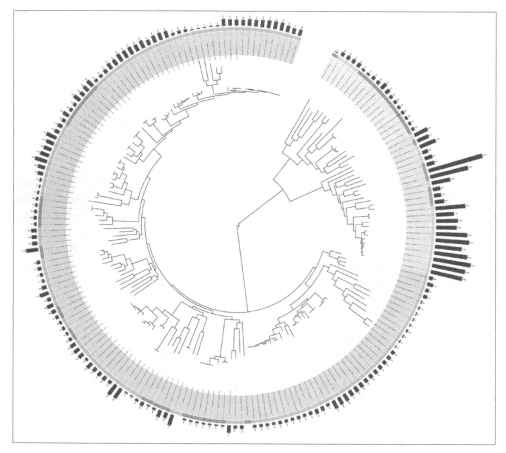

Figure 6-7. The phylogenetic Tree of Life, a huge hierarchical clustering of species, displayed radially.

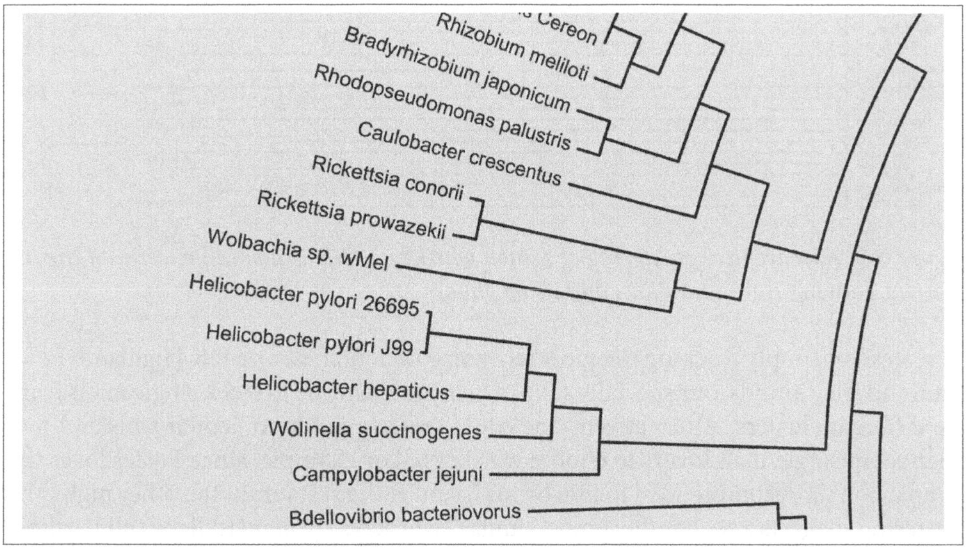

Figure 6-8. A portion of the Tree of Life.

Returning to our example from the outset of the chapter, the top of Figure 6-9 shows, as a dendrogram, the 50 single malt Scotch whiskeys clustered using the methodology described by Lapointe and Legendre (1994). By clipping the dendrogram we can obtain any number of clusters we would like, so for example, removing the top-most 11 connecting segments leaves us with 12 clusters.

At the bottom of Figure 6-9 is a close up of a portion of the hierarchy, focusing on Foster's new favorite, Bunnahabhain. Previously in "Example: Whiskey Analytics" on page 145 we retrieved whiskeys similar to it. This excerpt shows that most of its nearest neighbors (Tullibardine, Glenglassaugh, etc.) do indeed cluster near it in the hierarchy. (You may wonder why the clusters don't correspond *exactly* to the similarity ranking. The reason is that, while the five whiskeys we found are the most similar to Bunnahabhain, some of these five are more similar to other whiskeys in the dataset, so they are clustered with these closer neighbors before joining Bunnahabhain.)

Interestingly from the point of view of whiskey classification, the groups of single malts resulting from this taste-based clustering do not correspond neatly with regions of Scotland—the basis of the usual categorizations of Scotch whiskeys. There is a correlation, however, as Lapointe and Legendre (1994) point out.

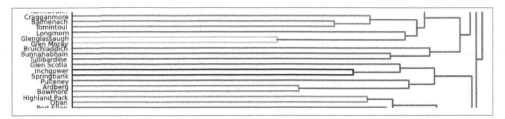

Figure 6-9. Hierarchical clustering of Scotch whiskeys. This is a small excerpt of the hierarchy showing Bunnahabhain and its neighbors.

So instead of simply stocking the most recognizable Scotches, or a few Highland, Lowland, and Islay brands, our specialty shop owner could choose to stock single malts from the different clusters. Alternatively, one could create a guide to Scotch whiskeys that might help single malt lovers to choose whiskeys.[6] For example, since Foster loves the Bunnahabhain recommended to him by his friend at the restaurant the other night, the clustering suggests a set of other "most similar" whiskeys (Bruichladdich, Tullibardine, etc.) The most unusual tasting single malt in the data appears to be Aultmore, at the very top, which is the last whiskey to join any others.

Nearest Neighbors Revisited: Clustering Around Centroids

Hierarchical clustering focuses on the similarities between the individual instances and how similarities link them together. A different way of thinking about clustering data is to focus on the clusters themselves—the groups of instances. The most common method for focusing on the clusters themselves is to represent each cluster by its "cluster center," or *centroid*. Figure 6-10 illustrates the idea in two dimensions: here we have three clusters, whose instances are represented by the circles. Each cluster has a centroid, represented by the solid-lined star. The star is not necessarily one of the instances; it is the geometric center of a group of instances. This same idea applies to any number of dimensions, as long as we have a numeric instance space and a distance measure (of course, we can't visualize the clusters so nicely, if at all, in high-dimensional space).

The most popular centroid-based clustering algorithm is called *k-means* clustering (MacQueen, 1967; Lloyd, 1982; MacKay, 2003), and the main idea behind it deserves some discussion as *k*-means clustering is mentioned frequently in data science. In *k*-means the "means" are the centroids, represented by the arithmetic means (averages) of the values along each dimension for the instances in the cluster. So in Figure 6-10, to compute the centroid for each cluster, we would average all the *x* values of the points in the cluster to form the *x* coordinate of the centroid, and average all the *y* values to form

---

6. This has been done: see David Wishart's (2006) book *Whisky Classified: Choosing Single Malts by Flavour*.

the centroid's *y* coordinate. Generally, the centroid is the average of the values for each feature of each example in the cluster. The result is shown in Figure 6-10.

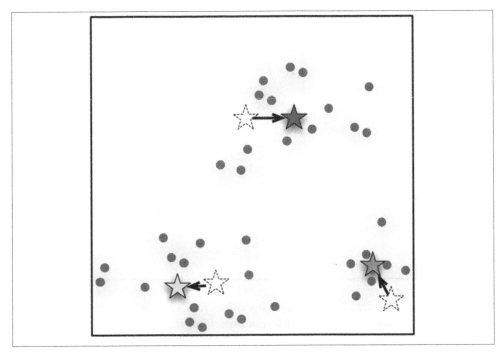

Figure 6-10. The second step of the k-means algorithm: find the actual center of the clusters found in the first step.

The *k* in *k*-means is simply the number of clusters that one would like to find in the data. Unlike hierarchical clustering, *k*-means starts with a desired number of clusters *k*. So, in Figure 6-11, the analyst would have specified *k*=3, and the *k*-means clustering method would return (i) the three cluster centroids when cluster method terminates (the three solid-lined stars in Figure 6-10), plus (ii) information on which of the data points belongs to each cluster. This is sometimes referred to as nearest-neighbor clustering because the answer to (ii) is simply that each cluster contains those points that are nearest to its centroid (rather than to one of the other centroids).

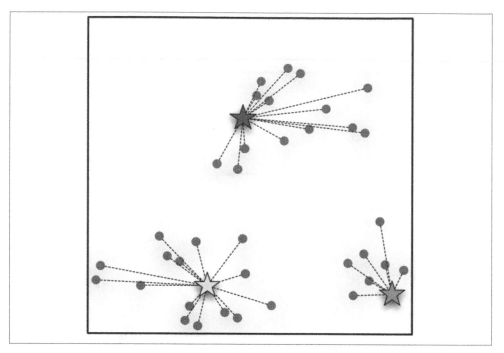

Figure 6-11. The first step of the k-means algorithm: find the points closest to the chosen centers (possibly chosen randomly). This results in the first set of clusters.

The k-means algorithm for finding the clusters is simple and elegant, and therefore is worth mentioning. It is represented by Figure 6-11 and Figure 6-10. The algorithm starts by creating k initial cluster centers, usually randomly, but sometimes by choosing k of the actual data points, or by being given specific initial starting points by the user, or via a pre-processing of the data to determine a good set of starting centers (Arthur & Vassilvitskii, 2007). Think of the stars in Figure 6-11 as being these initial ($k=3$) cluster centers. Then the algorithm proceeds as follows. As shown in Figure 6-11, the clusters corresponding to these cluster centers are formed, by determining which is the closest center to each point.

Next, for each of these clusters, its center is recalculated by finding the actual centroid of the points in the cluster. As shown in Figure 6-10, the cluster centers typically shift; in the figure, we see that the new solid-lined stars are indeed closer to what intuitively seems to be the center of each cluster. And that's pretty much it. The process simply iterates: since the cluster centers have shifted, we need to recalculate which points belong to each cluster (as in Figure 6-11). Once these are reassigned, we might have to shift the cluster centers again. The k-means procedure keeps iterating until there is no change in the clusters (or possibly until some other stopping criterion is met).

Figure 6-12 and Figure 6-13 show an example run of *k*-means on 90 data points with *k*=3. This dataset is a little more realistic in that it does not have such well-defined clusters as in the previous example. Figure 6-12 shows the initial data points before clustering. Figure 6-13 shows the final results of clustering after 16 iterations. The three (erratic) lines show the path from each centroid's initial (random) location to its final location. The points in the three clusters are denoted by different symbols (circles, x's, and triangles).

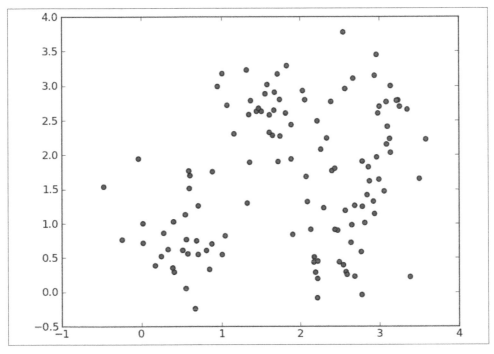

Figure 6-12. A k-means clustering example using 90 points on a plane and k=3 centroids. This figure shows the initial set of points.

There is no guarantee that a single run of the *k*-means algorithm will result in a good clustering. The result of a single clustering run will find a local optimum—a locally best clustering—but this will be dependent upon the initial centroid locations. For this reason, *k*-means is usually run many times, starting with different random centroids each time. The results can be compared by examining the clusters (more on that in a minute), or by a numeric measure such as the clusters' *distortion*, which is the sum of the squared differences between each data point and its corresponding centroid. In the latter case, the clustering with the lowest distortion value can be deemed the best clustering.

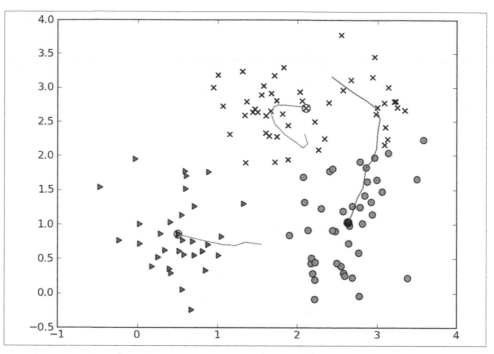

Figure 6-13. A k-means clustering example using 90 points on a plane and k=3 centroids. This figure shows the movement paths of centroids (each of three lines) through 16 iterations of the clustering algorithm. The marker shape of each point represents the cluster identity to which it is finally assigned.

In terms of run time, the k-means algorithm is efficient. Even with multiple runs it is generally relatively fast, because it only computes the distances between each data point and the cluster centers on each interaction. Hierarchical clustering is generally slower, as it needs to know the distances between all pairs of clusters on each iteration, which at the start is all pairs of data points.

A common concern with centroid algorithms such as k-means is how to determine a good value for k. One answer is simply to experiment with different k values and see which ones generate good results. Since k-means is often used for exploratory data mining, the analyst must examine the clustering results anyway to determine whether the clusters make sense. Usually this can reveal whether the number of clusters is appropriate. The value for k can be decreased if some clusters are too small and overly specific, and increased if some clusters are too broad and diffuse.

For a more objective measure, the analyst can experiment with increasing values of k and graph various metrics (sometimes obliquely called *indices*) of the quality of the resulting clusterings. As k increases the quality metrics should eventually stabilize or plateau, either bottoming out if the metric is to be minimized or topping out if maximized. Some judgment will be required, but the minimum k where the stabilization begins is often a good choice. Wikipedia's article *Determining the number of clusters in a data set* (*https://en.wikipedia.org/w/index.php?title=Determining_the_num ber_of_clusters_in_a_data_set&oldid=526596002*) describes various metrics for evaluating sets of candidate clusters.

Example: Clustering Business News Stories

As a concrete example of centroid-based clustering, consider the task of identifying some natural groupings of business news stories released by a news aggregator. The objective of this example is to identify, informally, different groupings of news stories released about a particular company. This may be useful for a specific application, for example: to get a quick understanding of the news about a company without having to read every news story; to categorize forthcoming news stories for a news prioritization process; or simply to understand the data before undertaking a more focused data mining project, such as relating business news stories to stock performance.

For this example we chose a large collection of (text) news stories: the Thomson Reuters Text Research Collection (TRC2) (*http://trec.nist.gov/data/reuters/reuters.html*), a corpus of news stories created by the Reuters news agency, and made available to researchers. The entire corpus comprises 1,800,370 news stories from January of 2008 through February of 2009 (14 months). To make the example tractable but still realistic, we're going to extract only those stories that mention a particular company—in this case, Apple (whose stock symbol is AAPL).

Data preparation

For this example, it is useful to discuss data preparation in a little detail, as we will be treating text as data, and we have not previously discussed that. See Chapter 10 for more details on mining text.

In this corpus, large companies are always mentioned when they are the primary subject of a story, such as in earnings reports and merger announcements; but they are often mentioned peripherally in weekly business summaries, lists of active stocks, and stories mentioning significant events within their industry sectors. For example, many stories about the personal computer industry mention how HP's and Dell's stock prices reacted on that day even if neither company was involved in the event. For this reason, we extracted stories whose headlines specifically mentioned Apple—thus assuring that the story is very likely news about Apple itself. There were 312 such stories but they covered a wide variety of topics, as we shall see.

Prior to clustering, the stories underwent basic web text preprocessing, with HTML and URLs stripped out and the text case-normalized. Words that occurred rarely (fewer than two documents) or too commonly (more than 50% documents) in the corpus were eliminated, and the rest formed the *vocabulary* for the next step. Then each document was represented by a numeric feature vector using "TFIDF scores" scoring for each vocabulary word in the document. TFIDF (Term Frequency times Inverse Document Frequency) scores represent the frequency of the word in the document, penalized by the frequency of the word in the corpus. TFIDF is explained in detail later in Chapter 10.

The similarity metric used was Cosine Similarity, introduced in "* Other Distance Functions" on page 158 (Equation 6-5). It is commonly used in text applications to measure the similarity of documents.

The news story clusters

We chose to cluster the stories into nine groups (so $k=9$ for k-means). Here we present a description of the clusters, along with some headlines of the stories contained in that cluster. It is important to remember that the entire news story was used in the clustering, not just the headline.

Cluster 1. These stories are analysts' announcements concerning ratings changes and price target adjustments:

- RBC RAISES APPLE <AAPL.O> PRICE TARGET TO $200 FROM $190; KEEPS OUT PERFORM RATING
- THINKPANMURE ASSUMES APPLE <AAPL.O> WITH BUY RATING; $225 PRICE TARGET
- AMERICAN TECHNOLOGY RAISES APPLE <AAPL.O> TO BUY FROM NEUTRAL
- CARIS RAISES APPLE <AAPL.O> PRICE TARGET TO $200 FROM $170; RATING ABOVE AVERAGE
- CARIS CUTS APPLE <AAPL.O> PRICE TARGET TO $155 FROM $165; KEEPS ABOVE AVERAGE RATING

Cluster 2. This cluster contains stories about Apple's stock price movements, during and after each day of trading:

- Apple shares pare losses, still down 5 pct
- Apple rises 5 pct following strong results
- Apple shares rise on optimism over iPhone demand
- Apple shares decline ahead of Tuesday event
- Apple shares surge, investors like valuation

Cluster 3. In 2008, there were many stories about Steve Jobs, Apple's charismatic CEO, and his struggle with pancreatic cancer. Jobs' declining health was a topic of frequent discussion, and many business stories speculated on how well Apple would continue without him. Such stories clustered here:

- ANALYSIS-Apple success linked to more than just Steve Jobs
- NEWSMAKER-Jobs used bravado, charisma as public face of Apple
- COLUMN-What Apple loses without Steve: Eric Auchard
- Apple could face lawsuits over Jobs' health
- INSTANT VIEW 1-Apple CEO Jobs to take medical leave
- ANALYSIS-Investors fear Jobs-less Apple

Cluster 4. This cluster contains various Apple announcements and releases. Superficially, these stories were similar, though the specific topics varied:

- Apple introduces iPhone "push" e-mail software
- Apple CFO sees 2nd-qtr margin of about 32 pct
- Apple says confident in 2008 iPhone sales goal
- Apple CFO expects flat gross margin in 3rd-quarter
- Apple to talk iPhone software plans on March 6

Cluster 5. This cluster's stories were about the iPhone and deals to sell iPhones in other countries:

- MegaFon says to sell Apple iPhone in Russia
- Thai True Move in deal with Apple to sell 3G iPhone
- Russian retailers to start Apple iPhone sales Oct 3
- Thai AIS in talks with Apple on iPhone launch
- Softbank says to sell Apple's iPhone in Japan

Cluster 6. One class of stories reports on stock price movements outside of normal trading hours (known as Before and After the Bell):

- Before the Bell-Apple inches up on broker action
- Before the Bell-Apple shares up 1.6 pct before the bell
- BEFORE THE BELL-Apple slides on broker downgrades
- After the Bell-Apple shares slip
- After the Bell-Apple shares extend decline

Centroid 7. This cluster contained little thematic consistency:

- ANALYSIS-Less cheer as Apple confronts an uncertain 2009

- TAKE A LOOK - Apple Macworld Convention
- TAKE A LOOK-Apple Macworld Convention
- Apple eyed for slim laptop, online film rentals
- Apple's Jobs finishes speech announcing movie plan

Cluster 8. Stories on iTunes and Apple's position in digital music sales formed this cluster:

- PluggedIn-Nokia enters digital music battle with Apple
- Apple's iTunes grows to No. 2 U.S. music retailer
- Apple may be chilling iTunes competition
- Nokia to take on Apple in music, touch-screen phones
- Apple talking to labels about unlimited music

Cluster 9. A particular kind of Reuters news story is a News Brief, which is usually just a few itemized lines of very terse text (e.g. "• Says purchase new movies on itunes same day as dvd release"). The contents of these New Briefs varied, but because of their very similar form they clustered together:

- BRIEF-Apple releases Safari 3.1
- BRIEF-Apple introduces ilife 2009
- BRIEF-Apple announces iPhone 2.0 software beta
- BRIEF-Apple to offer movies on iTunes same day as DVD release
- BRIEF-Apple says sold one million iPhone 3G's in first weekend

As we can see, some of these clusters are interesting and thematically consistent while others are not. Some are just collections of superficially similar text. There is an old cliché in statistics: *Correlation is not causation*, meaning that just because two things co-occur doesn't mean that one causes another. A similar caveat in clustering could be: *Syntactic similarity is not semantic similarity*. Just because two things—particularly text passages—have common surface characteristics doesn't mean they're necessarily related semantically. We shouldn't expect every cluster to be meaningful and interesting. Nevertheless, clustering is often a useful tool to uncover structure in our data that we did not foresee. Clusters can suggest new and interesting data mining opportunities.

Understanding the Results of Clustering

Once we have formulated the instances and clustered them, then what? As we mentioned above, the result of clustering is either a dendrogram or a set of cluster centers plus the corresponding data points for each cluster. How can we understand the clustering? This is particularly important because clustering often is used in exploratory analysis, so the whole point is to understand whether something was discovered, and if so, what?

How to understand clusterings and clusters depends on the sort of data being clustered and the domain of application, but there are several methods that apply broadly. We have seen some of them in action already.

Consider our whiskey example. Our whiskey researchers Lapointe and Legendre cut their dendrogram into 12 clusters; here are two of them:

Group A
> **Scotches:** Aberfeldy, Glenugie, Laphroaig, Scapa

Group H
> **Scotches:** Bruichladdich, Deanston, Fettercairn, Glenfiddich, Glen Mhor, Glen Spey, Glentauchers, Ladyburn, Tobermory

Thus, to examine the clusters, we simply can look at the whiskeys in each cluster. That seems rather easy, but remember that this whiskey example was chosen as an illustration in a book. What is it about the application that allowed relatively easy examination of the clusters (and thereby made it a good example in the book)? We might think, well, there are only a small number of whiskeys in total; that allows us to actually look at them all. This is true, but it actually is not so critical. If we had had massive numbers of whiskeys, we still could have sampled whiskeys from each cluster to show the composition of each.

The more important factor to understanding these clusters—at least for someone who knows a little about single malts—is that the elements of the cluster can be represented by the *names* of the whiskeys. In this case, the names of the data points are meaningful in and of themselves, and convey meaning to an expert in the field.

This gives us a guideline that can be applied to other applications. For example, if we are clustering customers of a large retailer, probably a list of the names of the customers in a cluster would have little meaning, so this technique for understanding the result of clustering would not be useful. On the other hand, if IBM is clustering business customers it may be that the names of the businesses (or at least many of them) carry considerable meaning to a manager or member of the sales force.

What can we do in cases where we cannot simply show the names of our data points, or for which showing the names does not give sufficient understanding? Let's look again at our whiskey clusters, but this time looking at more information on the clusters:

Group A
> - Scotches: Aberfeldy, Glenugie, Laphroaig, Scapa
> - The best of its class: Laphroaig (Islay), 10 years, 86 points

- Average characteristics: full gold; fruity, salty; medium; oily, salty, sherry; dry

Group H
- Scotches: Bruichladdich, Deanston, Fettercairn, Glenfiddich, Glen Mhor, Glen Spey, Glentauchers, Ladyburn, Tobermory
- The best of its class: Bruichladdich (Islay), 10 years, 76 points
- Average characteristics: white wyne, pale; sweet; smooth, light; sweet, dry, fruity, smoky; dry, light

Here we see two additional pieces of information useful for understanding the results of clustering. First, in addition to listing out the members, an "exemplar" member is listed. Here it is the "best of its class" whiskey, taken from Jackson (1989) (this additional information was not provided to the clustering algorithm). Alternatively, it could be the best known or highest-selling whiskey in the cluster. These techniques could be especially useful when there are massive numbers of instances in each cluster, so randomly sampling some may not be as telling as carefully selecting exemplars. However, this still presumes that the names of the instances are meaningful. Our other example, clustering the business news stories, shows a slight twist on this general idea: show exemplar stories and their headlines, because there the headlines can be meaningful summaries of the stories.

The example also illustrates a different way of understanding the result of the clustering: it shows the average characteristics of the members of the cluster—essentially, it shows the cluster centroid. Showing the centroid can be applied to any clustering; whether it is meaningful depends on whether the data values themselves are meaningful.

* Using Supervised Learning to Generate Cluster Descriptions

Technical Details Ahead

This section describes a way to automatically generate cluster descriptions. It is more complicated than the ones already discussed. It involves mixing unsupervised learning (the clustering) with supervised learning in order to create differential descriptions of the clusters. If this chapter is your first introduction to clustering and unsupervised learning, this may seem confusing to you, so we've made it a starred (advanced material) chapter. It may be skipped without loss of continuity.

However clustering was done, it provides us with a list of assignments indicating which examples belong to which cluster. A cluster centroid, in effect, describes the average cluster member. The problem is that these descriptions may be very detailed and they don't tell us how the clusters differ. What we may want to know is, for each cluster, *what differentiates this cluster from all the others?* This is essentially what supervised learning methods do so we can use them here.

The general strategy is this: we use the cluster assignments to label examples. Each example will be given a label of the cluster it belongs to, and these can be treated as class labels. Once we have a labeled set of examples, we run a supervised learning algorithm on the example set to generate a classifier for each class/cluster. We can then inspect the classifier descriptions to get a (hopefully) intelligible and concise description of the corresponding cluster. The important thing to note is that these will be *differential* descriptions: for each cluster, what differentiates it from the others?

In this section, from this point on we equate clusters with classes. We will use the terms interchangeably.

In principle we could use any predictive (supervised) learning method for this, but what is important here is *intelligibility*: we're going to use the learned classifier definition as a cluster description so we want a model that will serve this purpose. "Trees as Sets of Rules" on page 71 showed how rules could be extracted from classification trees, so this is a useful method for the task.

There are two ways to set up the classification task. We have *k* clusters so we could set up a *k*-class task (one class per cluster). Alternatively, we could set up a *k* separate learning tasks, each trying to differentiate one cluster from all the other *(k–1)* clusters.

We'll use the second approach on the whiskey-clustering task, using Lapointe and Legendre's cluster assignments (Appendix A of *A Classification of Pure Malt Scotch Whiskies* (*http://www.dcs.ed.ac.uk/home/jhb/whisky/lapointe/text.html*)). This gives us 12 whiskey clusters labeled A through L. We go back to our raw data and append each whiskey description with its cluster assignment. We're going to use the binary approach: choose each cluster in turn to classify against the others. We'll choose cluster J, which Lapointe and Legendre describe this way:

Group J
- Scotches: Glen Albyn, Glengoyne, Glen Grant, Glenlossie, Linkwood, North Port, Saint Magdalene, Tamdhu.
- The best of its class: Linkwood (Speyside), 12 years, 83 points.
- Average characteristics: full gold; dry, peaty, sherry; light to medium, round; sweet; dry.

You may recall from "Example: Whiskey Analytics" on page 145 that each whiskey is described using 68 binary features. The dataset now has a label (**J** or **not_J**) for each whiskey indicating whether it belongs to the J cluster. An excerpt of the dataset looks like this:

```
0,0,0,...,0,0,0,0,0,1,0,0,0,0,0,0,1,0,0,0,0,0,0,0,0,0,0,J      % Glen Grant
0,0,0,...,0,0,0,0,0,1,1,0,0,0,0,0,0,0,0,0,0,0,0,0,1,0,0,not_J  % Glen Keith
0,0,0,...,0,0,0,0,0,0,0,0,1,0,0,0,0,0,0,0,0,0,1,0,0,0,0,not_J  % Glen Mhor
```

The text after the "%" is a comment indicating the name of the whiskey.

This dataset is passed to a classification tree learner.[7] The result is shown in Figure 6-14.

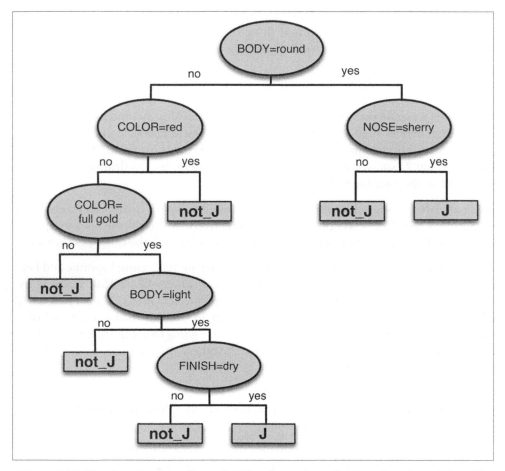

Figure 6-14. The decision tree learned from cluster J on the Scotches data. The right-most leaf corresponds to the segment of the population with round body and sherry nose. The whiskeys in this segment are mostly from cluster J.

---

7. Specifically, the J48 procedure of Weka (*http://www.cs.waikato.ac.nz/ml/weka/*) with pruning turned off.

From this tree we concentrate only on the leaves labeled **J** (ignoring the ones labeled **not_J**). There are only two such leaves. Tracing paths from the root to these leaves, we can extract the two rules:

1. `(BODY=round) AND (NOSE=sherry = 1)` $\Rightarrow$ `J`
2. `(BODY=round) AND (COLOR=red) AND (COLOR=full_gold) AND (BODY=light)`
   `AND (FINISH=dry)` $\Rightarrow$ `J`

Translating these loosely into English, the J cluster is distinguished by Scotches having either:

1. A round body and a sherry nose, or
2. A full gold (but not red) color with a light (but not round) body and a dry finish.

Is this description of cluster J better than the one given by Lapointe and Legendre, above? You can decide which you prefer, but it's important to point out they are different *types* of descriptions. Lapointe and Legendre's is a **characteristic** description; it describes what is typical or characteristic of the cluster, ignoring whether other clusters might share some of these characteristics. The one generated by the decision tree is a **differential** description; it describes only what differentiates this cluster from the others, ignoring the characteristics that may be shared by whiskeys within it. To put it another way: characteristic descriptions concentrate on intragroup commonalities, whereas differential descriptions concentrate on intergroup differences. Neither is inherently better —it depends on what you're using it for.

Stepping Back: Solving a Business Problem Versus Data Exploration

We now have seen various examples of our fundamental concepts of data science in action. You may have realized that the clustering examples seem somehow different from the predictive modeling examples, and even the examples of finding similar objects. Let's examine why.

In our predictive modeling examples, as well as our examples of using similarity directly, we focused on solving a very specific business problem. As we have emphasized, one of the fundamental concepts of data science is that one should work to define as precisely as possible the goal of any data mining. Recall the CRISP data mining process, replicated in Figure 6-15. We should spend as much time as we can in the business understanding/ data understanding mini-cycle, until we have a concrete, specific definition of the problem we are trying to solve. In predictive modeling applications, we are aided by our need to define the target variable precisely, and we will see in Chapter 7 that we can get more and more precise about defining the problem as we get more sophisticated in our un-

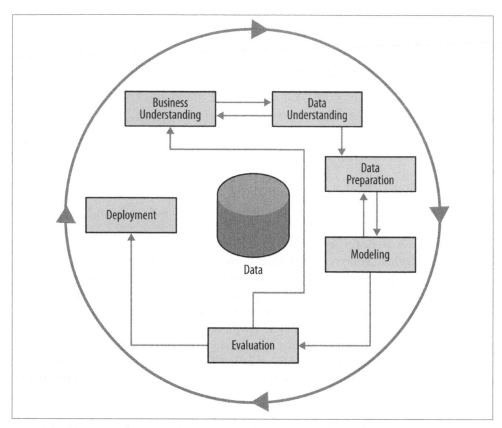

Business
Understanding

Data
Understanding

Data
Preparation

Deployment

Data

Modeling

Evaluation

Figure 6-15. The CRISP data mining process.

derstanding of data science. In our similarity-matching examples, again we had a very concrete notion of what exactly we were looking for: we want to find similar companies to optimize our efforts, and we will define specifically what it means to be similar. We want to find similar whiskeys—specifically in terms of taste—and we again work to gather and represent the data so that we can find exactly these. Later in the book we will discuss how we often expend considerable effort applying data science frameworks to decompose business problems into multiple, well-defined components, each of which we might apply data science methods to solve.

However, not all problems are so well defined. What do we do when in the business understanding phase we conclude: *we would like to explore our data, possibly with only a vague notion of the exact problem we are solving*? The problems to which we apply clustering often fall into this category. We want to perform *unsupervised* segmentation: finding groups that "naturally" occur (subject, of course, to how we define our similarity measures).

For the sake of discussion, let's simplify by separating our problems into supervised (e.g., predictive modeling) and unsupervised (e.g., clustering). The world is not so cut-and-dried and just about any of the data mining techniques we have presented could be used for data exploration, but the discussion will be much clearer if we do simply separate into supervised versus unsupervised. There is a direct trade-off in where and how effort is expended in the data mining process. For the supervised problems, since we spent so much time defining precisely the problem we were going to solve, in the Evaluation stage of the data mining process we already have a clear-cut evaluation question: do the results of the modeling seem to solve the problem we have defined? For example, if we had defined our goal as improving prediction of defection when a customer's contract is about to expire, we could assess whether our model has done this.

In contrast, unsupervised problems often are much more exploratory. We may have a notion that if we could cluster companies, news stories, or whiskeys, we would understand our business better, and therefore be able to improve something. However, we may not have a precise formulation. We should not let our desire to be concrete and precise keep us from making important discoveries from data. But there is a trade-off. The tradeoff is that for problems where we did not achieve a precise formulation of the problem in the early stages of the data mining process, we have to spend more time later in the process—in the Evaluation stage.

For clustering, specifically, it often is difficult even to understand what (if anything) the clustering reveals. Even when the clustering does seem to reveal interesting information, it often is not clear how to use that to make better decisions. Therefore, for clustering, additional creativity and business knowledge must be applied in the Evaluation stage of the data mining process.

Ira Haimowitz and Henry Schwartz (1997) show a concrete example of how clustering was used to improve decisions about how to set credit lines for new credit customers. They clustered existing GE Capital customers based on similarity in their use of their cards, payment of their bills, and profitability to the company. After some work, they settled on five clusters that represented very different consumer credit behavior (e.g., those who spend a lot but pay off their cards in full each month versus those who spend a lot and keep their balance near their credit limit). These different sorts of customers can tolerate very different credit lines (in the two examples, extra care must be taken with the latter to avoid default). The problem with using this clustering immediately for decision making is that the data are not available when the initial credit line is set. Briefly, Haimowitz and Schwarz took this new knowledge and cycled back to the beginning of the data mining process. They used the knowledge to define a precise predictive modeling problem: using data that *are* available at the time of credit approval, predict the probability that a customer will fall into each of these clusters. This predictive model then can be used to improve initial credit line decisions.

Summary

The fundamental concept of similarity between data items occurs throughout data mining. In this chapter we first discussed a wide variety of uses of similarity ranging from finding similar entities (or objects) based on their data descriptions, to predictive modeling, to clustering entities. We discussed these various uses and illustrated with examples.

A very common proxy for the similarity of two entities is the distance between them in the instance space defined by their feature vector representation. We presented similarity and distance computations, generally and in technical detail. We also introduced a family of methods, called nearest-neighbor methods, that perform prediction tasks by calculating explicitly the similarity between a new example and a set of training examples (with known values for the target). Once we can retrieve a set of nearest neighbors (most similar examples) we can use these for various data mining tasks: classification, regression and instance scoring. Finally, we showed how the same fundamental concept—similarity—also underlies the most common methods for unsupervised data mining: clustering.

We also discussed another important concept that raises its head once we begin to look seriously at methods (such as clustering) that are employed for more exploratory data analysis. When exploring the data, especially with unsupervised methods, we usually end up spending less time at the outset in the business understanding phase of the data mining process, but more time in the evaluation stage, and in iterating around the cycle. To illustrate, we discussed a variety of methodologies for understanding the results of clusterings.

CHAPTER 7

Decision Analytic Thinking I: What Is a Good Model?

Fundamental concepts: *Careful consideration of what is desired from data science results; Expected value as a key evaluation framework; Consideration of appropriate comparative baselines.*

Exemplary techniques: *Various evaluation metrics; Estimating costs and benefits; Calculating expected profit; Creating baseline methods for comparison.*

Recall from the beginning of Chapter 5: as a manager at MegaTelCo, you wanted to assess whether the model my consulting firm had produced was any good. Overfitting aside, how would you go about measuring that?

For data science to add value to an application, it is important for the data scientists and other stakeholders to consider carefully what they would like to achieve by mining data. This sounds obvious, so it is sometimes surprising how often it is ignored. Both data scientists themselves and the people who work with them often avoid—perhaps without even realizing it—connecting the results of mining data back to the goal of the undertaking. This may manifest itself in the reporting of a statistic without a clear understanding of why it is the right statistic, or in the failure to figuring out how to measure performance in a meaningful way.

We should be careful with such a criticism, though. Often it is not possible to measure perfectly one's ultimate goal, for example because the systems are inadequate, or because it is too costly to gather the right data, or because it is difficult to assess causality. So, we might conclude that we need to measure some surrogate for what we'd really like to measure. It is nonetheless crucial to think carefully about what we'd really like to measure. If we have to choose a surrogate, we should do it via careful, data-analytic thinking.

A challenge with writing a chapter on this topic is that every application is different. We cannot offer a single evaluation metric that is "right" for any classification problem, or regression problem, or whatever problem you may encounter. Nevertheless, there are various common issues and themes in evaluation, and frameworks and techniques for dealing with them.

We will work through a set of such frameworks and metrics for tasks of classification (in this chapter) and instance scoring (e.g., ordering consumers by their likelihood of responding to an offer), and class probability estimation (in the following chapter). The specific techniques should be seen as examples illustrating the general concept of thinking deeply about the needs of the application. Fortunately, these specific techniques do apply quite broadly. We also will describe a very general framework for thinking about evaluation, using expected value, that can cover a very wide variety of applications. As we will show in a later chapter, it also can be used as an organizational tool for data-analytic thinking generally, all the way back to problem formulation.

Evaluating Classifiers

Recall that a classification model takes an instance for which we do not know the class and predicts its class. Let's consider binary classification, for which the classes often are simply called "positive" and "negative." How shall we evaluate how well such a model performs? In Chapter 5 we discussed how for evaluation we should use a holdout test set to assess the generalization performance of the model. But how should we measure generalization performance?

Sidebar: Bad Positives and Harmless Negatives

In discussing classifiers, we often refer to a bad outcome as a "positive" example, and a normal or good outcome as "negative." This may seem odd to you, given the everyday definitions of positive and negative. Why, for example, is a case of fraud considered positive and a legitimate case considered negative? This terminology is conventional in many fields, including machine learning and data mining, and we will use it throughout this book. Some explanation may be useful to avoid confusion.

It is useful to think of a positive example as one worthy of attention or *alarm*, and a negative example as uninteresting or benign. For example, a medical test (which is a type of classifier) performed on a biological sample tries to detect disease or an unusual condition by examining certain aspects of the sample. If the test comes back positive it means the disease or condition is present; if the test is negative there is no cause for alarm and usually no need for treatment. Similarly, if a fraud detector finds unusual activity on a customer account and decides there is cause for alarm, this is called a positive. On the other hand, negatives (accounts with only legitimate activity) are profitable but from a fraud detection perspective they are unworthy of attention.

There are advantages to maintaining this general orientation rather than redefining the meaning of positive and negative for every domain we introduce. You can think of a classifier as sifting through a large population consisting mostly of negatives—the un-

---

interesting cases—looking for a small number of positive instances. By convention, then, the positive class is often rare, or at least rarer than the negative class. In consequence, the *number* of mistakes made on negative examples (the *false positive* errors) may dominate, though the *cost* of each mistake made on a positive example (a *false negative* error) will be higher.

Plain Accuracy and Its Problems

Up to this point we have assumed that some simple metric, such as classifier error rate or accuracy, was being used to measure a model's performance.

Classification accuracy is a popular metric because it's very easy to measure. Unfortunately, it is usually too simplistic for applications of data mining techniques to real business problems. This section discusses it and some of the alternatives.

The term "classifier accuracy" is sometimes used informally to mean any general measure of classifier performance. Here we will reserve *accuracy* for its specific technical meaning as the proportion of correct decisions:

$$\text{accuracy} = \frac{\text{Number of correct decisions made}}{\text{Total number of decisions made}}$$

This is equal to 1–*error rate*. Accuracy is a common evaluation metric that is often used in data mining studies because it reduces classifier performance to a single number and it is very easy to measure. Unfortunately, it is simplistic and has some well-known problems (Provost, Fawcett, & Kohavi, 1998). To understand these problems we need a way to decompose and count the different types of correct and incorrect decisions made by a classifier. For this we use the confusion matrix.

The Confusion Matrix

To evaluate a classifier properly it is important to understand the notion of *class confusion* and the *confusion matrix*, which is one sort of contingency table. A confusion matrix for a problem involving n classes is an $n \times n$ matrix with the columns labeled with actual classes and the rows labeled with predicted classes. Each example in a test set has an actual class label as well as the class predicted by the classifier (the predicted class), whose combination determines which matrix cell the instance counts into. For simplicity we will deal with two-class problems having 2×2 confusion matrices.

A confusion matrix separates out the decisions made by the classifier, making explicit how one class is being confused for another. In this way different sorts of errors may be dealt with separately. Let's differentiate between the true classes and the classes predicted by the model by using different symbols. We will consider two-class problems, and will denote the true classes as **p**(ositive) and **n**(egative), and the classes predicted by the model (the "predicted" classes) as **Y**(es) and **N**(o), respectively (think: the model says "**Yes**, it is a positive" or "**No**, it is not a positive").

Table 7-1. The layout of a 2 × 2 confusion matrix showing the names of the correct predictions (main diagonal) and errors (off-diagonal) entries.

	p	n
Y	True positives	False positives
N	False negatives	True negatives

In the confusion matrix, the main diagonal contains the counts of correct decisions. The errors of the classifier are the **false positives** (negative instances classified as positive) and **false negatives** (positives classified as negative).

Problems with Unbalanced Classes

As an example of how we need to think carefully about model evaluation, consider a classification problem where one class is rare. This is a common situation in applications, because classifiers often are used to sift through a large population of normal or uninteresting entities in order to find a relatively small number of unusual ones; for example, looking for defrauded customers, checking an assembly line for defective parts, or targeting consumers who actually would respond to an offer. Because the unusual or interesting class is rare among the general population, the class distribution is unbalanced or *skewed* (Ezawa, Singh, & Norton, 1996; Fawcett & Provost, 1996; Japkowicz & Stephen, 2002).

Unfortunately, as the class distribution becomes more skewed, evaluation based on accuracy breaks down. Consider a domain where the classes appear in a 999:1 ratio. A simple rule—always choose the most prevalent class—gives 99.9% accuracy. Presumably this is not satisfactory if a nontrivial solution is sought. Skews of 1:100 are common in fraud detection, and skews greater than $1:10^6$ have been reported in other classifier learning applications (Clearwater & Stern, 1991; Attenberg & Provost, 2010). Chapter 5 mentioned the "base rate" of a class, which corresponds to how well a classifier would perform by simply choosing that class for every instance. With such skewed domains the base rate for the majority class could be very high, so a report of 99.9% accuracy may tell us little about what data mining has really accomplished.

Even when the skew is not so great, in domains where one class is more prevalent than another accuracy can be greatly misleading. Consider again our cellular-churn example. Let's say you are a manager at MegaTelCo and as an analyst I report that our churn-prediction model generates 80% accuracy. This sounds good, but is it? My coworker reports that her model generates an accuracy of 64%. That's pretty bad, isn't it?

You might say, wait—we need more information about the data. And you would be exactly right to do so (and would be engaging in data-analytic thinking). What do we need? Considering the line of discussion so far in this subsection, you might rightly say: we need to know what is the proportion of churn in the population we are considering. Let's say you know that in these data the baseline churn rate is approximately 10% per month. Let's consider a customer who churns to be a positive example, so within our population of customers we expect a positive to negative class ratio of 1:9. So if we simply classify everyone as negative we could achieve a base rate accuracy of 90%!

Digging deeper, you discover that my coworker and I evaluated on two different datasets. This would not be suprising if we had not coordinated our data analysis efforts. My coworker calculated the accuracy on a representative sample from the population, whereas I created artificially balanced datasets for training and testing (both common practices). Now my coworker's model looks really bad—she could have achieved 90% accuracy, but only got 64%. However, when she applies her model to my balanced data set, she also sees an accuracy of 80%. Now it's really confusing.

The bottom line is that accuracy simply is the wrong thing to measure. In this admittedly contrived example, my coworker's model (call it Model A) achieves 80% accuracy on the balanced sample by correctly identifying all positive examples but only 60% of the negative examples. My model (Model B) does this, conversely, by correctly identifying all the negative examples but only 60% of the positive examples.

Let's look at these two models more carefully, using confusion matrices as a conceptual tool. In a training population of 1,000 customers, the confusion matrices are as follows. Recall that a model's predicted classes are denoted **Y** and **N**.

Table 7-2. Confusion matrix of A

	churn	not churn
Y	500	200
N	0	300

Table 7-3. Confusion matrix of B

	churn	not churn
Y	300	0
N	200	500

Figure 7-1 illustrates these classifications on a balanced population and on a representative population. As mentioned, both models correctly classify 80% of the balanced population. But the confusion matrices and the figure show that they operate very differently. Classifier A often falsely predicts that customers will churn when they will not, while classifier B makes opposite errors of predicting that customers will not churn when in fact they will. When applied to the original, unbalanced population of customers, model A's accuracy declines to 64% while model B's rises to 96%. This is a huge change. So which model is better?

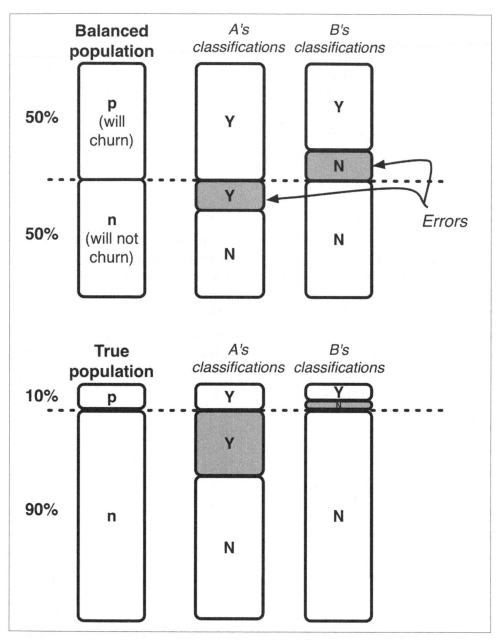

Figure 7-1. An example of why accuracy is misleading. At top, two churn models, A and B, make an equal number of errors (shaded regions) when classes are balanced. But A and B make different types of errors, so when the class proportion changes (bottom) their relative performance changes greatly.

My model (B) now appears to be better than A because B seems to have greater performance on the population we care about—the 1:9 mix of customers we expect to see. But we still can't say for sure because of another problem with accuracy: we don't know how much we *care* about the different errors and correct decisions. This issue is the topic of the next section.

Problems with Unequal Costs and Benefits

Another problem with simple classification accuracy as a metric is that it makes no distinction between false positive and false negative errors. By counting them together, it makes the tacit assumption that both errors are equally important. With real-world domains this is rarely the case. These are typically very different kinds of errors with very different costs because the classifications have consequences of differing severity.

Consider a medical diagnosis domain where a patient is wrongly informed he has cancer when he does not. This is a false positive error. The result would likely be that the patient would be given further tests or a biopsy, which would eventually disconfirm the initial diagnosis of cancer. This mistake might be expensive, inconvenient, and stressful for the patient, but it would not be life threatening. Compare this with the opposite error: a patient who has cancer but she is wrongly told she does not. This is a false negative. This second type of error would mean a person with cancer would miss early detection, which could have far more serious consequences. These two errors are very different, should be counted separately, and should have different costs.

Returning to our cellular-churn example, consider the cost of giving a customer a retention incentive which still results in departure (a false positive error). Compare this with the cost of losing a customer because no incentive was offered (a false negative). Whatever costs you might decide for each, it is unlikely they would be equal; and the errors should be counted separately regardless.

Indeed, it is hard to imagine any domain in which a decision maker can safely be indifferent to whether she makes a false positive or a false negative error. Ideally, we should estimate the cost or benefit of each decision a classifier can make. Once aggregated, these will produce an *expected profit* (or *expected benefit* or *expected cost*) estimate for the classifier.

Generalizing Beyond Classification

We have been using classification modeling to illustrate many data science issues concretely. Most of these issues are applicable beyond classification.

The general principle we're developing here is that when we are applying data science to an actual application it is vital to return to the question: what is important in the application? What is the goal? Are we assessing the results of data mining appropriately given the actual goal?

As another example, let's apply this thinking to regression modeling rather than classification. Say our data science team has to build a movie recommendation model. It predicts how much a given customer will like a given movie, which we will use to help us provide personalized recommendations. Let's say each customer rates a movie by giving it one to five stars, and the recommendation model predicts how many stars a user will give an unseen movie. One of our analysts describes each model by reporting the mean-squared-error (or root-mean-squared-error, or R^2, or whatever metric) for the model. We should ask: mean-squared-error of what? The analyst replies: the value of the target variable, which is the number of stars that a user would give as a rating for the movie. Why is the mean-squared-error on the predicted number of stars an appropriate metric for our recommendation problem? Is it meaningful? Is there a better metric? Hopefully, the analyst has thought this through carefully. It is surprising how often one finds that an analyst has not, and is simply reporting some measure he learned about in a class in school.

A Key Analytical Framework: Expected Value

We now are ready to discuss a very broadly useful conceptual tool to aid data analytic thinking: expected value. The expected value computation provides a framework that is extremely useful in organizing thinking about data-analytic problems. Specifically, it decomposes data-analytic thinking into (i) the structure of the problem, (ii) the elements of the analysis that can be extracted from the data, and (iii) the elements of the analysis that need to be acquired from other sources (e.g., business knowledge of subject matter experts).

In an expected value calculation the possible outcomes of a situation are enumerated. The expected value is then the weighted average of the values of the different possible outcomes, where the weight given to each value is its probability of occurrence. For example, if the outcomes represent different possible levels of profit, an expected profit calculation weights heavily the highly likely levels of profit, while unlikely levels of profit are given little weight. For this book, we will assume that we are considering repeated tasks (like targeting a large number of consumers, or diagnosing a large number of problems) and we are interested in maximizing expected profit.[1]

The expected value framework provides structure to an analyst's thinking (i) via the general form shown in Equation 7-1 .

Equation 7-1. The general form of an expected value calculation

$$EV = p(o_1) \cdot v(o_1) + p(o_2) \cdot v(o_2) + p(o_3) \cdot v(o_3) \ldots$$

1. A course in decision theory would lead you into a thicket of interesting related issues.

Each o_i is a possible decision outcome; $p(o_i)$ is its probability and $v(o_i)$ is its value. The probabilities often can be estimated from the data (ii), but the business values often need to be acquired from other sources (iii). As we will see in Chapter 11, data-driven modeling may help estimate business values, but usually the values must come from external domain knowledge.

We now will illustrate the use of expected value as an analytical framework with two different data science scenarios. The two scenarios are often confused but it is vital to be able to distinguish them. To do so, recall the difference from Chapter 2 between the *mining* (or induction) of a model, and the model's *use*.

Using Expected Value to Frame Classifier Use

In use, we have many individual cases for which we would like to predict a class, which may then lead to an action. In targeted marketing, for example, we may want to assign each consumer a class of *likely responder* versus *not likely responder*, then we could target the likely responders. Unfortunately, for targeted marketing often the probability of response for any individual consumer is very low—maybe one or two percent—so no consumer may seem like a likely responder. If we choose a "common sense" threshold of 50% for deciding what a likely responder is, we would probably not target anyone. Many inexperienced data miners are surprised when the application of data mining models results in everybody being classified as *not likely responder* (or a similar negative class).

However, with the expected value framework we can see the crux of the problem. Let's walk through a targeted marketing scenario.[2] Consider that we have an offer for a product that, for simplicity, is only available via this offer. If the offer is not made to a consumer, the consumer will not buy the product. We have a model, mined from historical data, that gives an estimated probability of response ($p_R(\mathbf{x})$) for any consumer whose feature vector description $\mathbf{x}$ is given as input. The model could be a classification tree or a logistic regression model or some other model we haven't talked about yet. Now we would like to decide whether to target a particular consumer described by feature vector $\mathbf{x}$.

Expected value provides a framework for carrying out the analysis. Specifically, let's calculate the expected benefit (or cost) of targeting consumer $\mathbf{x}$:

$$\text{Expected benefit of targeting} = p_R(\mathbf{x}) \cdot v_R + [1 - p_R(\mathbf{x})] \cdot v_{NR}$$

---

2. We use targeted marketing here, rather than the churn example, because the expected value framework actually reveals an important complexity to the churn example that we're not ready to deal with. We will return to that later in Chapter 11 when we're ready to deal with it.

where v_R is the value we get from a response and v_{NR} is the value we get from no response. Since everyone either responds or does not, our estimate of the probability of not responding is just $((1 - p_R(\mathbf{x})))$. As mentioned, the probabilities came from the historical data, as summarized in our predictive model. The benefits v_R and v_{NR} need to be determined separately, as part of the Business Understanding step (recall Chapter 2). Since a customer can only purchase the product by responding to the offer (as discussed above), the expected benefit of not targeting her conveniently is zero.

To be concrete, let's say that a consumer buys the product for $200 and our product-related costs are $100. To target the consumer with the offer, we also incur a cost. Let's say that we mail some flashy marketing materials, and the overall cost including postage is $1, yielding a value (profit) of v_R = $99 if the consumer responds (buys the product). Now, what about v_{NR}, the value to us if the consumer does not respond? We still mailed the marketing materials, incurring a cost of $1 or equivalently a benefit of -$1.

Now we are ready to say precisely whether we want to target this consumer: do we expect to make a profit? Technically, is the expected value (profit) of targeting greater than zero? Mathematically, this is:

$$p_R(\mathbf{x}) \cdot \$99 - \left[1 - p_R(\mathbf{x}) \right] \cdot \$1 > 0$$

A little rearranging of the equation gives us a decision rule: Target a given customer $\mathbf{x}$ only if:

$$p_R(\mathbf{x}) \cdot \$99 > \left[1 - p_R(\mathbf{x}) \right] \cdot \$1$$

$$p_R(\mathbf{x}) > 0.01$$

With these example values, we should target the consumer as long as the estimated probability of responding is greater than 1%.

This shows how an expected value calculation can express how we will *use* the model. Making this explicit helps to organize problem formulation and analysis. We will return to this in Chapter 11. Now, let's move on to the other important application of the expected value framework, to organize our analysis of whether the model we have induced from the data is any good.

Using Expected Value to Frame Classifier Evaluation

At this point we want to shift our focus from individual decisions to collections of decisions. Specifically, we need to evaluate the set of decisions made by a model when applied to a set of examples. Such an evaluation is necessary in order to compare one model to another. For example, does our data-driven model perform better than the hand-crafted model suggested by the marketing group? Does a classification tree work better than a linear discriminant model for a particular problem? Do any of the models do substantially better than a baseline "model," such as randomly choosing consumers to target? It is likely that each model will make some decisions better than the other model. What we care about is, *in aggregate*, how well does each model do: what is its *expected* value.

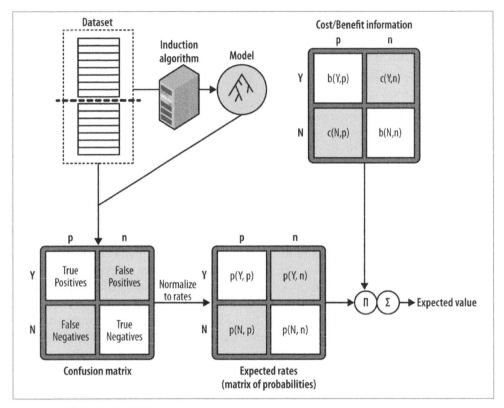

Figure 7-2. A diagram of the expected value calculation. The Π and Σ refer to the multiplication and summation in the expected value calculation.

We can use the expected value framework just described to determine the best decisions for each particular model, and then use the expected value in a different way to compare the models. If we are to calculate the expected profit for a model in aggregate, each o_i in Equation 7-1 corresponds to one of the possible combinations of the class we predict, and the actual class. We want to aggregate all the different possible cases: overall, when we decide to target consumers, what is the probability that they respond? What is the probability that they do not? What about when we do not target consumers, would they have responded? Fortunately, as you may recall, we already have the counts necessary to calculate all these—in the confusion matrix. Each o_i corresponds to one cell of the confusion matrix. For example, what is the probability associated with the particular combination of a consumer being *predicted to churn* and *actually does not churn*? That would be estimated by the number of test-set consumers who fell into the confusion matrix cell (**Y**, **n**), divided by the total number of test-set consumers.

Let's walk through an entire expected profit calculation at the aggregate (model) level, in the process computing these probabilities. Figure 7-2 shows a schematic diagram of the expected value calculation in the context of model induction and evaluation. At the top left of the diagram, a training portion of a dataset is taken as input by an induction algorithm, which produces the model that we will evaluate. That model is applied to a holdout (test) portion of the data, and the counts for the different cells of the confusion matrix are tallied. Let's consider a concrete example of a classifier confusion matrix in Table 7-4.

Table 7-4. A sample confusion matrix with counts.

	p	n
Y	56	7
N	5	42

Error rates

When calculating expected values for a business problem, the analyst is often faced with the question: where do these probabilities actually come from? When evaluating a model on testing data, the answer is straightforward: these probabilities (of errors and correct decisions) can be estimated from the tallies in the confusion matrix by computing the rates of the errors and correct decisions. Each cell of the confusion matrix contains a count of the number of decisions corresponding to the corresponding combination of (predicted, actual), which we will express as *count(h,a)* (we use h for "hypothesized" since p is already being used). For the expected value calculation we reduce these counts to rates or estimated probabilities, *p(h,a)*. We do this by dividing each count by the total number of instances:

$$p(h, a) = count(h, a) / T$$

Here are the calculations of the rates for each of the raw statistics in the confusion matrix. These rates are estimates of the probabilities that we will use in the expected value computation of Equation 7-1.

T = 110

$p(\mathbf{Y,p}) = 56/110 = 0.51$ $p(\mathbf{Y,n}) = 7/110 = 0.06$

$p(\mathbf{N,p}) = 5/110 = 0.05$ $p(\mathbf{N,n}) = 42/110 = 0.38$

Costs and benefits

To compute expected profit (recall Equation 7-1), we also need the cost and benefit values that go with each decision pair. These will form the entries of a cost-benefit matrix with the same dimensions (rows and columns) as the confusion matrix. However, the cost-benefit matrix specifies, for each (predicted,actual) pair, the cost or benefit of making such a decision (see Figure 7-3). Correct classifications (true positives and true negatives) correspond to the benefits $b(\mathbf{Y}, \mathbf{p})$ and $b(\mathbf{N}, \mathbf{n})$, respectively. Incorrect classifications (false positives and false negatives) correspond to the "benefit" $b(\mathbf{Y}, \mathbf{n})$ and $b(\mathbf{N}, \mathbf{p})$, respectively, which may well actually be a cost (a negative benefit), and often are explicitly referred to as costs $c(\mathbf{Y}, \mathbf{n})$ and $c(\mathbf{N}, \mathbf{p})$.

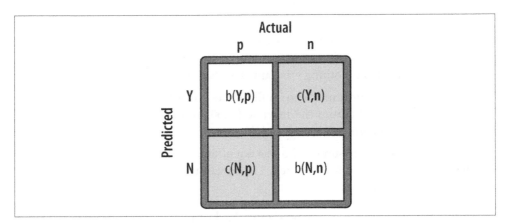

Figure 7-3. A cost-benefit matrix.

While the probabilities can be estimated from data, *the costs and benefits often cannot.* They generally depend on external information provided via analysis of the consequences of decisions in the context of the specific business problem. Indeed, specifying the costs and benefits may take a great deal of time and thought. In many cases they cannot be specified exactly but only as approximate ranges. Chapter 8 will return to address what we might do when these values are not known exactly. For example, in our churn problem, how much is it really worth us to retain a customer? The value depends on future cell phone usage and probably varies a great deal between customers. It may be that data on customers' prior usage can be helpful in this estimation. In many cases, average estimated costs and benefits are used rather than individual-specific costs and benefits, for simplicity of problem formulation and calculation. Therefore, we will ignore customer-specific cost/benefit calculations for the rest of our example, but will return to it in Chapter 11.

Mathematically, there is no difference between a cost and a benefit except for the sign. For simplicity, from this point on, we will express all values as **benefits**, with costs being negative benefits. We only have to specify a single function, which is b(predicted, actual).

So, let's return to our targeted marketing example. What are the costs and benefits? For simplicity, all numbers will be expressed as dollars.

- A *false positive* occurs when we classify a consumer as a likely responder and therefore target her, but she does not respond. We've said that the cost of preparing and mailing the marketing materials is a fixed cost of $1 per consumer. The benefit in this case is negative: $b(\mathbf{Y}, \mathbf{n}) = -1$.

- A *false negative* is a consumer who was predicted not to be a likely responder (so was not offered the product), but would have bought it if offered. In this case, no money was spent and nothing was gained, so $b(\mathbf{N}, \mathbf{p}) = 0$.

- A *true positive* is a consumer who is offered the product and buys it. The benefit in this case is the profit from the revenue ($200) minus the product-related costs ($100) and the mailing costs ($1), so $b(\mathbf{Y}, \mathbf{p}) = 99$.

- A *true negative* is a consumer who was not offered a deal and who would not have bought it even if it had been offered. The benefit in this case is zero (no profit but no cost), so $b(\mathbf{N}, \mathbf{n}) = 0$.

These cost-benefit estimations can be summarized in a 2 × 2 cost-benefit matrix, as in Figure 7-4. Note that the rows and columns are the same as for our confusion matrix, which is exactly what we'll need to compute the overall expected value for the classification model.

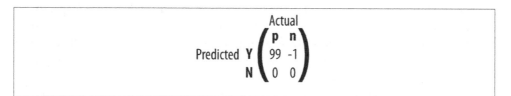

Figure 7-4. A cost-benefit matrix for the targeted marketing example.

Given a matrix of costs and benefits, these are multiplied cell-wise against the matrix of probabilities, then summed into a final value representing the total expected profit. The result is:

$$Expected\ profit = p(\mathbf{Y,p}) \cdot b(\mathbf{Y,p}) + p(\mathbf{N,p}) \cdot b(\mathbf{N,p}) +$$
$$p(\mathbf{N,n}) \cdot b(\mathbf{N,n}) + p(\mathbf{Y,n}) \cdot b(\mathbf{Y,n})$$

Using this equation, we can now compute and compare the expected profits for various models and other targeting strategies. All we need is to be able to compute the confusion matrices over a set of test instances, and to generate the cost-benefit matrix.

This equation is sufficient for comparing classifiers, but let's continue along this path a little further, because an alternative calculation of this equation is often used in practice. This alternative view is closely related to some techniques used to visualize classifier performance (see Chapter 8). Furthermore, by examining the alternative formulation we can see exactly how to deal with the model comparison problem we introduced at the beginning of the chapter—where one analyst had reported performance statistics over a representative (but unbalanced) population, and another had used a class-balanced population.

A common way of expressing expected profit is to factor out the probabilities of seeing each class, often referred to as the *class priors*. The class priors, $p(\mathbf{p})$ and $p(\mathbf{n})$, specify the likelihood of seeing positive and negative instances, respectively. Factoring these out allows us to separate the influence of class imbalance from the fundamental predictive power of the model, as we will discuss in more detail in Chapter 8.

A rule of basic probability is:

$$p(x, y) = p(y) \cdot p(x \mid y)$$

This says that the probability of two different events both occurring is equal to the probability of one of them occurring times the probability of the other occurring if we know that the first occurs. Using this rule we can re-express our expected profit as:

$$\text{Expected profit} = p(\mathbf{Y}|\mathbf{p}) \cdot p(\mathbf{p}) \cdot b(\mathbf{Y}, \mathbf{p}) + p(\mathbf{N}|\mathbf{p}) \cdot p(\mathbf{p}) \cdot b(\mathbf{N},\mathbf{p}) + \\ p(\mathbf{N}|\mathbf{n}) \cdot p(\mathbf{n}) \cdot b(\mathbf{N},\mathbf{n}) + p(\mathbf{Y}|\mathbf{n}) \cdot p(\mathbf{n}) \cdot b(\mathbf{Y},\mathbf{n})$$

Factoring out the class priors $p(\mathbf{p})$ and $p(\mathbf{n})$, we get the final equation:

Equation 7-2. Expected profit equation with priors p(p) and p(n) factored.

$$\text{Expected profit} = p(\mathbf{p}) \cdot [p(\mathbf{Y}|\mathbf{p}) \cdot b(\mathbf{Y},\mathbf{p}) + p(\mathbf{N}|\mathbf{p}) \cdot b(\mathbf{N},\mathbf{p})] + \\ p(\mathbf{n}) \cdot [p(\mathbf{N}|\mathbf{n}) \cdot b(\mathbf{N},\mathbf{n}) + p(\mathbf{Y}|\mathbf{n}) \cdot b(\mathbf{Y},\mathbf{n})]$$

From this mess, notice that we now have one component (the first one) corresponding to the expected profit from the positive examples, and another (the second one) corresponding to the expected profit from the negative examples. Each of these is weighted by the probability that we see that sort of example. So, if positive examples are very rare, their contribution to the overall expected profit will be correspondingly small. In this alternative formulation, the quantities $p(\mathbf{Y}|\mathbf{p})$, $p(\mathbf{Y}|\mathbf{n})$, etc. correspond directly to the true positive rate, the false positive rate, etc., that also can be calculated directly from the confusion matrix (see "Sidebar: Other Evaluation Metrics" on page 203).

Here again is our sample confusion matrix in Table 7-5.

Table 7-5. Our sample confusion matrix (raw counts)

	p	n
Y	56	7
N	5	42

Table 7-6 shows the class priors and various error rates we need.

Table 7-6. The class priors and the rates of true positives, false positives, and so on.

T = 110

P = 61	N = 49
$p(\mathbf{p}) = 0.55$	$p(\mathbf{n}) = 0.45$
tp rate = 56/61 = 0.92	fp rate = 7/49 = 0.14
fn rate = 5/61 = 0.08	tn rate = 42/49 = 0.86

Returning to the targeted marketing example, what is the expected profit of the model learned? We can calculate it using Equation 7-2:

$$
\begin{aligned}
\text{expected profit} \ &= \ p(\mathbf{p}) \cdot [\,p(\mathbf{Y}|\mathbf{p}) \cdot b(\mathbf{Y}, \mathbf{p}) + p(\mathbf{N}|\mathbf{p}) \cdot b(\mathbf{N}, \mathbf{p})\,] + \\
&\quad\ p(\mathbf{n}) \cdot [\,p(\mathbf{N}|\mathbf{n}) \cdot b(\mathbf{N}, \mathbf{n}) + p(\mathbf{Y}|\mathbf{n}) \cdot b(\mathbf{Y}, \mathbf{n})\,] \\
&= \ 0.55 \cdot [0.92 \cdot b(\mathbf{Y}, \mathbf{p}) + 0.08 \cdot b(\mathbf{N}, \mathbf{p})] + \\
&\quad\ 0.45 \cdot [0.86 \cdot b(\mathbf{N}, \mathbf{n}) + 0.14 \cdot b(\mathbf{Y}, \mathbf{n})] \\
&= \ 0.55 \cdot [0.92 \cdot 99 + 0.08 \cdot 0] + \\
&\quad\ 0.45 \cdot [0.86 \cdot 0 + 0.14 \cdot -1] \\
&= \ 50.1 - 0.063 \\
&\approx \ \$50.04
\end{aligned}
$$

This expected value means that if we apply this model to a population of prospective customers and mail offers to those it classifies as positive, we can expect to make an average of about $50 profit per consumer.

We now can see one way to deal with our motivating example from the beginning of the chapter. Instead of computing accuracies for the competing models, we would compute expected values. Furthermore, using this alternative formulation, we can compare the two models even though one analyst tested using a representative distribution and the other tested using a class-balanced distribution. In each calculation, we simply can replace the priors. Using a balanced distribution corresponds to priors of $p(\mathbf{p}) = 0.5$ and $p(\mathbf{n}) = 0.5$. The mathematically savvy reader is encouraged to convince herself that the other factors in the equation will not change if the test-set priors change.

 To close this section on estimated profit, we emphasize two pitfalls that are common when formulating cost-benefit matrices:

- It is important to make sure the signs of quantities in the cost-benefit matrix are consistent. In this book we take benefits to be positive and costs to be negative. In many data mining studies, the focus is on minimizing cost rather than maximizing profit, so the signs are reversed. Mathematically, there is no difference. However, it is important to pick one view and be consistent.

- An easy mistake in formulating cost-benefit matrices is to "double count" by putting a benefit in one cell and a negative cost *for the same thing* in another cell (or vice versa). A useful practical test is to compute the *benefit improvement* for changing the decision on an example test instance.

For example, say you've built a model to predict which accounts have been defrauded. You've determined that a fraud case costs $1,000 on average. If you decide that the benefit of catching fraud is therefore +$1,000/case on average, *and* the cost of missing fraud is -$1,000/case, then what would be the *improvement in benefit* for catching a case of fraud? You would calculate:

$b(\mathbf{Y},\mathbf{p}) - b(\mathbf{N},\mathbf{p}) = \$1000 - (-\$1000) = \$2000$

But intuitively you know that this improvement should only be about $1,000, so this error indicates double counting. The solution is to specify either that the benefit of catching fraud is $1,000 *or* that the cost of missing fraud is -$1,000, but not both. One should be zero.

Sidebar: Other Evaluation Metrics

There are many evaluation metrics you will likely encounter in data science. All of them are fundamentally summaries of the confusion matrix. Referring to the counts in the confusion matrix, let's abbreviate the number of true positives, false positives, true negatives, and false negatives by *TP*, *FP*, *TN*, and *FN*, respectively. We can describe various evaluation metrics using these counts. *True positive rate* and *False negative rate* refer to the frequency of being correct and incorrect, respectively, when the instance is actually positive: $TP/(TP + FN)$ and $FN/(TP + FN)$. The *True negative rate* and *False positive rate* are analogous for the instances that are actually negative. These are often taken as estimates of the probability of predicting **Y** when the instance is actually **p**, that is $p(\mathbf{Y}|\mathbf{p})$, etc. We will continue to explore these measures in Chapter 8.

The metrics *Precision* and *Recall* are often used, especially in text classification and information retrieval. Recall is the same as true positive rate, while precision is $TP/(TP + FP)$, which is the accuracy over the cases predicted to be positive. The *F-measure* is the harmonic mean of precision and recall at a given point, and is:

$$\text{F-measure} = 2 \cdot \frac{\text{precision} \cdot \text{recall}}{\text{precision} + \text{recall}}$$

Practitioners in many fields such as statistics, pattern recognition, and epidemiology speak of the sensitivity and specificity of a classifier:

$$\text{Sensitivity} = TN/(TN + FP) = \text{True negative rate} = 1 - \text{False positive rate}$$
$$\text{Specificity} = TP/(TP + FN) = \text{True positive rate}$$

You may also hear about the *positive predictive value*, which is the same as precision.

Accuracy, as mentioned before, is simply the count of correct decisions divided by the total number of decisions, or:

$$Accuracy = \frac{TP + TN}{P + N}$$

Swets (1996) lists many other evaluation metrics and their relationships to the confusion matrix.

Evaluation, Baseline Performance, and Implications for Investments in Data

Up to this point we have talked about model evaluation in isolation. In some cases just demonstrating that a model generates *some* (nonzero) profit, or a positive return on investment, will be informative by itself. Nevertheless, another fundamental notion in data science is: *it is important to consider carefully what would be a reasonable baseline against which to compare model performance.* This is important for the data science team in order to understand whether they indeed are improving performance, and is equally important for demonstrating to stakeholders that mining the data has added value. So, what is an appropriate baseline for comparison?

The answer of course depends on the actual application, and coming up with suitable baselines is one task for the business understanding phase of the data mining process. However, there are some general principles that can be very helpful.

For classification models it is easy to simulate a completely random model and measure its performance. The visualization frameworks we will discuss in Chapter 8 have natural baselines showing what random classification should achieve. This is useful for very difficult problems or initial explorations. Comparison against a random model establishes that there is some information to be extracted from the data.

However, beating a random model may be easy (or may seem easy), so demonstrating superiority to it may not be very interesting or informative. A data scientist will often need to implement an alternative model, usually one that is simple but not simplistic, in order to justify continuing the data mining effort.

In Nate Silver's book on prediction, *The Signal and the Noise* (2012), he mentions the baseline issue with respect to weather forecasting:

> There are two basic tests that any weather forecast must pass to demonstrate its merit: It must do better than what meteorologists call persistence: the assumption that the weather will be the same tomorrow (and the next day) as it was today. It must also beat climatology, the long-term historical average of conditions on a particular date in a particular area.

In other words, weather forecasters have two simple—but not simplistic—baseline models that they compare against. One (persistence) predicts that the weather tomorrow is going to be whatever it was today. The other (climatology) predicts whatever the average historical weather has been on this day from prior years. Each model performs considerably better than random guessing, and both are so easy to compute that they make natural baselines of comparison. Any new, more complex model must beat these.

What are some general guidelines for good baselines? For classification tasks, one good baseline is the *majority classifier*, a naive classifier that always chooses the majority class of the training dataset (see Note: Base rate in "Holdout Data and Fitting Graphs" on page 113). This may seem like advice so obvious it can be passed over quickly, but it is worth spending an extra moment here. There are many cases where smart, analytical people have been tripped up in skipping over this basic comparison. For example, an analyst may see a classification accuracy of 94% from her classifier and conclude that it is doing fairly well—when in fact only 6% of the instances are positive. So, the simple majority prediction classifier also would have an accuracy of 94%. Indeed, many beginning data science students are surprised to find that the models they build from the data simply predict everything to be of the majority class. Note that this may make sense if the modeling procedure is set up to build maximum accuracy models—it may be hard to beat 94% accuracy. The answer, of course, is to apply the central idea of this chapter: consider carefully what is desired from the data mining results. Maximizing simple prediction accuracy is usually not an appropriate goal. If that's what our algorithm is doing, we're using the wrong algorithm. For regression problems we have a directly analogous baseline: predict the average value over the population (usually the mean or median).

In some applications there are multiple simple averages that one may want to combine. For example, when evaluating recommendation systems that internally predict how many "stars" a particular customer would give to a particular movie, we have the average number of stars a movie gets across the population (how well liked it is) and the average number of stars a particular customer gives to movies (what that customer's overall bias is). A simple prediction based on these two may do substantially better than using one or the other in isolation.

Moving beyond these simple baseline models, a slightly more complex alternative is a model that only considers a very small amount of feature information. For example, recall from Chapter 3 our very first example of a data mining procedure: finding informative variables. If we find the one variable that correlates best with the target, we can build a classification or regression model that uses just that variable, which gives another view of baseline performance: how well does a simple "conditional" model perform? "Conditional" here means that it predicts differently based on, or conditioned on, the value of the feature(s). The overall population average is therefore sometimes called the "unconditional" average.

One example of mining such single-feature predictive models from data is to use tree induction to build a "decision stump"—a decision tree with only one internal node, the root node. A tree limited to one internal node simply means that the tree induction selects the single most informative feature to make a decision. In a well-known paper in machine learning, Robert Holte (1993) showed that decision stumps often produce quite good baseline performance on many of the test datasets used in machine learning research. A decision stump is an example of the strategy of choosing the single most informative piece of information available (recall Chapter 3) and basing all decisions on it. In some cases most of the leverage may be coming from a single feature, and this method assesses whether and to what extent that is the case.

This idea can be extended to data *sources*, and relates to our fundamental principle from Chapter 1 that we should regard data as an asset to be invested in. If you are considering building models that integrate data from various sources, you should compare the result to models built from the individual sources. Often there are substantial costs to acquiring new sources of data. In some cases these are actual monetary costs; in other cases they involve commitments of personnel time for managing relationships with data providers and monitoring data feeds. To be thorough, for each data source the data science team should compare a model that uses the source to one that does not. Such comparisons help to justify the cost of each source by quantifying its value. If the contribution is negligible, the team may be able to reduce costs by eliminating it.

Beyond comparing simple models (and reduced-data models), it is often useful to implement simple, inexpensive models based on domain knowledge or "received wisdom" and evaluate their performance. For example, in one fraud detection application it was commonly believed that most defrauded accounts would experience a sudden increase in usage, and so checking accounts for sudden jumps in volume was sufficient for catching a large proportion of fraud. Implementing this idea was straightforward and it provided a useful baseline for demonstrating the benefit of data mining. (This essentially was a single-feature predictive model.) Similarly, an IBM team that used data mining to direct sales efforts chose to implement a simple sales model that prioritized existing customers by the size of previous revenue and other companies by annual sales.[3] They were able to demonstrate that their data mining added significant value beyond this simpler strategy. Whatever the data mining group chooses as a baseline for comparison, it should be something the stakeholders find informative, and hopefully persuasive.

Summary

A vital part of data science is arranging for proper evaluation of models. This can be surprisingly difficult to get right and will often require multiple iterations. It is tempting to use simple measures, such as classification accuracy, since these are simple to calculate, are used in many research papers, and may be what one learned in school. However, in real-world domains simplistic measures rarely capture what is actually important for the problem at hand, and often mislead. Instead, the data scientist should give careful thought to how the model will be used in practice and devise an appropriate metric.

The *expected value* calculation is a good framework for organizing this thinking. It will help to frame the evaluation, and in the event that the final deployed model produces unacceptable results, it will help identify what is wrong.

The characteristics of the data should be taken into account carefully when evaluating data science results. For example, real classification problems often present data with very unbalanced class distributions (that is, the classes will not occur with equal prevalence). Adjusting class proportions may be useful (or even necessary) to learn a model from the data; however, evaluation should use the original, realistic population so that the results reflect what will actually be achieved.

To calculate the overall expected value of a model, the costs and benefits of decisions must be specified. If this is possible, the data scientist can calculate an expected cost per instance for each model and choose whichever model produces the lowest expected cost or greatest profit.

It also is vital to consider what one should compare a data-driven model against, to judge whether it performs well or better. The answer to this question is intimately tied

---

3. They refer to these as Willy Sutton models, after the famed bank robber who robbed banks because "that's where the money is."

to the business understanding, but there are a variety of general best practices that data science teams should follow.

We illustrated the ideas of this chapter with applications of the concepts presented in the chapters that preceded. The concepts are more general of course, and relate to our very first fundamental concept: data should be considered an asset and we need to consider how to invest. We illustrated this point by discussing briefly that one not only can compare different models and different baselines, but also compare results with different data sources. Different data sources may have different associated costs, and careful evaluation may show which can be chosen to maximize the return on investment.

As a final summary point, this chapter has discussed single quantitative numbers as summary estimates of model performance. They can answer questions like "How much profit can I expect to make?" and "Should I use model A or model B?" Such answers are useful but provide only "single-point values" that hold under a specific set of assumptions. It is often revealing to visualize model behavior under a broad range of conditions. The next chapter discusses graphical views of model behavior that can do just this.

CHAPTER 8

Visualizing Model Performance

Fundamental concepts: *Visualization of model performance under various kinds of uncertainty; Further consideration of what is desired from data mining results.*

Exemplary techniques: *Profit curves; Cumulative response curves; Lift curves; ROC curves.*

The previous chapter introduced basic issues of model evaluation and explored the question of what makes for a good model. We developed detailed calculations based on the expected value framework. That chapter was much more mathematical than previous ones, and if this is your first introduction to that material you may have felt overwhelmed by the equations. Though they form the basis for what comes next, by themselves they may not be very intuitive. In this chapter we will take a different view to increase our understanding of what they are revealing.

The expected profit calculation of Equation 7-2 takes a specific set of conditions and generates a single number, representing the expected profit in that scenario. Stakeholders outside of the data science team may have little patience for details, and will often want a higher-level, more intuitive view of model performance. Even data scientists who are comfortable with equations and dry calculations often find such single estimates to be impoverished and uninformative, because they rely on very stringent assumptions (e.g., of precise knowledge of the costs and benefits, or that the models' estimates of probabilities are accurate). In short, it is often useful to present *visualizations* rather than just calculations, and this chapter presents some useful techniques.

Ranking Instead of Classifying

"A Key Analytical Framework: Expected Value" on page 194 discussed how the score assigned by a model can be used to compute a decision for each individual case based on its expected value. A different strategy for making decisions is to *rank* a set of cases by these scores, and then take actions on the cases at the top of the ranked list. Instead of deciding each case separately, we may decide to take the top *n* cases (or, equivalently, all cases that score above a given threshold). There are several practical reasons for doing this.

It may be that the model gives a score that ranks cases by their likelihood of belonging to the class of interest, but which is not a true probability (recall our discussion in Chapter 4 of the distance from the separating boundary as a classifier score). More importantly, for some reason we may not be able to obtain accurate probability estimates from the classifier. This happens, for example, in targeted marketing applications when one cannot get a sufficiently representative training sample. The classifier scores may still be very useful for deciding which prospects are better than others, even if a 1% probability estimate doesn't exactly correspond to a 1% probability of responding.

A common situation is where you have a *budget* for actions, such as a fixed marketing budget for a campaign, and so you want to target the most promising candidates. If one is going to target the highest expected value cases using costs and benefits that are constant for each class, then ranking cases by likelihood of the target class is sufficient. There is no great need to care about the precise probability estimates. The only caveat is that the budget be small enough so that the actions do not go into negative expected-value territory. For now, we will leave that as a business understanding task.

It also may be that costs and benefits cannot be specified precisely, but nevertheless we would like to take actions (and are happy to do so on the highest likelihood cases). We'll return to this situation in the next section.

 If *individual* cases have different costs and benefits, then our expected value discussion in "A Key Analytical Framework: Expected Value" on page 194 should make it clear that simply ranking by likelihood will not be sufficient.

When working with a classifier that gives scores to instances, in some situations the classifier decisions should be very conservative, corresponding to the fact that the classifier should have high certainty before taking the positive action. This corresponds to using a high threshold on the output score. Conversely, in some situations the classifier can be more permissive, which corresponds to lowering the threshold.[1]

This introduces a complication for which we need to extend our analytical framework for assessing and comparing models. "The Confusion Matrix" on page 189 stated that a classifier produces a confusion matrix. With a ranking classifier, a classifier *plus a threshold* produces a single confusion matrix. Whenever the threshold changes, the

---

1. Indeed, in some applications, scores from the same model may be used in several places with different thresholds to make different decisions. For example, a model may be used first in a decision to grant or deny credit. The same model may be used later in setting a new customer's credit line.

confusion matrix may change as well because the numbers of true positives and false positives change.

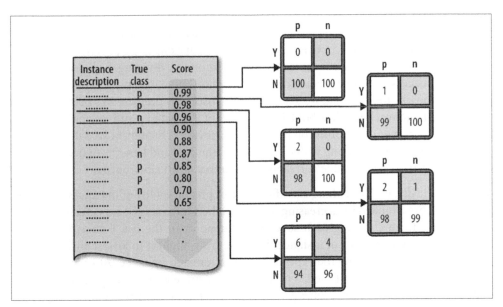

Figure 8-1. Thresholding a list of instances sorted by scores. Here, a set of test instances is scored by a model and sorted decreasing by these scores. We then apply a series of thresholds (represented by each horizontal line) to classify all instances above it as positive and those below it as negative. Each threshold results in a specific confusion matrix.

Figure 8-1 illustrates this basic idea. As the threshold is lowered, instances move up from the **N** row into the **Y** row of the confusion matrix: an instance that was considered a negative is now classified as positive, so the counts change. Which counts change depends on the example's true class. If the instance was a positive (in the "**p**" column) it moves up and becomes a true positive (**Y,p**). If it was a negative (**n**), it becomes a false positive (**Y,n**). Technically, each different threshold produces a different classifier, represented by its own confusion matrix.

This leaves us with two questions: how do we compare different *rankings*? And, how do we choose a proper *threshold*? If we have accurate probability estimates and a well-specified cost-benefit matrix, then we already answered the second question in our discussion of expected value: we determine the threshold where our expected profit is above a desired level (usually zero). Let's explore and extend this idea.

Profit Curves

From "A Key Analytical Framework: Expected Value" on page 194, we know how to compute expected profit, and we've just introduced the idea of using a model to rank instances. We can combine these ideas to construct various performance visualizations in the form of curves. Each curve is based on the idea of examining the effect of thresholding the value of a classifier at successive points, implicitly dividing the list of instances into many successive sets of predicted positive and negative instances. As we move the threshold "down" the ranking, we get additional instances predicted as being positive rather than negative. Each threshold, i.e., each set of predicted positives and negatives, will have a corresponding confusion matrix. The previous chapter showed that once we have a confusion matrix, along with knowledge of the cost and benefits of decisions, we can generate an expected value corresponding to that confusion matrix.

More specifically, with a ranking classifier, we can produce a list of instances and their predicted scores, ranked by decreasing score, and then measure the expected profit that would result from choosing each successive cut-point in the list. Conceptually, this amounts to ranking the list of instances by score from highest to lowest and sweeping down through it, recording the expected profit after each instance. At each cut-point we record the percentage of the list predicted as positive and the corresponding estimated profit. Graphing these values gives us a *profit curve*. Three profit curves are shown in Figure 8-2.

This graph is based on a test set of 1,000 consumers—say, a small random population of people to whom you test-marketed earlier. (When interpreting results, we normally will talk about percentages of consumers, so as to generalize to the population as a whole.) For each curve, the consumers are ordered from highest to lowest probability of accepting an offer based on some model. For this example, let's assume our profit margin is small: each offer costs $5 to make and market, and each accepted offer earns $9, for a profit of $4. The cost matrix is thus:

	p	n
Y	$4	-$5
N	$0	$0

The curves show that profit can go negative—not always, but sometimes they will, depending on the costs and the class ratio. In particular, this will happen when the profit margin is thin and the number of responders is small, because the curves show you "going into the red" by working too far down the list and making offers to too many people who won't respond, thereby spending too much on the costs of the offers.[2]

---

2. For simplicity in the example we will ignore inventory and other realistic issues that would require a more complicated profit calculation.

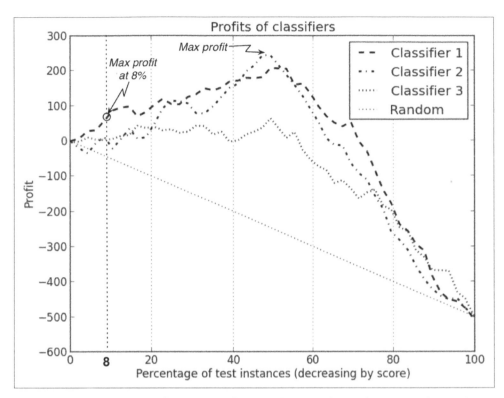

Figure 8-2. Profit curves of three classifiers. Each curve shows the expected cumulative profit for that classifier as progressively larger proportions of the consumer base are targeted.

Notice that all four curves begin and end at the same point. This should make sense because, at the left side, when no customers are targeted there are no expenses and zero profit; at the right side everyone is targeted, so every classifier performs the same. In between, we'll see some differences depending on how the classifiers order the customers. The random classifier performs worst because it has an even chance of choosing a responder or a nonresponder. Among the classifiers tested here, the one labeled Classifier 2 produces the maximum profit of $200 by targeting the top-ranked 50% of consumers. If your goal was simply to maximize profit and you had unlimited resources, you should choose Classifier 2, use it to score your population of customers, and target the top half (highest 50%) of customers on the list.

Now consider a slightly different but very common situation where you're constrained by a *budget*. You have a fixed amount of money available and you must plan how to spend it before you see any profit. This is common in situations such as marketing campaigns. As before, you still want to target the highest-ranked people, but now you have a budgetary constraint[3] that may affect your strategy. Say you have 100,000 total customers and a budget of $40,000 for the marketing campaign. You want to use the modeling results (the profit curves in Figure 8-2) to figure out how best to spend your budget. What do you do in this case? Well, first you figure out how many offers you can afford to make. Each offer costs $5 so you can target at most $40,000/$5 = 8,000 customers. As before, you want to identify the customers most likely to respond, but each model ranks customers differently. Which model should you use for this campaign? 8,000 customers is 8% of your total customer base, so check the performance curves at $x=8\%$. The best-performing model at this performance point is Classifier 1. You should use it to score the entire population, then send offers to the highest-ranked 8,000 customers.

In summary, from this scenario we see that adding a budgetary constraint causes not only a change in the operating point (targeting 8% of the population instead of 50%) but also a change in the choice of classifier to do the ranking.

ROC Graphs and Curves

Profit curves are appropriate when you know fairly certainly the conditions under which a classifier will be used. Specifically, there are two critical conditions underlying the profit calculation:

1. The *class priors*; that is, the proportion of positive and negative instances in the target population, also known as the *base rate* (usually referring to the proportion of positives). Recall that Equation 7-2 is sensitive to $p(\mathbf{p})$ and $p(\mathbf{n})$.

2. The *costs and benefits*. The expected profit is specifically sensitive to the relative levels of costs and benefits for the different cells of the cost-benefit matrix.

If both class priors and cost-benefit estimates are known and are expected to be stable, profit curves may be a good choice for visualizing model performance.

However, in many domains these conditions are uncertain or unstable. In fraud detection domains, for example, the amount of fraud changes from place to place, and from one month to the next (Leigh, 1995; Fawcett & Provost, 1997). The amount of fraud influences the priors. In the case of mobile phone churn management, marketing campaigns can have different budgets and offers may have different costs, which will change the expected costs.

---

3. Another common situation is to have a *workforce constraint*. It's the same idea: you have a fixed allocation of resources (money or personnel) available to address a problem and you want the most "bang for the buck." An example might be that you have a fixed workforce of fraud analysts, and you want to give them the top-ranked cases of potential fraud to process.

One approach to handling uncertain conditions is to generate many different expected profit calculations for each model. This may not be very satisfactory: the sets of models, sets of class priors, and sets of decision costs multiply in complexity. This often leaves the analyst with a large stack of profit graphs that are difficult to manage, difficult to understand the implications of, and difficult to explain to a stakeholder.

Another approach is to use a method that can accomodate uncertainty by showing the entire space of performance possibilities. One such method is the Receiver Operating Characteristics (ROC) graph (Swets, 1988; Swets, Dawes, & Monahan, 2000; Fawcett, 2006). A ROC graph is a two-dimensional plot of a classifier with false positive rate on the x axis against true positive rate on the y axis. As such, a ROC graph depicts relative trade-offs that a classifier makes between benefits (true positives) and costs (false positives). Figure 8-3 shows a ROC graph with five classifiers labeled **A** through **E**.

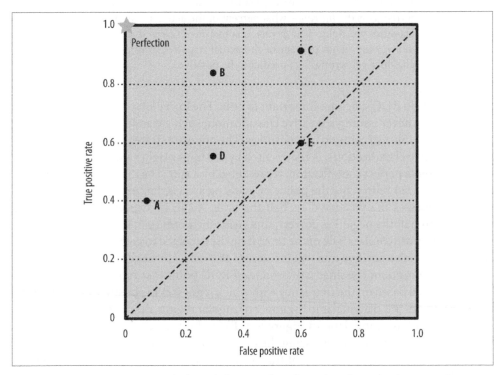

Figure 8-3. ROC space and five different classifiers (A-E) with their performance shown.

A *discrete* classifier is one that outputs only a class label (as opposed to a ranking). As already discussed, each such classifier produces a confusion matrix, which can be summarized by certain statistics regarding the numbers and rates of true positives, false positives, true negatives, and false negatives. Note that although the confusion matrix contains four numbers, we really only need two of the rates: either the true positive rate or the false negative rate, and either the false positive rate or the true negative rate. Given one from either pair the other can be derived since they sum to one. It is conventional to use the true positive rate (*tp rate*) and the false positive rate (*fp rate*), and we will keep to that convention so the ROC graph will make sense. Each discrete classifier produces an (*fp rate*, *tp rate*) pair corresponding to a single point in ROC space. The classifiers in Figure 8-3 are all discrete classifiers. Importantly for what follows, the *tp rate* is computed using only the actual positive examples, and the *fp rate* is computed using only the actual negative examples.

 Remembering exactly what statistics the *tp rate* and *fp rate* refer to can be confusing for someone who does not deal with such things on a daily basis. It can be easier to remember by using less formal but more intuitive names for the statistics: the *tp rate* is sometimes referred to as the *hit rate*—what percent of the actual positives does the classifier get right. The *fp rate* is sometimes referred to as the *false alarm rate*—what percent of the actual negative examples does the classifier get wrong (i.e., predict to be positive).

Several points in ROC space are important to note. The lower left point (0, 0) represents the strategy of never issuing a positive classification; such a classifier commits no false positive errors but also gains no true positives. The opposite strategy, of unconditionally issuing positive classifications, is represented by the upper right point (1, 1). The point (0, 1) represents perfect classification, represented by a star. The diagonal line connecting (0, 0) to (1, 1) represents the policy of guessing a class. For example, if a classifier randomly guesses the positive class half the time, it can be expected to get half the positives and half the negatives correct; this yields the point (0.5, 0.5) in ROC space. If it guesses the positive class 90% of the time, it can be expected to get 90% of the positives correct but its false positive rate will increase to 90% as well, yielding (0.9, 0.9) in ROC space. Thus a random classifier will produce a ROC point that moves back and forth on the diagonal based on the frequency with which it guesses the positive class. In order to get away from this diagonal into the upper triangular region, the classifier must exploit some information in the data. In Figure 8-3, **E**'s performance at (0.6, 0.6) is virtually random. **E** may be said to be guessing the positive class 60% of the time. Note that no classifier should be in the lower right triangle of a ROC graph. This represents performance that is worse than random guessing.

One point in ROC space is superior to another if it is to the northwest of the first (*tp rate* is higher and *fp rate* is no worse; *fp rate* is lower and *tp rate* is no worse, or both are better). Classifiers appearing on the lefthand side of a ROC graph, near the *x* axis, may be thought of as "conservative": they raise alarms (make positive classifications) only with strong evidence so they make few false positive errors, but they often have low true positive rates as well. Classifiers on the upper righthand side of a ROC graph may be thought of as "permissive": they make positive classifications with weak evidence so they classify nearly all positives correctly, but they often have high false positive rates. In Figure 8-3, **A** is more conservative than **B**, which in turn is more conservative than **C**. Many real-world domains are dominated by large numbers of negative instances (see the discussion in "Sidebar: Bad Positives and Harmless Negatives" on page 188), so performance in the far left-hand side of the ROC graph is often more interesting than elsewhere. If there are many negative examples, even a moderate false alarm *rate* can be unmanageable. A ranking model produces a set of points (a curve) in ROC space. As discussed previously, a ranking model can be used with a threshold to produce a discrete (binary) classifier: if the classifier output is above the threshold, the classifier produces a **Y**, else an **N**. Each threshold value produces a different point in ROC space, as shown in Figure 8-4.

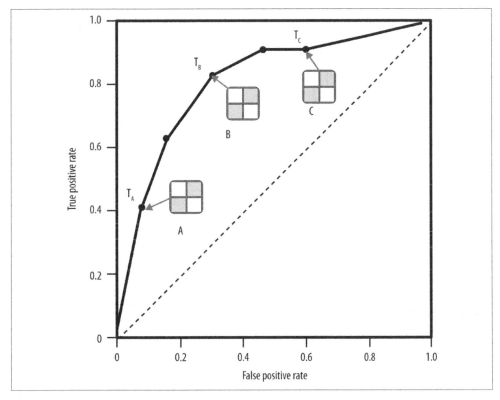

Figure 8-4. Each different point in ROC space corresponds to a specific confusion matrix.

Conceptually, we may imagine sorting the instances by score and varying a threshold from $-\infty$ to $+\infty$ while tracing a curve through ROC space, as shown in Figure 8-5. Whenever we pass a positive instance, we take a step upward (increasing true positives);

whenever we pass a negative instance, we take a step rightward (increasing false positives). Thus the "curve" is actually a step function for a single test set, but with enough instances it appears smooth.[4]

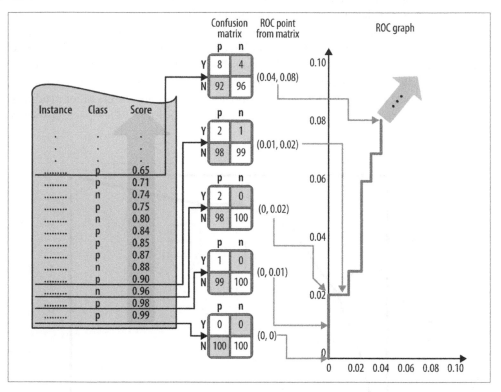

*Figure 8-5. An illustration of how a ROC "curve" (really, a stepwise graph) is constructed from a test set. The example set, at left, consists of 100 positives and 100 negatives. The model assigns a score to each instance and the instances are ordered decreasing from bottom to top. To construct the curve, start at the bottom with an initial confusion matrix where everything is classified as **N**. Moving upward, every instance moves a count of 1 from the **N** row to the **Y** row, resulting in a new confusion matrix. Each confusion matrix maps to a (fp rate, tp rate) pair in ROC space.*

An advantage of ROC graphs is that they decouple classifier performance from the conditions under which the classifiers will be used. Specifically, they are independent of the class proportions as well as the costs and benefits. A data scientist can plot the performance of classifiers on a ROC graph as they are generated, knowing that the

---

4. Technically, if there are runs of examples with the same score, we should count the positive and negatives across the entire run, and thus the ROC curve will have a sloping step rather than square step.

positions and relative performance of the classifiers will not change. The region(s) on the ROC graph that are of interest may change as costs, benefits, and class proportions change, but the curves themselves should not.

Both Stein (2005) and Provost & Fawcett (1997, 2001) show how the operating conditions of the classifier (the class priors and error costs) can be combined to identify the region of interest on its ROC curve. Briefly, knowledge about the range of possible class priors can be combined with knowledge about the cost and benefits of decisions; together these describe a family of tangent lines that can identify which classifier(s) should be used under those conditions. Stein (2005) presents an example from finance (loan defaulting) and shows how this technique can be used to choose models.

The Area Under the ROC Curve (AUC)

An important summary statistic is the *area under the ROC curve* (AUC). As the name implies, this is simply the area under a classifier's curve expressed as a fraction of the unit square. Its value ranges from zero to one. Though a ROC curve provides more information than its area, the AUC is useful when a single number is needed to summarize performance, or when nothing is known about the operating conditions. Later, in "Example: Performance Analytics for Churn Modeling" on page 223, we will show a use of the AUC statistic. For now it is enough to realize that it's a good general summary statistic of the predictiveness of a classifier.

 As a technical note, the AUC is equivalent to the Mann-Whitney-Wilcoxon measure, a well-known ordering measure in Statistics (Wilcoxon, 1945). It is also equivalent to the Gini Coefficient, with a minor algebraic transformation (Adams & Hand, 1999; Stein, 2005). Both are equivalent to the probability that a randomly chosen positive instance will be ranked ahead of a randomly chosen negative instance.

Cumulative Response and Lift Curves

ROC curves are a common tool for visualizing model performance for classification, class probability estimation, and scoring. However, as you may have just experienced if you are new to all this, ROC curves are not the most intuitive visualization for many business stakeholders who really ought to understand the results. It is important for the data scientist to realize that clear communication with key stakeholders is not only a primary goal of her job, but also is essential for doing the right modeling (in addition to doing the modeling right). Therefore, it can be useful also to consider visualization frameworks that might not have all of the nice properties of ROC curves, but are more intuitive. (It is important for the business stakeholder to realize that the theoretical properties that are sacrificed sometimes are important, so it may be necessary in certain circumstances to pull out the more complex visualizations.)

One of the most common examples of the use of an alternate visualization is the use of the "cumulative response curve," rather than the ROC curve. They are closely related, but the cumulative response curve is more intuitive. Cumulative response curves plot the hit rate (*tp* rate; *y* axis), *i.e.*, the *percentage of positives correctly classified*, as a function of the percentage of the population that is targeted (*x* axis). So, conceptually as we move down the list of instances ranked by the model, we target increasingly larger proportions of all the instances. Hopefully in the process, if the model is any good, when we are at the top of the list we will target a larger proportion of the actual positives than actual negatives. As with ROC curves, the diagonal line $x=y$ represents random performance. In this case, the intuition is clear: if you target 20% of all instances completely randomly, you should target 20% of the positives as well. Any classifier above the diagonal is providing some advantage.

 The cumulative response curve is sometimes called a *lift curve*, because one can see the increase over simply targeting randomly as how much the line representing the model performance is lifted up over the random performance diagonal. We will call these curves cumulative response curves, because "lift curve" also refers to a curve that specifically plots the numeric lift.

Intuitively, the lift of a classifier represents the advantage it provides over random guessing. The lift is the degree to which it "pushes up" the positive instances in a list above the negative instances. For example, consider a list of 100 customers, half of whom churn (positive instances) and half who do not (negative instances). If you scan down the list and stop halfway (representing 0.5 targeted), how many positives would you expect to have seen in the first half? If the list were sorted randomly, you would expect to have seen only half the positives (0.5), giving a lift of 0.5/0.5 = 1. If the list had been ordered by an effective ranking classifier, more than half the positives should appear in the top half of the list, producing a lift greater than 1. If the classifier were *perfect*, all positives would be ranked at the top of the list so by the midway point we would have seen all of them (1.0), giving a lift of 1.0/0.5 = 2.

Figure 8-6 shows four sample cumulative response curves, and Figure 8-7 shows the lift curves of the same four.

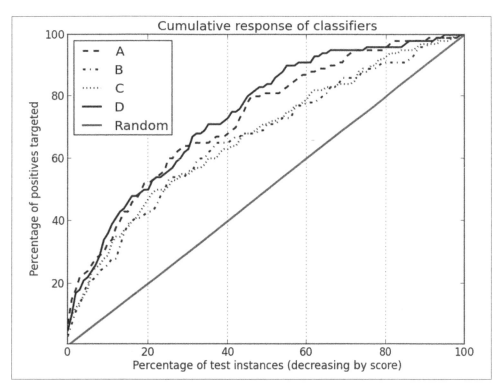

Figure 8-6. Four example classifiers (A–D) and their cumulative response curves.

The lift curve is essentially the value of the cumulative response curve at a given x point divided by the diagonal line ($y=x$) value at that point. The diagonal line of a cumulative response curve becomes a horizontal line at $y=1$ on the lift curve.

Sometimes you will hear claims like "our model gives a two times (or a 2X) lift"; this means that at the chosen threshold (often not mentioned), the lift curve shows that the model's targeting is twice as good as random. On the cumulative response curve, the corresponding *tp rate* for the model will be twice the *tp rate* for the random-performance diagonal. (You might also compute a version of lift with respect to some other baseline.) The lift curve plots this numeric lift on the y axis, against the percent of the population targeted on the x axis (the same x axis as the cumulative response curve).

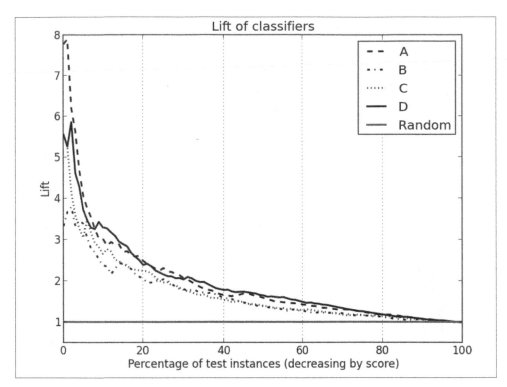

Figure 8-7. The four classifiers (A–D) of Figure 8-6 and their lift curves.

Both lift curves and cumulative response curves must be used with care if the exact proportion of positives in the population is unknown or is not represented accurately in the test data. Unlike for ROC curves, these curves assume that the test set has exactly the same target class priors as the population to which the model will be applied. This is one of the simplifying assumptions that we mentioned at the outset, that can allow us to use a more intuitive visualization.

As an example, in online advertising the base rate of observed response to an advertisement may be very small. One in ten million ($1:10^7$) is not unusual. Modelers may not want to have to manage datasets that have ten million nonresponders for every responder, so they down-sample the nonresponders, and create a more balanced dataset for modeling and evaluation. When visualizing classifier performance with ROC curves, this will have no effect (because as mentioned above, the axes each correspond only to proportions of one class). However, lift and cumulative response curves will be different —the basic shapes of the curves may still be informative, but the relationships between the values on the axes will not be valid.

Example: Performance Analytics for Churn Modeling

The last few chapters have covered a lot of territory in evaluation. We've introduced several important methods and issues in evaluating models. In this section we tie them together with a single application case study to show the results of different evaluation methods. The example we'll use is our ongoing domain of cell phone churn. However, in this section we use a different (and more difficult) churn dataset than was used in previous chapters. It is a dataset from the 2009 KDD Cup data mining competition (*http://www.kddcup-orange.com/*). We did not use this dataset in earlier examples, such as Table 3-2 and Figure 3-18, because these attribute names and values have been anonymized extensively to preserve customer privacy. This leaves very little meaning in the attributes and their values, which would have interfered with our discussions. However, we can demonstrate the model performance analytics with the sanitized data. From the website:

> The KDD Cup 2009 offers the opportunity to work on large marketing databases from the French Telecom company Orange to predict the propensity of customers to switch provider (churn), buy new products or services (appetency), or buy upgrades or add-ons proposed to them to make the sale more profitable (up-selling). The most practical way, in a CRM system, to build knowledge on customer is to produce scores.
>
> A score (the output of a model) is an evaluation for all instances of a target variable to explain (i.e., churn, appetency or up-selling). Tools which produce scores allow to project, on a given population, quantifiable information. The score is computed using input variables which describe instances. Scores are then used by the information system (IS), for example, to personalize the customer relationship.

Little of the dataset is worth describing because it has been thoroughly sanitized, but its class skew is worth mentioning. There are about 47,000 instances altogether, of which about 7% are marked as churn (positive examples) and the remaining 93% are not (negatives). This is not severe skew, but it's worth noting for reasons that will become clear.

We emphasize that the intention is not to propose good solutions for this problem, or to suggest which models might work well, but simply to use the domain as a testbed to illustrate the ideas about evaluation we've been developing. Little effort has been done to tune performance. We will train and test several models: a classification tree, a logistic regression equation, and a nearest-neighbor model. We will also use a simple Bayesian classifier called Naive Bayes, not discussed until Chapter 9. For the purpose of this section, details of the models are unimportant; all the models are "black boxes" with different performance characteristics. We're using the evaluation and visualization techniques introduced in the last chapters to understand their characteristics.

Let's begin with a very naive evaluation. We'll train on the complete dataset and then test on the *same* dataset we trained on. We'll also measure simple classification accuracies. The results are shown in Table 8-1.

Table 8-1. Accuracy values of four classifiers trained and tested on the complete KDD Cup 2009 churn problem.

Model	Accuracy
Classification tree	95%
Logistic regression	93%
k-Nearest Neighbor	100%
Naive Bayes	76%

Several things are striking here. First, there appears to be a wide range of performance —from 76% to 100%. Also, since the dataset has a base rate of 93%, any classifier should be able to achieve at least this minimum accuracy. This makes the Naive Bayes result look strange since it's significantly worse. Also, at 100% accuracy, the *k*-Nearest Neighbor classifier looks suspiciously good.[5]

But this test was performed on the training set, and by now (having read Chapter 5) you realize such numbers are unreliable, if not completely meaningless. They are more likely to be an indication of how well each classifier can memorize (overfit) the training set than anything else. So instead of investigating these numbers further, let's redo the evaluation properly using separate training and test sets. We could just split the dataset in half, but instead we'll use the cross-validation procedure discussed in "From Holdout Evaluation to Cross-Validation" on page 126. This will not only ensure proper separation of datasets but also provide a measure of variation in results. The results are shown in Table 8-2.

Table 8-2. Accuracy and AUC values of four classifiers on the KDD Cup 2009 churn problem. These values are from ten-fold cross-validation.

Model	Accuracy (%)	AUC
Classification Tree	91.8 ± 0.0	0.614 ± 0.014
Logistic Regression	93.0 ± 0.1	0.574 ± 0.023
k-Nearest Neighbor	93.0 ± 0.0	0.537 ± 0.015
Naive Bayes	76.5 ± 0.6	0.632 ± 0.019

5. Optimism can be a fine thing, but as a rule of thumb in data mining, any results that show perfect performance on a real-world problem should be mistrusted.

Each number is an average of ten-fold cross validation followed by a "±" sign and the standard deviation of the measurements. Including a standard deviation may be regarded as a kind of "sanity check": a large standard deviation indicates the test results are very erratic, which could be the source of various problems such as the dataset being too small or the model being a very poor match to a portion of the problem.

The accuracy numbers have all dropped considerably, except for Naive Bayes, which is still oddly low. The standard deviations are fairly small compared to the means so there is not a great deal of variation in the performance on the folds. This is good.

At the far right is a second value, the Area Under the ROC Curve (commonly abbreviated AUC). We briefly discussed this AUC measure back in "The Area Under the ROC Curve (AUC)" on page 219, noting it as a good general summary statistic of the predictiveness of a classifier. It varies from zero to one. A value of 0.5 corresponds to randomness (the classifier cannot distinguish at all between positives and negatives) and a value of one means that it is perfect in distinguishing them. One of the reasons accuracy is a poor metric is that it is misleading when datasets are skewed, which this one is (93% negatives and 7% positives).

Recall that we introduced fitting curves back in "Overfitting Examined" on page 113 as a way to detect when a model is overfitting. Figure 8-8 shows fitting curves for the classification tree model on this churn domain. The idea is that as a model is allowed to get more and more complex it typically fits the data more and more closely, but at some point it is simply memorizing idiosyncracies of the particular training set rather than learning general characteristics of the population. A fitting curve plots model complexity (in this case, the number of nodes in the tree) against a performance measure (in this case, AUC) using two datasets: the set it was trained upon and a separate holdout set. When performance on the holdout set starts to decrease, overfitting is occurring, and Figure 8-8 does indeed follow this general pattern.[6] The classification tree definitely *is* overfitting, and the other models probably are too. The "sweet spot" where holdout performance is maximum is at about 100 tree nodes, beyond which the performance on the holdout data declines.

---

6. Note that the *x* axis is log scale so the righthand side of the graph looks compressed.

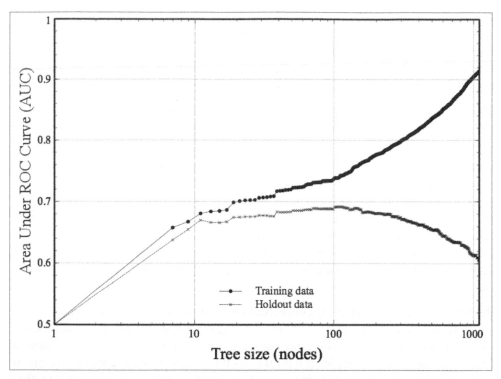

Figure 8-8. Fitting curves for a classification tree on the churn data: the change in the area under the ROC curve (AUC) as we increase the allowed complexity (size) of the tree. The performance on the training data (upper curve) continues to increase whereas the performance on the holdout data peaks and then declines.

Let's return to the model comparison figures in Table 8-2. These values are taken from a reasonably careful evaluation using holdout data, so they are less suspicious. However, they do raise some questions. There are two things to note about the AUC values. One is that they are all fairly modest. This is unsurprising with real-world domains: many datasets simply have little signal to be exploited, or the data science problem is formulated after the easier problems have already been solved. Customer churn is a difficult problem so we shouldn't be too surprised by these modest AUC scores. Even modest AUC scores may lead to good business results.

The second interesting point is that Naive Bayes, which has the *lowest* accuracy of the group, has the *highest* AUC score in Table 8-2. What's going on here? Let's take a look at a sample confusion matrix of Naive Bayes, with the highest AUC and lowest accuracy, and compare it with the confusion matrix of *k*-NN (lowest AUC and high accuracy) on the same dataset. Here is the Naive Bayes confusion matrix:

	p	n
Y	127 (3%)	848 (18%)
N	200 (4%)	3518 (75%)

Here is the *k*-Nearest Neighbors confusion matrix on the same test data:

	p	n
Y	3 (0%)	15 (0%)
N	324 (7%)	4351 (93%)

We see from the *k*-NN matrix that it rarely predicts churn—the Y row is almost empty. In other words, it is performing very much like a base-rate classifier, with a total accuracy of just about 93%. On the other hand, the Naive Bayes classifier makes more mistakes (so its accuracy is lower) but it identifies many more of the churners. Figure 8-9 shows the ROC curves of a typical fold of the cross-validation procedure. Note that the curves corresponding to Naive Bayes (NB) and Classification Tree (Tree) are somewhat more "bowed" than the others, indicating their predictive superiority.

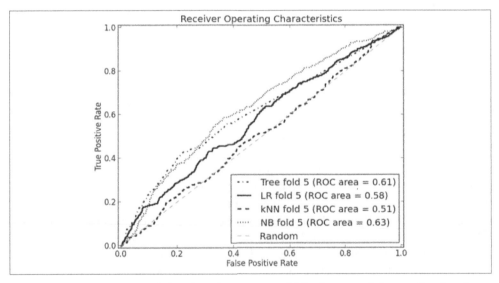

Figure 8-9. ROC curves of the classifiers on one fold of cross-validation for the churn problem.

As we said, ROC curves have a number of nice technical properties but they can be hard to read. The degree of "bowing" and the relative superiority of one curve to another can be difficult to judge by eye. Lift and profit curves are sometimes preferable, so let's examine these.

Lift curves have the advantage that they don't require us to commit to any costs yet so we begin with those, shown in Figure 8-10.

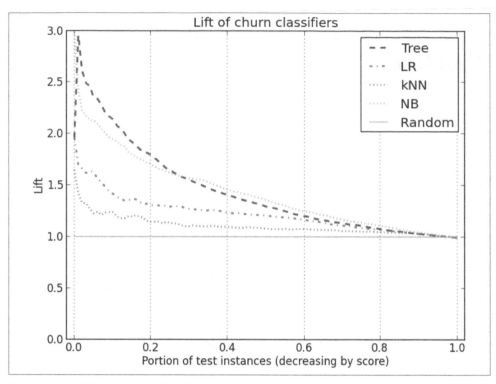

Figure 8-10. Lift curves for the churn domain.

These curves are averaged over the 10 test sets of the cross-validation. The classifiers generally peak very early then trail off down to random performance (Lift=1). Both Tree (Classification tree) and NB (Naive Bayes) perform very well. Tree is superior up through about the first 25% of the instances, after which it is dominated by NB. Both k-NN and Logistic Regression (LR) perform poorly here and have no regions of superiority. Looking at this graph, if you wanted to target the top 25% or less of customers, you'd choose the classification tree model; if you wanted to go further down the list you should choose NB. Lift curves are sensitive to the class proportions, so if the ratio of churners to nonchurners changed these curves would change also.

A note on combining classifiers

Looking at these curves, you might wonder, *"If Tree is best for the top 25%, and NB is best for the remainder, why don't we just use Tree's top 25% then switch to NB's list for the rest?"* This is a clever idea, but you won't necessarily get the best of both classifiers that way. The reason, in short, is that the two orderings are different and you can't simply pick-and-choose segments from each and expect the result to be optimal. The evaluation curves are only valid for each model individually, and all bets are off when you start mixing orderings from each.

But classifiers *can* be combined in principled ways, such that the combination outperforms any individual classifier. Such combinations are called ensembles, and they are discussed in "Bias, Variance, and Ensemble Methods" on page 308.

Although the lift curve shows you the relative advantage of each model, it does *not* tell you how much profit you should expect to make—or even whether you'd make a profit at all. For that purpose we use a profit curve, which incorporates assumptions about costs and benefits and displays expected value.

Let's ignore the actual details of churn in wireless for the moment (we will return to these explicitly in Chapter 11). To make things interesting with this dataset, let's make two sets of assumptions about costs and benefits. In the first scenario, let's assume an expense of $3 for each offer and a gross benefit of $30, so a true positive gives us a net profit of $27 and a false positive gives a net loss of $3. This is a 9-to-1 profit ratio. The resulting profit curves are shown in Figure 8-11. The classification tree is superior for the highest cutoff thresholds, and Naive Bayes dominates for the remainder of the possible cutoff thresholds. Maximum profit would be achieved in this scenario by targeting roughly the first 20% of the population.

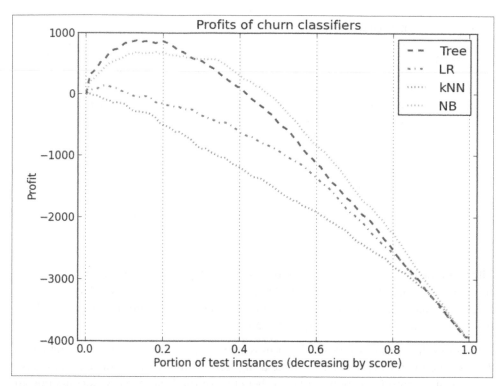

Figure 8-11. Profit curves of four classifiers on the churn domain, assuming a 9-to-1 ratio of benefit to cost.

In the second scenario, we assume the same expense of $3 for each offer (so the false positive cost doesn't change) but we assume a higher gross benefit ($39), so a true positive now nets us a profit of $36. This is a 12-to-1 profit ratio. The curves are shown in Figure 8-12. As you might expect, this scenario has much higher maximum profit than the previous scenario. More importantly it demonstrates different profit *maxima*. One peak is with the Classification Tree at about 20% of the population and the second peak, slightly higher, occurs when we target the top 35% of the population with NB. The crossover point between Tree and LR occurs at the same place on both graphs, however: at about 25% of the population. This illustrates the sensitivity of profit graphs to the particular assumptions about costs and benefits.

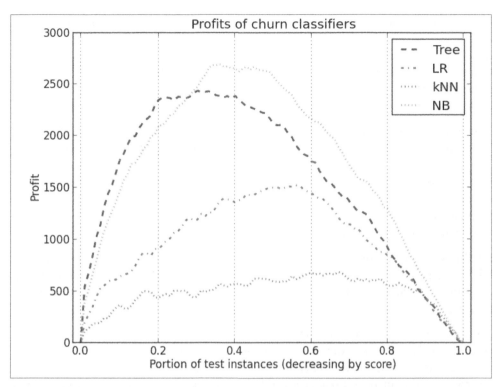

Figure 8-12. Profit curves of four classifiers on the churn domain. These curves assume a more lucrative 12-to-1 ratio (compare with Figure 8-11).

We conclude this section by reiterating that these graphs are just meant to illustrate the different techniques for model evaluation. Little effort was made to tune the induction methods to the problem, and no general conclusions should be drawn about the relative merits of these model types or their suitability for churn prediction. We deliberately produced a range of classifier performance to illustrate how the graphs could reveal their differences.

Summary

A critical part of the data scientist's job is arranging for proper evaluation of models and conveying this information to stakeholders. Doing this well takes experience, but it is vital in order to reduce surprises and to manage expectations among all concerned. Visualization of results is an important piece of the evaluation task.

When building a model from data, adjusting the training sample in various ways may be useful or even necessary; but evaluation should use a sample reflecting the original, realistic population so that the results reflect what will actually be achieved.

When the costs and benefits of decisions can be specified, the data scientist can calculate an expected cost per instance for each model and simply choose whichever model produces the best value. In some cases a basic *profit* graph can be useful to compare models of interest under a range of conditions. These graphs may be easy to comprehend for stakeholders who are not data scientists, since they reduce model performance to their basic "bottom line" cost or profit.

The disadvantage of a profit graph is that it requires that operating conditions be known and specified exactly. With many real-world problems, the operating conditions are imprecise or change over time, and the data scientist must contend with uncertainty. In such cases other graphs may be more useful. When costs and benefits cannot be specified with confidence, but the class mix will likely not change, a *cumulative response* or *lift* graph is useful. Both show the relative advantages of classifiers, independent of the value (monetary or otherwise) of the advantages.

Finally, ROC curves are a valuable visualization tool for the data scientist. Though they take some practice to interpret readily, they separate out performance from operating conditions. In doing so they convey the fundamental trade-offs that each model is making.

A great deal of work in the Machine Learning and Data Mining communities involves comparing classifiers in order to support various claims about learning algorithm superiority. As a result, much has been written about the methodology of classifier comparison. For the interested reader a good place to start is Thomas Dietterich's (1998) article "Approximate Statistical Tests for Comparing Supervised Classification Learning Algorithms," and the book *Evaluating Learning Algorithms: A Classification Perspective* (Japkowicz & Shah, 2011).

CHAPTER 9

Evidence and Probabilities

Fundamental concepts: *Explicit evidence combination with Bayes' Rule; Probabilistic reasoning via assumptions of conditional independence.*

Exemplary techniques: *Naive Bayes classification; Evidence lift.*

So far we have examined several different methods for using data to help draw conclusions about some unknown quantity of a data instance, such as its classification. Let's now examine a different way of looking at drawing such conclusions. We could think about the things that we know about a data instance as *evidence* for or against different values for the target. The things that we know about the data instance are represented as the features of the instance. If we knew the strength of the evidence given by each feature, we could apply principled methods for combining evidence probabilistically to reach a conclusion as to the value for the target. We will determine the strength of any particular piece of evidence from the training data.

Example: Targeting Online Consumers With Advertisements

To illustrate, let's consider another business application of classification: targeting online display advertisements to consumers, based on what webpages they have visited in the past. As consumers, we have become used to getting a vast amount of information and services on the Web seemingly for free. Of course, the "for free" part is very often due to the existence or promise of revenue from online advertising, similar to how broadcast television is "free." Let's consider *display advertising*—the ads that appear on the top, sides, and bottom of pages full of content that we are reading or otherwise consuming.

Display advertising is different from search advertising (e.g., the ads that appear with the results of a Google search) in an important way: for most webpages, the user has not typed in a phrase related to exactly what she is looking for. Therefore, the targeting of an advertisement to the user needs to be based on other sorts of inference. For several chapters now we have been talking about a particular sort of inference: inferring the value of an instance's target variable from the values of the instance's features. Therefore, we could apply the techniques we already have covered to infer whether a particular user would be interested in an advertisement. In this chapter we introduce a different way of looking at the problem that has wide applicability and is quite easy to apply.

Let's define our ad targeting problem more precisely. What will be an instance? What will be the target variable? What will be the features? How will we get the training data?

Let's assume that we are working for a very large content provider (a "publisher") who has a wide variety of content, sees many online consumers, and has many opportunities to show advertisements to these consumers. For example, Yahoo! has a vast number of different advertisement-supported web "properties," which we can think of as different "content pieces." In addition, recently (as of this writing) Yahoo! agreed to purchase the blogging site Tumblr, which has 50 billion blog posts across over 100 million blogs. Each of these might also be seen as a "content piece" that gives some view into the interests of a consumer who reads it. Similarly, Facebook might consider each "Like" that a consumer makes as a piece of evidence regarding the consumer's tastes, which might help target ads as well.

For simplicity, assume we have one advertising campaign for which we would like to target some subset of the online consumers that visit our sites. This campaign is for the upscale hotel chain, Luxhote. The goal of Luxhote is for people to book rooms. We have run this campaign in the past, selecting online consumers randomly. We now want to run a targeted campaign, hopefully getting more bookings per dollar spent on ad impressions.[1]

Therefore, we will consider a consumer to be an instance. Our target variable will be: did/will the consumer book a Luxhote room within one week after having seen the Luxhote advertisement? Through the magic of browser cookies,[2] in collaboration with Luxhote we can observe which consumers book rooms. For training, we will have a binary value for this target variable for each consumer. In use, we will estimate the probability that a consumer will book a room after having seen an ad, and then, as our budget allows, target some subset of the highest probability consumers.

We are left with a key question: what will be the features we will use to describe the consumers, such that we might be able to differentiate those that are more or less likely to be good customers for Luxhote? For this example, we will consider a consumer to be described by the set of content pieces that we have observed her to have viewed (or Liked) previously, again as recorded via browser cookies or some other mechanism. We

---

1. An ad *impression* is when an ad is displayed somewhere on a page, regardless of whether a user clicks it.

2. A browser exchanges small amounts of information ("cookies") with the sites that are visited, and saves site-specific information that can be retrieved later by the same website.

have many different kinds of content: finance, sports, entertainment, cooking blogs, etc. We might pick several thousand content pieces that are very popular, or we may consider hundreds of millions. We believe that some of these (e.g., finance blogs) are more likely to be visited by good prospects for Luxhote, while others (e.g., a tractor-pull fan page) are less likely.

However, for this exercise we do not want to rely on our presumptions about such content, nor do we have the resources to estimate the evidence potential for each content piece manually. Furthermore, while humans are quite good at using our knowledge and common sense to recognize whether evidence is likely to be "for" or "against," humans are notoriously bad at estimating the precise *strength* of the evidence. We would like our historical data to estimate both the direction and the strength of the evidence. We next will describe a very broadly applicable framework both for evaluating the evidence, and for combining it to estimate the resulting likelihood of class membership (here, the likelihood that a consumer will book a room after having seen the ad).

It turns out that there are many other problems that fit the mold of our example: classification/class probability estimation problems where each instance is described by a set of pieces of evidence, possibly taken from a very large total collection of possible evidence. For example, text document classification fits exactly (which we'll discuss next in Chapter 10). Each document is a collection of words, from a very large total vocabulary. Each word can possibly provide some evidence for or against the classification, and we would like to combine the evidence. The techniques that we introduce next are exactly those used in many spam detection systems: an instance is an email message, the target classes are **spam** or **not-spam**, and the features are the words and symbols in the email message.

Combining Evidence Probabilistically

More math than usual ahead
To discuss the ideas of combining evidence probabilistically, we need to introduce some probability notation. You do not have to have learned (or remember) probability theory—the notions are quite intuitive, and we will not get beyond the basics. The notation allows us to be precise. It might look like there's a lot of math in what follows, but you'll see that it's quite straightforward.

We are interested in quantities such as the probability of a consumer booking a room after being shown an ad. We actually need to be a little more specific: some particular consumer? Or just any consumer? Let's start with just any consumer: what is the probability that if you show an ad to just any consumer, she will book a room? As this is our desired classification, let's call this quantity C. We will represent the probability of an event C as $p(C)$. If we say $p(C) = 0.0001$, that means that if we were to show ads randomly to consumers, we would expect about 1 in 10,000 to book rooms.[3]

Now, we are interested in the probability of C given some evidence E, such as the set of websites visited by a *particular* consumer. The notation for this quantity is $p(C|E)$, which is read as "the probability of C given E," or "the probability of C conditioned on E." This is an example of a conditional probability, and the "|" is sometimes called the "conditioning bar." We would expect that $p(C|E)$ would be different based on different collections of evidence E—in our example, different sets of websites visited.

As mentioned above, we would like to use some labeled data, such as the data from our randomly targeted campaign, to associate different collections of evidence E with different probabilities. Unfortunately, this introduces a key problem. For any particular collection of evidence E, we probably have not seen enough cases with exactly that same collection of evidence to be able to infer the probability of class membership with any confidence. In fact, we may not have seen this particular collection of evidence at all! In our example, if we are considering thousands of different websites, what is the chance that in our training data we have seen a consumer with *exactly* the same visiting patterns as a consumer we will see in the future? It is infinitesimal. Therefore, what we will do is to consider the different pieces of evidence separately, and then combine evidence. To discuss this further, we need a few facts about combining probabilities.

Joint Probability and Independence

Let's say we have two events, A and B. If we know $p(A)$ and $p(B)$, can we say what is the probability that both A and B occur? Let's call that $p(AB)$. This is called the *joint* probability.

There is one special case when we can: if events A and B are *independent*. A and B being independent means that knowing about one of them tells you nothing about the likelihood of the other. The typical example used to illustrate independence is rolling a fair die; knowing the value of the first roll tells you nothing about the value of the second. If event A is "roll #1 shows a six" and event B is "roll #2 shows a six", then $p(A) = 1/6$ and $p(B) = 1/6$, and importantly, even if we *know* that roll #1 shows a six, still $p(B) = 1/6$. In this case, the events are independent, and in the case of independent events, $p(AB) = p(A) \cdot p(B)$—we can calculate the probability of the "joint" event AB by multiplying the probabilities of the individual events. In our example, $p(AB) = 1/36$.

However, we cannot in general compute the probabilities of joint events in this way. If this isn't clear, think about the case of rolling a trick die. In my pocket I have six trick dice. Each trick die has one of the numbers from one to six on all faces—all faces show

---

3. This is not necessarily a reasonable response rate for any particular advertisement, just an illustrative example. Purchase rates attributable to online advertisements generally seem very small to those outside the industry. It is important to realize that the cost of placing one ad often is quite small as well.

---

the same number. I pull a die at random from my pocket, and then roll it twice. In this case, $p(A) = p(B) = 1/6$ (because I could have pulled any of the six dice out with equal likelihood). However, $p(AB) = 1/6$ as well, because the events are completely dependent! If the first roll is a six, so will be the second (and vice versa).

The general formula for combining probabilities that takes care of dependencies between events is:

Equation 9-1. Joint probability using conditional probability

$$p(AB) = p(A) \cdot p(B \mid A)$$

This is read as: the probability of A and B is the probability of A times the probability of B *given A*. In other words, given that you know A, what is the probability of B? Take a minute to make sure that has sunk in.

We can illustrate with our two dice examples. In the independent case, since knowing A tells us nothing about $p(B)$, then $p(B|A) = p(B)$, and we get our formula from above, where we simply multiply the individual probabilities. In our trick die case, $p(B|A) = 1.0$, since if the first roll was a six, then the second roll is guaranteed to be a six. Thus, $p(AB) = p(A) \cdot 1.0 = p(A) = 1/6$, just as expected.

In general, events may be completely independent, completely dependent, or somewhere in between. If events are not completely independent, knowing something about one event changes the likelihood of the other. In all cases, our formula $p(AB) = p(A) \cdot p(B|A)$ combines the probabilities properly.

We've gone through this detail for a very important reason. This formula is the basis for one of the most famous equations in data science, and in fact in science generally.

Bayes' Rule

Notice that in $p(AB) = p(A)p(B|A)$ the order of A and B seems rather arbitrary—and it is. We could just as well have written:

$$p(AB) = p(B) \cdot p(A \mid B)$$

This means:

$$p(A) \cdot p(B \mid A) = p(AB) = p(B) \cdot p(A \mid B)$$

And so:

$$p(A) \cdot p(B \mid A) = p(B) \cdot p(A \mid B)$$

If we divide both sides by $p(A)$ we get:

$$p(B \mid A) = \frac{p(A \mid B) \cdot p(B)}{p(A)}$$

Now, let's consider B to be some hypothesis that we are interested in assessing the likelihood of, and A to be some evidence that we have observed. Renaming with H for hypothesis and E for evidence, we get:

$$p(H \mid E) = \frac{p(E \mid H) \cdot p(H)}{p(E)}$$

This is the famous *Bayes' Rule*, named after the Reverend Thomas Bayes who derived a special case of the rule back in the 18th century. Bayes' Rule says that we can compute the probability of our hypothesis H given some evidence E by instead looking at the probability of the evidence given the hypothesis, as well as the unconditional probabilities of the hypothesis and the evidence.

Note: Bayesian methods

Bayes' Rule, combined with the fundamental principle of thinking carefully about conditional independence, is the foundation for a large number of more advanced data science techniques that we will not cover in this book. These include Bayesian networks, probabilistic topic models, probabilistic relational models, Hidden Markov Models, Markov random fields, and others.

Importantly, the last three quantities may be easier to determine than the quantity of ultimate interest—namely, $p(H|E)$. To see this, consider a (simplified) example from medical diagnosis. Assume you're a doctor and a patient arrives with red spots. You guess (hypothesize) that the patient has measles. We would like to determine the probability of our hypothesized diagnosis (H = measles), given the evidence (E = red spots). In order to directly estimate p(measles|red spots) we would need to think through all the different reasons a person might exhibit red spots and what proportion of them would be measles. This is likely impossible even for the most broadly knowledgeable physician.

However, consider instead the task of estimating this quantity using the righthand side of Bayes' Rule.

- $p(E|H)$ is the probability that one has red spots given that one has measles. An expert in infectious diseases may well know this or be able to estimate it relatively accurately.

- $p(H)$ is simply the probability that someone has measles, without considering any evidence; that's just the prevalence of measles in the population.

- $p(E)$ is the probability of the evidence: what's the probability that someone has red spots—again, simply the prevalence of red spots in the population, which does not require complicated reasoning about the different underlying causes, just observation and counting.

Bayes' Rule has made estimating $p(H|E)$ much easier. We need three pieces of information, but they're much easier to estimate than the original value is.

$p(E)$ may still be difficult to compute. In many cases, though, it does not have to be computed, because we are interested in comparing the probabilities of different hypotheses given the same evidence. We will see this later.

Applying Bayes' Rule to Data Science

It is possibly quite obvious now that Bayes' Rule should be critical in data science. Indeed, a very large portion of data science is based on "Bayesian" methods, which have at their core reasoning based on Bayes' Rule. Describing Bayesian methods broadly is well beyond the scope of this book. We will introduce the most fundamental ideas, and then show how they apply in the most basic of Bayesian techniques—which is used a great deal. Let's rewrite Bayes' Rule yet again, but now returning to classification. Let's for the moment emphasize the application to classification by writing out "$C = c$" — the event that the target variable takes on the particular value c.

Equation 9-2. Bayes Rule for classification

$$p(C = c \mid \mathbf{E}) = \frac{p(\mathbf{E} \mid C = c) \cdot p(C = c)}{p(\mathbf{E})}$$

In Equation 9-2, we have four quantities. On the lefthand side is the quantity we would like to estimate. In the context of a classification problem, this is the probability that the target variable C takes on the class of interest c *after* taking the evidence $\mathbf{E}$ (the **vector** of feature values) into account. This is called the *posterior* probability.

Bayes' Rule decomposes the posterior probability into the three quantities that we see on the righthand side. We would like to be able to compute these quantities from the data:

1. $p(C = c)$ is the *"prior"* probability of the class, i.e., the probability we would assign to the class before seeing any evidence. In Bayesian reasoning generally, this could

come from several places. It could be (i) a "subjective" prior, meaning that it is the belief of a particular decision maker based on all her knowledge, experience, and opinions; (ii) a "prior" belief based on some previous application(s) of Bayes' Rule with other evidence, or (iii) an unconditional probability inferred from data. The specific method we introduce below takes approach (iii), using as the *class prior* the "base rate" of c—the prevalence of c in the population as a whole. This is calculated easily from the data as the percentage of all examples that are of class c.

2. $p(\mathbf{E} \mid C = c)$ is the *likelihood* of seeing the evidence $\mathbf{E}$—the particular features of the example being classified—when the class $C = c$. One might see this as a "generative" question: if the world (the "data generating process") generated an instance of class c, how often would it look like $\mathbf{E}$? This likelihood might be calculated from the data as the percentage of examples of class c that have feature vector $\mathbf{E}$.

3. Finally, $p(\mathbf{E})$ is the likelihood of the evidence: how common is the feature representation $\mathbf{E}$ among all examples? This might be calculated from the data as the percentage occurrence of $\mathbf{E}$ among all examples.

Estimating these three values from training data, we could calculate an estimate for the posterior $p(C = c \mid \mathbf{E})$ for a particular example in use. This could be used directly as an estimate of class probability, possibly in combination with costs and benefits as described in Chapter 7. Alternatively, $p(C = c \mid \mathbf{E})$ could be used as a score to rank instances (e.g., estimating those that are most likely to respond to our advertisement). Or, we could choose as the classification the maximum $p(C = c \mid \mathbf{E})$ across the different values c.

Unfortunately, we return to the major difficulty we mentioned above, which keeps Equation 9-2 from being used directly in data mining. Consider $\mathbf{E}$ to be our usual vector of attribute values $<e_1, e_2, \cdots, e_k>$, a possibly large, specific collection of conditions. Applying Equation 9-2 directly would require knowing the $p(\mathbf{E}|c)$ as $p(e_1 \wedge e_2 \wedge \cdots \wedge e_k|c)$.[4] This is very specific and very difficult to measure. We may never see a specific example in the training data that exactly matches a given $\mathbf{E}$ in our testing data, and even if we do it may be unlikely we'll see enough of them to estimate a probability with any confidence.

Bayesian methods for data science deal with this issue by making assumptions of probabilistic independence. The most broadly used method for dealing with this complication is to make a particularly strong assumption of independence.

---

4. The $\wedge$ operator means "and."

Conditional Independence and Naive Bayes

Recall from above the notion of independence: two events are independent if knowing one does not give you information on the probability of the other. Let's extend that notion ever so slightly.

Conditional independence is the same notion, except using conditional probabilities. For our purposes, we will focus on the class of the example as the condition (since in Equation 9-2 we are looking at the probability of the evidence *given* the class). Conditional independence is directly analogous to the unconditional independence we discussed above. Specifically, without assuming independence, to combine probabilities we need to use Equation 9-1 from above, augmented with the $|C$ condition:

$$p(AB \mid C) = p(A \mid C) \cdot p(B \mid AC)$$

However, as above, if we assume that A and B are conditionally independent given C,[5] we can now combine the probabilities much more easily:

$$p(AB \mid C) = p(A \mid C) \cdot p(B \mid C)$$

This makes a huge difference in our ability to compute the probabilities from the data. In particular, for the conditional probability $p(\mathbf{E} \mid C=c)$ in Equation 9-2, let's assume that the attributes are conditionally independent, given the class. In other words, in $p(e_1 \wedge e_2 \wedge \cdots \wedge e_k \mid c)$, each e_i is independent of every other e_j given the class c. For simplicity of presentation, let's replace $C=c$ simply by c, as long as it won't lead to confusion.

$$
\begin{aligned}
p(\mathbf{E} \mid c) &= p(e_1 \wedge e_2 \wedge \cdots \wedge e_k \mid c) \\
&= p(e_1 \mid c) \cdot p(e_2 \mid c) \cdots p(e_k \mid c)
\end{aligned}
$$

Each of the $p(e_i \mid c)$ terms can be computed directly from the data, since now we simply need to count up the proportion of the time that we see individual feature e_i in the instances of class c, rather than looking for an entire matching feature vector. There are likely to be relatively many occurrences of e_i.[6] Combining this with Equation 9-2 we get the *Naive Bayes equation* as shown in Equation 9-3.

---

5. This is a weaker assumption than assuming unconditional independence, by the way.

6. And in the cases where there are not we can use a statistical correction for small counts; see "Probability Estimation" on page 71.

Equation 9-3. Naive Bayes equation

$$p(c \mid \mathbf{E}) = \frac{p(e_1 \mid c) \cdot p(e_2 \mid c) \cdots p(e_k \mid c) \cdot p(c)}{p(\mathbf{E})}$$

This is the basis of the *Naive Bayes classifier*. It classifies a new example by estimating the probability that the example belongs to each class and reports the class with highest probability.

If you will allow two paragraphs on a technical detail: at this point you might notice the $p(\mathbf{E})$ in the denominator of Equation 9-3 and say, whoa there—if I understand you, isn't that going to be almost as difficult to compute as $p(\mathbf{E} \mid C)$? It turns out that generally $p(\mathbf{E})$ never actually has to be calculated, for one of two reasons. First, if we are interested in classification, what we mainly care about is: of the different possible classes c, for which one is $p(C \mid \mathbf{E})$ the greatest? In this case, $\mathbf{E}$ is the same for all, and we can just look to see which numerator is larger.

In cases where we would like the actual probability estimates, we still can get around computing $p(\mathbf{E})$ in the denominator. This is because the classes often are mutually exclusive and exhaustive, meaning that every instance will belong to one and only one class. In our Luxhote example, a consumer either books a room or does not. Informally, if we see evidence $\mathbf{E}$ it belongs either to c_0 or c_1. Mathematically:

$$\begin{aligned} p(\mathbf{E}) &= p(\mathbf{E} \wedge c_0) + p(\mathbf{E} \wedge c_1) \\ &= p(\mathbf{E} \mid c_0) \cdot p(c_0) + p(\mathbf{E} \mid c_1) \cdot p(c_1) \end{aligned}$$

Our independence assumption allows us to rewrite this as:

$$\begin{aligned} p(\mathbf{E}) = \ & p(e_1 \mid c_0) \cdot p(e_2 \mid c_0) \cdots p(e_k \mid c_0) \cdot p(c_0) \\ & + p(e_1 \mid c_1) \cdot p(e_2 \mid c_1) \cdots p(e_k \mid c_1) \cdot p(c_1) \end{aligned}$$

Combining this with Equation 9-3, we get a version of the Naive Bayes equation with which we can compute the posterior probabilities easily from the data:

$$p(c_0 \mid \mathbf{E}) = \frac{p(e_1 \mid c_0) \cdot p(e_2 \mid c_0) \cdots p(e_k \mid c_0) \cdot p(c_0)}{p(e_1 \mid c_0) \cdot p(e_2 \mid c_0) \cdots p(e_k \mid c_0) \cdot p(c_0) + p(e_1 \mid c_1) \cdot p(e_2 \mid c_1) \cdots p(e_k \mid c_1) \cdot p(c_1)}$$

Although it has lots of terms in it, each one is either the evidence "weight" of some particular individual piece of evidence, or a class prior.

Advantages and Disadvantages of Naive Bayes

Naive Bayes is a very simple classifier, yet it still takes all the feature evidence into account. It is very efficient in terms of storage space and computation time. Training consists only of storing counts of classes and feature occurrences as each example is seen. As mentioned, $p(c)$ can be estimated by counting the proportion of examples of class c among all examples. $p(e_i|c)$ can be estimated by the proportion of examples in class c for which feature e_i appears.

In spite of its simplicity and the strict independence assumptions, the Naive Bayes classifier performs surprisingly well for classification on many real-world tasks. This is because the violation of the independence assumption tends not to hurt classification performance, for an intuitively satisfying reason. Specifically, consider that two pieces of evidence are actually strongly dependent—what does that mean? Roughly, that means that when we see one we're also likely to see the other. Now, if we treat them as being independent, we're going to see one and say "there's evidence for the class" and see the other and say "there's more evidence for the class." So, to some extent we'll be double-counting the evidence. *However*, as long as the evidence is generally pointing us in the right direction, for classification the double-counting won't tend to hurt us. In fact, it will tend to make the probability estimates more extreme in the correct direction: the probability will be overestimated for the correct class and underestimated for the incorrect class(es). But for classification we're choosing the class with the greatest probability estimate, so making them more extreme in the correct direction is OK.

This does become a problem, though, if we're going to be using the probability estimates themselves—so Naive Bayes should be used with caution for actual decision-making with costs and benefits, as discussed in Chapter 7. Practitioners do use Naive Bayes regularly for ranking, where the actual values of the probabilities are not relevant—only the relative values for examples in the different classes.

Another advantage of Naive Bayes is that it is naturally an "incremental learner." An incremental learner is an induction technique that can update its model one training example at a time. It does not need to reprocess all past training examples when new training data become available.

Incremental learning is especially advantageous in applications where training labels are revealed in the course of the application, and we would like the model to take into account this new information as quickly as possible. For example, consider creating a personalized junk email classifier. When I receive a piece of junk email, I can click the "junk" button in my browser. Besides removing this email from my Inbox, this also creates a training data point: a positive instance of spam. It would be quite useful if the model could be updated immediately, on the fly, and immediately start classifying similar emails as spam. Naive Bayes is the basis of many personalized spam detection systems, such as the one in Mozilla's Thunderbird.

Naive Bayes is included in nearly every data mining toolkit and serves as a common baseline classifier against which more sophisticated methods can be compared. We have discussed Naive Bayes using binary attributes. The basic idea presented above can be extended easily to multi-valued categorical attributes, as well as to numeric attributes, as you can read about in a textbook on data mining algorithms.

Sidebar: Variants of Naive Bayes

There actually are several slightly different classifiers that all are called Naive Bayes. The differences are small and often are overlooked (except for this sidebar, we ignore them in this chapter); however, they can make a difference.

In short, Naive Bayes (NB) is based on a "generative" model—a model of how the data are generated. The different versions of NB are based on different generative statistical models, all of which make the main NB assumption that we have discussed (namely, that the features are generated conditionally independently for each class). We will not discuss the actual statistical models here. However, it is useful to consider one key difference.

You'll notice that the NB model we describe considers the value of each feature as evidence for or against each class. What if there are very many features: say every word in the language, or every web page someone might visit? In such applications, features often represent the presence or the frequency of these words, pages, etc. It turns out that in such applications, often the vast majority of the words, webpages, etc. simply do not occur for any particular instance (document, online consumer).

It turns out that there are some math tricks in calculating the Naive Bayes scores that allow us only to consider the evidence that is present. The interested reader is encouraged to read about them, and about different Naive Bayes models more generally (McCallum & Nigam, 1998; Junqué de Fortuny et al., 2013). The upshot is that common practice in such large sparse domains is only to consider explicitly the evidence that is present. So, for example, in our advertising example from above, often we only focus on sites that a consumer *does* visit, and do not mention the many websites the consumer does *not* visit. The latter are taken care of implicitly in the math and via some assumptions on how the data are actually generated. Similarly, below we will consider only the evidence from those items that a Facebook user Likes, but will not consider explicitly the evidence from all the possible things that one did not Like.

A Model of Evidence "Lift"

"Cumulative Response and Lift Curves" on page 219 presented the notion of *lift* as a metric for evaluating a classifier. Lift measures how much more prevalent the positive class is in the selected subpopulation over the prevalence in the population as a whole. If the prevalence of hotel bookings in a randomly targeted set of consumers is 0.01%

and in our selected population it is 0.02%, then the classifier gives us a lift of 2—the selected population has double the booking rate.

With a slight modification, we can adapt our Naive Bayes equation to model the different lifts attributable to the different pieces of evidence. The slight modification is to assume full feature independence, rather than the weaker assumption of conditional independence used for Naive Bayes. Let's call this Naive-Naive Bayes, since it's making stronger simplifying assumptions about the world. Assuming full feature independence, Equation 9-3 becomes the following for Naive-Naive Bayes:

$$p(c \mid \mathbf{E}) = \frac{p(e_1 \mid c) \cdot p(e_2 \mid c) \cdots p(e_k \mid c) \cdot p(c)}{p(e_1) \cdot p(e_2) \cdots p(e_k)}$$

The terms in this equation can be rearranged to yield:

Equation 9-4. Probability as a product of evidence lifts

$$p(c \mid \mathbf{E}) = p(c) \cdot \text{lift}_c(e_1) \cdot \text{lift}_c(e_2) \cdots$$

where $\text{lift}_c(x)$ is defined as:

$$\text{lift}_c(x) = \frac{p(x \mid c)}{p(x)}$$

Consider how these evidence lifts will apply to a new example $\mathbf{E} = <e_1, e_2, \cdots, e_k>$. Starting at the prior probability, each piece of evidence—each feature e_i—raises or lowers the probability of the class by a factor equal to that piece of evidence's lift (which may be less than one).

Conceptually, we start off with a number—call it z—set to the prior probability of class c. We go through our example, and for each new piece of evidence e_i we multiply z by $\text{lift}_c(e_i)$. If the lift is greater than one, the probability z is increased; if less than one, z is diminished.

In the case of our Luxhote example, z is the probability of booking, and it is initialized to 0.0001 (the prior probability, before seeing evidence, that a website visitor will book a room). Visited a finance site? Multiply the probability of booking by a factor of two. Visit a truck-pull site? Multiply the probability by a factor of 0.25. And so on. After processing all of the e_i evidence bits of $\mathbf{E}$, the resulting product (call that z_j) is the final probability (belief) that **E** is a member of class c—in this case, that visitor **E** will book a room.[7]

Considered this way, it may become clearer what the independence assumption is doing. We are treating each bit of evidence e_i as independent of the others, so we can just multiply z by their individual lifts. But any dependencies among them will result in some distortion of the final value, z_f. It will end up either higher or lower than it properly should be. Thus the evidence lifts and their combination are very useful for understanding the data, and for *comparing* instance scores, but the actual final value of the probability should be taken with a large grain of salt.

Example: Evidence Lifts from Facebook "Likes"

Let's examine some evidence lifts from real data. To freshen things up a little, let's consider a brand new domain of application. Researchers Michal Kosinski, David Stillwell, and Thore Graepel recently published a paper (Kosinski et al., 2013) in the *Proceedings of the National Academy of Sciences* showing some striking results. What people "Like" on the social-networking site Facebook[8] is quite predictive of all manner of traits that usually are not directly apparent:

- How they score on intelligence tests
- How they score on psychometric tests (e.g., how extroverted or conscientious they are)
- Whether they are (openly) gay
- Whether they drink alcohol or smoke
- Their religion and political views
- And many more.

We encourage you to read the paper to understand their experimental design. You should be able to understand most of the results now that you have read this book. (For example, for evaluating how well they can predict many of the binary traits they report the area under the ROC curve, which you can now interpret properly.)

---

7. Technically, we may also need to consider the evidence from not having visited other websites, which also can be taken care of by some math tricks; see "Sidebar: Variants of Naive Bayes" on page 244.

8. For those unfamiliar with the workings of Facebook, it allows people to share a wide variety of information on their interests and activities and to connect with "friends." Facebook also has pages devoted to special interests such as TV shows, movies, bands, hobbies, and so on. What's relevant here is that each such page has a "Like" button, and users can declare themselves to be fans by clicking it. Such "Likes" can usually be seen by one's friends. And if you "Like" a fan page, you'll start see postings associated with that fan page in your news feed.

What we would like to do is to look to see what are the Likes that give strong evidence lifts for "high IQ," or more specifically for scoring high on an IQ test. Taking a sample of the Facebook population, let's define our target variable as the binary variable $IQ>130$.

So let's examine the Likes that give the highest evidence lifts…[9]

Table 9-1. Some Facebook page "Likes" and corresponding lifts.

Like	Lift	Like	Lift
Lord Of The Rings	1.69	Wikileaks	1.59
One Manga	1.57	Beethoven	1.52
Science	1.49	NPR	1.48
Psychology	1.46	Spirited Away	1.45
The Big Bang Theory	1.43	Running	1.41
Paulo Coelho	1.41	Roger Federer	1.40
The Daily Show	1.40	Star Trek (Movie)	1.39
Lost	1.39	Philosophy	1.38
Lie to Me	1.37	The Onion	1.37
How I Met Your Mother	1.35	The Colbert Report	1.35
Doctor Who	1.34	Star Trek	1.32
Howl's Moving Castle	1.31	Sheldon Cooper	1.30
Tron	1.28	Fight Club	1.26
Angry Birds	1.25	Inception	1.25
The Godfather	1.23	Weeds	1.22

So, recalling Equation 9-4 above, and the independence assumptions made, we can calculate the lift in probability that someone has very high intelligence based on the things they Like. On Facebook, the probability of a high-IQ person liking *Sheldon Cooper* is 30% higher than the probability in the general population. The probability of a high-IQ person liking *The Lord of the Rings* is 69% higher than that of the general population.

Of course, there are also Likes that would drag *down* one's probabability of **High-IQ**. So as not to depress you, we won't list them here.

This example also illustrates how it is important to think carefully about exactly what the results mean in light of the data collection process. The result above does not really mean that liking *The Lord of the Rings* is necessarily a strong indication of high IQ. It means clicking "Like" on Facebook's page called **The Lord of the Rings** is a strong indication of a high IQ. This difference is important: the act of clicking "Like" on a page

---

9. Thanks to Wally Wang for his generous help with generating these results.

is different from simply liking it, and the data we have are on the former and not the latter.

Evidence in Action: Targeting Consumers with Ads

In spite of the math that appears in this chapter, the calculations are quite simple to implement—so simple they can be implemented directly in a spreadsheet. So instead of presenting a static example here, we have prepared a spreadsheet with a simple numerical example illustrating Naive Bayes and evidence lift on a toy version of the online ad-targeting example. You'll see how straightforward it is to use these calculations, because they just involve counting things, computing proportions, and multiplying and dividing.

 The spreadsheet can be downloaded here (*http://www.data-science-for-biz.com/NB-advertising.html*).

The spreadsheet lays out all the "evidence" (website visits for multiple visitors) and shows the intermediate calculations and final probability of a ficticious advertising response. You can experiment with the technique by tweaking the numbers, adding or deleting visitors, and seeing how the estimated probabilities of response and the evidence lifts adjust in response.

Summary

Prior chapters presented modeling techniques that basically ask the question: *"What is the best way to distinguish target values?"* in different segments of the population of instances. Classification trees and linear equations both create models this way, trying to minimize loss or entropy, which are functions of discriminability. These are termed *discriminative* methods, in that they try directly to discriminate different targets.

This chapter introduced a new family of methods that essentially turns the question around and asks: "How do different target segments *generate* feature values?" They attempt to model how the data was generated. In the use phase, when faced with a new example to be classified, they use the models to answer the question: "Which class most likely generated this example?" Thus, in data science this approach to modeling is called *generative*. The large family of popular methods known as *Bayesian* methods, because they depend critically on Bayes' Rule, are usually generative methods. The literature on Bayesian methods is both broad and deep, and you will encounter them often in data science.

This chapter focused primarily on a particularly common and simple but very useful Bayesian method called the Naive Bayes classifier. It is "naive" in the sense that it models each feature as being generated independently (for each target), so the resulting classifier tends to double-count evidence when features are correlated. Because of its simplicity it is very fast and efficient, and in spite of its naïveté it is surprisingly (almost embarrassingly) effective. In data science it is so simple as to be a common "baseline" method —one of the first methods to be applied to any new problem.

We also discussed how Bayesian reasoning using certain independence assumptions can allow us to compute "evidence lifts" to examine large numbers of possible pieces of evidence for or against a conclusion. As an example, we showed that the probability of "Liking" *Fight Club*, *Star Trek*, or *Sheldon Cooper* on Facebook each is about 30% higher for high-IQ people than for the general population.

CHAPTER 10

Representing and Mining Text

Fundamental concepts: *The importance of constructing mining-friendly data representations; Representation of text for data mining.*

Exemplary techniques: *Bag of words representation; TFIDF calculation; N-grams; Stemming; Named entity extraction; Topic models.*

Up to this point we've ignored or side-stepped an important stage of the data mining process: data preparation. The world does not always present us with data in the feature vector representation that most data mining methods take as input. Data are represented in ways natural to problems from which they were derived. If we want to apply the many data mining tools that we have at our disposal, we must either engineer the data representation to match the tools, or build new tools to match the data. Top-notch data scientists employ both of these strategies. It generally is simpler to first try to engineer the data to match existing tools, since they are well understood and numerous.

In this chapter, we will focus on one particular sort of data that has become extremely common as the Internet has become a ubiquitous channel of communication: text data. Examining text data allows us to illustrate many real complexities of data engineering, and also helps us to understand better a very important type of data. We will see in Chapter 14 that although in this chapter we focus exclusively on text data, the fundamental principles indeed generalize to other important sorts of data.

We've encountered text once before in this book, in the example involving clustering news stories about Apple Inc. ("Example: Clustering Business News Stories"). There we deliberately avoided a detailed discussion of how the news stories were prepared because the focus was on clustering, and text preparation would have been too much of a digression. This chapter is devoted to the difficulties and opportunities of dealing with text.

In principle, text is just another form of data, and text processing is just a special case of representation engineering. In reality, dealing with text requires dedicated preprocessing steps and sometimes specific expertise on the part of the data science team.

Entire books and conferences (and companies) are devoted to text mining. In this chapter we can only scratch the surface, to give a basic overview of the techniques and issues involved in typical business applications.

First, let's discuss why text is so important and why it's difficult.

Why Text Is Important

Text is everywhere. Many legacy applications still produce or record text. Medical records, consumer complaint logs, product inquiries, and repair records are still mostly intended as communication between people, not computers, so they're still "coded" as text. Exploiting this vast amount of data requires converting it to a meaningful form.

The Internet may be the home of "new media," but much of it is the same form as old media. It contains a vast amount of text in the form of personal web pages, Twitter feeds, email, Facebook status updates, product descriptions, Reddit comments, blog postings —the list goes on. Underlying the search engines (Google and Bing) that we use everyday are massive amounts of text-oriented data science. Music and video may account for a great deal of traffic volume, but when people communicate with each other on the Internet it is usually via text. Indeed, the thrust of Web 2.0 was about Internet sites allowing users to interact with one another as a community, and to generate much added content of a site. This user-generated content and interaction usually takes the form of text.

In business, understanding customer feedback often requires understanding text. This isn't always the case; admittedly, some important consumer attitudes are represented explicitly as data or can be inferred through behavior, for example via five-star ratings, click-through patterns, conversion rates, and so on. We can also pay to have data collected and quantified through focus groups and online surveys. But in many cases if we want to "listen to the customer" we'll actually have to read what she's written—in product reviews, customer feedback forms, opinion pieces, and email messages.

Why Text Is Difficult

Text is often referred to as "unstructured" data. This refers to the fact that text does not have the sort of structure that we normally expect for data: tables of records with fields having fixed meanings (essentially, collections of feature vectors), as well as links between the tables. Text of course has plenty of structure, but it is *linguistic* structure— intended for human consumption, not for computers.

Words can have varying lengths and text fields can have varying numbers of words. Sometimes word order matters, sometimes not.

As data, text is relatively *dirty*. People write ungrammatically, they misspell words, they run words together, they abbreviate unpredictably, and punctuate randomly. Even when text is flawlessly expressed it may contain synonyms (multiple words with the same meaning) and homographs (one spelling shared among multiple words with different meanings). Terminology and abbreviations in one domain might be meaningless in another domain—we shouldn't expect that medical recordkeeping and computer repair records would share terms in common, and in the worst case they would conflict.

Because text is intended for communication between people, *context* is important, much more so than with other forms of data. Consider this movie review excerpt:

> "The first part of this movie is far better than the second. The acting is poor and it gets out-of-control by the end, with the violence overdone and an incredible ending, but it's still fun to watch."

Consider whether the overall sentiment is for or against the film. Is the word *incredible* positive or negative? It is difficult to evaluate any particular word or phrase here without taking into account the entire context.

For these reasons, text must undergo a good amount of preprocessing before it can be used as input to a data mining algorithm. Usually the more complex the featurization, the more aspects of the text problem can be included. This chapter can only describe some of the basic methods involved in preparing text for data mining. The next few subsections describe these steps.

Representation

Having discussed how difficult text can be, let's go through the basic steps to transform a body of text into a set of data that can be fed into a data mining algorithm. The general strategy in text mining is to use the simplest (least expensive) technique that works. Nevertheless, these ideas are the key technology underlying much of web search, like Google and Bing. A later example will demonstrate basic query retrieval.

First, some basic terminology. Most of this is borrowed from the field of Information Retrieval (IR). A *document* is one piece of text, no matter how large or small. A document could be a single sentence or a 100 page report, or anything in between, such as a YouTube comment or a blog posting. Typically, all the text of a document is considered together and is retrieved as a single item when matched or categorized. A document is composed of individual *tokens* or *terms*. For now, think of a token or term as just a word; as we go on we'll show how they can be different from what are customarily thought of as words. A collection of documents is called a *corpus*.[1]

---

1. Latin for "body." The plural is *corpora*.

Bag of Words

It is important to keep in mind the purpose of the text representation task. In essence, we are taking a set of documents—each of which is a relatively free-form sequence of words—and turning it into our familiar feature-vector form. Each document is one instance but we don't know in advance what the features will be.

The approach we introduce first is called "bag of words." As the name implies, the approach is to treat every document as just a collection of individual words. This approach ignores grammar, word order, sentence structure, and (usually) punctuation. It treats every word in a document as a potentially important keyword of the document. The representation is straightforward and inexpensive to generate, and tends to work well for many tasks.

> **Note: Sets and bags**
> The terms *set* and *bag* have specific meanings in mathematics, neither of which we exactly mean here. A set allows only one instance of each item, whereas we want to take into account the number of occurrences of words. In mathematics a *bag* is a *multiset*, where members are allowed to appear more than once. The bag-of-words representation initially treats documents as bags—multisets—of words, thereby ignoring word order and other linguistic structure. However, the representation used for mining the text often is more complex than just counting the number of occurrences, as we will describe.

So if every word is a possible feature, what will be the feature's value in a given document? There are several approaches to this. In the most basic approach, each word is a token, and each document is represented by a one (if the token is present in the document) or a zero (the token is not present in the document). This approach simply reduces a document to the set of words contained in it.

Term Frequency

The next step up is to use the word count (frequency) in the document instead of just a zero or one. This allows us to differentiate between how many times a word is used; in some applications, the importance of a term in a document should increase with the number of times that term occurs. This is called the *term frequency* representation. Consider the three very simple sentences (documents) shown in Table 10-1.

Table 10-1. Three simple documents.

d1　jazz music has a swing rhythm

d2　swing is hard to explain

d3　swing rhythm is a natural rhythm

Each sentence is considered a separate document. A simple bag-of-words approach using term frequency would produce a table of term counts shown in Table 10-2.

Table 10-2. Term count representation.

	a	explain	hard	has	is	jazz	music	natural	rhythm	swing	to
d1	1	0	0	1	0	1	1	0	1	1	0
d2	0	1	1	0	1	0	0	0	0	1	1
d3	1	0	0	0	1	0	0	1	2	1	0

Usually some basic processing is performed on the words before putting them into the table. Consider this more complex sample document:

> Microsoft Corp and Skype Global today announced that they have entered into a definitive agreement under which Microsoft will acquire Skype, the leading Internet communications company, for $8.5 billion in cash from the investor group led by Silver Lake. The agreement has been approved by the boards of directors of both Microsoft and Skype.

Table 10-3 shows a reduction of this document to a term frequency representation.

Table 10-3. Terms after normalization and stemming, ordered by frequency

Term	Count	Term	Count	Term	Count	Term	Count
skype	3	microsoft	3	agreement	2	global	1
approv	1	announc	1	acquir	1	lead	1
definit	1	lake	1	communic	1	internet	1
board	1	led	1	director	1	corp	1
compani	1	investor	1	silver	1	billion	1

To create this table from the sample document, the following steps have been performed:

- First, the case has been normalized: every term is in lowercase. This is so that words like Skype and SKYPE are counted as the same thing. Case variations are so common (consider iPhone, iphone, and IPHONE) that case normalization is usually necessary.

- Second, many words have been *stemmed*: their suffixes removed, so that verbs like *announces, announced* and *announcing* are all reduced to the term announc. Similarly, stemming transforms noun plurals to the singular forms, which is why *directors* in the text becomes director in the term list.

- Finally, *stopwords* have been removed. A stopword is a very common word in English (or whatever language is being parsed). The words *the, and, of,* and *on* are considered stopwords in English so they are typically removed.

Note that the "$8.5" in the story has been discarded entirely. Should it have been? Numbers are commonly regarded as unimportant details for text processing, but the purpose of the representation should decide this. You can imagine contexts where terms like "4TB" and "1Q13" would be meaningless, and others where they could be critical modifiers.

Note: Careless Stopword Elimination

A word of caution: stopword elimination is not always a good idea. In titles, for example, common words may be very significant. For example, *The Road*, Cormac McCarthy's story of a father and son surviving in a post-apocalyptic world, is very different from John Kerouac's famous novel *On the Road*— though careless stopword removal may cause them to be represented identically. Similarly, the recent movie thriller *Stoker* should not be confused with the 1935 film comedy *The Stoker*.[2]

Table 10-3 shows raw counts of terms. Instead of raw counts, some systems perform a step of normalizing the term frequencies with respect to document length. The purpose of term frequency is to represent the relevance of a term to a document. Long documents usually will have more words—and thus more word occurrences—than shorter ones. This doesn't mean that the longer document is necessarily more important or relevant than the shorter one. In order to adjust for document length, the raw term frequencies are normalized in some way, such as by dividing each by the total number of words in the document.

Measuring Sparseness: Inverse Document Frequency

So term *frequency* measures how prevalent a term is in a single document. We may also care, when deciding the weight of a term, how common it is in the entire corpus we're mining. There are two opposing considerations.

First, a term should not be too *rare*. For example, say the unusual word *prehensile* occurs in only one document in your corpus. Is it an important term? This may depend on the application. For retrieval, the term may be important since a user may be looking for that exact word. For clustering, there is no point keeping a term that occurs only once: it will never be the basis of a meaningful cluster. For this reason, text processing systems usually impose a small (arbitrary) lower limit on the number of documents in which a term must occur.

Another, opposite consideration is that a term should not be too *common*. A term occurring in every document isn't useful for classification (it doesn't distinguish anything) and it can't serve as the basis for a cluster (the entire corpus would cluster together).

---

2. Both of these examples appeared in recent search results on the film review site of a popular search engine. Not everyone is careful with stopword elimination.

Overly common terms are typically eliminated. One way to do this is to impose an arbitrary upper limit on the number (or fraction) of documents in which a word may occur.

In addition to imposing upper and lower limits on term frequency, many systems take into account the distribution of the term over a corpus as well. The fewer documents in which a term occurs, the more significant it likely is to be to the documents is does occur in. This sparseness of a term t is measured commonly by an equation called *inverse document frequency* (IDF), which is shown in Equation 10-1.

Equation 10-1. Inverse Document Frequency (IDF) of a term

$$IDF(t) = 1 + \log\left(\frac{\text{Total number of documents}}{\text{Number of documents containing } t}\right)$$

IDF may be thought of as the boost a term gets for being rare. Figure 10-1 shows a graph of IDF(t) as a function of the number of documents in which t occurs, in a corpus of 100 documents. As you can see, when a term is very rare (far left) the IDF is quite high. It decreases quickly as t becomes more common in documents, and asymptotes at 1.0. Most stopwords, due to their prevalence, will have an IDF near one.

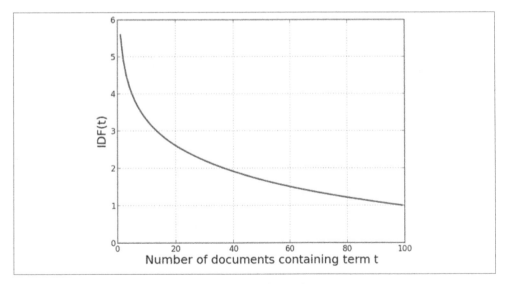

Figure 10-1. IDF of a term t within a corpus of 100 documents.

Combining Them: TFIDF

A very popular representation for text is the product of Term Frequency (TF) and Inverse Document Frequency (IDF), commonly referred to as TFIDF. The TFIDF value of a term t in a given document d is thus:

$$\text{TFIDF}(t, d) = \text{TF}(t, d) \times \text{IDF}(t)$$

Note that the TFIDF value is specific to a single document (d) whereas IDF depends on the entire corpus. Systems employing the bag-of-words representation typically go through steps of stemming and stopword elimination before doing term counts. Term counts within the documents form the TF values for each term, and the document counts across the corpus form the IDF values.

Each document thus becomes a feature vector, and the corpus is the set of these feature vectors. This set can then be used in a data mining algorithm for classification, clustering, or retrieval.

Because there are very many potential terms with text representation, feature selection is often employed. Systems do this in various ways, such as imposing minimum and maximum thresholds of term counts, and/or using a measure such as information gain[3] to rank the terms by importance so that low-gain terms can be culled.

The bag-of-words text representation approach treats every word in a document as an independent potential keyword (feature) of the document, then assigns values to each document based on frequency and rarity. TFIDF is a very common value representation for terms, but it is not necessarily optimal. If someone describes mining a text corpus using bag of words it just means they're treating each word individually as a feature. Their values could be binary, term frequency, or TFIDF, with normalization or without. Data scientists develop intuitions about how best to attack a given text problem, but they'll typically experiment with different representations to see which produces the best results.

Example: Jazz Musicians

Having introduced a few basic concepts, let's now illustrate them with a concrete example: representing jazz musicians. Specifically, we're going to look at a small corpus of 15 prominent jazz musicians and excerpts of their biographies from Wikipedia. Here are excerpts from a few jazz musician biographies:

---

3. See "Example: Attribute Selection with Information Gain" on page 56.

Charlie Parker

Charles "Charlie" Parker, Jr., was an American jazz saxophonist and composer. Miles Davis once said, "You can tell the history of jazz in four words: Louis Armstrong. Charlie Parker." Parker acquired the nickname "Yardbird" early in his career and the shortened form, "Bird," which continued to be used for the rest of his life, inspired the titles of a number of Parker compositions, [...]

Duke Ellington

Edward Kennedy "Duke" Ellington was an American composer, pianist, and big-band leader. Ellington wrote over 1,000 compositions. In the opinion of Bob Blumenthal of *The Boston Globe*, "in the century since his birth, there has been no greater composer, American or otherwise, than Edward Kennedy Ellington." A major figure in the history of jazz, Ellington's music stretched into various other genres, including blues, gospel, film scores, popular, and classical.[...]

Miles Davis

Miles Dewey Davis III was an American jazz musician, trumpeter, bandleader, and composer. Widely considered one of the most influential musicians of the 20th century, Miles Davis was, with his musical groups, at the forefront of several major developments in jazz music, including bebop, cool jazz, hard bop, modal jazz, and jazz fusion.[...]

Even with this fairly small corpus of fifteen documents, the corpus and its vocabulary are too large to show here (nearly 2,000 features after stemming and stopword removal) so we can only illustrate with a sample. Consider the sample phrase *"Famous jazz saxophonist born in Kansas who played bebop and latin."* We could imagine it being typed as a query to a search engine. How would it be represented? It is treated and processed just like a document, and goes through many of the same steps.

First, basic stemming is applied. Stemming methods are not perfect, and can produce terms like kansa and famou from "Kansas" and "famous." Stemming perfection usually isn't important as long as it's consistent among all the documents. The result is shown in Figure 10-2.

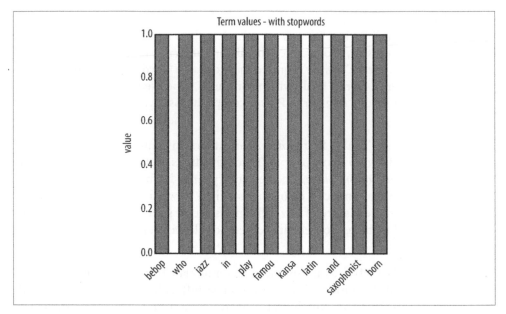

Figure 10-2. Representation of the query "Famous jazz saxophonist born in Kansas who played bebop and latin" after stemming.

Next, stopwords (in and and) are removed, and the words are normalized with respect to document length. The result is shown in Figure 10-3.

These values would typically be used as the Term Frequency (TF) feature values if we were to stop here. Instead, we'll generate the full TFIDF representation by multiplying each term's TF value by its IDF value. As we said, this boosts words that are rare.

Jazz and *play* are very frequent in this corpus of jazz musician biographies so they get no boost from IDF. They are almost stopwords in this corpus.

The terms with the highest TFIDF values ("latin," "famous," and "kansas") are the rarest in this corpus so they end up with the highest weights among the terms in the query. Finally, the terms are renormalized, producing the final TFIDF weights shown in Figure 10-4. This is the feature vector representation of this sample "document" (the query).

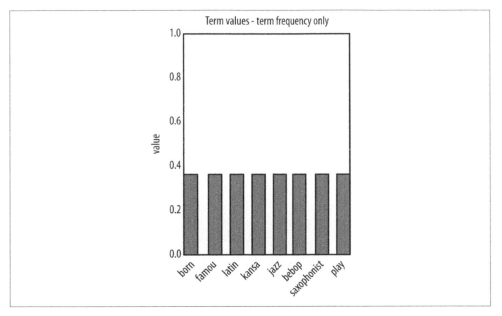

Figure 10-3. Representation of the query "Famous jazz saxophonist born in Kansas who played bebop and latin" after stopword removal and term frequency normalization.

Having shown how this small "document" would be represented, let's use it for something. Recall in Chapter 6, we discussed doing nearest-neighbor retrievals by employing a distance metric, and we showed how similar whiskies could be retrieved. We can do the same thing here. Assume our sample phrase *"Famous jazz saxophonist born in Kansas who played bebop and latin"* was a search query typed by a user and we were implementing a simple search engine. How might it work? First, we would translate the query to its TFIDF representation, as shown graphically in Figure 10-4. We've already computed TFIDF representations of each of our jazz musician biography documents. Now all we need to do is to compute the similarity of our query term to each musician's biography and choose the closest one!

For doing this matching, we'll use the Cosine Similarity function (Equation 6-5) discussed back in the starred section "* Other Distance Functions" on page 158. Cosine similarity is commonly used in text classification to measure the distance between documents.

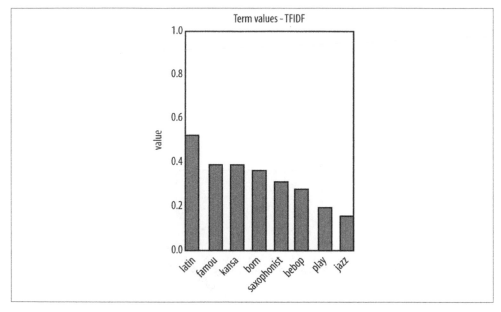

Figure 10-4. Final TFIDF representation of the query "Famous jazz saxophonist born in Kansas who played bebop and latin."

Table 10-4. Similarity of each musician's text to the query 'Famous jazz saxophonist born in Kansas who played bebop and latin,' ordered by decreasing similarity.

Musician	Similarity	Musician	Similarity
Charlie Parker	0.135	Count Basie	0.119
Dizzie Gillespie	0.086	John Coltrane	0.079
Art Tatum	0.050	Miles Davis	0.050
Clark Terry	0.047	Sun Ra	0.030
Dave Brubeck	0.027	Nina Simone	0.026
Thelonius Monk	0.025	Fats Waller	0.020
Charles Mingus	0.019	Duke Ellington	0.017
Benny Goodman	0.016	Louis Armstrong	0.012

As you can see, the closest matching document is Charlie Parker—who was, in fact, a saxophonist born in Kansas and who played the bebop style of jazz. He sometimes combined other genres, including Latin, a fact that is mentioned in his biography.

* The Relationship of IDF to Entropy

Technical Details Ahead

Back in "Selecting Informative Attributes" on page 49, we introduced the entropy measure when we began discussing predictive modeling. The curious reader (with a long memory) may notice that Inverse Document Frequency and entropy are somewhat similar—they both seem to measure how "mixed" a set is with respect to a property. Is there any connection between the two? Maybe they're the same? They are not identical, but they are related, and this section will show the relationship. If you're not curious about this you can skip this section.

Figure 10-5 shows some graphs related to the equations we're going to talk about. To begin, consider a term t in a document set. What is the probability that a term t occurs in a document set? We can estimate it as:

$$p(t) = \frac{\text{Number of documents containing } t}{\text{Total number of documents}}$$

To simplify things, from here on we'll refer to this estimate $p(t)$ simply as p. Recall that the definition of IDF of some term t is:

$$\text{IDF}(t) = 1 + \log\left(\frac{\text{Total number of documents}}{\text{Number of documents containing } t}\right)$$

The 1 is just a constant so let's discard it. We then notice that IDF(t) is basically $log(1/p)$. You may recall from algebra that $log(1/p)$ is equal to $-log(p)$.

Consider again the document set with respect to a term t. Each document either contains t (with probability p) or does not contain it (with probability $1-p$). Let's create a pseudo, mirror-image term *not_t* that, by definition, occurs in every document that does *not* contain t. What's the IDF of this new term? It is:

$$\text{IDF}(not\_T) = \log 1 / (1 - p) = -\log(1 - p)$$

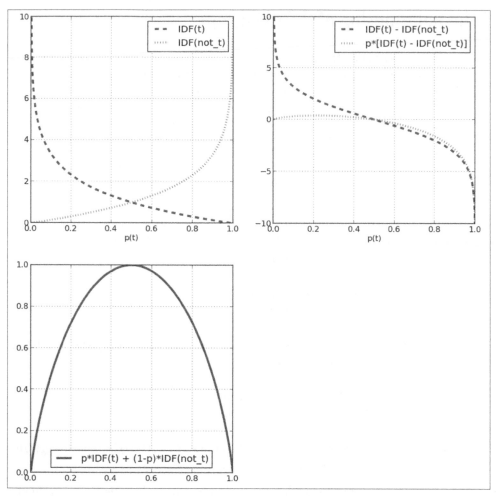

Figure 10-5. Plots of various values related to IDF(t) and IDF(not_t).

See the upper left graph of Figure 10-5. The two graphs are mirror images of each other, as we might expect. Now recall the definition of entropy from Equation 3-1. For a binary term where $p_2=1-p_1$, the entropy becomes:

$$\text{entropy} = -p_1 \log (p_1) - p_2 \log (p_2)$$

In our case, we have a binary term t that either occurs (with probability p) or does not (with probability $1-p$). So the definition of entropy of a set partitioned by t reduces to:

$$\text{entropy}(t) = -p \log (p) - (1 - p) \log (1 - p)$$

Now, given our definitions of IDF(*t*) and IDF(*not_t*), we can start substituting and simplifying (for reference, various of these subexpressions are plotted in the top right graph of Figure 10-5).

$$\text{entropy}(t) \quad = \quad -p \log (p) - (1 - p) \log (1 - p)$$
$$= \quad p \cdot \text{IDF}(t) - (1 - p)[\,-\text{IDF}(not\_t)]$$
$$= \quad p \cdot \text{IDF}(t) + (1 - p)[\text{IDF}(not\_t)]$$

Note that this is now in the form of an *expected value* calculation! We can express entropy as the expected value of IDF(*t*) and IDF(*not_t*) based on the probability of its occurrence in the corpus. Its graph at the bottom left in Figure 10-5 does match the entropy curve of Figure 3-3 back in Chapter 3.

Beyond Bag of Words

The basic bag of words approach is relatively simple and has much to recommend it. It requires no sophisticated parsing ability or other linguistic analysis. It performs surprisingly well on a variety of tasks, and is usually the first choice of data scientists for a new text mining problem.

Still, there are applications for which bag of words representation isn't good enough and more sophisticated techniques must be brought to bear. Here we briefly discuss a few of them.

N-gram Sequences

As presented, the bag-of-words representation treats every individual word as a term, discarding word order entirely. In some cases, word order is important and you want to preserve some information about it in the representation. A next step up in complexity is to include *sequences* of adjacent words as terms. For example, we could include pairs of adjacent words so that if a document contained the sentence *"The quick brown fox jumps."* it would be transformed into the set of its constitutent words {quick, brown, fox, jumps}, plus the tokens quick_brown, brown_fox, and fox_jumps.

This general representation tactic is called *n-grams*. Adjacent pairs are commonly called bi-grams. If you hear a data scientist mention representing text as "bag of n-grams up to three" it simply means she's representing each document using as features its individual words, adjacent word pairs, and adjacent word triples.

N-grams are useful when particular phrases are significant but their component words may not be. In a business news story, the appearance of the tri-gram exceed_ana lyst_expectation is more meaningful than simply knowing that the individual words analyst, expectation, and exceed appeared somewhere in a story. An advantage of using n-grams is that they are easy to generate; they require no linguistic knowledge or complex parsing algorithm.

The main disadvantage of n-grams is that they greatly increase the size of the feature set. There are many adjacent word pairs, and still more adjacent word triples. The number of features generated can quickly get out of hand, and many of them will be very rare, occuring only once in the corpus. Data mining using n-grams almost always needs some special consideration for dealing with massive numbers of features, such as a feature selection stage or special consideration to computational storage space.

Named Entity Extraction

Sometimes we want still more sophistication in phrase extraction. We want to be able to recognize common named entities in documents. *Silicon Valley*, *New York Mets*, *Department of the Interior*, and *Game of Thrones* are significant phrases. Their component words mean one thing, and may not be significant, but in sequence they name unique entities with interesting identities. The basic bag-of-words (or even n-grams) representation may not capture these, and we'd want a preprocessing component that knows when word sequences constitute proper names.

Many text-processing toolkits include a named entity extractor of some sort. Usually these can process raw text and extract phrases annotated with terms like `person` or `organization`. In some cases normalization is done so that, for example, phrases like "HP," "H-P," and "Hewlett-Packard" all link to some common representation of the Hewlett-Packard Corporation.

Unlike bag of words and n-grams, which are based on segmenting text on whitespace and punctuation, named entity extractors are knowledge intensive. To work well, they have to be trained on a large corpus, or hand coded with extensive knowledge of such names. There is no linguistic principle dictating that the phrase "*oakland raiders*" should refer to the Oakland Raiders professional football team, rather than, say, a group of aggressive California investors. This knowledge has to be learned, or coded by hand. The quality of entity recognition can vary, and some extractors may have particular areas of expertise, such as industry, government, or popular culture.

Topic Models

So far we've dealt with models created directly from words (or named entities) appearing from a document. The resulting model—whatever it may be—refers directly to words. Learning such direct models is relatively efficient, but is not always optimal. Because of the complexity of language and documents, sometimes we want an additional layer between the document and the model. In the context of text we call this the *topic* layer (see Figure 10-6).

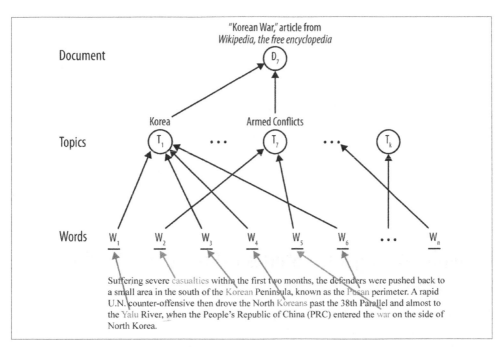

Figure 10-6. Modeling documents with a topic layer.

The main idea of a topic layer is first to model the set of topics in a corpus separately. As before, each document constitutes a sequence of words, but instead of the words being used directly by the final classifier, the words map to one or more topics. The topics also are learned from the data (often via unsupervised data mining). The final classifier is defined in terms of these intermediate topics rather than words. One advantage is that in a search engine, for example, a query can use terms that do not exactly match the specific words of a document; if they map to the correct topic(s), the document will still be considered relevant to the search.

General methods for creating topic models include matrix factorization methods, such as Latent Semantic Indexing and Probabilistic Topic Models, such as Latent Dirichlet Allocation. The math of these approaches is beyond the scope of this book, but we can think of the topic layer as being a clustering of words. In topic modeling, the terms associated with the topic, and any term weights, are *learned* by the topic modeling process. As with clusters, the topics emerge from statistical regularities in the data. As such, they are not necessarily intelligible, and they are not guaranteed to correspond to topics familiar to people, though in many cases they are.

Note: Topics as Latent Information

Topic models are a type of *latent information* model, which we'll discuss a bit more in Chapter 12 (along with a movie recommendation example). You can think of latent information as a type of intermediate, unobserved layer of information inserted between the inputs and outputs. The techniques are essentially the same for finding latent topics in text and for finding latent "taste" dimensions of movie viewers. In the case of text, words map to topics (unobserved) and topics map to documents. This makes the entire model more complex and more expensive to learn, but can yield better performance. In addition, the latent information is often interesting and useful in its own right (as we will see again in the movie recommendation example in Chapter 12).

Example: Mining News Stories to Predict Stock Price Movement

To illustrate some issues in text mining, we introduce a new predictive mining task: we're going to predict stock price fluctuations based on the text of news stories. Roughly speaking, we are going to "predict the stock market" based on the stories that appear on the news wires. This project contains many common elements of text processing and of problem formulation.

The Task

Every trading day there is activity in the stock market. Companies make and announce decisions—mergers, new products, earnings projections, and so forth—and the financial news industry reports on them. Investors read these news stories, possibly change their beliefs about the prospects of the companies involved, and trade stock accordingly. This results in stock price changes. For example, announcements of acquisitions, earnings, regulatory changes, and so on can all affect the price of a stock, either because it directly affects the earnings potential or because it affects what traders think other traders are likely to pay for the stock.

This is a very simplified view of the financial markets, of course, but it's enough to lay out a basic task. We want to predict stock price changes based on financial news. There are many ways we could approach this based on the ultimate purpose of the project. If we wanted to make *trades* based on financial news, ideally we'd like to predict—in advance and with precision—the change in a company's stock price based on the stream of news. In reality there are many complex factors involved in stock price changes, many of which are not conveyed in news stories.

Instead, we'll mine the news stories for a more modest purpose, that of *news recommendation*. From this point of view, there is a huge stream of market news coming in

—some interesting, most not. We'd like predictive text mining to recommend interesting news stories that we should pay attention to. What's an interesting story? Here we'll define it as *news that will likely result in a significant change in a stock's price.*

We have to simplify the problem further to make it more tractable (in fact, this task is a good example of problem formulation as much as it is of text mining). Here are some of the problems and simplifying assumptions:

1. It is difficult to predict the effect of news far in advance. With many stocks, news arrives fairly often and the market responds quickly. It is unrealistic, for example, to predict what price a stock will have a week from now based on a news release today. Therefore, we'll try to predict what effect a news story will have on stock price the *same day*.

2. It is difficult to predict exactly what the stock price will be. Instead, we will be satisfied with the *direction* of movement: up, down, or no change. In fact, we'll simplify this further into **change** and **no change**. This works well for our example application: recommending a news story if it looks like it will trigger, or indicate, a subsequent change in the stock price.

3. It is difficult to predict small changes in stock price, so instead we'll predict *relatively large* changes. This will make the signal a bit cleaner at the expense of yielding fewer events. We will deliberately ignore the subtlety of small fluctuations.

4. It is difficult to associate a specific piece of news with a price change. In principle, any piece of news could affect any stock. If we accepted this idea it would leave us with a huge problem of credit assignment: how do you decide which of today's thousands of stories are relevant? We need to narrow the "causal radius."

   We will assume that only news stories mentioning a specific stock will affect that stock's price. This is inaccurate, of course—companies are affected by the actions of their competitors, customers, and clients, and it's rare that a news story will mention all of them. But for a first pass this is an acceptable simplifying assumption.

We still have to nail some of this down. Consider issue two. What is a "relatively large" change? We can (somewhat arbitrarily) place a threshold of 5%. If a stock's price increases by five percent or more, we'll call it a **surge**; if it declines by five percent or more, we'll call it a **plunge**. What if it changes by some amount in between? We could call any value in between **stable**, but that's cutting it a little close—a 4.9% change and a 5% change shouldn't really be distinct classes. Instead, we'll designate some "gray zones" to make the classes more separable (see Figure 10-7). Only if a stock's price stays between 2.5% and −2.5% will it be called **stable**. Otherwise, for the zones between 2.5% to 5% and −2.5% to −5%, we'll refuse to label it.

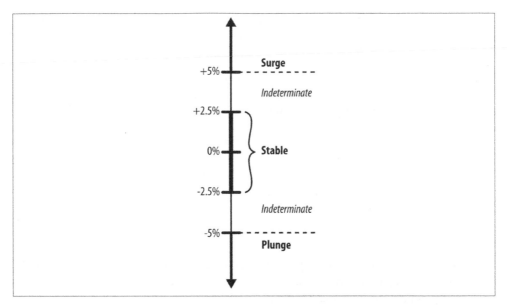

Figure 10-7. Percentage change in price, and corresponding label.

For the purpose of this example, we'll create a two-class problem by merging surge and plunge into a single class, **change**. It will be the positive class, and **stable** (**no change**) will be the negative class.

The Data

The data we'll use comprise two separate time series: the stream of news stories (text documents), and a corresponding stream of daily stock prices. The Internet has many sources of financial data, such as Google Finance and Yahoo! Finance. For example, to see what news stories are available about Apple Computer, Inc., see the corresponding Yahoo! Finance page (*http://finance.yahoo.com/q?s=AAPL*). Yahoo! aggregates news stories from a variety of sources such as Reuters, PR Web, and Forbes. Historical stock prices can be acquired from many sources, such as Google Finance (*https://www.google.com/finance*).

The data to be mined are historical data from 1999 for stocks listed on the New York Stock Exchange and NASDAQ. This data was used in a prior study (Fawcett & Provost, 1999). We have open and close prices for stocks on the major exchanges, and a large compendium of financial news stories throughout the year—nearly 36,000 stories altogether. Here is a sample news story from the corpus:

```
1999-03-30 14:45:00
WALTHAM, Mass.--(BUSINESS WIRE)--March 30, 1999--Summit Technology,
Inc. (NASDAQ:BEAM) and Autonomous Technologies Corporation
(NASDAQ:ATCI) announced today that the Joint Proxy/Prospectus for
```

```
Summit's acquisition of Autonomous has been declared effective by the
Securities and Exchange Commission. Copies of the document have been
mailed to stockholders of both companies. "We are pleased that these
proxy materials have been declared effective and look forward to the
shareholder meetings scheduled for April 29," said Robert Palmisano,
Summit's Chief Executive Officer.
```

As with many text sources, there is a lot of miscellaneous material since it is intended
for human readers and not machine parsing (see "Sidebar: The News Is Messy" on page
272 for more details). The story includes the date and time, the news source (Reuters),
stock symbols and link (NASDAQ:BEAM), as well as background material not strictly
germane to the news. Each such story is tagged with the stock mentioned.

Figure 10-8. Graph of stock price of Summit Technologies, Inc., (NASDAQ:BEAM) annotated with news story summaries.

1   Summit Tech announces revenues for the three months ended Dec 31, 1998 were $22.4 million, an increase of 13%.

2   Summit Tech and Autonomous Technologies Corporation announce that the Joint Proxy/Prospectus for Summit's acquisition
    of Autonomous has been declared effective by the SEC.

3   Summit Tech said that its procedure volume reached new levels in the first quarter and that it had concluded its acquisition
    of Autonomous Technologies Corporation.

4   Announcement of annual shareholders meeting.

5   Summit Tech announces it has filed a registration statement with the SEC to sell 4,000,000 shares of its common stock.

6   A US FDA panel backs the use of a Summit Tech laser in LASIK procedures to correct nearsightedness with or without
    astigmatism.

7   Summit up 1-1/8 at 27-3/8.

8   Summit Tech said today that its revenues for the three months ended June 30, 1999 increased 14%…

9   Summit Tech announces the public offering of 3,500,000 shares of its common stock priced at $16/share.

10 Summit announces an agreement with Sterling Vision, Inc. for the purchase of up to six of Summit's state of the art, Apex Plus Laser Systems.

11 Preferred Capital Markets, Inc. initiates coverage of Summit Technology Inc. with a Strong Buy rating and a 12-16 month price target of $22.50.

Sidebar: The News Is Messy

The financial news corpus is actually far messier than this one story implies, for several reasons.

First, financial news comprises a wide variety of stories, including earnings announcements, analysts' assessments ("We are reiterating our Buy rating on Apple"), market commentary ("Other stocks featured in this morning's MarketMovers include Lycos Inc. and Staples Inc."), SEC filings, financial balance sheets, and so on. Companies are mentioned for many different reasons and a single document ("story") may actually comprise multiple unrelated news blurbs of the day.

Second, stories come in different formats, some with tabular data, some in a multi-paragraph "lead stories of the day" format, and so on. Much of the meaning is imparted by context. Our text processing won't pick this up.

Finally, stock tagging is not perfect. It tends to be overly permissive, such that stories are included in the news feed of stocks that were not actually referenced in the story. As an extreme example, American blogger Perez Hilton uses the expression "cray cray" to mean crazy or disgusting, and some of his blog postings end up in the story feed of Cray Computer Corporation.

In short, the relevance of a stock to a document may not be clear without a careful reading. With deep parsing (or at least story segmentation) we could eliminate some of the noise, but with bag of words (or even named entity extraction) we cannot hope to remove all of it.

Figure 10-8 shows the kind of data we have to work with. They are basically two linked time series. At the top is a graph of the stock price of Summit Technologies, Inc., a manufacturer of excimer laser systems for use in laser vision correction. Some points on the graph are annotated with story numbers on the date the story was released. Below the graph are summaries of each story.

Data Preprocessing

As mentioned, we have two streams of data. Each stock has an opening and closing price for the day, measured at 9:30 am EST and 4:00 pm EST, respectively. From these values we can easily compute a percentage change. There is one minor complication. We're trying to predict stories that produce a substantial change in a stock's value. Many events occur outside of trading hours, and fluctuations near the opening of trading can be erratic. For this reason, instead of measuring the opening price at the opening bell (9:30 am EST) we measure it at 10:00 am, and track the difference between the day's prices at 4 pm and 10 am. Divided by the stock's closing price, this becomes the daily percent change.

The stories require much more care. The stories are pre-tagged with stocks, which are mostly accurate ("Sidebar: The News Is Messy" on page 272 goes into some details on why this is a difficult text mining problem). Almost all stories have timestamps (those without are discarded) so we can align them with the correct day and trading window. Because we want a fairly tight association of a story with the stock(s) it might affect, we reject any stories mentioning more than two stocks. This gets rid of many stories that are just summaries and news aggregations.

The basic steps outlined in "Bag of Words" on page 254 were applied to reduce each story to a TFIDF representation. In particular, each word was case-normalized and stemmed, and stopwords were removed. Finally, we created n-grams up to two, such that every individual term and pair of adjacent terms were used to represent each story.

Subject to this preparation, each story is tagged with a label (**change** or **no change**) based on the associated stock(s) price movement, as depicted in Figure 10-7. This results in about 16,000 usable tagged stories. For reference, the breakdown of stories was about 75% no change, 13% surge, and 12% plunge. The surge and plunge stories were merged to form **change**, so 25% of the stories were followed by a significant price change to the stocks involved, and 75% were not.

Results

Before we dig into results, a short digression.

Previous chapters (particularly Chapter 7) stressed the importance of thinking carefully about the business problem being solved in order to frame the evaluation. With this example we have not done such careful specification. If the purpose of this task were to trigger stock trades, we might propose an overall trading strategy involving thresholds, time limits, and transaction costs, from which we could produce a complete cost-benefit analysis.[4] But the purpose is news recommendation (answering "which stories lead to

---

4. Some researchers have done this, evaluating their systems by simulating stock trades and calculating the return on investment. See, for example, Schumaker & Chen's (2010) work on AZFinText.

substantial stock price changes?") and we've left this pretty open, so we won't specify exact costs and benefits of decisions. For this reason, expected value calculations and profit graphs aren't really appropriate here.

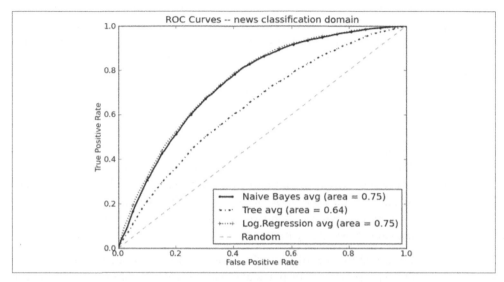

Figure 10-9. ROC curves for the stock news classification task.

Instead, let's look at predictability, just to get a sense of how well this problem can be solved. Figure 10-9 shows the ROC curves of three sample classifiers: Logistic Regression, Naive Bayes, and a Classification Tree, as well as the random classification line. These curves are averaged from ten-fold cross-validation, using **change** as the positive class and **no change** as the negative class. Several things are apparent. First, there is a significant "bowing out" of the curves away from the diagonal (Random) line, and the ROC curve areas (AUCs) are all substantially above 0.5, so there *is* predictive signal in the news stories. Second, logistic regression and Naive Bayes perform similarly, whereas the classification tree (Tree) is considerably worse. Finally, there is no obvious region of superiority (or deformity) in the curves. Bulges or concavities can sometimes reveal characteristics of the problem, or flaws in the data representation, but we see none here.

Figure 10-10 shows the corresponding lift curves of these three classifiers, again averaged from ten-fold cross-validation. Recall that one in four (25%) of the stories in our population is positive, (i.e., it is followed by a significant change in stock price). Each curve shows the lift in precision[5] we would get if we used the model to score and order the news stories. For example, consider the point at $x=0.2$, where the lifts of Logistic

---

5. Recall from Chapter 7, precision is the percentage of the cases that are above the classification threshold that are actually positive examples, and the lift is how many times more this is than you would expect by chance.

Regression and Naive Bayes are both around 2.0. This means that, if you were to score all the news stories and take the top 20% (*x*=0.2), you'd have *twice* the precision (lift of two) of finding a positive story in that group than in the population as a whole. Therefore, among the top 20% of the stories as ranked by the model, *half* are significant.

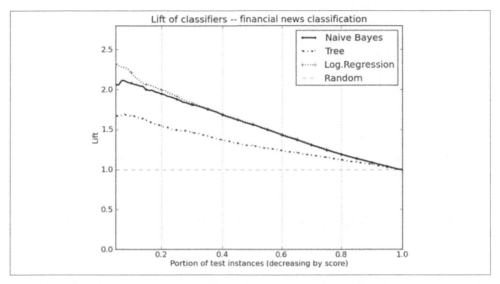

Figure 10-10. Lift curves for the stock news prediction task.

Before concluding this example, let's look at some of the important terms found from this task. The goal of this example was not to create intelligible rules from the data, but prior work on the same corpus by Macskassy et al. (2001) did just that. Here is a list of terms with high information gain[6] taken from their work. Each term is either a word or a stem followed by suffixes in parentheses:

    alert(s,ed), architecture, auction(s,ed,ing,eers), average(s,d), award(s,ed),
    bond(s), brokerage, climb(ed,s,ing), close(d,s), comment(ator,ed,ing,s),
    commerce(s), corporate, crack(s,ed,ing), cumulative, deal(s), dealing(s),
    deflect(ed,ing), delays, depart(s,ed), department(s), design(ers,ing),
    economy, econtent, edesign, eoperate, esource, event(s), exchange(s),
    extens(ion,ive), facilit(y,ies), gain(ed,s,ing), higher, hit(s), imbalance(s),
    index, issue(s,d), late(ly), law(s,ful), lead(s,ing), legal(ity,ly), lose,
    majority, merg(ing,ed,es), move(s,d), online, outperform(s,ance,ed),
    partner(s), payments, percent, pharmaceutical(s), price(d), primary,
    recover(ed,s), redirect(ed,ion), stakeholder(s), stock(s), violat(ing,ion,ors)

Many of these are suggestive of significant announcements of good or bad news for a company or its stock price. Some of them (econtent, edesign, eoperate) are also sug-

6. Recall Chapter 3.

gestive of the "Dotcom Boom" of the late 1990s, from which this corpus is taken, when the e- prefix was in vogue.

Though this example is one of the most complex presented in this book, it is still a fairly simple approach to mining financial news stories. There are many ways this project could be extended and refined. The bag-of-words representation is primitive for this task; named entity recognition could be used to better extract the names of the companies and people involved. Better still, event parsing should provide real leverage, since news stories usually report events rather than static facts about companies. It is not clear from individual words who are the subjects and objects of the events, and important modifiers like *not*, *despite*, and *expect* may not be adjacent to the phrases they modify, so the bag of words representation is at a disdvantage. Finally, to calculate price changes we considered only daily opening and closing stock prices, rather than hourly or instantaneous ("tick level") price changes. The market responds quickly to news, and if we wanted to trade on the information we'd need to have fine-grained, reliable timestamps on both stock prices and news stories.

Sidebar: Prior Work on Predicting Stock Prices from Financial News

The problem of relating financial news stories to market activity has been tackled by many people in the past 15 years or so. Your authors even did some early work on the task (Fawcett & Provost, 1999). Most of the prior work has been published outside the data mining literature, so the data mining community may remain largely unaware of the task and the work. We mention a few articles here for anyone interested in pursuing the topic.

A survey by Mittermayer and Knolmayer (2006) is a good place to start, though it is a bit dated by now. It provides a good overview of approaches up to that point.

Most researchers view the problem as predicting the stock market from news. In this chapter, we've taken an inverse view as that of recommending news stories based on their future effects. This task was termed *information triage* by Macskassy et al. (2001).

Early work looked at the effect of financial news in the mainstream media. Later work takes into account opinions and sentiment from other sources on the Internet, such as Twitter updates, blog postings, and search engine trends. A paper by Mao et al. (2011) provides a good analysis and comparison of the effect of these additional sources.

Finally, though it's not text mining per se, let us mention the paper "Legislating Stock Prices" by Cohen, Diether, and Malloy (2012). These researchers examined the relationship of politicians, legislation, and firms affected by the legislation. Obviously, these three groups are interrelated and should affect each other, but surprisingly, the relationship had not been exploited by Wall Street. From publicly available data the researchers discovered a "simple, yet previously undetected impact on firm stock prices"

---

that they report to be able to trade upon profitably. This suggests that there are undiscovered relationships remaining to be mined.

Summary

Our problems do not always present us with data in a neat feature vector representation that most data mining methods take as input. Real-world problems often require some form of data representation engineering to make them amenable to mining. Generally it is simpler to first try to engineer the data to match existing tools. Data in the form of text, images, sound, video, and spatial information usually require special preprocessing —and sometimes special knowledge on the part of the data science team.

In this chapter, we discussed one especially prevalent type of data that requires preprocessing: text. A common way to turn text into a feature vector is to break each document into individual words (its "bag of words" representation), and assign values to each term using the TFIDF formula. This approach is relatively simple, inexpensive and versatile, and requires little knowledge of the domain, at least initially. In spite of its simplicity, it performs surprisingly well on a variety of tasks. In fact, we will revisit these ideas on a completely different, nontext task in Chapter 14.

CHAPTER 11

Decision Analytic Thinking II: Toward Analytical Engineering

Fundamental concept: *Solving business problems with data science starts with analytical engineering: designing an analytical solution, based on the data, tools, and techniques available.*

Exemplary technique: *Expected value as a framework for data science solution design.*

Ultimately, data science is about extracting information or knowledge from data, based on principled techniques. However, as we've discussed throughout the book, seldom does the world provide us with important business problems perfectly aligned with these techniques, or with data represented such that the techniques can be applied directly. Ironically, this fact often is better accepted by the business users (for whom it is often obvious) than by entry-level data scientists—because academic programs in statistics, machine learning, and data mining often present students with problems ready for the application of the tools that the programs teach.

Reality is much messier. Business problems rarely are classification problems or regression problems or clustering problems. They're just business problems. Recall the mini-cycle in the first stages of the data mining process, where we focus on business understanding and data understanding. In these stages we must *design* or *engineer* a solution to the business problem. As with engineering more broadly, the data science team considers the needs of the business as well as the tools that might be brought to bear to solve the problem.

In this chapter, we will illustrate such *analytical engineering* with two case studies. In these case studies, we will see the application of the fundamental principles presented throughout the book, as well as some of the specific techniques that we have introduced. One common theme that runs through these case studies is how our expected value framework (recall from Chapter 7) helps to decompose each of the business problems into subproblems, such that the subproblems can be attacked with tried-and-true data science techniques. Then the expected value framework guides the recombination of the results into a solution to the original problem.

Targeting the Best Prospects for a Charity Mailing

A classic business problem for applying data science principles and techniques is targeted marketing. Targeted marketing makes for a perfect case study for two reasons. First, a very large number of businesses have problems that look similar to targeted marketing problems—traditional targeted (database) marketing, customer-specific coupon offers, online ad targeting, and so on. Second, the fundamental structure of the problem occurs in many other problems as well, such as our running example problem of churn management.

For this case study, let's consider a real example of targeted marketing: targeting the best prospects for a charity mailing. Fundraising organizations (including those in universities) need to manage their budgets and the patience of their potential donors. In any given campaign segment, they would like to solicit from a "good" subset of the donors. This could be a very large subset for an inexpensive, infrequent campaign, or a smaller subset for a focused campaign that includes a not-so-inexpensive incentive package.

The Expected Value Framework: Decomposing the Business Problem and Recomposing the Solution Pieces

We would like to "engineer" an analytic solution to the problem, and our fundamental concepts will provide the structure to do so. To frame our data-analytic thinking, we begin by using the data-mining process (Chapter 2) to provide structure to the overall analysis: we start with business and data understanding. More specifically, we need to focus using one of our fundamental principles: what exactly is the business problem that we would like to solve (Chapter 7)?

So let's get specific. A data miner might immediately think: we want to model the probability that each prospective customer, a prospective donor in this case, will respond to the offer. However, thinking carefully about the business problem we realize that in this case, the response can vary—some people might donate $100 while others might donate $1. We need to take this into account.

Would we like to maximize the total amount of donations? (The amount could be either in this particular campaign or over the lifetime of the donor prospects; let's assume the first for simplicity.) What if we did that by targeting a massive number of people, and these each give just $1, and our costs are about $1 per person? We would make almost no money. So let's revise our thinking.

Focusing on the business problem that we want to solve may have given us our answer right away, because to a business-savvy person it may seem rather obvious: we would like to maximize our donation *profit*—meaning the net after taking into account the costs. However, while we have methods for estimating the probability of response (that's a clear application of class probability estimation over a binary outcome), it is not clear that we have methods to estimate profit.

Again, our fundamental concepts allow us to structure our thinking and engineer a data-analytic solution. Applying another one of our fundamental notions, we can structure this data analysis using the framework of expected value. We can apply the concepts introduced in Chapter 7 to our problem formulation: we can use expected value as a framework for structuring our approach to engineering a solution to the problem. Recall our formulation of the expected benefit (or cost) of targeting consumer $\mathbf{x}$:

$$\text{Expected benefit of targeting} = p(R \mid \mathbf{x}) \cdot v_R + [1 - p(R \mid \mathbf{x})] \cdot v_{NR}$$

where $(p(R \mid \mathbf{x}))$ is the probability of response given consumer $\mathbf{x}$, v_R is the value we get from a response, and v_{NR} is the value we get from no response. Since everyone either responds or does not, our estimate of the probability of not responding is just $((1 - p(R \mid \mathbf{x})))$. As we discussed in Chapter 7, we can model the probabilities by mining historical data using one of the many techniques discussed through the book.

However, the expected value framework helps us realize that this business problem is slightly different from problems we have considered up to this point. In this case, the value varies from consumer to consumer, and we do not know the value of the donation that any particular consumer will give until after she is targeted! Let's modify our formulation to make this explicit:

$$\text{Expected benefit of targeting} = p(R \mid \mathbf{x}) \cdot v_R(\mathbf{x}) + [1 - p(R \mid \mathbf{x})] \cdot v_{NR}(\mathbf{x})$$

where $v_R(\mathbf{x})$ is the value we get from a response from consumer $\mathbf{x}$ and $v_{NR}(\mathbf{x})$ is the value we get if consumer $\mathbf{x}$ does not respond. The value of a response, $v_R(\mathbf{x})$, would be the consumer's donation minus the cost of the solicitation. The value of no response, $v_{NR}(\mathbf{x})$, in this application would be zero minus the cost of the solicitation. To be complete, we also want to estimate the benefit of *not* targeting, and then compare the two to make the decision of whether to target or not. The expected benefit of not targeting is simply zero—in this application, we do not expect consumers to donate spontaneously without a solicitation. That may not always be the case, but let's assume it is here.

Why exactly does the expected value framework help us? Because we may be able to estimate $v_R(\mathbf{x})$ and/or $v_{NR}(\mathbf{x})$ from the data as well. Regression modeling estimates such values. Looking at historical data on consumers who have been targeted, we can use regression modeling to estimate how much a consumer will respond. Moreover, the expected value framework gives us even more precise direction: $v_R(\mathbf{x})$ is the value we would predict to get *if a consumer were to respond* — this would be estimated using a model trained only on consumers who have responded. This turns out to be a more useful prediction problem than the problem of estimating the response from a targeted consumer generally, because in this application the vast majority of consumers do not respond at all, and so the regression modeling would need somehow to differentiate between the cases where the value is zero because of non-response or the value is small because of the characteristics of the consumer.

Stepping back for a moment, this example illustrates why the expected value framework is so useful for decomposing business problems: as discussed in Chapter 7, the expected value is a summation of products of probabilities and values, and data science gives us methods to estimate both probabilities and values. To be clear, we may not need to estimate some of these quantities (like $v_{NR}(\mathbf{x})$, which we assume in this example is always zero), and estimating them well may be a nontrivial undertaking. The point is that the expected value framework provides a helpful decomposition of possibly complicated business problems into subproblems that we understand better how to solve. The framework also shows exactly how to put the pieces together. For our example problem (chosen for its straightforward derivation), the answer works out to the intuitively satisfying result: mail to those people whose estimated expected donation is greater than the cost associated with mailing! Mathematically, we simply look for those whose expected benefit of targeting is greater than zero, and simplify the inequality algebraically. Let $d_R(\mathbf{x})$ be the estimated donation if consumer $\mathbf{x}$ were to respond, and let c be the mailing cost. Then:

$$\text{Expected benefit of targeting} = p(R \mid \mathbf{x}) \cdot v_R(\mathbf{x}) + [1 - p(R \mid \mathbf{x})] \cdot v_{NR}(\mathbf{x})$$

We always want this benefit to be greater than zero, so:

$$p(R \mid \mathbf{x}) \cdot (d_R(\mathbf{x}) - c) + [1 - p(R \mid \mathbf{x})] \cdot (-c) > 0$$
$$p(R \mid \mathbf{x}) \cdot d_R(\mathbf{x}) - p(R \mid \mathbf{x}) \cdot c - c + p(R \mid \mathbf{x}) \cdot c > 0$$
$$p(R \mid \mathbf{x}) \cdot d_R(\mathbf{x}) > c$$

That is, the expected donation (lefthand side) should be greater than the solicitation cost (righthand side).

A Brief Digression on Selection Bias

This example brings up an important data science issue whose detailed treatment is beyond the scope of this book, but nevertheless is important to discuss briefly. For modeling the predicted donation, notice that the data may well be biased—meaning that they are not a random sample from the population of all donors. Why? Because the data are from past donations—from the individuals who *did respond* in the past. This is similar to the idea of modeling creditworthiness based on the experience with past credit customers: those are likely the people whom you had deemed to be creditworthy in the past! However, you want to apply the model to the general population to find good prospects. Why would those who happened to have been selected in the past be a good sample from which to model the general population? This is an example of *selection bias*—the data were not selected randomly from the population to which you intend to apply the model, but instead were biased in some way (by who happened to donate, and perhaps by those who were targeted using past methods; by who was granted credit in the past).

One important question for the data scientist is: do you expect the particular selection procedure that biases the data also to have a bearing on the value of the target variable? In modeling creditworthiness, the answer is absolutely *yes*—the past customers were selected precisely because they were predicted to be creditworthy. The donation case is not as straightforward, but it seems reasonable to expect that people who donate larger sums do not donate as often. For example, some people may donate $10 each and every time they're asked. Others may give $100 and then feel they need not donate for a while, ignoring many subsequent campaigns. The result would be that those who happened to donate in some past campaign will be biased towards those who donate *less*.

Fortunately, there are data science techniques to help modelers deal with selection bias. They are beyond the scope of this book, but the interested reader might start by reading (Zadrozny & Elkan, 2001; Zadrozny, 2004) for an illustration of dealing with selection bias in this exact donation solicitation case study.

Our Churn Example Revisited with Even More Sophistication

Let's return to our example of churn and apply what we've learned to examine it data-analytically. In our prior forays, we did not treat the problem as comprehensively as we might. That was by design, of course, because we had not learned everything we needed yet, and the intermediate attempts were illustrative. But now let's examine the problem in more detail, applying the exact same fundamental data science concepts as we just applied to the case of soliciting donations.

The Expected Value Framework: Structuring a More Complicated Business Problem

First, what exactly is the business problem we would like to solve? Let's keep our basic example problem setting: we're having a serious problem with churn in our wireless business. Marketing has designed a special retention offer. Our task is to target the offer to some appropriate subset of our customer base.

Initially, we had decided that we would try to use our data to determine which customers would be the most likely to defect shortly after their contracts expire. Let's continue to focus on the set of customers whose contracts are about to expire, because this is where most of the churn occurs. However, do we really want to target our offer to those with the highest probability of defection?

We need to go back to our fundamental concept: what exactly is the business problem we want to solve. Why is churn a problem? Because it causes us to lose money. The real business problem is losing money. If a customer actually were costly to us rather than profitable, we may not mind losing her. We would like to limit the amount of money we are losing—not simply to keep the most customers. Therefore, as in the donation problem, we want to take the *value* of the customer into account. Our expected value framework helps us to frame that analysis, similar to how it did above. In the case of churn, the value of an individual may be much easier to estimate: these are our customers, and since we have their billing records we can probably forecast their future value pretty well (contingent on their staying with the company) with a simple extrapolation of their past value. However, in this case we have not completely solved our problem, and framing the analysis using expected value shows why.

Let's apply our expected value framework to really dig down into the business understanding/data understanding segment of the data mininig process. Is there any problem with treating this case exactly as we did the donation case? As with the donation case study, we might represent the expected benefit of targeting a customer with the special offer as:

$$\text{Expected benefit of targeting} = p(S \mid \mathbf{x}) \cdot v_S(\mathbf{x}) + [1 - p(S \mid \mathbf{x})] \cdot v_{NS}(\mathbf{x})$$

where ($p(S \mid \mathbf{x})$) is the probability that the customer will **S**tay with the company after being targeted, $v_S(\mathbf{x})$ is the value we get if consumer $\mathbf{x}$ stays with the company and $v_{NS}(\mathbf{x})$ is the value we get if consumer $\mathbf{x}$ does not stay (defects or churns).

Can we use this to target customers with the special offer? All else being equal, targeting those with the highest value seems like it simply targets those with the highest probability of *staying*, rather than the highest probability of leaving! To see this let's oversimplify by assuming that the value if the customer does not stay is zero. Then our expected value becomes:

$$\text{Expected benefit of targeting} = p(S \mid \mathbf{x}) \cdot v_s(\mathbf{x})$$

That does not jibe with our prior intuition that we want to target those who have the highest probability of leaving. What's wrong? Our expected value framework tells us exactly—let's be more careful. We don't want to just apply what we did in the donation problem, but to think carefully about this problem. We don't want to target those with the highest value if they were to stay. We want to target those where we would lose the most value if they were to leave. That's complicated, but our expected value framework can help us to work through the thinking systematically, and as we will see that will cast an interesting light on the solution. Recall that in the donation example we said, "To be complete, we would also want to assess the expected benefit of not targeting, and then compare the two to make the decision of whether to target or not." We allowed ourselves to ignore this in the donation setting because we assumed that consumers were not going to donate spontaneously without a solicitation. However, in the business understanding phase we need to think through the specifics of each particular business problem.

Let's think about the "not targeting" case of the churn problem. Is the value zero if we don't target? No, not necessarily. If we do not target and the customer stays anyway, then we actually achieve higher value because we did not expend the cost of the incentive!

Assessing the Influence of the Incentive

Let's dig even deeper, calculating both the benefit of targeting a customer with the incentive and of not targeting her, and making the cost of the incentive explicit. Let's call $u_S(\mathbf{x})$ the profit from customer $\mathbf{x}$ if she stays, not including the incentive cost; and $u_{NS}(\mathbf{x})$ the profit from customer $\mathbf{x}$ if she leaves, not including the incentive cost. Furthmore, for simplicity, let's assume that we incur the incentive cost c no matter whether the customer stays or leaves.

 For churn this is not completely realistic, as the incentives usually include a large cost component that is contingent upon staying, such as a new phone. Expanding the analysis to include this small complication is straightforward, and we would draw the same qualitative conclusions. Try it.

So let's compute separately the expected benefit if we target or if we do not target. In doing so, we need to clarify that there (hopefully) will be different estimated probabilities of staying and churning depending on whether we target (i.e., hopefully the incentive actually has an effect), which we indicate by conditioning the probability of staying on the two possibilities (target, T, or not target, $notT$). The expected benefit of targeting is:

$$EB_T(\mathbf{x}) = p(S \mid \mathbf{x}, T) \cdot (u_s(\mathbf{x}) - c) + [1 - p(S \mid \mathbf{x}, T)] \cdot (u_{NS}(\mathbf{x}) - c)$$

The expected benefit of not targeting is:

$$EB_{notT}(\mathbf{x}) = p(S \mid \mathbf{x}, notT) \cdot u_s(\mathbf{x}) + [1 - p(S \mid \mathbf{x}, notT)] \cdot u_{NS}(\mathbf{x})$$

So, now to complete our business problem formulation, we would like to target those customers for whom we would see the greatest expected benefit *from targeting them*. These are specifically those customers where $EB_T(\mathbf{x}) - EB_{notT}(\mathbf{x})$ is the largest. This is a substantially more complex problem formulation than we have seen before—but the expected value framework structures our thinking so we can think systematically and engineer our analysis focusing precisely on the goal.

The expected value framework also allows us to see what is different about this problem structure than those that we have considered in the past. Specifically, we need to consider what would happen if we did *not target* (looking at both EB_T and EB_{notT}), as well as what is the actual *influence* of the incentive (taking the difference of EB_T and EB_{notT}).[1]

Let's take another brief mathematical digression to illustrate. Consider the conditions under which this "value of targeting," $VT = EB_T(\mathbf{x}) - EB_{notT}(\mathbf{x})$, would be the largest. Let's expand the equation for VT, but at the same time simplify by assuming that we get no value from a customer if she does not stay.

Equation 11-1. VT decomposition

$$
\begin{aligned}
VT &= p(S \mid \mathbf{x}, T) \cdot u_S(\mathbf{x}) - p(S \mid \mathbf{x}, notT) \cdot u_S(\mathbf{x}) - c \\
&= [p(S \mid \mathbf{x}, T) - p(S \mid \mathbf{x}, notT)] \cdot u_S(\mathbf{x}) - c \\
&= \Delta(p) \cdot u_S(\mathbf{x}) - c
\end{aligned}
$$

where $(\Delta(p))$ is the difference in the predicted probabilities of staying, depending on whether the customer is targeted or not. Again we see an intuitive result: we want to target those customers with the greatest change in their probability of staying, moderated by their value if they were to stay! In other words, target those with the greatest change in their expected value as a result of targeting. (The $-c$ is the same for everyone in our scenario, and including it here simply assures that the VT is not expected to be a monetary loss.)

It's important not to lose track: this was all work in our Business Understanding phase. Let's turn to the implications for the rest of the data mining process.

From an Expected Value Decomposition to a Data Science Solution

The prior discussion and specifically the decomposition highlighted in Equation 11-1 guide us in our data understanding, data formulation, modeling, and evaluation. In particular, from the decomposition we can see precisely what models we will want to

---

1. This also is an essential starting point for *causal analysis*: create a so-called counterfactual situation assessing the difference in expected values between two otherwise identical settings. These settings are often called the "treated" and "untreated" cases, in analogy to medical inference, where one often wants to assess the causal influence of the treatment. The many different frameworks for causal analysis, from randomized experimentation, to regression-based causal analysis, to more modern causal modeling approaches, all have this difference in expected values at their core. We will discuss causal data analysis further in Chapter 12.

build: models to estimate ($p(S \mid \mathbf{x}, T)$) and ($p(S \mid \mathbf{x}, notT)$), the probability that a customer will stay if targeted and the probability that a customer will stay anyway, even if not targeted. Unlike our prior data mining solutions, here we want to build two separate probability estimation models. Once these models are built, we can use them to compute the expected value of targeting.

Importantly, the expected value decomposition focuses our Data Understanding efforts. What data do we need to build these models? In both cases, we need samples of customers who have reached contract expiration. Indeed, we need samples of customers who have gone far enough beyond contract expiration that we are satisfied with concluding they have definitely "stayed" or "left." For the first model we need a sample of customers who were targeted with the offer. For the second model, we need a sample of customers who were *not* targeted with the offer. Hopefully this would be a representative sample of the customer base to which the model was applied (see the above discussion of selection bias). Developing our Data Understanding, let's think more deeply about each of these in turn.

How can we obtain a sample of such customers who have not been targeted with the offer? First, we should assure ourselves that nothing substantial has changed in the business environment that would call into question the use of historical data for churn prediction (e.g., the introduction of the iPhone only to AT&T customers would have been such an event for the other phone companies). Assuming there has been no such event, gathering the requisite data should be relatively straightforward: the phone company keeps substantial data on customers for many months, for billing, fraud detection, and other purposes. Given that this is a new offer, none of them would have been targeted with it. We would want to double-check that none of our customers was made some other offer that would affect the likelihood of churning.

The situation with modeling ($p(S \mid \mathbf{x}, T)$) is quite different, and again highlights how the expected value framework can focus our thinking early, highlighting issues and challenges that we face. What's the challenge here? This is a new offer. No one has seen it yet. We do not have the data to build a model to estimate ($p(S \mid \mathbf{x}, T)$)!

Nonetheless, business exigencies may force us to proceed. We need to reduce churn; Marketing has confidence in this offer, and we certainly have some data that might inform how we proceed. This is not an uncommon situation in the application of data science to solving a real business problem. The expected value decomposition can lead us to a complex formulation that helps us to understand the problem, but for which we are not willing or able to address the full complexity. It may be that we simply do not have the resources (data, human, or computing). In our churn example, we do not have the data necessary.

A different scenario might be that we do not believe that the added complexity of the full formulation will add substantially to our effectiveness. For example, we might conclude, "*Yes, the formulation of Equation 11-1 helps me understand what I should do, but*

I believe I will do just about as well with a simpler or cheaper formulation." For example, what if we were to assume that when given the offer, everyone would Stay with certainty, $(p(S \mid \mathbf{x}, T) = 1)$? This is obviously an oversimplification, but it may allow us to act— and in business we need to be ready to act even without ideal information. You could verify via Equation 11-1 that the result of applying this assumption would be simply to target those customers with the largest $(1 - p(S \mid \mathbf{x}, notT) \cdot u_S(\mathbf{x}))$— i.e., the customers with the largest expected loss if they were to leave. That makes a lot of sense if we do not have data on the actual differential effect of the offer.

Consider an alternative course of action in a case such as this, where sufficient data are not available on a modeling target. One can instead label the data with a "proxy" for the target label of interest. For example, perhaps Marketing had come up with a similar, but not identical, offer in the past. If this offer had been made to customers in a similar situation (and recall the selection bias concern discussed above), it may be useful to build a model using the proxy label.[2]

The expected value decomposition highlights yet another option. What would we need to do to model $(p(S \mid \mathbf{x}, T))$? We need to *obtain* data. Specifically, we need to obtain data for customers who are targeted. That means we have to target customers. However, this would incur a cost. What if we target poorly and waste money targeting customers with lower probabilities of responding? This situation relates back to our very first fundamental principle of data science: data should be treated as an asset. We need to think not only about taking advantage of the assets that we already have, but also about investing in data assets from which we can generate important returns. Recall from Chapter 1 the situation Signet Bank faced in "Data and Data Science Capability as a Strategic Asset" on page 9. They did not have data on the differential response of customers to the various new sorts of offers they had designed. So they invested in data, taking losses by making offers broadly, and the data assets they acquired are considered to be the reason they became the wildly successful Capital One. Our situation may not be so grand, in that we have a single offer, and in making the offer we are not likely to lose the sort of money that Signet Bank did when their customers defaulted. Nonetheless, the lesson is the same: if we are willing to invest in data on how people will respond to this offer, we may be able to better target the offer to future customers.

---

2. For some applications, proxy labels might come from completely different events from the event on which the actual target label is based. For example, for building models to predict who will purchase after being targeted with an advertisement, data on actual conversions are scarce. It is surprisingly effective to use visiting the compaign's brand's website as a modeling proxy for purchasing (Dalessandro, Hook, Perlich, & Provost, 2012).

It's worth reiterating the importance of deep business understanding. Depending on the structure of the offer, we may not lose that much if the offer is not taken, so the simpler formulation above may be quite satisfactory.

Note that this investment in data can be managed carefully, also applying conceptual tools developed through the book. Recall the notion of visualizing performance via the learning curve, from Chapter 8. The learning curve helps us to understand the relationship between the amount of data—in this case, the amount of investment in data so far—and the resultant improvement in generalization performance. We can easily extend the notion of generalization performance to include the improvement in performance over a baseline (recall our fundamental concept: think carefully about what you will compare to). That baseline could be our alternative, simple churn model. Thus, we would slowly invest in data, examining whether increasing our data is improving our performance, and whether extrapolating the curve indicates that there are more improvements to come. If this analysis suggests that the investment is not worthwhile, it can be aborted.

Importantly, that does not mean the investment was wasteful. We invested in information: here, information about whether the additional data would pay off for our ultimate task of cost-effective churn reduction.

Furthermore, framing the problem using expected value allows extensions to the formulation to provide a structured way to approach the question of: *what is the right offer to give*. We could expand the formulation to include multiple offers, and judge which gives the best value for any particular customer. Or we could parameterize the offers (for example with a variable discount amount) and then work to optimize what discount will yield the best expected value. This would likely involve additional investment in data, running experiments to judge different customers' probabilities of staying or leaving at different offer levels—again similar to what Signet Bank did in becoming Capital One.

Summary

By following through the donation and churn examples, we have seen how the expected value framework can help articulate the true business problem and the role(s) data mining will play in its solution.

It is possible to keep elaborating the business problem into greater and greater detail, uncovering additional complexity in the problem (and greater demands on its solution). You may wonder, "*Where does this all end? Can't I keep pushing the analysis on forever?*" In principle, yes, but modeling always involves making some simplifying assumptions to keep the problem tractable. There will always be points in analytical engineering at which you should conclude:

- We can't get data on this event,
- It would be too expensive to model this aspect accurately,
- This event is so improbable we're just going to ignore it, or
- This formulation seems sufficient for the time being, and we should proceed with it.

The point of analytical engineering is not to develop complex solutions by addressing every possible contingency. Rather, the point is to promote thinking about problems data analytically so that the role of data mining is clear, the business constraints, cost, and benefits are considered, and any simplifying assumptions are made consciously and explicitly. This increases the chance of project success and reduces the risk of being blindsided by problems during deployment.

CHAPTER 12

Other Data Science Tasks and Techniques

Fundamental concepts: *Our fundamental concepts as the basis of many common data science techniques; The importance of familiarity with the building blocks of data science.*

Exemplary techniques: *Association and co-occurrences; Behavior profiling; Link prediction; Data reduction; Latent information mining; Movie recommendation; Bias-variance decomposition of error; Ensembles of models; Causal reasoning from data.*

As discussed in the previous chapter, a useful way to think of a team approaching a business problem data analytically is that they are faced with an *engineering* problem—not mechanical engineering or even software engineering, but *analytical engineering*. The business problem itself provides the goal as well as constraints on its solution. The data and domain knowledge provide raw materials. And data science provides frameworks for decomposing the problem into subproblems, as well as tools and techniques for solving them. We have discussed some of the most valuable conceptual frameworks and some of the most common building blocks for solutions. However, data science is a vast field, with entire degree programs devoted to it, so we cannot hope to be exhaustive in a book like this. Fortunately, the fundamental principles we have discussed undergird most of data science.

As with other engineering problems, it is often more efficient to cast a new problem into a set of problems for which we already have good tools, rather than trying to build a custom solution completely from scratch. Analytical engineering is not different: data science provides us with an abundance of tools to solve particular, common tasks. So we have illustrated the fundamental principles with some of the most common tools, methods for finding correlations/finding informative variables, finding similar entities, classification, class-probability estimation, regression, and clustering.

These are tools for the most common data science tasks, but as described in Chapter 2 there are others as well. Fortunately, the same fundamental concepts that underlie the tasks we have used for illustration also underlie these others. So now that we've presented the fundamentals, let's briefly discuss some of the other tasks and techniques we haven't yet discussed.

Co-occurrences and Associations: Finding Items That Go Together

Co-occurrence grouping or *association discovery* attempts to find associations between entities based on transactions involving them. Why would we want to find such co-occurrences? There are many applications. Consider a consumer-facing application. Let's say that we run an online retailer. Based on shopping cart data, we might tell a customer, "Customers who bought the new eWatch also bought the eBracelet Bluetooth speaker companion." If the associations indeed capture true consumer preferences, this might increase revenue from cross-selling. It also could enhance the consumer experience (in this case, by allowing stereo music listening from their otherwise monaural eWatch), and thus leverage our data asset to create additional customer loyalty.

Consider an operations application where we ship products to online customers from many distribution centers across the globe. Not every distribution center stocks every product. Indeed, the smaller, regional distribution centers only stock the more frequently purchased products. We built these regional distribution centers to reduce shipping expense, but in practice we see that for many orders we end up either having to ship from the main distribution center anyway, or to make multiple deliveries for many orders. The reason is that even when people order popular items, they often include less-popular items as well. This is a business problem we can try to address by mining associations from our data. If there are particular less-popular items that co-occur often with the most-popular items, these also could be stocked in the regional distribution centers, achieving a substantial reduction in our shipping costs.

The co-occurrence grouping is simply a search through the data for combinations of items whose statistics are "interesting." There are different ways of framing the task, but let's think of the co-occurrence as a rule: *"If A occurs then B is likely to occur as well."* So A might be the sale of an eWatch, and B the sale of the eBracelet.[1] The statistics on "interesting" generally follow our fundamental principles.

First, we need to consider complexity control: there are likely to be a tremendous number of co-occurrences, many of which might simply be due to chance, rather than to a generalizable pattern. A simple way to control complexity is to place a constraint that such rules must apply to some minimum percentage of the data—let's say that we require rules to apply to at least 0.01% of all transactions. This is called the *support* of the association.

---

1. *A* and *B* could be multiple items as well. We will presume that they are single items for the moment. The Facebook Likes example below generalizes to multiple items.

We also have the notion of "likely" in the association. If a customer buys the eWatch then she is likely to buy the eBracelet. Again, we may want to require a certain minimum degree of likelihood for the associations we find. We can quantify this notion again using the same notions we have already seen. The probability that B occurs when A occurs we've seen before; it is $p(B|A)$, which in association mining is called the *confidence* or *strength* of the rule. Let's call that "strength," so as not to confuse it with statistical confidence. So we might say we require the strength to be above some threshold, such as 5% (so that 5% or more of the time, a buyer of A also buys B).

Measuring Surprise: Lift and Leverage

Finally, we would like the association to be in some sense "surprising." There are many notions of surprisingness that have been pursued in data mining, but unfortunately most of them involve matching the discovered knowledge to our prior background knowledge, intuition, and common sense. In other words, an association is surprising if it contradicts something we already knew or believed. Researchers study how to address this difficult-to-codify knowledge, but dealing with it automatically is not common in practice. Instead, data scientists and business users pore over long lists of associations, culling the unsurprising ones.

However, there is a weaker but nonetheless intuitive notion of surprisingness that can be computed from the data alone, and which we already have encountered in other contexts: **lift** — how much more frequently does this association occur than we would expect by chance? If associations from supermarket shopping cart data revealed that bread and milk are often bought together, we might say: "Of course." Many people buy milk and many people buy bread. So we would expect them to occur together frequently just by chance. We would be more surprised if we found associations that occur much more frequently than chance would dictate. Lift is calculated simply by applying basic notions of probability.

Equation 12-1. Lift

$$\text{Lift}(A, B) = \frac{p(A, B)}{p(A)p(B)}$$

In English, the lift of the co-occurrence of A and B is the probability that we actually see the two together, compared to the probability that we would see the two together if they were unrelated to (independent of) each other. As with other uses of lift we've seen, a lift greater than one is the factor by which seeing A "boosts" the likelihood of seeing B as well.

This is only one possible way to compute how much more likely than chance a discovered association is. An alternative is to look at the difference of these quantities rather than their ratio. This measure is called **leverage**.

Equation 12-2. Leverage

$$\text{Leverage}(A, B) = p(B, A) - p(A)p(B)$$

Take a minute to convince yourself that one of these would be better for associations that are very unlikely to occur by chance, and one better for those rather likely to occur by chance.

Example: Beer and Lottery Tickets

As we've already seen from the "eWatch and eBracelet" example, association discovery is often used in market basket analysis to find and analyze co-ocurrences of bought items. Let's work through a concrete example.

Suppose we operate a small convenience store where people buy groceries, liquor, lottery tickets, and so on. Let's say we analyze all of our transactions over a year's time. We discover that people often buy beer and lottery tickets together. However, we know that in our store, people buy beer often and people buy lottery tickets often. Let's say we find that 30% of all transactions involve beer, and 20% of the transactions include both beer and lottery tickets! Is this co-occurrence an interesting one? Or is it simply due to the commonality of these two purchases? Association statistics can help us.

First, let's state an association rule representing this belief: "Customers who buy beer are also likely to buy lottery tickets"; or more tersely, "beer $\Rightarrow$ lottery tickets." Next, let's calculate the lift of this association. We already know one value we need: $p(\text{beer})=0.3$. Let's say that lottery tickets also are very popular: $p(\text{lottery tickets})=0.4$. If these two items were completely unrelated (independent), the chance that they would be bought together would be the product of these two: $p(\text{beer}) \times p(\text{lottery tickets})=0.12$.

We also have the actual probability (frequency in the data) of people buying the two items together, $p(\text{lottery tickets, beer})$, which we found by combing through the register receipt data looking for all transactions including beer and lottery tickets. As mentioned above, 20% of the transactions included both, and this is our probability: $p(\text{lottery tickets, beer}) = 0.2$. So the lift is 0.2 / 0.12, which is about 1.67. This means that buying lottery tickets and beer together is about 1 2/3 times more likely than one would expect by chance. We might conclude that there is some relationship there, but much of the co-occurrence is due to the fact that these are each very popular items.

What about leverage? This is $p(\text{lottery tickets, beer}) - p(\text{lottery tickets}) \times p(\text{beer})$, which is 0.2 − 0.12, or 0.08. Whatever is driving the co-occurrence results in an eight percentage-point increase in the probability of buying both together over what we would expect simply because they are popular items.

There are two other significant statistics we should calculate too: the support and the strength. The *support* of the association is just the prevalence in the data of buying the two items together, p(lottery tickets, beer), which is 20%. The *strength* is the conditional probability, p(lottery tickets|beer), which is 67%.

Associations Among Facebook Likes

Although finding associations is often used with market basket data—and sometimes is even called *market-basket analysis*—the technique is much more general. We can use our example from Chapter 9 of "Likes" on Facebook to illustrate. Recall that we have data on the things that were "Liked" by a large collection of users of Facebook (Kosinski, Stillwell, & Graepel, 2013). By analogy to market basket data, we can consider each of these users to have a "basket" of Likes, by aggregating all the Likes of each user. Now we can ask, do certain Likes tend to co-occur more frequently than we would expect by chance? We will use this simply as an interesting example to illustrate association finding, but the process could actually have an important business application. If you are a marketer looking to understand the consumers in a particular market, you might be interested in finding patterns of things people Like. If you are thinking data-analytically, you will apply exactly the sort of thinking we've illustrated so far in this chapter: you'll want to know what things co-occur more frequently than you would expect by chance.

Before we get to the mining of the data, let's introduce one more useful idea for association finding. Since we're using the market basket as an analogy at this point, we should consider broadening our thinking of what might be an item. Why can't we put just about anything we might be interested in finding associations with into our "basket"? For example, we might put a user's location into the basket, and then we could see associations between Likes and locations. For actual market basket data, these sometimes are called *virtual* items, to distinguish from the actual items that people put into their basket in the store. For our Facebook data, recall that we might obtain psychometric data on many of the consumers, such as their degree of extroversion or agreableness, or their score on an IQ test. It may be interesting to allow the association search to find associations with these psychometric characteristics as well.

Note: Supervised Versus Unsupervised?

We should keep in mind our distinction between supervised and unsupervised data mining. If we want specifically to understand what correlates most with agreeableness or with Liking our brand, we should formulate this as a supervised problem, with the corresponding target variable. This is what we did when looking at the evidence lifts in Chapter 9, and at supervised segmentation throughout the book. If we want to explore the data without such a specific goal, then association finding may be more appropriate. See the discussion in Chapter 6 on the differences between supervised and unsupervised mining—there in the context of clustering, but the fundamental concepts apply to association mining as well.

OK, so let's see what associations we get among Facebook Likes.[2] These associations were found using the popular association mining system Magnum Opus.[3] Magnum Opus allows searching for associations that give the highest lift or highest leverage, while filtering out associations that cover too few cases to be interesting. The list below shows some of the highest lift associations among Facebook Likes with the constraint that they have to cover at least 1% of the users in the dataset. Do these associations make sense? Do they give us a picture of the relationships among the users' tastes? Note that the lifts are all above 20, meaning that all of these associations are at least *20 times more likely* than we would expect by chance:

```
Family Guy & The Daily Show -> The Colbert Report
Support=0.010; Strength=0.793; Lift=31.32; Leverage=0.0099

Spirited Away -> Howl's Moving Castle
Support=0.011; Strength=0.556; Lift=30.57; Leverage=0.0108

Selena Gomez -> Demi Lovato
Support=0.010; Strength=0.419; Lift=27.59; Leverage=0.0100

I really hate slow computers & Random laughter when remembering something ->
    Finding Money In Your Pocket
Support=0.010; Strength=0.726; Lift=25.80; Leverage=0.0099

Skittles & Glowsticks -> Being Hyper!
Support=0.011; Strength=0.529; Lift=25.53; Leverage=0.0106

Linkin Park & Disturbed & System of a Down & Korn -> Slipknot
Support=0.011; Strength=0.862; Lift=25.50; Leverage=0.0107

Lil Wayne & Rihanna -> Drake
```

2. Thanks to Wally Wang for help with this.

3. See this page (*http://www.giwebb.com/*).

Support=0.011; Strength=0.619; Lift=25.33; Leverage=0.0104

Skittles & Mountain Dew -> Gatorade
Support=0.010; Strength=0.519; Lift=25.23; Leverage=0.0100

SpongeBob SquarePants & Converse -> Patrick Star
Support=0.010; Strength=0.654; Lift=24.94; Leverage=0.0097

Rihanna & Taylor Swift -> Miley Cyrus
Support=0.010; Strength=0.490; Lift=24.90; Leverage=0.0100

Disturbed & Three Days Grace -> Breaking Benjamin
Support=0.012; Strength=0.701; Lift=24.64; Leverage=0.0117

Eminem & Lil Wayne -> Drake
Support=0.014; Strength=0.594; Lift=24.30; Leverage=0.0131

Adam Sandler & System of a Down & Korn -> Slipknot
Support=0.010; Strength=0.819; Lift=24.23; Leverage=0.0097

Pink Floyd & Slipknot & System of a Down -> Korn
Support=0.010; Strength=0.810; Lift=24.05; Leverage=0.0097

Music & Anime -> Manga
Support=0.011; Strength=0.675; Lift=23.99; Leverage=0.0110

Medium IQ & Sour Gummy Worms -> I Love Cookie Dough
Support=0.012; Strength=0.568; Lift=23.86; Leverage=0.0118

Rihanna & Drake -> Lil Wayne
Support=0.011; Strength=0.849; Lift=23.55; Leverage=0.0104

I Love Cookie Dough -> Sour Gummy Worms
Support=0.014; Strength=0.569; Lift=23.28; Leverage=0.0130

Laughing until it hurts and you can't breathe! & I really hate slow computers ->
    Finding Money In Your Pocket
Support=0.010; Strength=0.651; Lift=23.12; Leverage=0.0098

Evanescence & Three Days Grace -> Breaking Benjamin
Support=0.012; Strength=0.656; Lift=23.06; Leverage=0.0117

Disney & Disneyland -> Walt Disney World
Support=0.011; Strength=0.615; Lift=22.95; Leverage=0.0103

i finally stop laughing... look back over at you and start all over again ->
    That awkward moment when you glance at someone staring at you.
Support=0.011; Strength=0.451; Lift=22.92; Leverage=0.0104

Selena Gomez -> Miley Cyrus
Support=0.011; Strength=0.443; Lift=22.54; Leverage=0.0105

```
Reese's & Starburst -> Kelloggs Pop-Tarts
Support=0.011; Strength=0.493; Lift=22.52; Leverage=0.0102

Skittles & SpongeBob SquarePants -> Patrick Star
Support=0.012; Strength=0.590; Lift=22.49; Leverage=0.0112

Disney & DORY & Toy Story -> Finding Nemo
Support=0.011; Strength=0.777; Lift=22.47; Leverage=0.0104

Katy Perry & Taylor Swift -> Miley Cyrus
Support=0.011; Strength=0.441; Lift=22.43; Leverage=0.0101

AKON & Black Eyed Peas -> Usher
Support=0.010; Strength=0.731; Lift=22.42; Leverage=0.0097

Eminem & Drake -> Lil Wayne
Support=0.014; Strength=0.807; Lift=22.39; Leverage=0.0131
```

Most association mining examples use domains (such as Facebook Likes) where readers already have a fair knowledge of the domain. This is because otherwise, since the mining is unsupervised, evaluation depends much more critically on domain knowledge validation (recall the discussion in Chapter 6)—we do not have a well-defined target task for an objective evaluation. However, one interesting practical use of association mining is to explore data that we do not understand so well. Consider going into a new job. Exploring the company's customer transaction data and examining the strong co-occurrences can quickly give broad overview of the taste relationships in the customer base. So, with that in mind, look back at the co-occurrences in the Facebook Likes and pretend that this was not a domain of popular culture: these and others like them (there are huge numbers of such associations) would give you a very broad view of the related tastes of the customers.

Profiling: Finding Typical Behavior

Profiling attempts to characterize the typical behavior of an individual, group, or population. An example profiling question might be: *What is the typical credit card usage of this customer segment?* This could be a simple average of spending, but such a simple description might not represent the behavior well for our business task. For example, fraud detection often uses profiling to characterize normal behavior and then looks for instances that deviate substantially from the normal behavior—especially in ways that previously have been indicative of fraud (Fawcett & Provost, 1997; Bolton & Hand, 2002). Profiling credit card usage for fraud detection might require a complex description of weekday and weekend averages, international usage, usage across merchant and product categories, usage from suspicious merchants, and so on. Behavior can be described generally over an entire population, at the level of small groups, or even for each individual. For example, each credit card user might be profiled with respect to his international usage, so as not to create many false alarms for an individual who commonly travels abroad.

Profiling combines concepts discussed previously. Profiling can essentially involve clustering, if there are subgroups of the population with different behaviors. Many profiling methods seem complicated, but in essence are simply instantiations of the fundamental concept introduced in Chapter 4: define a numeric function with some parameters, define a goal or objective, and find the parameters that best meet the objective.

So let's consider a simple example from business operations management. Businesses would like to use data to help to understand how well their call centers are supporting their customers.[4] One aspect of supporting customers well is to not leave them sitting on hold for long periods of time. So how might we profile the typical wait time of our customers who call into the call center? We might calculate the mean and standard deviation of the wait time.

That seems like exactly what a manager with basic statistical training might do—it turns out to be a simple instance of model fitting. Here's why. Let's assume that customer wait times follow a Normal or Gaussian distribution. Saying such things can cause a non-mathematical person to fear what's to come, but that just means the distribution follows a bell curve with some particularly nice properties. Importantly, it is a "profile" of the wait times that (in this case) has only two important parameters: the mean and the standard deviation. When we calculate the mean and standard deviation, we are finding the "best" profile or model of wait time under the assumption that it is Normally distributed. In this case "best" is the same notion that we discussed for logistic regression, for example, the mean we calculate from the spending gives us the mean of the Gaussian distribution that is most likely to have generated the data (the "maximum likelihood" model).

This view illustrates why a data science perspective can help even in simple scenarios: it is much clearer now what we are doing when we are calculating averages and standard deviations, even if our memory of the details from statistics classes is hazy. We also need to keep in mind our fundamental principles introduced in Chapter 4 and elaborated in Chapter 7: we need to consider carefully what we desire from our data science results. Here we would like to profile the "normal" wait time of our customers. If we plot the data and they do not look like they came from a Gaussian (a symmetric bell curve that goes to zero very quickly in the "tails"), we might want to reconsider simply reporting the mean and standard deviation. We might instead report the median, which is not so sensitive to the skew, or possibly even better, fit a different distribution (maybe after talking to a statistically oriented data scientist about what might be appropriate).

---

4. The interested reader is encouraged to read Brown et al. (2005) for a technical treatment and details on this application.

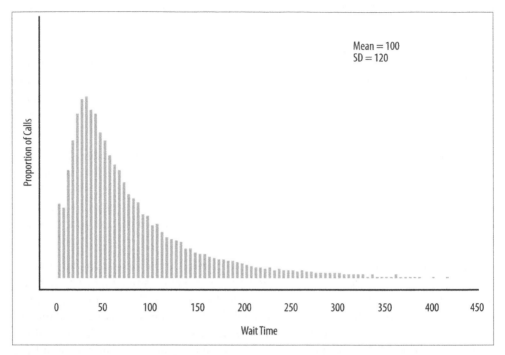

Figure 12-1. A distribution of wait times for callers into a bank's call center.

To illustrate how a data science savvy manager might proceed, let's look at a distribution of wait times for callers into a bank's call center over a couple of months. Figure 12-1 shows such a distribution. Importantly, we see how visualizing the distribution should cause our data science radar to issue an alert. The distribution is *not* a symmetric bell curve. We should then worry about simply profiling wait times by reporting the mean and standard deviation. For example, the mean (100) does not seem to satisfy our desire to profile how long our customers normally wait; it seems too large. Technically, the long "tail" of the distribution skews the mean upward, so it does not represent faithfully where most of the data really lie. It does not represent faithfully the normal wait time of our customers.

To give more depth to what our data science-savvy manager might do, let's go a little further. We will not get into the details here, but a common trick for dealing with data that are skewed in this way is to take the logarithm (log) of the wait times. Figure 12-2 shows the same distribution as Figure 12-1, except using the logarithms of the wait times. We now see that after the simple transformation, the wait times look very much like the classic bell curve.

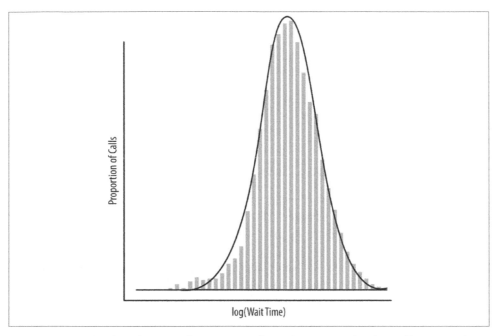

Figure 12-2. The distribution of wait times for callers into a bank's call center after a quick redefinition of the data.

Indeed, Figure 12-2 also shows an actual Gaussian distribution (the bell curve) fit to the bell-shaped distribution, as described above. It fits very well, and thus we have a justification for reporting the mean and standard deviation as summary statistics of the profile of (log) wait times.[5]

This simple example extends nicely to more complex situations. Shifting contexts, let's say we want to profile customer behavior in terms of their spending and their time on our website. We believe these to be correlated, but not perfectly, as with the points plotted in Figure 12-3. Again, a very common tack is to apply the fundamental notion of Chapter 4: choose a parameterized numeric function and an objective, and find parameters that maximize the objective. For example, we can choose a two-dimensional Gaussian, which is essentially a bell *oval* instead of a bell curve—an oval-shaped blob that is very dense in the center and thins out toward the edges. This is represented by the contour lines in Figure 12-3.

---

5. A statistically trained data scientist might have noticed immediately the shape of the distribution of the original data, shown in Figure 12-1. This is a so-called log-normal distribution, which just means that the logs of the quantities in question are normally distributed.

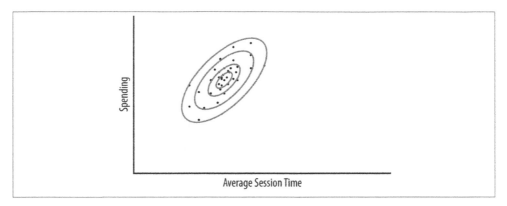

Figure 12-3. A profile of our customers with respect to their spending and the time they spend on our web site, represented as a two-dimensional Gaussian fit to the data.

We can keep extending the idea to more and more sophisticated profiling. What if we believe there are different subgroups of customers with different behaviors? We may not be willing to simply fit a Gaussian distribution to the behavior. However, maybe we are comfortable assuming that there are k groups of customers, each of whose behavior is normally distributed. We can fit a model with multiple Gaussians, called a *Gaussian Mixture Model* (GMM). Applying our fundamental concept again, finding the maximum-likelihood parameters identifies the k Gaussians that fit the data best (with respect to this particular objective function). We see an example with $k=2$ in Figure 12-4. The figure shows how the fitting procedure identifies two different groups of customers, each modeled by a two-dimensional Gaussian distribution.

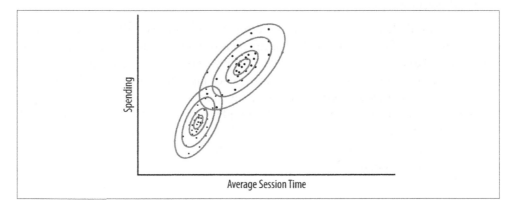

Figure 12-4. A profile of our customers with respect to their spending and the time they spend on our web site, represented as a Gaussian Mixture Model (GMM), with 2 two-dimensional Gaussians fit to the data. The GMM provides a "soft" clustering of our customers along two these two dimensions.

Now we have a rather sophisticated profile, which we can understand as a surprisingly straightforward application of our fundamental principles. An interesting side note is that this GMM has produced for us a clustering, but in a different way from the clusterings presented in Chapter 6. This illustrates how fundamental principles, rather than specific tasks or algorithms, form the basis for data science. In this case, clustering can be done in many different ways, just as classification and regression can be.

Note: "Soft" Clustering

Incidentally, you may notice that the clusters in the GMM overlap with each other. The GMM provides what is called a "soft" or probabilistic clustering. Each point does not strictly belong to a single cluster, but instead has a degree or probability of membership in each cluster. In this particular clustering, we can think that a point is more likely to have come from some clusters than others. However, there still is a possibility, perhaps remote, that the point may have come from any of them.

Link Prediction and Social Recommendation

Sometimes, instead of predicting a property (target value) of a data item, it is more useful to predict *connections* between data items. A common example of this is predicting that a link should exist between two individuals. Link prediction is common in social networking systems: *Since you and Karen share 10 friends, maybe you'd like to be Karen's friend?* Link prediction can also estimate the strength of a link. For example, for recommending movies to customers one can think of a graph between customers and the movies they've watched or rated. Within the graph, we search for links that do *not* exist between customers and movies, but that we predict should exist and should be strong. These links form the basis for recommendations.

There are many approaches to link prediction, and even an entire chapter of this book would not do them justice. However, we can understand a wide variety of approaches using our fundamental concepts of data science. Let's consider the social network case. Knowing what you know now, if you had to predict either the presence or the strength of a link between two individuals, how would you go about framing the problem? We have several alternatives. We could presume that links should be between similar individuals. We know then that we need to define a similarity measure that takes into account the important aspects of our application.

Could we define a similarity measure between two individuals that would indicate that they might like to be friends? (Or are already friends, depending on the application.) Sure. Using the example above directly, we could consider the similarity to be the number of shared friends. Of course, the similarity measure could be more sophisticated: we could weight the friends by the amount of communication, geographical proximity, or some other factor, and then find or devise a similarity function that takes these strengths into account. We could use this friend strength as one aspect of similarity while also including others (since after Chapter 6 we are comfortable with multivariate similarity), such as shared interests, shared demographics, etc. In essence, we could apply knowledge of "finding similar data items" to people, by considering the different ways in which we could represent the people as data.

That is one way to attack the link prediction problem. Let's consider another, just to continue to illustrate how the fundamental principles apply to other tasks. Since we want to *predict* the existence (or strength) of a link, we might well decide to cast the task as a predictive modeling problem. So we can apply our framework for thinking about predictive modeling problems. As always, we start with business and data understanding. What would we consider to be an instance? At first, we might think: wait a minute —here we are looking at the *relationship* between *two* instances. Our conceptual framework comes in very handy: let's stick to our guns, and define an instance for prediction. What exactly is it that we want to predict? We want to predict the existence of a relationship (or its strength, but let's just consider the existence here) between two people. So, an instance should be a pair of people!

Once we have defined an instance to be a pair of people, we can proceed smoothly. Next, what would be the target variable? Whether the relationship exists, or would be formed if recommended. Would this be a supervised task? Yes, we can get training data where links already do or do not exist, or if we wanted to be more careful we could invest in acquiring labels specifically for the recommendation task (we would need to spend a bit more time than we have here on defining the exact semantics of the link). What would be the features? These would be features *of the pair of people*, such as how many common friends the two individuals have, what is the similarity in their interests, and so on. Now that we have cast the problem in the form of a predictive modeling task, we can start to ask what sorts of models we would apply and how we would evaluate them. This is the same conceptual procedure we go through for any predictive modeling task.

Data Reduction, Latent Information, and Movie Recommendation

For some business problems, we would like to take a large set of data and replace it with a smaller set that preserves much of the important information in the larger set. The smaller dataset may be easier to deal with or to process. Moreover, the smaller dataset may better reveal the information contained within it. For example, a massive dataset on consumer movie-viewing preferences may be reduced to a much smaller dataset revealing the consumer taste preferences that are latent in the viewing data (for example, viewer preferences for movie genre). Such data reduction usually involves sacrificing some information, but what is important is the trade-off between the insight or manageability gained against the information lost. This is often a trade worth making.

As with link prediction, data reduction is a general task, not a particular technique. There are many techniques, and we can use our fundamental principles to understand them. Let's discuss a popular technique as an example.

Let's continue to talk about movie recommendations. In a now famous (at least in data science circles) contest, the movie rental company Netflix™ offered a million dollars to the individual or team that could best predict how consumers would rate movies. Specifically, they set a prediction performance goal on a holdout data set and awarded the prize to the team that first reached this goal.[6] Netflix made available historical data on movie ratings assigned by their customers. The winning team[7] produced an extremely complicated technique, but much of the success is attributed to two aspects of the solution: (i) the use of ensembles of models, which we will discuss in "Bias, Variance, and Ensemble Methods" on page 308, and (ii) data reduction. The main data reduction technique that the winners used can be described easily using our fundamental concepts.

The problem to be solved was essentially a link prediction problem, where specifically we would like to predict the strength of the link between a user and a movie—the strength representing how much the user would like it. As we just discussed, this can be cast as a predictive modeling problem. However, what would the features be for the relationship between a user and a movie?

One of the most popular approaches for providing recommendations, described in detail in a very nice article by several of the Netflix competition winners (Koren, Bell, & Volinsky, 2009), is to base the model on *latent* dimensions underlying the preferences. The term "latent," in data science, means "relevant but not observed explicitly in the data." Chapter 10 discussed topic models, another form of latent model, where the latent information is the set of topics in the documents. Here the latent dimensions of movie preference include possible characterizations like serious versus escapist, comedy versus drama, orientation towards children, or gender orientation. Even if these are not represented explicitly in the data, they may be important for judging whether a particular user will like the movie. The latent dimensions also could include possibly ill-defined things like depth of character development or quirkiness, as well as dimensions never explicitly articulated, since the latent dimensions will emerge from the data.

Again, we can understand this advanced data science approach as a combination of fundamental concepts. The idea of the latent dimension approaches to recommendation is to represent each movie as a feature vector using the latent dimensions, and also to represent each user's preferences as a feature vector using the latent dimensions. Then

---

6. There are some technicalities to the rules of the Netflix Challenge, which you can find on the Wikipedia page (*https://en.wikipedia.org/wiki/Netflix_prize*).

7. The winning team, Bellkor's Pragmatic Chaos, had seven members. The history of the contest and the team evolution is complicated and fascinating. See this Wikipedia page (*http://en.wikipedia.org/wiki/Netflix_Prize*) on the Netflix Prize.

it is easy to find movies to recommend to any user: compute a similarity score between the user and all the movies; the movies that best match the users' preferences would be those movies most similar to the user, when both are represented by the same latent dimensions.

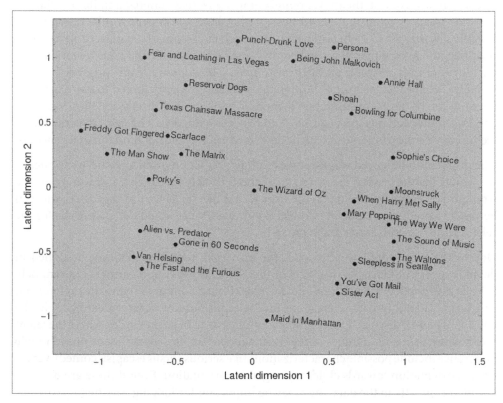

Figure 12-5. A collection of movies placed in a "taste space" defined by the two strongest latent dimensions mined from the Netflix Challenge data. See the text for a detailed discussion. A customer would also be placed somewhere in the space, based on the movies she has previously viewed or rated. A similarity-based recommendation approach would suggest the closest movies to the customer as candidate recommendations.

Figure 12-5 shows a two-dimensional latent space actually mined from the Netflix movie data,[8] as well as a collection of movies represented in this new space. The interpretation of such latent dimensions mined from data must be inferred by the data scientists or business users. The most common way is to observe how the dimensions separate the movies, then apply domain knowledge.

---

8. Thanks to one of the members of the winning team, Chris Volinsky, for his help here.

In Figure 12-5, the latent dimension represented by the horizontal axis seems to separate the movies into drama-oriented films on the right and action-oriented films on the left. At the extremes, on the far right we see films of the heart such as *The Sound of Music*, *Moonstruck*, and *When Harry Met Sally*. On the far left we see whatever is the opposite of films of the heart (films of the gut?), including films focusing on the stereotypical likes of men and adolescent boys (*The Man Show, Porky's*), killing (*Texas Chainsaw Massacre, Reservoir Dogs*), speed (*The Fast and the Furious*), and monster hunting (*Van Helsing*). The latent dimension represented by the vertical axis seems to separate the movies by intellectual appeal versus emotional appeal, with movies like *Being John Malkovich, Fear and Loathing in Los Vegas*, and *Annie Hall* at one extreme, and *Maid in Manhattan, The Fast and the Furious*, and *You've Got Mail* at the other. Feel free to disagree with those interpretations of the dimensions—they are completely subjective. One thing is clear, though: *The Wizard of Oz* captures an unusual balance of whatever tastes are represented by the latent dimensions.

To use this latent space for recommendation, a customer also would be placed somewhere in the space, based on the movies she has rented or rated. The closest movies to the position of the customer would be good candidates for making recommendations. Note that for making recommendations, as always we need to keep thinking back to our business understanding. For example, different movies have different profit margins, so we may want to combine this knowledge with the knowledge of the most similar movies.

But how do we *find* the right latent dimensions in the data? We apply the fundamental concept introduced in Chapter 4: we represent the similarity calculation between a user and a movie as a mathematical formula using some number d of as-yet-unknown latent dimensions. Each dimension would be represented by a set of weights (the coefficients) on each movie and a set of weights on each customer. A high weight would mean this dimension is strongly associated with the movie or the customer. The meaning of the dimension would be purely implicit in the weights on the movies and customers. For example, we might look at the movies that are weighted highly on some dimension versus low-weighted movies and decide, "the highly rated movies are all 'quirky.'" In this case, we could think of the dimension as the degree of *quirkiness* of the movie, although it is important to keep in mind that this interpretation of the dimension was imposed by us. The dimension is simply some way in which the movies clustered in the data on how customers rated movies.

Recall that to fit a numeric-function model to data, we find the optimal set of parameters for the numeric function. Initially, the d dimensions are purely a mathematical abstraction; only after the parameters are selected to fit the data can we try to formulate an interpretation of the meaning of the latent dimensions (and sometimes such an effort is fruitless). Here, the parameters of the function would be the (unknown) weights for each customer and each movie along these dimensions. Intuitively, data mining is determining simultaneously (i) how quirky the movie is, and (ii) how much this viewer likes quirky movies.

We also need an objective function to determine what is a good fit. We define our objective function for training based on the set of movie ratings we have observed. We find a set of weights that characterizes the users and the movies along these dimensions. There are different objective functions used for the movie-recommendation problem. For example, we can choose the weights that allow us to best predict the observed ratings in the training data (subject to regularization, as discussed in Chapter 4). Alternatively, we could choose the dimensions that best explain the variation in the observed ratings. This is often called "matrix factorization," and the interested reader might start with the paper about the Netflix Challenge (Koren, Bell, & Volinsky, 2009).

The result is that we have for each movie a representation along some reduced set of dimensions—maybe how quirky it is, maybe whether it is a "tear-jerker" or a "guy flick," or whatever—the best d latent dimensions that the training finds. We also have a representation of each user in terms of their preferences along these dimensions. We can now look back at Figure 12-5 and the associated discussion. These are the two latent dimensions that best fit the data, i.e., the dimensions that result from fitting the data with $d=2$.

Bias, Variance, and Ensemble Methods

In the Netflix competition, the winners also took advantage of another common data science technique: they built lots of different recommendation models and combined them into one super model. In data mining parlance, this is referred to as creating an *ensemble* model. Ensembles have been observed to improve generalization performance in many situations—not just for recommendations, but broadly across classification, regression, class probability estimation, and more.

Why is a collection of models often better than a single model? If we consider each model as a sort of "expert" on a target prediction task, we can think of an ensemble as a collection of experts. Instead of just asking one expert, we find a group of experts and then somehow combine their predictions. For example, we could have them vote on a classification, or we could average their numeric predictions. Notice that this is a generalization of the method introduced in Chapter 6 to turn similarity computations into "nearest neighbor" predictive models. To make a k-NN prediction, we find a group of similar examples (very simple experts) and then apply some function to combine their individual predictions. Thus a k-nearest-neighbor model is a simple ensemble method. Generally, ensemble methods use more complex predictive models as their "experts"; for example, they may build a group of classification trees and then report an average (or weighted average) of the predictions.

When might we expect ensembles to improve our performance? Certainly, if each expert knew exactly the *same* things, they would all give the same predictions, and the ensemble would provide no advantage. On the other hand, if each expert was knowledgeable in a slightly different aspect of the problem, they might give complementary predictions, and the whole group might provide more information than any individual expert. Technically, we would like the experts to make different sorts of *errors*—we would like their errors to be as unrelated as possible, and ideally to be completely independent. In averaging the predictions, the errors would then tend to cancel out, the predictions indeed would be complementary, and the ensemble would be superior to using any one expert.

 Ensemble methods have a long history and are an active area of research in data science. Much has been written about them. The interested reader may want to start with the review article by Dietterich (2000).

One way to understand why ensembles work is to understand that the errors a model makes can be characterized by three factors:

1. Inherent randomness,

2. Bias, and

3. Variance.

The first, inherent randomness, simply covers cases where a prediction is not "deterministic," (i.e., we simply do not always get the same value for the target variable every time we see the same set of features). For example, customers described by a certain set of characteristics may not always either purchase our product or not. The prediction may simply be inherently probabilistic given the information we have. Thus, a portion of the observed "error" in prediction is simply due to this inherent probabilistic nature of the problem. We can debate whether a particular data-generating process is truly probabilistic—as opposed to our simply not seeing all the requisite information—but that debate is largely academic,[9] because the process may be essentially probabilistic based on the data we have available. Let's proceed assuming that we've reduced the randomness as much as we can, and there simply is some theoretical maximum accuracy that we can achieve for this problem. This accuracy is called the *Bayes rate*, and it is generally unknown. For the rest of this section we will consider the Bayes rate as being "perfect" accuracy.

---

9. The debate sometimes can bear fruit. For example, thinking whether we have all the requisite information might reveal a new attribute that could be obtained that would increase the possible predictability.

Beyond inherent randomness, models make errors for two other reasons. The modeling procedure may be "biased." What this means can be understood best in reference to learning curves (recall "Learning Curves" on page 130). Specifically, a modeling procedure is biased if no matter how much training data we give it, the learning curve will never reach perfect accuracy (the Bayes rate). For example, we learn a (linear) logistic regression to predict response to an advertising campaign. If the true response really is more complex than the linear model can represent, the model will never achieve perfect accuracy.

The other source of error is due to the fact that we do not have an infinite amount of training data; we have some finite sample that we want to mine. Modeling procedures usually give different models from even slightly different samples. These different models will tend to have different accuracies. How much the accuracy tends to vary across different training sets (let's say, of the same size) is referred to as the modeling procedure's variance. Procedures with more variance tend to produce models with larger errors, all else being equal.

You might see now that we would like to have a modeling procedure that has no bias and no variance, or at least low bias and low variance. Unfortunately (and intuitively), there typically is a trade-off between the two. Lower variance models tend to have higher bias, and vice versa. As a very simple example, we might decide that we want to estimate the response to our advertising campaign simply by ignoring all the customer features and simply predict the (average) purchase rate. This will be a very low-variance model, because we will tend to get about the same average from different datasets of the same size. However, we have no hope to get perfect accuracy if there are customer-specific differences in propensity to purchase. On the other hand, we might decide to model customers based on one thousand detailed variables. We may now have the opportunity to get much better accuracy, but we would expect there to be much greater variance in the models we obtain based on even slightly different training sets. Thus, we won't necessarily expect the thousand-variable model to be better; we don't know exactly which source of error (bias or variance) will dominate.

You may be thinking: *Of course. As we learned in Chapter 5, the thousand-variable model will overfit. We should apply some sort of complexity control, such as selecting a subset of the variables to use.* That is exactly right. More complexity generally gives us lower bias but higher variance. Complexity control generally tries to manage the (usually unknown) trade-off between bias and variance, to find a "sweet spot" where the combination of the errors from each is smallest. So, we could apply variable selection to our thousand-variable problem. If there truly are customer-specific differences in purchase rate, and we have enough training data, hopefully the variable selection will not throw away all variables, which would leave us with just the average over the population. Hopefully, instead we would get a model with a subset of the variables that allow us to predict as well as possible, given the training data available.

Technically, the accuracies we discuss in this section are the expected values of the accuracies of the models. We omit that qualification because the discussion otherwise becomes technically baroque. The reader interested in understanding bias, variance, and the trade-off between them might start with the technical but quite readable article by Friedman (1997).

Now we can see why ensemble techniques might work. If we have a modeling method with high variance, averaging over multiple predictions reduces the variance in the predictions. Indeed, ensemble methods tend to improve the predictive ability more for higher-variance methods, such as in cases where you would expect more overfitting (Perlich, Provost, & Simonoff, 2003). Ensemble methods are often used with tree induction, as classification and regression trees tend to have high variance. In the field you may hear about random forests, bagging, and boosting. These are all ensemble methods popular with trees (the latter two are more general). Check out Wikipedia to find out more about them.

Data-Driven Causal Explanation and a Viral Marketing Example

One important topic that we have only touched on in this book (in Chapter 2 and Chapter 11) is *causal explanation* from data. Predictive modeling is extremely useful for many business problems. However, the sort of predictive modeling that we have discussed so far is based on correlations rather than on knowledge of causation. We often want to look more deeply into a phenomenon and ask what influences what. We may want to do this simply to understand our business better, or we may want to use data to improve decisions about how to intervene to cause a desired outcome.

Consider a detailed example. Recently there has been much attention paid to "viral" marketing. One common interpretation of viral marketing is that consumers can be helped to influence each other to purchase a product, and so a marketer can get significant benefit by "seeding" certain consumers (e.g., by giving them the product for free), and they then will be "influencers"— they will cause an increase in the likelihood that the people they know will purchase the product. The holy grail of viral marketing is to be able to create campaigns that spread like an epidemic, but the critical assumption behind "virality" is that consumers actually influence each other. How much do they? Data scientists work to measure such influence, by observing in the data whether once a consumer has the product, her social network neighbors indeed have increased likelihood to purchase the product.

Unfortunately, a naive analysis of the data can be tremendously misleading. For important sociological reasons (McPherson, Smith-Lovin, & Cook, 2001), people tend to cluster in social networks with people who are similar to them. Why is this important?

This means that social network neighbors are likely to have similar product preferences, and we would *expect* the neighbors of people who choose or like a product also to choose or like the product, *even in the absence of any causal influence* among the consumers! Indeed, based on the careful application of causal analysis, it was shown in the *Proceedings of the National Academy of Sciences* (Aral, Muchnik, & Sundararajan, 2009) that traditional methods for estimating the influence in viral marketing analysis overestimated the influence by at least 700%!

There are various methods for careful causal explanation from data, and they can all be understood within a common data science framework. The point of discussing this here toward the end of the book is that understanding these sophisticated techniques requires a grasp of the fundamental principles presented so far. Careful causal data analysis requires the understanding of investments in acquiring data, of similarity measurements, of expected value calculations, of correlation and finding informative variables, of fitting equations to data, and more.

Chapter 11 gave a taste of this more sophisticated causal analysis when we returned to the telecommunications churn problem and asked: shouldn't we be targeting those customers whom the special offer is most likely to influence? This illustrated the key role the expected value framework played, along with several other concepts. There are other techniques for causal understanding that use similarity matching (Chapter 6) to simulate the "counterfactual" that someone might both receive a "treatment" (e.g., an incentive to stay) and not receive the treatment. Still other causal analysis methods fit numeric functions to data and interpret the coefficients of the functions.[10]

The point is that we cannot understand causal data science without first understanding the fundamental principles. Causal data analysis is just one such example; the same applies to other more sophisticated methods you may encounter.

Summary

There are very many specific techniques used in data science. To achieve a solid understanding of the field, it is important to step back from the specifics and think about the sorts of tasks to which the techniques are applied. In this book, we have focused on a collection of the most common tasks (finding correlations and informative attributes, finding similar data items, classification, probability estimation, regression, clustering), showing that the concepts of data science provide a firm foundation for understanding both the tasks and the methods for solving the tasks. In this chapter, we presented several

---

10. It is beyond the scope of this book to explain the conditions under which this can be given a causal interpretation. But if someone presents a regression equation to you with a causal interpretation of the equation's parameters, ask questions about exactly what the coefficients mean and why one can interpret them causally until you are satisfied. For such analyses, comprehension by decision makers is paramount; insist that you understand any such results.

other important data science tasks and techniques, and illustrated that they too can be understood based on the foundation provided by our fundamental concepts.

Specifically, we discussed: finding interesting co-occurrences or associations among items, such as purchases; profiling typical behavior, such as credit card usage or customer wait time; predicting links between data items, such as potential social connections between people; reducing our data to make it more manageable or to reveal hidden information, such as latent movie preferences; combining models as if they were experts with different expertise, for example to improve movie recommendations; and drawing causal conclusions from data, such as whether and to what extent the fact that socially connected people buy the same products is actually because they influence each other (necessary for viral campaigns), or simply because socially connected people have very similar tastes (which is well known in sociology). A solid understanding of the basic principles helps you to understand more complex techniques as instances or combinations of them.

CHAPTER 13

Data Science and Business Strategy

Fundamental concepts: *Our principles as the basis of success for a data-driven business; Acquiring and sustaining competitive advantage via data science; The importance of careful curation of data science capability.*

In this chapter we discuss the interaction between data science and business strategy, including a high-level perspective on choosing problems to be solved with data science. We see that the fundamental concepts of data science allow us to think clearly about strategic issues. We also show how, taken as a whole, the array of concepts is useful for thinking about tactical business decisions such as evaluating proposals for data science projects from consultants or internal data science teams. We also discuss in detail the curation of data science capability.

Increasingly we see stories in the press about how yet another aspect of business has been addressed with a data science-based solution. As we discussed in Chapter 1, a confluence of factors has led contemporary businesses to be strikingly data rich, as compared to their predecessors. But the availability of data alone does not ensure successful data-driven decision-making. How does a business ensure that it gets the most from the wealth of data? The answer of course is manifold, but two important factors are: (i) the firm's management must think data-analytically, and (ii) the management must create a culture where data science, and data scientists, will thrive.

Thinking Data-Analytically, Redux

Criterion (i) does not mean that the managers have to be data scientists. However, managers have to understand the fundamental principles well enough to envision and/ or appreciate data science opportunities, to supply the appropriate resources to the data science teams, and to be willing to invest in data and experimentation. Furthermore, unless the firm has on its management team a seasoned, practical data scientist, often the management must steer the data science team carefully to make sure that the team stays on track toward an eventually useful business solution. This is very difficult if the managers don't really understand the principles. Managers need to be able to ask probing questions of a data scientist, who often can get lost in technical details. We need to accept that each of us has strengths and weaknesses, and as data science projects span so much of a business, a diverse team is essential. Just as we can't expect a manager necessarily to have deep expertise in data science, we can't expect a data scientist *necessarily* to have deep expertise in business solutions. However, an effective data science team involves collaboration between the two, and each needs to have some understanding of the fundamentals of the other's area of responsibility. Just as it would be a Sisyphean task to manage a data science team where the team had no understanding of the fundamental concepts of business, it likewise is extremely frustrating at best, and often a tremendous waste, for data scientists to struggle under a management that does not understand basic principles of data science.

For example, it is not uncommon for data scientists to struggle under a management that (sometimes vaguely) sees the potential benefit of predictive modeling, but does not have enough appreciation for the process to invest in proper training data or in proper evaluation procedures. Such a company may "succeed" in engineering a model that is predictive enough to produce a viable product or service, but will be at a severe disadvantage to a competitor who invests in doing the data science well.

A solid grounding in the fundamentals of data science has much more far-reaching strategic implications. We know of no systematic scientific study, but broad experience has shown that as executives, managers, and investors increase their exposure to data science projects, they see more and more opportunities in turn. We see extreme cases in companies like Google and Amazon (there is a vast amount of data science underlying web search, as well as Amazon's product recommendations and other offerings). Both of these companies eventually built subsequent products offering "big data" and data-science related services to other firms. Many, possibly most, data-science oriented startups use Amazon's cloud storage and processing services for some tasks. Google's "Prediction API" is increasing in sophistication and utility (we don't know how broadly used it is).

Those are extreme cases, but the basic pattern is seen in almost every data-rich firm. Once the data science capability has been developed for one application, other applications throughout the business become obvious. Louis Pasteur famously wrote, "Fortune favors the prepared mind." Modern thinking on creativity focuses on the juxtaposition of a new way of thinking with a mind "saturated" with a particular problem. Working through case studies (either in theory or in practice) of data science applications helps prime the mind to see opportunities and connections to new problems that could benefit from data science.

For example, in the late 1980s and early 1990s, one of the largest phone companies had applied predictive modeling—using the techniques we've described in this book—to the problem of reducing the cost of repairing problems in the telephone network and to the design of speech recognition systems. With the increased understanding of the use of data science for helping to solve business problems, the firm subsequently applied similar ideas to decisions about how to allocate a massive capital investment to best improve its network, and how to reduce fraud in its burgeoning wireless business. The progression continued. Data science projects for reducing fraud discovered that incorporating features based on social-network connections (via who-calls-whom data) into fraud prediction models improved the ability to discover fraud substantially. In the early 2000s, telecommunications firms produced the first solutions using such social connections to improve marketing—and improve marketing it did, showing huge performance lifts over traditional targeted marketing based on socio-demographic, geographic, and prior purchase data. Next, in telecommunications, such social features were added to models for churn prediction, with equally beneficial results. The ideas diffused to the online advertising industry, and there was a subsequent flurry of development of online advertising based on the incorporation of data on online social connections (at Facebook and at other firms in the online advertising ecosystem).

This progression was driven both by experienced data scientists moving among business problems as well as by data science savvy managers and entrepreneurs, who saw new opportunities for data science advances in the academic and business literature.

Achieving Competitive Advantage with Data Science

Increasingly, firms are considering whether and how they can obtain competitive advantage from their data and/or from their data science capability. This is important strategic thinking that should not be superficial, so let's spend some time digging into it.

Data and data science capability are (complementary) strategic assets. Under what conditions can a firm achieve competitive advantage from such an asset? First of all, the asset has to be valuable to the firm. This seems obvious, but note that the value of an asset to a firm depends on the other strategic decisions that the firm has made. Outside of the context of data science, in the personal computer industry in the 1990s, Dell famously got substantial competitive advantage early over industry leader Compaq from using web-based systems to allow customers to configure computers to their personal needs and liking. Compaq could not get the same value from web-based systems. One main reason was that Dell and Compaq had implemented different strategies: Dell already was a direct-to-customer computer retailer, selling via catalogs; web-based systems held tremendous value given this strategy. Compaq sold computers mainly via retail outlets; web-based systems were not nearly as valuable given this alternative strategy. When Compaq tried to replicate Dell's web-based strategy, it faced a severe backlash from its retailers. The upshot is that the value of the new asset (web-based systems) was dependent on each company's other strategic decisions.

The lesson is that we need to think carefully in the business understanding phase as to how data and data science can provide value in the context of our business strategy, and also whether it would do the same in the context of our competitors' strategies. This can identify both possible opportunities and possible threats. A direct data science analogy of the Dell-Compaq example is Amazon versus Borders. Even very early, Amazon's data on customers' book purchases allowed personalized recommendations to be delivered to customers while they were shopping online. Even if Borders were able to exploit its data on who bought what books, its brick-and-mortar retail strategy did not allow the same seamless delivery of data science-based recommendations.

So, a prerequisite for a competitive advantage is that the asset be valuable in the context of our strategy. We've already begun to talk about the second set of criteria: in order to gain competitive advantage, competitors either must not possess the asset, or must not be able to obtain the same value from it. We should think both about the data asset(s) and the data science capability. Do we have a unique data asset? If not, do we have an asset the utilization of which is better aligned with our strategy than with the stragegy of our competitors? Or are we better able to take advantage of the data asset due to our better data science capability?

The flip side of asking about achieving competitive advantage with data and data science is asking whether we are at a competitive disadvantage. It may be that the answers to the previous questions are affirmative for our competitors and not for us. In what follows we will assume that we are looking to achieve competitive advantage, but the arguments apply symmetrically if we are trying to achieve parity with a data-savvy competitor.

Sustaining Competitive Advantage with Data Science

The next question is: even if we can achieve competitive advantage, can we *sustain* it? If our competitors can easily duplicate our assets and capabilities, our advantage may be short-lived. This is an especially critical question if our competitors have greater resources than we do: by adopting our strategy, they may surpass us if they have greater resources.

One strategy for competing based on data science is to plan to always keep one step ahead of the competition: always be investing in new data assets, and always be developing new techniques and capabilities. Such a strategy can provide for an exciting and possibly fast-growing business, but generally few companies are able to execute it. For example, you must have confidence that you have one of the best data science teams, since the effectiveness of data scientists has a huge variance, with the best being much more talented than the average. If you have a great team, you may be willing to bet that you can keep ahead of the competition. We will discuss data science teams more below.

The alternative to always keeping one step ahead of the competition is to achieve sustainable competitive advantage due to a competitor's inability to replicate, or their elevated expense of replicating, the data asset or the data science capability. There are several avenues to such sustainability.

Formidable Historical Advantage

Historical circumstances may have placed our firm in an advantageous position, and it may be too costly for competitors to reach the same position. Amazon again provides an outstanding example. In the "Dotcom Boom" of the 1990s, Amazon was able to sell books below cost, and investors continued to reward the company. This allowed Amazon to amass tremendous data assets (such as massive data on online consumers' buying preferences and online product reviews), which then allowed them to create valuable data-based products (such as recommendations and product ratings). These historical circumstances are gone: it is unlikely today that investors would provide the same level of support to a competitor that was trying to replicate Amazon's data asset by selling books below cost for years on end (not to mention that Amazon has moved far beyond books).

This example also illustrates that the data products themselves can increase the cost to competitors of replicating the data asset. Consumers value the data-driven recommendations and product reviews/ratings that Amazon provides. This creates switching costs: competitors would have to provide extra value to Amazon's customers to entice them to shop elsewhere—either with lower prices or with some other valuable product or service that Amazon does not provide. Thus, when the data acquisition is tied directly to the value provided by the data, the resulting virtuous cycle creates a catch-22 for competitors: competitors need customers in order to acquire the necessary data, but they need the data in order to provide equivalent service to attract the customers.

Entrepreneurs and investors might turn this strategic consideration around: what historical circumstances now exist that may not continue indefinitely, and which may allow me to gain access to or to build a data asset more cheaply than will be possible in the future? Or which will allow me to build a data science team that would be more costly (or impossible) to build in the future?

Unique Intellectual Property

Our firm may have unique intellectual property. Data science intellectual property can include novel techniques for mining the data or for using the results. These might be patented, or they might just be trade secrets. In the former case, a competitor either will be unable to (legally) duplicate the solution, or will have an increased expense of doing so, either by licensing our technology or by developing new technology to avoid infringing on the patent. In the case of a trade secret, it may be that the competitor simply does not know how we have implemented our solution. With data science solutions, the actual mechanism is often hidden; with only the result being visible.

Unique Intangible Collateral Assets

Our competitors may not be able to figure out how to put our solution into practice. With successful data science solutions, the actual source of good performance (for example with effective predictive modeling) may be unclear. The effectiveness of a predictive modeling solution may depend critically on the problem engineering, the attributes created, the combining of different models, and so on. It often is not clear to a competitor how performance is achieved in practice. Even if our algorithms are published in detail, many implementation details may be critical to get a solution that works in the lab to work in production.

Furthermore, success may be based on intangible assets such as a company culture that is particularly suitable to the deployment of data science solutions. For example, a culture that embraces business experimentation and the (rigorous) supporting of claims with data will naturally be an easier place for data science solutions to succeed. Alternatively, if developers are encouraged to understand data science, they are less likely to screw up an otherwise top-quality solution. Recall our maxim: *Your model is not what your data scientists design, it's what your engineers implement.*

Superior Data Scientists

Maybe our data scientists simply are much better than our competitors'. There is a huge variance in the quality and ability of data scientists. Even among well-trained data scientists, it is well accepted within the data science community that certain individuals have the combination of innate creativity, analytical acumen, business sense, and perseverence that enables them to create remarkably better solutions than their peers.

This extreme difference in ability is illustrated by the year-after-year results in the KDD Cup data mining competition. Every year, the top professional society for data scientists, the ACM SIGKDD (*http://www.sigkdd.org/*), holds its annual conference (the ACM SIGKDD International Conference on Knowledge Discovery and Data Mining). Each year the conference holds a data mining competition. Some data scientists love to compete, and there are many competitions. The Netflix competition, discussed in Chapter 12, is one of the most famous, and such competitions have even been turned into a crowd-sourcing business (see Kaggle (*http://www.kaggle.com*)). The KDD Cup (*http://www.sigkdd.org/kddcup/index.php*) is the granddaddy of data mining competitions and has been held every year since 1997. Why is this relevant? Some of the best data scientists in the world participate in these competitions. Depending on the year and the task, hundreds or thousands of competitors try their hand at solving the problem. If data science talent were evenly distributed, then one would think it unlikely to see the same individuals repeatedly winning the competitions. But that's exactly what we see. There are individuals who have been on winning teams repeatedly, sometimes multiple years in a row and for multiple tasks each year (sometimes the competition has more than one task).[1] The point is that there is substantial variation in the ability even of the best data scientists, and this is illustrated by the "objective" results of the KDD Cup competitions. The upshot is that because of the large variation in ability, the best data scientists can pick and choose the employment opportunities that suit their desires with respect to salary, culture, advancement opportunities, and so on.

The variation in the quality of data scientists is amplified by the simple fact that top-notch data scientists are in high demand. Anyone can call himself a data scientist, and few companies can really evaluate data scientists well as potential hires. This leads to another catch: you need at least one top-notch data scientist to truly evaluate the quality of prospective hires. Thus, if our company has managed to build a strong data science capability, we have a substantial and sustained advantage over competitors who are having trouble hiring data scientists. Further, top-notch data scientists like to work with other top-notch data scientists, which compounds our advantage.

We also must embrace the fact that data science is in part a craft. Analytical expertise takes time to acquire, and all the great books and video lectures alone will not turn someone into a master. The craft is learned by experience. The most effective learning path resembles that in the classic trades: aspiring data scientists work as apprentices to masters. This could be in a graduate program with a top applications-oriented professor, in a postdoctoral program, or in industry working with one of the best industrial data scientists. At some point the apprentice is skilled enough to become a "journeyman," and will then work more independently on a team or even lead projects of her own. Many high-quality data scientists happily work in this capacity for their careers. Some small subset become masters themselves, because of a combination of their talent at recognizing the potential of new data science opportunities (more on that in a moment) and their mastery of theory and technique. Some of these then take on apprentices. Understanding this learning path can help to focus on hiring efforts, looking for data scientists who have apprenticed with top-notch masters. It also can be used tactically in a less obvious way: if you can hire one master data scientist, top-notch aspiring data scientists may come to apprentice with her.

In addition to all this, a top-notch data scientist needs to have a strong professional network. We don't mean a network in the sense of what one might find in an online professional networking system; an effective data scientist needs to have deep connections to other data scientists throughout the data science community. The reason is simply that the field of data science is immense and there are far too many diverse topics for any individual to master. A top-notch data scientist is a master of some area of technical expertise, and is familiar with many others. (Beware of the "jack-of-all-trades, master of none.") However, we do not want the data scientist's mastery of some area of

---

1. This is not to say that one should look at the KDD Cup winners as necessarily the best data miners in the world. Many top-notch data scientists have never competed in such a competition; some compete once and then focus their efforts on other things.

technical expertise to turn into the proverbial hammer for which all problems are nails. A top-notch data scientist will pull in the necessary expertise for the problem at hand. This is facilitated tremendously by strong and deep professional contacts. Data scientists call on each other to help in steering them to the right solutions. The better a professional network is, the better will be the solution. And, the best data scientists have the best connections.

Superior Data Science Management

Possibly even more critical to success for data science in business is having good *management* of the data science team. Good data science managers are especially hard to find. They need to understand the fundamentals of data science well, possibly even being competent data scientists themselves. Good data science managers also must possess a set of other abilities that are rare in a single individual:

- They need to truly understand and appreciate the needs of the business. What's more, they should be able to anticipate the needs of the business, so that they can interact with their counterparts in other functional areas to develop ideas for new data science products and services.

- They need to be able to communicate well with and be respected by both "techies" and "suits"; often this means translating data science jargon (which we have tried to minimize in this book) into business jargon, and vice versa.

- They need to coordinate technically complex activities, such as the integration of multiple models or procedures with business constraints and costs. They often need to understand the technical architectures of the business, such as the data systems or production software systems, in order to ensure that the solutions the team produces are actually useful in practice.

- They need to be able to anticipate outcomes of data science projects. As we have discussed, data science is more similar to R&D than to any other business activity. Whether a particular data science project will produce positive results is highly uncertain at the outset, and possibly even well into the project. Elsewhere we discuss how it is important to produce proof-of-concept studies quickly, but neither positive nor negative outcomes of such studies are highly predictive of success or failure of the larger project. They just give guidance to investments in the next cycle of the data mining process (recall Chapter 2). If we look to R&D management for clues about data science management, we find that there is only one reliable predictor of the success of a research project, and it is *highly* predictive: the prior success of the investigator. We see a similar situation with data science projects. There are individuals who seem to have an intuitive sense of which projects will pay off. We do not know of a careful analysis of why this is the case, but experience shows that it is. As with data science competitions, where we see remarkable repeat performances by the same individuals, we also see individuals repeatedly envisioning new data science opportunities and managing them to great success—and this is particularly impressive as many data science managers never see even one project through to great success.

- They need to do all this within the culture of a particular firm.

Finally, our data science capability may be difficult or expensive for a competitor to duplicate because *we can hire data scientists and data science managers better*. This may be due to our reputation and brand appeal with data scientists—a data scientist may prefer to work for a company known as being friendly to data science and data scientists. Or our firm may have a more subtle appeal. So let's examine in a little more detail what it takes to attract top-notch data scientists.

Attracting and Nurturing Data Scientists and Their Teams

At the beginning of the chapter, we noted that the two most important factors in ensuring that our firm gets the most from its data assets are: (i) the firm's management must think data-analytically, and (ii) the firm's management must create a culture where data science, and data scientists, will thrive. As we mentioned above, there can be a huge difference between the effectiveness of a great data scientist and an average data scientist, and between a great data science team and an individually great data scientist. But how can one confidently engage top-notch data scientists? How can we create great teams?

This is a very difficult question to answer in practice. At the time of this writing, the supply of top-notch data scientists is quite thin, resulting in a very competitive market for them. The best companies at hiring data scientists are the IBMs, Microsofts, and Googles of the world, who clearly demonstrate the value they place in data science via compensation, perks, and/or intangibles, such as one particular factor not to be taken lightly: data scientists like to be around other top-notch data scientists. One might argue that they *need* to be around other top-notch data scientists, not only to enjoy their day-to-day work, but also because the field is vast and the collective mind of a group of data scientists can bring to bear a much broader array of particular solution techniques.

However, just because the market is difficult does not mean all is lost. Many data scientists want to have more individual influence than they would have at a corporate behemoth. Many want more responsibility (and the concomitant experience) with the broader process of producing a data science solution. Some have visions of becoming Chief Scientist for a firm, and understand that the path to Chief Scientist may be better paved with projects in smaller and more varied firms. Some have visions of becoming entrepreneurs, and understand that being an early data scientist for a startup can give them invaluable experience. And some simply will enjoy the thrill of taking part in a fast-growing venture: working in a company growing at 20% or 50% a year is much different from working in a company growing at 5% or 10% a year (or not growing at all).

In all these cases, the firms that have an advantage in hiring are those that create an environment for nurturing data science and data scientists. If you do not have a critical mass of data scientists, be creative. Encourage your data scientists to become part of local data science technical communities and global data science academic communities.

 A note on publishing
Science is a social endeavor, and the best data scientists often want to stay engaged in the community by publishing their advances. Firms sometimes have trouble with this idea, feeling that they are "giving away the store" or tipping their hand to competitors by revealing what they are doing. On the other hand, if they do not, they may not be able to hire or retain the very best. Publishing also has some advantages for the firm, such as increased publicity, exposure, external validation of ideas, and so on. There is no clear-cut answer, but the issue needs to be considered carefully. Some firms file patents aggressively on their data science ideas, after which academic publication is natural if the idea is truly novel and important.

A firm's data science presence can be bolstered by engaging academic data scientists. There are several ways of doing this. For those academics interested in practical applications of their work, it may be possible to fund their research programs. Both of your authors, when working in industry, funded academic programs and essentially extended the data science team that was focusing on their problems and interacting. The best arrangement (by our experience) is a combination of data, money, and an interesting business problem; if the project ends up being a portion of the Ph.D. thesis of a student in a top-notch program, the benefit to the firm can far outweigh the cost. Funding a Ph.D. student might cost a firm in the ballpark of $50K/year, which is a fraction of the fully loaded cost of a top data scientist. A key is to have enough understanding of data science to select the right professor—one with the appropriate expertise for the problem at hand.

Another tactic that can be very cost-effective is to take on one or more top-notch data scientists as scientific advisors. If the relationship is structured such that the advisors truly interact on the solutions to problems, firms that do not have the resources or the clout to hire the very best data scientists can substantially increase the quality of the eventual solutions. Such advisors can be data scientists at partner firms, data scientists from firms who share investors or board members, or academics who have some consulting time.

A different tack altogether is to hire a third party to conduct the data science. There are various third-party data science providers, ranging from massive firms specializing in business analytics (such as IBM), to data-science-specific consulting firms (such as Elder Research), to boutique data science firms who take on a very small number of clients to help them develop their data science capabilities (such as Data Scientists, LLC).[2] You can find a large list of data-science service companies, as well as a wide variety of other data science resources, at KDnuggets (*http://kdnuggets.com*). A caveat about engaging data science consulting firms is that their interests are not always well aligned with their customers' interests; this is obvious to seasoned users of consultants, but not to everyone.

Savvy managers employ all of these resources tactically. A chief scientist or empowered manager often can assemble for a project a substantially more powerful and diverse team than most companies can hire.

Examine Data Science Case Studies

Beyond building a solid data science team, how can a manager ensure that her firm is best positioned to take advantage of opportunities for applying data science? Make sure that there is an understanding of and appreciation for the fundamental principles of data science. Empowered employees across the firm often see novel applications.

After gaining command of the fundamental principles of data science, the best way to position oneself for success is to work through many examples of the application of data science to business problems. Read case studies that actually walk through the data mining process. Formulate your own case studies. Actually mining data is helpful, but even more important is working through the connection between the business problem and the possible data science solutions. The more, different problems you work through, the better you will be at naturally seeing and capitalizing on opportunities for bringing to bear the information and knowledge "stored" in the data—often the same problem formulation from one problem can be applied by analogy to another, with only minor changes.

It is important to keep in mind that the examples we have presented in this book were chosen or designed for illustration. In reality, the business and data science team should be prepared for all manner of mess and contraints, and must be flexible in dealing with them. Sometimes there is a wealth of data and data science techniques available to be brought to bear. Other times the situation seems more like the critical scene from the movie *Apollo 13*. In the movie, a malfunction and explosion in the command module leave the astronauts stranded a quarter of a million miles from Earth, with the CO_2 levels rising too rapidly for them to survive the return trip. In a nutshell, because of the constraints placed by what the astronauts have on hand, the engineers have to figure out how to use a large cubic filter in place of a narrower cylindrical filter (to literally put a square peg in a round hole). In the key scene, the head engineer dumps out onto a table all the "stuff" that's there in the command module, and tells his team: "OK, people …

---

2. Disclaimer: The authors have a relationship with Data Scientists, LLC.

we got to find a way to make *this* fit into the hole for *this*, using nothing but *that*." Real data science problems often seem more like the Apollo 13 situation than a textbook situation.

For example, Perlich et al. (2013) describe a study of just such a case. For targeting consumers with online display advertisements, obtaining an adequate supply of the ideal training data would have been prohibitively expensive. However, data were available at much lower cost from various other distributions and for other target variables. Their very effective solution cobbled together models built from these surrogate data, and "transferred" these models for use on the desired task. The use of these surrogate data allowed them to operate with a substantially reduced investment in data from the ideal (and expensive) training distribution.

Be Ready to Accept Creative Ideas from Any Source

Once different role players understand fundamental principles of data science, creative ideas for new solutions can come from any direction—such as from executives examining potential new lines of business, from directors dealing with profit and loss responsibility, from managers looking critically at a business process, and from line employees with detailed knowledge of exactly how a particular business process functions. Data scientists should be encouraged to interact with employees throughout the business, and part of their performance evaluation should be based on how well they produce ideas for improving the business with data science. Incidentally, doing so can pay off in unintended ways: the data processing skills possessed by data scientists often can be applied in ways that are not so sophisticated but nevertheless can help other employees without those skills. Often a manager may have no idea that particular data can even be obtained—data that might help the manager directly, without sophisticated data science.

Be Ready to Evaluate Proposals for Data Science Projects

Ideas for improving business decisions through data science can come from any direction. Managers, investors, and employees should be able to formulate such ideas clearly, and decision makers should be prepared to evaluate them. Essentially, we need to be able to formulate solid proposals and to evaluate proposals.

The data mining process, described in Chapter 2, provides a framework to direct this. Each stage in the process reveals questions that should be asked both in formulating proposals for projects and in evaluating them:

- Is the business problem well specified? Does the data science solution solve the problem?
- Is it clear how we would evaluate a solution?

- Would we be able see evidence of success before making a huge investment in deployment?
- Does the firm have the data assets it needs? For example, for supervised modeling, are there actually labeled training data? Is the firm ready to invest in the assets it does not have yet?

Appendix A provides a starting list of questions for evaluating data science proposals, organized by the data mining process. Let's walk through an illustrative example. (In Appendix B you will find another example proposal to evaluate, focusing on our running churn problem.)

Example Data Mining Proposal

Your company has an installed user base of 900,000 current users of your Whiz-bang® widget. You now have developed Whiz-bang® 2.0, which has substantially lower operating costs than the original. Ideally, you would like to convert ("migrate") your entire user base over to version 2.0; however, using 2.0 requires that users master the new interface, and there is a serious risk that in attempting to do so, the customers will become frustrated and not convert, become less satistified with the company, or in the worst case, switch to your competitor's popular Boppo® widget. Marketing has designed a brand-new migration incentive plan, which will cost $250 per selected customer. There is no guarantee that a customer will choose to migrate even if she takes this incentive.

An external firm, Big Red Consulting, is proposing a plan to target customers carefully for Whiz-bang® 2.0, and given your demonstrated fluency with the fundamentals of data science, you are called in to help assess Big Red's proposal. Do Big Red's choices seem correct?

Targeted Whiz-bang Customer Migration—prepared by Big Red Consulting, Inc.

We will develop a predictive model using modern data-mining technology. As discussed in our last meeting, we assume a budget of $5,000,000 for this phase of customer migration; adjusting the plan for other budgets is straightforward. Thus we can target 20,000 customers under this budget. Here is how we will select those customers:

We will use data to build a model of whether or not a customer will migrate given the incentive. The dataset will comprise a set of attributes of customers, such as the number and type of prior customer service interactions, level of usage of the widget, location of the customer, estimated technical sophistication, tenure with the firm, and other loyalty indicators, such as number of other firm products and services in use. The target will be whether or not the customer will migrate to the new widget if he/she is given the incentive. Using these data, we will build a linear regression to estimate the target variable. The model will be evaluated based on its accuracy on these data; in particular, we want to ensure that the accuracy is substantially greater than if we targeted randomly.

To use the model: for each customer we will apply the regression model to estimate the target variable. If the estimate is greater than 0.5, we will predict that the customer will migrate; otherwise, we will say the customer will not migrate. We then will select at random 20,000 customers from those predicted to migrate, and these 20,000 will be the recommended targets.

Flaws in the Big Red Proposal

We can use our understanding of the fundamental principles and other basic concepts of data science to identify flaws in the proposal. Appendix A provides a starting guide for reviewing such proposals, with some of the main questions to ask. However, this book as a whole really can be seen as a proposal review guide. Here are some of the most egregious flaws in Big Data's proposal:

Business Understanding

- The target variable definition is imprecise. For example, over what time period must the migration occur? (Chapter 3)
- The formulation of the data mining problem could be better-aligned with the business problem. For example, what if certain customers (or everyone) were likely to migrate anyway (without the incentive)? Then we would be wasting the cost of the incentive in targeting them. (Chapter 2, Chapter 11)

Data Understanding/Data Preparation

- There aren't any labeled training data! This is a brand-new incentive. We should invest some of our budget in obtaining labels for some examples. This can be done by targeting a (randomly) selected subset of customers with the incentive. One also might propose a more sophisticated approach (Chapter 2, Chapter 3, Chapter 11).
- If we are worried about wasting the incentive on customers who are likely to migrate without it, we also should observe a "control group" over the period where we are obtaining training data. This should be easy, since everyone we don't target to gather labels would be a "control" subject. We can build a separate model for migrate or not given no incentive, and combine the models in an expected value framework. (Chapter 11)

Modeling

- Linear regression is not a good choice for modeling a categorical target variable. Rather one should use a classification method, such as tree induction, logistic regression, k-NN, and so on. Even better, why not try a bunch of methods and evaluate them experimentally to see which performs best? (Chapter 2, Chapter 3, Chapter 4, Chapter 5, Chapter 6, Chapter 7, Chapter 8)

Evaluation

- The evaluation shouldn't be on the training data. Some sort of holdout approach should be used (e.g., cross-validation and/or a staged approach as discussed above). (Chapter 5)
- Is there going to be any domain-knowledge validation of the model? What if it is capturing some weirdness of the data collection process? (Chapter 7, Chapter 11, Chapter 14)

Deployment

- The idea of randomly selecting customers with regression scores greater than 0.5 is not well considered. First, it is not clear that a regression score of 0.5 really corresponds to a probability of migration of 0.5. Second, 0.5 is rather arbitrary in any case. Third, since our model is providing a ranking (e.g., by likelihood of migration, or by expected value if we use the more complex formulation), we should use the ranking to guide our targeting: choose the top-ranked candidates, as the budget will allow. (Chapter 2, Chapter 3, Chapter 7, Chapter 8, Chapter 11)

Of course, this is just one example with a particular set of flaws. A different set of concepts may need to be brought to bear for a different proposal that is flawed in other ways.

A Firm's Data Science Maturity

For a firm to realistically plan data science endeavors it should assess, frankly and rationally, its own *maturity* in terms of data science capability. It is beyond the scope of this book to provide a self-assessment guide, but a few words on the topic are important.

Firms vary widely in their data science capabilities along many dimensions. One dimension that is very important for strategic planning is the firm's "maturity," specifically, how systematic and well founded are the processes used to guide the firm's data science projects.[3]

At one end of the maturity spectrum, a firm's data science processes are completely ad hoc. In many firms, the employees engaged in data science and business analytics endeavors have no formal training in these areas, and the managers involved have little understanding of the fundamental principles of data science and data analytic thinking.

---

3. The reader interested in this notion of the maturity of a firm's capabilities is encouraged to read about the Capability Maturity Model (*http://en.wikipedia.org/wiki/Capability_Maturity_Model*) for software engineering, which is the inspiration for this discussion.

A note on "immature" firms

Being "immature" does *not* mean that a firm is destined to failure. It means that success is highly variable and is much more dependent on luck than in a mature firm. Project success will depend upon the heroic efforts by individuals who happen to have a natural acuity for data-analytic thinking. An immature firm may implement not-so-sophisticated data science solutions at a large scale, or may implement sophisticated solutions at a small scale. Rarely, though, will an immature firm implement sophisticated data science solutions at a large scale.

A firm with a medium level of maturity employs well-trained data scientists, as well as business managers and other stakeholders who understand the fundamental principles of data science. Both sides can think clearly about how to solve business problems with data science, and both sides participate in the design and implementation of solutions that directly address the problems of the business.

At the high end of maturity are firms who continually work to improve their data science *processes* (and not just the solutions). Executives at such firms continually challenge the data science team to instill processes that will align their solutions better with the business problems. At the same time they realize that pragmatic trade-offs may favor the choice of a suboptimal solution that can be realized today over a theoretically much better solution that won't be ready until next year. Data scientists at such a firm should have the confidence that when they propose an investments to improve data science processes, their suggestions will be met with open and informed minds. That's not to say that every such request will be approved, but that the proposal will be evaluated on its own merits in the context of the business.

Note: Data science is neither operations nor engineering.

There is some danger in making an analogy to the Capability Maturity Model from software engineering—danger that the analogy will be taken too literally. Trying to apply the same sort of processes that work for software engineering, or worse for manufacturing or operations, will fail for data science. Moreover, misguided attempts to do so will send a firm's best data scientists out the door before the management even knows what happened. The key is to understand *data science processes* and how to do data science well, and work to establish consistency and support. Remember that data science is more like R&D than like engineering or manufacturing. As a concrete example, management should consistently make available the resources needed for solid evaluation of data science projects early and often. Sometimes this involves investing in data that would not otherwise have been obtained. Often this involves assigning engineering resources to support the data science team. The data science team should in return work to provide management with evaluations that are as well aligned with the actual business problem(s) as possible.

As a concrete example, consider yet again our telecom churn problem and how firms of varying maturity might address it:

- An immature firm will have (hopefully) analytically adept employees implementing ad hoc solutions based on their intuitions about how to manage churn. These may work well or they may not. In an immature firm, it will be difficult for management to evaluate these choices against alternatives, or to determine when they've implemented a nearly optimal solution.

- A firm of medium maturity will have implemented a well-defined framework for testing different alternative solutions. They will test under conditions that mimic as closely as possible the actual business setting—for example, running the latest production data through a testbed platform that compares how different methods "would have done," and considering carefully the costs and benefits involved.

- A very mature organization may have deployed the exact same methods as the medium-maturity firm for identifying the customers with the highest probability of leaving, or even the highest expected loss if they were to churn. They would also be working to implement the processes, and gather the data, necessary to judge also the effect of the incentives and thereby work towards finding those individuals for which the incentives will produce the largest expected increase in value (over not giving the incentive). Such a firm may also be working to integrate such a procedure into an experimentation and/or optimization framework for assessing different offers or different parameters (like the level of discount) to a given offer.

A frank self-assessment of data science maturity is difficult, but it is essential to getting the best out of one's current capabilities, and to improving one's capabilities.

CHAPTER 14

Conclusion

*If you can't explain it simply, you don't understand
it well enough.*

—Albert Einstein

The practice of data science can best be described as a combination of analytical engineering and exploration. The business presents a problem we would like to solve. Rarely is the business problem directly one of our basic data mining tasks. We decompose the problem into subtasks that we think we can solve, usually starting with existing tools. For some of these tasks we may not know how *well* we can solve them, so we have to mine the data and conduct evaluation to see. If that does not succeed, we may need to try something completely different. In the process we may discover knowledge that will help us to solve the problem we had set out to solve, or we may discover something unexpected that leads us to other important successes.

Neither the analytical engineering nor the exploration should be omitted when considering the application of data science methods to solve a business problem. Omitting the engineering aspect usually makes it much less likely that the results of mining data will actually solve the business problem. Omitting the understanding of process as one of exploration and discovery often keeps an organization from putting the right management, incentives, and investments in place for the project to succeed.

The Fundamental Concepts of Data Science

Both the analytical engineering and the exploration and discovery are made more systematic and thereby more likely to succeed by the understanding and embracing of the fundamental concepts of data science. In this book we have introduced a collection of the most important fundamental concepts. Some of these concepts we made into headliners for the chapters, and others were introduced more naturally through the discussions (and not necessarily labeled as fundamental concepts). These concepts span the process from envisioning how data science can improve business decisions, to applying data science techniques, to deploying the results to improve decision-making. The concepts also undergird a large array of business analytics.

We can group our fundamental concepts roughly into three types:

1. General concepts about how data science fits in the organization and the competitive landscape, including ways to attract, structure, and nurture data science teams, ways for thinking about how data science leads to competitive advantage, ways that competitive advantage can be sustained, and tactical principles for doing well with data science projects.

2. General ways of thinking data-analytically, which help us to gather appropriate data and consider appropriate methods. The concepts include the *data mining process*, the collection of different *high-level data science tasks*, as well as principles such as the following.

   - *The data science team should keep in mind the problem to be solved and the use scenario throughout the data mining process*

   - *Data should be considered an asset, and therefore we should think carefully about what investments we should make to get the best leverage from our asset*

   - *The expected value framework can help us to structure business problems so we can see the component data mining problems as well as the connective tissue of costs, benefits, and constraints imposed by the business environment*

   - *Generalization and overfitting: if we look too hard at the data, we will find patterns; we want patterns that generalize to data we have not yet seen*

   - *Applying data science to a well-structured problem versus exploratory data mining require different levels of effort in different stages of the data mining process*

3. General concepts for actually extracting knowledge from data, which undergird the vast array of data science techniques. These include concepts such as the following.

   - *Identifying informative attributes—those that correlate with or give us information about an unknown quantity of interest*

   - *Fitting a numeric function model to data by choosing an objective and finding a set of parameters based on that objective*

   - *Controlling complexity is necessary to find a good trade-off between generalization and overfitting*

   - *Calculating similarity between objects described by data*

Once we think about data science in terms of its fundamental concepts, we see the same concepts underlying many different data science strategies, tasks, algorithms, and processes. As we have illustrated throughout the book, these principles not only allow us to understand the theory and practice of data science much more deeply, they also allow us to understand the methods and techniques of data science very broadly, because these methods and techniques are quite often simply particular instantiations of one or more of the fundamental principles.

At a high level we saw how structuring business problems using the expected value framework allows us to decompose problems into data science tasks that we understand better how to solve, and this applies across many different sorts of business problems.

For extracting knowledge from data, we saw that our fundamental concept of determining the similarity of two objects described by data is used directly, for example to find customers similar to our best customers. It is used for classification and for regression, via nearest-neighbor methods. It is the basis for clustering, the unsupervised grouping of data objects. It is the basis for finding documents most related to a search query. And it is the basis for more than one common method for making recommendations, for example by casting both customers and movies into the same "taste space," and then finding movies most similar to a particular customer.

When it comes to measurement, we see the notion of *lift*—determining how much more likely a pattern is than would be expected by chance—appearing broadly across data science, when evaluating very different sorts of patterns. One evaluates algorithms for targeting advertisements by computing the lift one gets for the targeted population. One calculates lift for judging the weight of evidence for or against a conclusion. One calculates lift to help judge whether a repeated co-occurrence is interesting, as opposed to simply being a natural consequence of popularity.

Understanding the fundamental concepts also facilitates communication between business stakeholders and data scientists, not only because of the shared vocabulary, but because both sides actually understand better. Instead of missing important aspects of a discussion completely, we can dig in and ask questions that will reveal critical aspects that otherwise would not have been uncovered.

For example, let's say your venture firm is considering investing in a data science-based company producing a personalized online news service. You ask how exactly they are personalizing the news. They say they use support vector machines. Let's even pretend that we had not talked about support vector machines in this book. You should feel confident enough in your knowledge of data science now that you should not simply say "Oh, OK." You should be able to confidently ask: "What's that exactly?" If they really do know what they are talking about, they should give you some explanation based upon our fundamental principles (as we did in Chapter 4). You also are now prepared to ask, "What exactly are the training data you intend to use?" Not only might that impress data scientists on their team, but it actually is an important question to be asked to see whether they are doing something credible, or just using "data science" as a smokescreen to hide behind. You can go on to think about whether you really believe building any predictive model from these data—regardless of what sort of model it is—would be likely to solve the business problem they're attacking. You should be ready to ask whether you really think they will have reliable training labels for such a task. And so on.

Applying Our Fundamental Concepts to a New Problem: Mining Mobile Device Data

As we've emphasized repeatedly, once we think about data science as a collection of concepts, principles, and general methods, we will have much more success both understanding data science activities broadly, and also applying data science to new business problems. Let's consider a fresh example.

Recently (as of this writing), there has been a marked shift in consumer online activity from traditional computers to a wide variety of mobile devices. Companies, many still working to understand how to reach consumers on their desktop computers, now are scrambling to understand how to reach consumers on their mobile devices: smart phones, tablets, and even increasingly mobile laptop computers, as WiFi access becomes ubiquitous. We won't talk about most of the complexity of that problem, but from our perspective, the data-analytic thinker might notice that mobile devices provide a new sort of data from which little leverage has yet been obtained. In particular, mobile devices are associated with data on their location.

For example, in the mobile advertising ecosystem, depending on my privacy settings, my mobile device may broadcast my exact GPS location to those entities who would like to target me with advertisements, daily deals, and other offers. Figure 14-1 shows a scatterplot of a small sample of locations that a potential advertiser might see, sampled from the mobile advertising ecosystem. Even if I do not broadcast my GPS location, my device broadcasts the IP address of the network it currently is using, which often conveys location information.

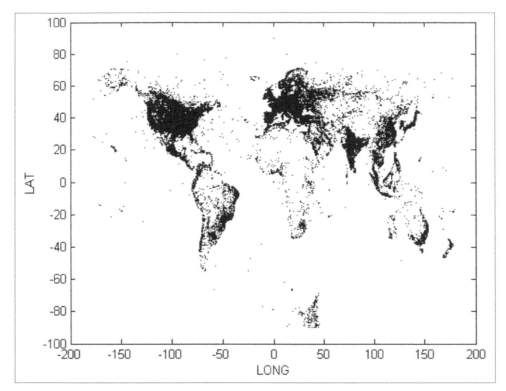

Figure 14-1. A scatterplot of a sample of GPS locations captured from mobile devices.

As an interesting side point, this is just a scatterplot of the latitude and longitudes broadcast by mobile devices; *there is no map!* It gives a striking picture of population density across the world. And it makes us wonder what's going on with mobile devices in Antarctica.

How might we use such data? Let's apply our fundamental concepts. If we want to get beyond exploratory data analysis (as we've started with the visualization in Figure 14-1), we need to think in terms of some concrete business problem. A particular firm might have certain problems to solve, and be focused on one or two. An entrepreneur or investor might scan across different possible problems she sees that businesses or consumers currently have. Let's pick one related to these data.

Advertisers face the problem that in this new world, we see a variety of different devices and a particular consumer's behavior may be fragmented across several. In the desktop world, once the advertisers identify a good prospect, perhaps via a cookie in a particular consumer's browser or a device ID, they can then begin to take action accordingly; for example, by presenting targeted ads. In the mobile ecosystem, this consumer's activity is fragmented across devices. Even if a good prospect is found on one device, how can she be targeted on her other devices?

One possibility is to use the location data to winnow the space of possible other devices that could belong to this prospect. Figure 14-1 suggests that a huge portion of the space of possible alternatives would be eliminated if we could profile the location visitation behavior of a mobile device. Presumably, my location behavior on my smart phone will be fairly similar to my location behavior on my laptop, especially if I am considering the WiFi locations that I use.[1] So I may want to draw on what I know about assessing the similarity of data items (Chapter 6).

When working through our data-understanding phase, we need to decide how exactly we will represent devices and their locations. Once we are able to step back from the details of algorithms and applications, and think instead about the fundamentals, we might notice that the ideas discussed in the example of problem formulation for text mining (Chapter 10) would apply very well here—even though this example has nothing to do with text. When mining data on documents, we often ignore much of the structure of the text, such as its sequence. For many problems we can simply treat each document as a collection of words from a potentially large vocabulary. The same thinking will apply here. Obviously there is considerable structure to the locations one visits, such as the sequence in which they are visited, but for data mining a simplest-first strategy is often best. Let's just consider each device to be a "bag of locations," in analogy to the bag-of-words representation discussed in Chapter 10.

If we are looking to try to find other instances of the same user, we might also profitably apply the ideas of TFIDF for text to our locations. WiFi locations that are very popular (like the Starbucks on the corner of Washington Square Park) are unlikely to be so informative in a similarity calculation focused on finding the same user on different devices. Such a location would get a low IDF score (think of the "D" as being for "Device" rather than "Document"). At the other end of the spectrum, for many people their apartment WiFi networks would have few different devices, and thereby be quite discriminative. TFIDF on location would magnify the importance of these locations in a similarity calculation. In between these two in discriminability might be an office WiFi network, which might get a middle-of-the-road IDF score.

Now, if our device profile is a TFIDF representation based on our bag of locations, as with using similarity over the TFIDF formulation for our search query for the jazz musician example in Chapter 10, we might look for the devices most similar to the one that we had identified as a good prospect. Let's say that my laptop was the device identified as a good prospect. My laptop is observed on my apartment WiFi network and on my work WiFi network. The only other devices that are observed there are my phone, my tablet, and possibly the mobile devices of my wife and a few friends and colleagues

---

1. Which incidentally can be anonymized if I am concerned about invasions of privacy. More on that later.

(but note that these will get low TF scores at one or the other location, as compared to my devices). Thus, it is likely that my phone and tablet will be strongly similar—possibly most similar—to the one identified as a prospect. If the advertiser had identified my laptop as a good prospect for a particular ad, then this formulation would also identify my phone and tablet as good prospects for the same ad.

This example isn't meant to be a definitive solution to the problem of finding corresponding users on different mobile devices;[2] it shows how having a conceptual toolkit can be helpful in thinking about a brand-new problem. Once these ideas are conceptualized, data scientists would dig in to figure out what really works and how to flesh out and extend the ideas, applying many of the concepts we have discussed (such as how to evaluate alternative implementation options).

Changing the Way We Think about Solutions to Business Problems

The example also provides a concrete illustration of yet another important fundamental concept (we haven't exhausted them even after this many pages of a detailed book). It is quite common that in the business understanding/data understanding subcycle of the data mining process, our notion of *what is the problem* changes to fit what we actually can do with the data. Often the change is subtle, but it is very important to (try to) notice when it happens. Why? Because all stakeholders are not involved with the data science problem formulation. If we forget that we have changed the problem, especially if the change is subtle, we may run into resistance down the line. And it may be resistance due purely to misunderstanding! What's worse, it may be perceived as due to stubbornness, which might lead to hard feelings that threaten the success of the project.

Let's look back at the mobile targeting example. The astute reader might have said: *Wait a minute. We started by saying that we were going to find the same users on different devices. What we've done is to find very similar users in terms of their location information. I may be willing to agree that the set of these similar users is very likely to contain the same user—more likely than any alternative I can think of—but that's not the same as finding the same user on different devices.* This reader would be correct. In working through our problem formulation the problem changed slightly. We now have made the identification of the same user probabilistic: there may be a very high probability that the subset of devices with very similar location profiles will contain other instances of the same user, but it is not guaranteed. This needs to be clear in our minds, and clarified to stakeholders.

It turns out that for targeting advertisements or offers, this change probably will be acceptable to all stakeholders. Recalling our cost/benefit framework for evaluating data mining solutions (Chapter 7), it's pretty clear that for many offers targeting some false

---

2. It is however the essence of a real-world solution to the problem implemented by one of the most advanced mobile advertising companies.

positives will be of relatively low cost as compared to the benefit of hitting more true positives. What's more, for many offers targeters may actually be happy to "miss," if each miss constitutes hitting other people with similar interests. And my wife and close friends and colleagues are pretty good hits for many of my tastes and interests![3]

What Data Can't Do: Humans in the Loop, Revisited

This book has focused on how, why, and when we can get business value from data science by enhancing data-driven decision-making. It is important also to consider the limits of data science and data-driven decision-making.

There are things computers are good at and things people are good at, but often these aren't the same things. For example, humans are much better at identifying—from everything out in the world—small sets of relevant aspects of the world from which to gather data in support of a particular task. Computers are much better at sifting through a massive collection of data, including a huge number of (possibly) relevant variables, and quantifying the variables' relevance to predicting a target.

 New York Times Op-Ed columnist David Brooks has written an excellent essay entitled "What Data Can't Do" (Brooks, 2013). You should read this if you are considering the magical application of data science to solve your problems.

Data science involves the judicious integration of human knowledge and computer-based techniques to achieve what neither of them could achieve alone. (And beware of any tool vendor who suggests otherwise!) The data mining process introduced in Chapter 2 helps direct the combination of humans and computers. The structure imposed by the process emphasizes the interaction of humans early, to ensure that the application of data science methods are focused on the right tasks. Examining the data mining process also reveals that task selection and specification is not the only place where human interaction is critical. As discussed in Chapter 2, one of the places where human creativity, knowledge, and common sense adds value is in selecting the right data to mine—which is far too often overlooked in discussions of data mining, especially considering its importance.

---

3. In an article in the *Proceedings of the National Academy of Sciences*, Crandall et al. (2010) show that geographic co-ocurrences between individuals are very strongly predictive of the individuals being friends: "The knowledge that two people were proximate at just a few distinct locations at roughly the same times can indicate a high conditional probability that they are directly linked in the underlying social network." This means that even "misses" due to location similarity may still contain some of the advantage of social network targeting —which has been shown to be extremely effective for marketing (Hill et al., 2006).

Human interaction is also critical in the evaluation stage of the process. The combination of the right data and data science techniques excels at finding models that optimize some objective criterion. Only humans can tell what is the best objective criterion to optimize for a particular problem. This involves substantial subjective human judgment, because often the true criterion to be optimized cannot be measured, so the humans have to pick the best proxy or proxies possible—and keep these decisions in mind as sources of risk when the models are deployed. And then we need careful, and sometimes creative, attention to whether the resultant models or patterns actually do help to solve the problem.

We also need to keep in mind that the data to which we will apply data science techniques are the product of some process that involved human decisions. We should not fall prey to thinking that the data represent objective truth.[4] Data incorporate the beliefs, purposes, biases, and pragmatics of those who designed the data collection systems. The meaning of data is colored by our own beliefs.

Consider the following simple example. Many years ago, your authors worked together as data scientists at one of the largest telephone companies. There was a terrible problem with fraud in the wireless business, and we applied data science methods to massive data on cell phone usage, social calling patterns, locations visited, etc. (Fawcett & Provost, 1996, 1997). A seemingly well-performing component of a model for detecting fraud indicated that "calling from cellsite number zero provides substantially increased risk of fraud." This was verified through careful holdout evaluation. Fortunately (in this instance), we followed good data science practice and in the evaluation phase worked to ensure domain-knowledge validation of the model. We had trouble understanding this particular model component. There were many cellsites that indicated elevated probability of fraud,[5] but cellsite zero stood out. Furthermore, the other cellsites made sense because when you looked up their locations, there at least was a good story—for example, the cellsite was in a high-crime area. Looking up cellsite zero resulted in nothing at all. It wasn't in the cellsite lists. We went to the top data guru to divine the answer. Indeed, *there was no cellsite zero*. But the data clearly have many fraudulent calls from cellsite zero!

---

4. The philosophically minded should read W. V. O. Quine's (1951) classic essay, "Two Dogmas of Empiricism," in which he presents a biting criticism of the common notion that there is a dichotomy between the empirical and the analytical.

5. Technically, the models were most useful if there was a significant *change* in behavior to more calling from these cellsites. If you are interested, the papers describe this in detail.

To make a quite long story short, our understanding of the data was wrong. Briefly, when fraud was resolved on a customer's account, often a substantial amount of time passed between their bill being printed, sent out, received by the customer, opened, read, and acted upon. During this time, fraudulent activity continued. Now that fraud had been detected, these calls should not appear on the customer's next bill, so they were removed from the billing system. They were not discarded however, but (fortunately for the data mining efforts) were kept in a different database. Unfortunately, whoever designed that database decided that it was not important to keep certain fields. One of these was the cellsite. Thus, when the data science effort asked for data on all the fraudulent calls, in order to build training and test sets, these calls were included. As they did not have a cellsite, another design decision (conscious or not) led the fields to be filled with zeros. Thus, many of the fraudulent calls seemed to be from cellsite zero!

This is a "leak," as introduced in Chapter 2. You might think that should have been easy to spot. It wasn't, for several reasons. Consider how many phone calls are made by *tens of millions* of customers over many months, and for each call there was a very large number of possible descriptive attributes. There was no possibility to manually examine the data. Further, the calls were grouped by customer, so there wasn't a bulk of cellsite-zero calls; they were interspersed with each customer's other calls. Finally, and possibly most importantly, as part of the data preparation the data were scrubbed to improve the quality of the target variable. Some calls credited as fraud to an account were not actually fraudulent. Many of these, in turn, could be identified by seeing that the customer called them in a prior, nonfraud period. The result was that calls from cellsite zero had an elevated probability of fraud, but were not a perfect predictor of fraud (which would have been a red flag).

The point of this mini-case study is to illustrate that "what the data is" is an interpretation that we place. This interpretation often changes through the process of data mining, and we need to embrace this malleability. Our fraud detection example showed a change in the interpretation of a data item. We often also change our understanding of how the data were sampled as we uncover biases in the data collection process. For example, if we want to model consumer behavior in order to design or deliver a marketing campaign, it is essential to understand exactly what was the consumer base from which the data were sampled. This again sounds obvious in theory, but in practice it may involve in-depth analysis of the systems and businesses from which the data came.

Finally we need to be discerning in *the sorts of problems for which data science, even with the integration of humans, is likely to add value*. We must ask: are there really sufficient data pertaining to the decision at hand? Very high-level strategic decisions may be placed in a unique context. Data analyses, as well as theoretical simulations, may provide insight, but often for the highest-level decisions the decision makers must rely on their experience, knowledge, and intuition. This applies certainly to strategic decisions such as whether to acquire a particular company: data analysis can support the decision, but ultimately each situation is unique and the judgment of an experienced strategist will be necessary.

This idea of unique situations should be carried through. At an extreme we might think of Steve Jobs' famous statement: "It's really hard to design products by focus groups. A lot of times, people don't know what they want until you show it to them... That doesn't mean we don't listen to customers, but it's hard for them to tell you what they want when they've never seen anything remotely like it." As we look to the future we may hope that with the increasing ability to do careful, automated experimentation we may move from asking people what they would like or would find useful to observing what they like or find useful. To do this well, we need to follow our fundamental principle: consider data as an asset, in which we may need to invest. Our Capital One case from Chapter 1 is an example of creating many products and investing in data and data science to determine both which ones people would want, and for each product which people would be appropriate (i.e., profitable) customers.

Privacy, Ethics, and Mining Data About Individuals

Mining data, especially data about individuals, raises important ethical issues that should not be ignored. There recently has been considerable discussion in the press and within government agencies about privacy and data (especially online data), but the issues are much broader. Most consumer-facing large companies collect or purchase detailed data on all of us. These data are used directly to make decisions regarding many of the business applications we have discussed through the book: should we be granted credit? If so, what should be our credit line? Should we be targeted with an offer? What content would we like to be shown on the website? What products should be recommended to us? Are we likely to defect to a competitor? Is there fraud on our account?

The tension between privacy and improving business decisions is intense because there seems to be a direct relationship between increased use of personal data and increased effectiveness of the associated business decisions. For example, a study by researchers at the University of Toronto and MIT showed that after particularly stringent privacy protection was enacted in Europe, online advertising became significantly less effective. In particular, "the difference in stated purchase intent between those who were exposed to ads and those who were not dropped by approximately 65%. There was no such change for countries outside Europe" (Goldfarb & Tucker, 2011).[6] This is not a phenomenon restricted to online advertising: adding fine-grained social network data (e.g., who communicates with whom) to more traditional data on individuals substantially increases the effectiveness of fraud detection (Fawcett & Provost, 1997) and targeted marketing (Hill et al., 2006). Generally, the more fine-grained data you collect on in-

---

6. See Mayer and Narayanan's web site (*http://donottrack.us/bib/#sec_economics*) for a criticism of this and other research claims about the value of behaviorally targeted online advertising.

dividuals, the better you can predict things about them that are important for business decision-making. This seeming direct relationship between reduced privacy and increased business performance elicits strong feelings from both the privacy and the business perspectives (sometimes within the same person).

It is far beyond the scope of this book to resolve this problem, and the issues are extremely complicated (for example, what sort of "anonymization" would be sufficient?) and diverse. Possibly the biggest impediment to the reasoned consideration of privacy-friendly data science designs is the difficulty with even defining what privacy is. Daniel Solove is a world authority on privacy. His article "A Taxonomy of Privacy" (2006) starts:

> Privacy is a concept in disarray. Nobody can articulate what it means. As one commentator has observed, privacy suffers from "an embarrassment of meanings."

Solove's article goes on to spend over 80 pages giving a taxonomy of privacy. Helen Nissenbaum is another world authority on privacy, who has concentrated recently specifically on the relationship of privacy and massive databases (and the mining thereof). Her book on this topic, *Privacy in Context*, is over 300 pages (and well worth reading). We bring this up to emphasize that privacy concerns are not some easy-to-understand or easy-to-deal-with issues that can be quickly dispatched, or even written about well as a section or chapter of a data science book. If you are either a data scientist or a business stakeholder in data science projects, you should care about privacy concerns, and you will need to invest serious time in thinking carefully about them.

Is There More to Data Science?

Although this book is fairly thick, we have tried hard to pick the most relevant fundamental concepts to help the data scientist and the business stakeholder to understand data science and to communicate well. Of course, we have not covered all the fundamental concepts of data science, and any given data scientist may dispute whether we have included exactly the right ones. But all should agree that these are some of the most important concepts and that they underlie a vast amount of the science.

There are all manner of advanced topics and closely related topics that build upon the fundamentals presented here. We will not try to list them—if you're interested, peruse the programs of recent top-notch data mining research conferences, such as the *ACM SIGKDD International Conference on Data Mining and Knowledge Discovery*, or the *IEEE International Conference on Data Mining*. Both of these conferences have top-notch Industry Tracks as well, focusing on applications of data science to business and government problems.

Let us give just one more concrete example of the sort of topic one might find when exploring further. Recall our first principle of data science: data (and data science capability) should be regarded as assets, and should be candidates for investment. Through the book we have discussed in increasing complexity the notion of investing in data. If we apply our general framework of considering the costs and benefits in data science projects explicitly, it leads us to new thinking about investing in data.

Final Example: From Crowd-Sourcing to Cloud-Sourcing

The connectivity between businesses and "consumers" brought about by the Internet has changed the economics of labor. Web-based systems like Amazon's Mechanical Turk and oDesk (among others) facilitate a type of crowd-sourcing that might be called "cloud labor"—harnessing via the Internet a vast pool of independent contractors. One sort of cloud labor that is particularly relevant to data science is "micro-outsourcing": the outsourcing of large numbers of very small, well-defined tasks. Micro-outsourcing is particularly relevant to data science, because it changes the economics, as well as the practicalities, of investing in data.[7]

As one example, recall the requirements for applying supervised modeling (see Chapter 2). We need to have specified a target variable precisely, and we need to actually have values for the target variable ("labels") for a set of training data. Sometimes we can specify the target variable precisely, but we find we do not have any labeled data. In certain cases, we can use micro-outsourcing systems such as Mechanical Turk to label data.

For example, advertisers would like to keep their advertisements off of objectionable web pages, like those that contain hate speech. However, with billions of pages to put their ads on, how can they know which ones are objectionable? It would be far too costly to have employees look at them all. We might immediately recognize this as a possible candidate for text classification (Chapter 10): we can get the text of the page, represent it as feature vectors as we have discussed, and build a hate-speech classifier. Unfortunately, we have no representative sample of hate speech pages to use as training data. However, if this problem is important enough[8] then we should consider investing in labeled training data to see whether we can build a model to identify pages containing hate speech.

---

7. The interested reader can go to Google Scholar and query on "data mining mechanical turk" or more broadly on "human computation" to find papers on the topic, and to follow the forward citation links ("Cited by") to find even more.

8. In fact, the problem of ads appearing on objectionable pages was reported to be a $2 billion problem (Winterberry Group, 2010).

Cloud labor changes the economics of investing in data in our example of getting labeled training data. We can engage very inexpensive labor via the Internet to invest in data in various ways. For example, we can have workers on Amazon Mechanical Turk label pages as objectionable or not, providing us with target labels, much more cheaply than hiring even student workers.

> The rate of completion, when done by a trained intern, was 250 websites per hour, at a cost of $15/hr. When posted on Amazon Mechanical Turk, the labeling rate went up to 2,500 websites per hour and the overall cost remained the same. (Ipeirotis et al., 2010)

The problem is that you get what you pay for, and low cost sometimes means low quality. There has been a surge of research over the past half decade on the problems of maintaining quality while taking advantage of cloud labor. Note that page labeling is just one example of enhancing data science with cloud labor. Even in this case study there are other options, such as using cloud labor to *search for* positive examples of hate speech, instead of labeling pages that we give them (Attenberg & Provost, 2010), or cloud laborers can be challenged in a game-like system to find cases where the current model makes mistakes—to "beat the machine" (Attenberg et al., 2011).

Final Words

Your authors have been working on applying data science to real business problems for more than two decades. You would think that it would all become second nature. It is striking how useful it still can be even for us to have this set of explicit fundamental concepts in hand. So many times when you reach a seeming impasse in thinking, pulling out the the fundamental concepts makes the way clear. "Well, let's go back to our business and data understanding…what exactly is the problem we are trying to solve" can resolve many problems, whether we then decide to work through the implications of the expected value framework, or to think more carefully about how the data are gathered, or about whether the costs and benefits are specified well, or about further investing in data, or to consider whether the target variable has been defined appropriately for the problem to be solved, etc. Knowing what are the different sorts of data science tasks helps to keep the data scientist from treating all business problems as nails for the particular hammers that he knows well. Thinking carefully about what is important to the business problem, when considering evaluation and "baselines" for comparison, brings interactions with stakeholders to life. (Compare that with the chilling effect of reporting some statistic like mean-squared error when it is meaningless to the problem at hand.) This facilitation of data-analytic thinking applies not just to the data scientists, but to everyone involved.

If you are a business stakeholder rather than a data scientist, don't let so-called data scientists bamboozle you with jargon: the concepts of this book plus knowledge of your own business and data systems should allow you to understand 80% or more of the data science at a reasonable enough level to be productive for your business. After having read this book, if you don't understand what a data scientist is talking about, be wary. There are of course many, many more complex concepts in data science, but a good data scientist should be able to describe the fundamentals of the problem and its solution at the level and in the terms of this book.

If you are a data scientist, take this as our challenge: think deeply about exactly why your work is relevant to helping the business and be able to present it as such.

Proposal Review Guide

Effective data analytic thinking should allow you to assess potential data mining projects systematically. The material in this book should give you the necessary background to assess proposed data mining projects, and to uncover potential flaws in proposals. This skill can be applied both as a self-assessment for your own proposals and as an aid in evaluating proposals from internal data science teams or external consultants.

What follows contains a set of questions that one should have in mind when considering a data mining project. The questions are framed by the data mining process discussed in detail in Chapter 2, and used as a conceptual framework throughout the book. After reading this book, you should be able to apply these conceptually to a new business problem. The list that follows is not meant to be exhaustive (in general, the book isn't meant to be exhaustive). However, the list contains a selection of some of the most important questions to ask.

Throughout the book we have concentrated on data science projects where the focus is to mine some regularities, patterns, or models from the data. The proposal review guide reflects this. There may be data science projects in an organization where these regularities are not so explicitly defined. For example, many data visualization projects initially do not have crisply defined objectives for modeling. Nevertheless, the data mining process can help to structure data-analytic thinking about such projects—they simply resemble unsupervised data mining more than supervised data mining.

Business and Data Understanding

- What exactly is the business problem to be solved?
- Is the data science solution formulated appropriately to solve this business problem? *NB: sometimes we have to make judicious approximations.*
- What business entity does an instance/example correspond to?

- Is the problem a supervised or unsupervised problem?
    - If supervised,
        - Is a *target* variable defined?
        - If so, is it defined precisely?
        - Think about the values it can take.
- Are the attributes defined precisely?
    - Think about the values they can take.
- For supervised problems: will modeling this target variable actually improve the stated business problem? An important subproblem? If the latter, is the rest of the business problem addressed?
- Does framing the problem in terms of expected value help to structure the subtasks that need to be solved?
- If unsupervised, is there an "exploratory data analysis" path well defined? (That is, *where is the analysis going?*)

Data Preparation

- Will it be practical to get values for attributes and create feature vectors, and put them into a single table?
- If not, is an alternative data format defined clearly and precisely? Is this taken into account in the later stages of the project? (Many of the later methods/techniques assume the dataset is in feature vector format.)
- If the modeling will be supervised, is the target variable well defined? Is it clear how to get values for the target variable (for training and testing) and put them into the table?
- How exactly will the values for the target variable be acquired? Are there any costs involved? If so, are the costs taken into account in the proposal?
- Are the data being drawn from a population similar to that to which the model will be applied? If there are discrepancies, are any selection biases noted clearly? Is there a plan for how to compensate for them?

Modeling

- Is the choice of model appropriate for the choice of target variable?
    - Classification, class probability estimation, ranking, regression, clustering, etc.

- Does the model/modeling technique meet the other requirements of the task?
  - — Generalization performance, comprehensibility, speed of learning, speed of application, amount of data required, type of data, missing values?
  - — Is the choice of modeling technique compatible with prior knowledge of the problem (e.g., is a linear model being proposed for a definitely nonlinear problem)?
- Should various models be tried and compared (in evaluation)?
- For clustering, is there a similarity metric defined? Does it make sense for the business problem?

Evaluation and Deployment

- Is there a plan for domain-knowledge validation?
  - — Will domain experts or stakeholders want to vet the model before deployment? If so, will the model be in a form they can understand?
- Is the evaluation setup and metric appropriate for the business task? Recall the original formulation.
  - — Are business costs and benefits taken into account?
  - — For classification, how is a classification threshold chosen?
  - — Are probability estimates used directly?
  - — Is ranking more appropriate (e.g., for a fixed budget)?
  - — For regression, how will you evaluate the quality of numeric predictions? Why is this the right way in the context of the problem?
- Does the evaluation use holdout data?
  - — Cross-validation is one technique.
- Against what baselines will the results be compared?
  - — Why do these make sense in the context of the actual problem to be solved?
  - — Is there a plan to evaluate the baseline methods objectively as well?
- For clustering, how will the clustering be understood?
- Will deployment as planned actually (best) address the stated business problem?
- If the project expense has to be justified to stakeholders, what is the plan to measure the final (deployed) business impact?

Another Sample Proposal

Appendix A presented a set of guidelines and questions useful for evaluating data science proposals. Chapter 13 contained a sample proposal ("Example Data Mining Proposal" on page 327) for a "customer migration" campaign and a critique of its weaknesses ("Flaws in the Big Red Proposal" on page 328).

We've used the telecommunications churn problem as a running example throughout this book. Here we present a second sample proposal and critique, this one based on the churn problem.

Scenario and Proposal

You've landed a great job with Green Giant Consulting (GGC), managing an analytical team that is just building up its data science skill set. GGC is proposing a data science project with TelCo, the nation's second-largest provider of wireless communication services, to help address their problem of customer churn. Your team of analysts has produced the following proposal, and you are reviewing it prior to presenting the proposed plan to TelCo. Do you find any flaws with the plan? Do you have any suggestions for how to improve it?

Churn Reduction via Targeted Incentives — A GGC Proposal

We propose that TelCo test its ability to control its customer churn via an analysis of churn prediction. The key idea is that TelCo can use data on customer behavior to predict when customers will leave, and then can target these customers with special incentives to remain with TelCo. We propose the following modeling problem, which can be carried out using data already in TelCo's possession.

We will model the probability that a customer will (or will not) leave within 90 days of contract expiration, with the understanding that there is a separate problem of retaining customers who are continuing their service month-to-month, long after contract expiration. We believe that predicting churn in this 90-day window is an appropriate starting point, and the lessons learned may apply to other churn-prediction cases as well. The model will be built on a database of historical cases of customers who have left the company. Churn probability will be predicted based on data 45 days prior to contract expiration, in order for TelCo to have sufficient lead time to affect customer behavior with an incentive offer. We will model churn probability by building an ensemble of trees (random forest) model, which is known to have high accuracy for a wide variety of estimation problems.

We estimate that we will be able to identify 70% of the customers who will leave within the 90-day time window. We will verify this by running the model on the database to verify that indeed the model can reach this level of accuracy. Through interactions with TelCo stakeholders, we understand that it is very important that the V.P. of Customer Retention sign off on any new customer retention procedures, and she has indicated that she will base her decision on her own assessment that the procedure used for identifying customers makes sense and on the opinions about the procedure from selected firm experts in customer retention. Therefore, we will give the V.P. and the experts access to the model, so that they can verify that it will operate effectively and appropriately. We propose that every week, the model be run to estimate the probabilities of churn of the customers whose contracts expire in 45 days (give or take a week). The customers will be ranked based on these probabilities, and the top N will be selected to receive the current incentive, with N based on the cost of the incentive and the weekly retention budget.

Flaws in the GGC Proposal

We can use our understanding of the fundamental principles and other basic concepts of data science to identify flaws in the proposal. Appendix A provides a starting "guide" for reviewing such proposals, with some of the main questions to ask. However, this book as a whole really can be seen as a proposal review guide. Here are some of the most egregious flaws in Green Giant's proposal:

1. The proposal currently only mentions modeling based on "customers who have left the company." For training (and testing) we will also want to have customers who did *not* leave the company, in order for the modeling to find discriminative information. (Chapter 2, Chapter 3, Chapter 4, Chapter 7)

2. Why rank customers by the highest probability of churn? Why not rank them by expected loss, using a standard expected value computation? (Chapter 7, Chapter 11)

3. Even better, should we not try to model those customers who are most likely to be influenced (positively) by the incentive? (Chapter 11, Chapter 12)

4. If we're going to proceed as in (3), we have the problem of not having the training data we need. We'll have to invest in obtaining training data. (Chapter 3, Chapter 11)

Note that the current proposal may well be just a first step toward the business goal, but this would need to be spelled out explicitly: *see if we can estimate the probabilities well.* If we can, then it makes sense to proceed. If not, we may need to rethink our investment in this project.

5. The proposal says nothing about assessing *generalization* performance (i.e., doing a holdout evaluation). It sounds like they are going to test on the training set ("… running the model on the database…"). (Chapter 5)

6. The proposal does not define (nor even mention) what attributes are going to be used! Is this just an omission? Is this because the team hasn't even thought about it? What is the plan? (Chapter 2, Chapter 3)

7. How does the team estimate that the model will be able to identify 70% of the customers who will leave? There is no mention that any pilot study already has been conducted, nor learning curves having been produced on data samples, nor any other support for this claim. It seems like a guess. (Chapter 2, Chapter 5, Chapter 7)

8. Furthermore, without discussing the error rate or the notion of false positives and false negatives, it's not clear what "identify 70% of the customers who will leave" really means. If I say nothing about the false-positive rate, I can identify 100% of them simply by saying everyone will leave. So talking about true-positive rate only makes sense if you also talk about false-positive rate. (Chapter 7, Chapter 8)

9. Why choose one particular model? With modern toolkits, we can easily compare various models on the same data. (Chapter 4, Chapter 7, Chapter 8)

10. The V.P. of Customer Retention must sign off on the procedure, and has indicated that she will examine the procedure to see if it makes sense (domain knowledge validation). However, ensembles of trees are black-box models. The proposal says nothing about how she is going to understand how the procedure is making its decisions. Given her desire, it would be better to sacrifice some accuracy to build a more comprehensible model. Once she is "on board" it may be possible to use less-comprehensible techniques to achieve higher accuracies. (Chapter 3, Chapter 7, Chapter 12)

Glossary

Note: This glossary is an extension to one compiled by Ron Kohavi and Foster Provost (1998), used with kind permission of Springer Science and Business Media.

a priori

A priori is a term borrowed from philosophy meaning "prior to experience." In data science, an *a priori* belief is one that is brought to the problem as background knowledge, as opposed to a belief that is formed after examining data. For example, you might say, "There is no *a priori* reason to believe that this relationship is linear." After examining data you might decide that two variables have a linear relationship (and so linear regression should work fairly well), but there was no reason to believe, from prior knowledge, that they should be so related. The opposite of *a priori* is *a posteriori*.

Accuracy (error rate)

The rate of correct (incorrect) predictions made by the model over a dataset (cf. coverage). Accuracy is usually estimated using an independent (holdout) dataset that was not used at any time during the learning process. More complex accuracy estimation techniques, such as cross-validation and the bootstrap, are commonly used, especially with datasets containing a small number of instances.

Association mining

Techniques that find conjunctive implication rules of the form "X and Y → A and B" (associations) that satisfy given criteria.

Attribute (field, variable, feature)

A quantity describing an instance. An attribute has a domain defined by the attribute type, which denotes the values that can be taken by an attribute. The following domain types are common:

- **Categorical (symbolic)**: A finite number of discrete values. The type *nominal* denotes that there is no ordering between the values, such as last names and colors. The type *ordinal* denotes that there is an ordering, such as in an attribute taking on the values low, medium, or high.

- **Continuous (quantitative)**: Commonly, subset of real numbers, where there is a measurable difference between the possible values. Integers are usually treated as continuous in practical problems.

We do not differentiate in this book, but often the distinction is made that a feature is the specification of an attribute and its value. For example, color is an attribute. "Color is blue" is a feature of an example. Many transformations to the attribute set leave the feature set unchanged (for example, regrouping attribute values or transforming multivalued attributes to binary attributes). In this book we follow the practice of many authors and practitioners, and use feature as a synonym for *attribute*.

Class (label)

One of a small, mutually exclusive set of labels used as possible values for the target variable in a classification problem. Labeled data has one class label assigned to each example. For example, in a dollar bill classification problem the classes could be *legitimate* and *counterfeit*. In a stock assessment task the classes might be *will gain substantially*, *will lose substantially*, and *will maintain its value*.

Classifier

A mapping from unlabeled instances to (discrete) classes. Classifiers have a form (e.g., classification tree) plus an interpretation procedure (including how to handle unknown values, etc.). Most classifiers also can provide probability estimates (or other likelihood scores), which can be thresholded to yield a discrete class decision thereby taking into account a cost/benefit or utility function.

Confusion matrix

A matrix showing the predicted and actual classifications. A confusion matrix is of size $l \times l$, where l is the number of different label values. A variety of classifier evaluation metrics are defined based on the contents of the confusion matrix, including *accuracy, true positive rate, false positive rate, true negative rate, false negative rate, precision, recall, sensitivity, specificity, positive predictive value,* and *negative predictive value*.

Coverage

The proportion of a dataset for which a classifier makes a prediction. If a classifier does not classify all the instances, it may be important to know its performance on the set of cases for which it is confident enough to make a prediction.

Cost (utility/loss/payoff)

A measurement of the cost to the performance task (and/or benefit) of making a prediction $\hat{y}$ when the actual label is y. The use of accuracy to evaluate a model assumes uniform costs of errors and uniform benefits of correct classifications.

Cross-validation

A method for estimating the accuracy (or error) of an inducer by dividing the data into k mutually exclusive subsets (the "folds") of approximately equal size. The inducer is trained and tested k times. Each time it is trained on the dataset minus one of the folds and tested on that fold. The accuracy estimate is the average accuracy for the k folds or the accuracy on the combined ("pooled") testing folds.

Data cleaning/cleansing

The process of improving the quality of the data by modifying its form or content, for example by removing or correcting data values that are incorrect. This step usually precedes the modeling step, although a pass through the data mining process may indicate that further cleaning is desired and may suggest ways to improve the quality of the data.

Data mining

The term data mining is somewhat overloaded. It sometimes refers to the whole data mining process and sometimes to the specific application of modeling techniques to data in order to build models or find other patterns/regularities.

Dataset

A schema and a set of instances matching the schema. Generally, no ordering on instances is assumed. Most data mining work uses a single fixed-format table or collection of feature vectors.

Dimension

An attribute or several attributes that together describe a property. For example, a geographical dimension might consist of three attributes: country, state, city. A time dimension might include 5 attributes: year, month, day, hour, minute.

Error rate

See Accuracy (error rate).

Example

See Instance (example, case, record).

Feature

See Attribute (field, variable, feature).

Feature vector (record, tuple)

A list of features describing an instance.

Field

See Attribute.

i.i.d. sample

A set of independent and identically distributed instances.

Induction

Induction is the process of creating a general model (such as a classification tree or an equation) from a set of data. Induction may be contrasted with deduction: deduction starts with a general rule or model and one or more facts, and creates other specific facts from them. Induction goes in the other direction: induction takes a collection of facts and creates a general rule or model. In the context of this book, model induction is synonymous with *learning* or *mining* a model, and the rules or models are generally statistical in nature.

Instance (example, case, record)

A single object of the world from which a model will be learned, or on which a model will be used (*e.g.*, for prediction). In most data science work, instances are described by feature vectors; some work uses more complex representations (*e.g.*, containing relations between instances or between parts of instances).

KDD

originally was an abbreviation for Knowledge Discovery from Databases. It is now used to cover broadly the discovery of knowledge from data, and often is used synonymously with data mining.

Knowledge discovery

The nontrivial process of identifying valid, novel, potentially useful, and ultimately understandable patterns in data. This is the definition used in "Advances in Knowledge Discovery and Data Mining," by Fayyad, Piatetsky-Shapiro, & Smyth (1996).

Loss

See Cost (utility/loss/payoff).

Machine learning

In data science, machine learning is most commonly used to mean the application of induction algorithms to data. The term is often used synonymously with the modeling stage of the data mining process. Machine Learning is the field of scientific study that concentrates on induction algorithms and on other algorithms that can be said to learn.

Missing value

The situation where the value for an attribute is not known or does not exist. There are several possible reasons for a value to be missing, such as: it was not measured; there was an instrument malfunction; the attribute does not apply, or the attribute's value cannot be known. Some algorithms have problems dealing with missing values.

Model

A structure and corresponding interpretation that summarizes or partially summarizes a set of data, for description or prediction. Most inductive algorithms generate models that can then be used as classifiers, as regressors, as patterns for human consumption, and/or as input to subsequent stages of the data mining process.

Model deployment

The use of a learned model to solve a real-world problem. Deployment often is used specifically to contrast with the "use" of a model in the Evaluation stage of the data mining process. In the latter, deployment usually is simulated on data where the true answer is known.

OLAP (MOLAP, ROLAP)

Online Analytical Processing. Usually synonymous with MOLAP (multidimensional OLAP). OLAP engines facilitate the exploration of data along several (predetermined) dimensions. OLAP commonly uses intermediate data structures to store precalculated results on multidimensional data, allowing fast computations. ROLAP (relational OLAP) refers to performing OLAP using relational databases.

Record

See Feature vector (record, tuple).

Schema

A description of a dataset's attributes and their properties.

Sensitivity

True positive rate (see Confusion matrix).

Specificity

True negative rate (see Confusion matrix).

Supervised learning

Techniques used to learn the relationship between independent attributes and a designated dependent attribute (the label). Most induction algorithms fall into the supervised learning category.

Tuple

See Feature vector (record, tuple).

Unsupervised learning

Learning techniques that group instances without a pre-specified target attribute. Clustering algorithms are usually unsupervised.

Utility

See Cost (utility/loss/payoff).

Bibliography

Aamodt, A., & Plaza, E. (1994). Case-based reasoning: Foundational issues, methodological variations, and system approaches. *Artificial Intelligence Communications, 7*(1), 39–59. Available: *http://www.iiia.csic.es/People/enric/AICom.html*.

Adams, N. M., & Hand, D. J. (1999). Comparing classifiers when the misallocations costs are uncertain. *Pattern Recognition, 32*, 1139–1147.

Aha, D. W. (Ed.). (1997). *Lazy learning.* Kluwer Academic Publishers, Norwell, MA, USA.

Aha, D. W., Kibler, D., & Albert, M. K. (1991). Instance-based learning algorithms. *Machine Learning, 6*, 37–66.

Aggarwal, C., & Yu, P. (2008). *Privacy-preserving Data Mining: Models and Algorithms.* Springer, USA.

Aral, S., Muchnik, L., & Sundararajan, A. (2009). Distinguishing influence-based contagion from homophily-driven diffusion in dynamic networks. *Proceedings of the National Academy of Sciences, 106*(51), 21544-21549.

Arthur, D., & Vassilvitskii, S. (2007). K-means++: the advantages of careful seeding. In *Proceedings of the Eighteenth Annual ACM-SIAM Symposium on Discrete Algorithms*, pp. 1027–1035.

Attenberg, J., Ipeirotis, P., & Provost, F. (2011). Beat the machine: Challenging workers to find the unknown unknowns. In *Workshops at the Twenty-Fifth AAAI Conference on Artificial Intelligence*.

Attenberg, J., & Provost, F. (2010). Why label when you can search?: Alternatives to active learning for applying human resources to build classification models under extreme class imbalance. In *Proceedings of the 16th ACM SIGKDD International Conference on Knowledge Discovery and Data Mining*, pp. 423–432. ACM.

Bache, K. & Lichman, M. (2013). UCI Machine Learning Repository. *http://archive.ics.uci.edu/ml.* Irvine, CA: University of California, School of Information and Computer Science.

Bolton, R., & Hand, D. (2002). Statistical Fraud Detection: A Review. *Statistical Science, 17*(3), 235-255.

Breiman, L., Friedman, J., Olshen, R., & Stone, C. (1984). *Classification and regression trees.* Wadsworth International Group, Belmont, CA.

Brooks, D. (2013). What Data Can't Do. *New York Times,* Feb. 18.

Brown, L., Gans, N., Mandelbaum, A., Sakov, A., Shen, H., Zeltyn, S., & Zhao, L. (2005). Statistical analysis of a telephone call center: A queueing-science perspective. *Journal of the American Statistical Association, 100*(469), 36-50.

Brynjolfsson, E., & Smith, M. (2000). Frictionless commerce? A comparison of internet and conventional retailers. *Management Science, 46,* 563–585.

Brynjolfsson, E., Hitt, L. M., & Kim, H. H. (2011). Strength in numbers: How does data-driven decision making affect firm performance? Tech. rep., available at SSRN: *http://ssrn.com/abstract=1819486* or *http://dx.doi.org/10.2139/ssrn.1819486.*

Business Insider (2012). The Digital 100: The world's most valuable private tech companies. *http://www.businessinsider.com/2012-digital-100.*

Ciccarelli, F. D., Doerks, T., Von Mering, C., Creevey, C. J., Snel, B., & Bork, P. (2006). Toward automatic reconstruction of a highly resolved tree of life. *Science, 311* (5765), 1283–1287.

Clearwater, S., & Stern, E. (1991). A rule-learning program in high energy physics event classification. *Comp Physics Comm, 67,* 159–182.

Clemons, E., & Thatcher, M. (1998). Capital One: Exploiting and Information-based Strategy. In *Proceedings of the 31st Hawaii International Conference on System Sciences.*

Cohen, L., Diether, K., & Malloy, C. (2012). Legislating Stock Prices. Harvard Business School Working Paper, No. 13–010.

Cover, T., & Hart, P. (1967). Nearest neighbor pattern classification. *Information Theory, IEEE Transactions on, 13*(1), 21–27.

Crandall, D., Backstrom, L., Cosley, D., Suri, S., Huttenlocher, D., & Kleinberg, J. (2010). Inferring social ties from geographic coincidences. *Proceedings of the National Academy of Sciences,* 107(52), 22436-22441.

Deza, E., & Deza, M. (2006). *Dictionary of distances.* Elsevier Science.

Dietterich, T. G. (1998). Approximate statistical tests for comparing supervised classification learning algorithms. *Neural Computation, 10*, 1895–1923.

Dietterich, T. G. (2000). Ensemble methods in machine learning. *Multiple Classifier Systems*, 1-15.

Duhigg, C. (2012). How Companies Learn Your Secrets. *New York Times*, Feb. 19.

Elmagarmid, A., Ipeirotis, P., & Verykios, V. (2007). Duplicate record detection: A survey. *Knowledge and Data Engineering, IEEE Transactions on, 19*(1), 1–16.

Evans, R., & Fisher, D. (2002). Using decision tree induction to minimize process delays in the printing industry. In Klosgen, W., & Zytkow, J. (Eds.), *Handbook of Data Mining and Knowledge Discovery*, pp. 874–881. Oxford University Press.

Ezawa, K., Singh, M., & Norton, S. (1996). Learning goal oriented Bayesian networks for telecommunications risk management. In Saitta, L. (Ed.), *Proceedings of the Thirteenth International Conference on Machine Learning*, pp. 139–147. San Francisco, CA. Morgan Kaufmann.

Fawcett, T. (2006). An introduction to ROC analysis. *Pattern Recognition Letters, 27*(8), 861–874.

Fawcett, T., & Provost, F. (1996). Combining data mining and machine learning for effective user profiling. In Simoudis, Han, & Fayyad (Eds.), *Proceedings of the Second International Conference on Knowledge Discovery and Data Mining*, pp. 8–13. Menlo Park, CA. AAAI Press.

Fawcett, T., & Provost, F. (1997). Adaptive fraud detection. *Data Mining and Knowledge Discovery, 1* (3), 291–316.

Fayyad, U., Piatetsky-shapiro, G., & Smyth, P. (1996). From data mining to knowledge discovery in databases. *AI Magazine, 17*, 37–54.

Frank, A., & Asuncion, A. (2010). UCI machine learning repository.

Friedman, J. (1997). On bias, variance, 0/1-loss, and the curse-of-dimensionality. *Data Mining and Knowledge Discovery, 1*(1), 55-77.

Gandy, O. H. (2009). *Coming to Terms with Chance: Engaging Rational Discrimination and Cumulative Disadvantage.* Ashgate Publishing Company.

Goldfarb, A. & Tucker, C. (2011). Online advertising, behavioral targeting, and privacy. *Communications of the ACM 54*(5), 25-27.

Haimowitz, I., & Schwartz, H. (1997). Clustering and prediction for credit line optimization. In Fawcett, Haimowitz, Provost, & Stolfo (Eds.), *AI Approaches to Fraud Detection and Risk Management*, pp. 29–33. AAAI Press. Available as Technical Report WS-97-07.

Hall, M., Frank, E., Holmes, G., Pfahringer, B., Reutemann, P. & Witten, I. (2009). The WEKA data mining software: An update. *SIGKDD Explorations*, 11 (1).

Hand, D. J. (2008). *Statistics: A Very Short Introduction*. Oxford University Press.

Hastie, T., Tibshirani, R., & Friedman, J. (2009). *The Elements of Statistical Learning: Data Mining, Inference, and Prediction* (Second Edition edition). Springer.

Hays, C. L. (2004). What they know about you. *The New York Times*.

Hernández, M. A., & Stolfo, S. J. (1995). The merge/purge problem for large databases. *SIGMOD Rec.*, *24*, 127–138.

Hill, S., Provost, F., & Volinsky, C. (2006). Network-based marketing: Identifying likely adopters via consumer networks. *Statistical Science*, *21* (2), 256–276.

Holte, R. C. (1993). Very simple classification rules perform well on most commonly used datasets. *Machine Learning*, *11*, 63–91.

Ipeirotis, P., Provost, F., & Wang, J. (2010). Quality management on Amazon Mechanical Turk. In *Proceedings of the 2010 ACM SIGKDD Workshop on Human Computation*, pp. 64-67. ACM.

Jackson, M. (1989). *Michael Jackson's Malt Whisky Companion: a Connoisseur's Guide to the Malt Whiskies of Scotland*. Dorling Kindersley, London.

Japkowicz, N., & Stephen, S. (2002). The class imbalance problem: A systematic study. *Intelligent Data Analysis*, *6* (5), 429–450.

Japkowicz, N., & Shah, M. (2011). *Evaluating Learning Algorithms: A Classification Perspective*. Cambridge University Press.

Jensen, D. D., & Cohen, P. R. (2000). Multiple comparisons in induction algorithms. *Machine Learning*, *38*(3), 309–338.

Junqué de Fortuny, E., Martens, D., & Provost, F. (2013). Predictive Modeling with Big Data: Is Bigger Really Better? *Big Data*, published online October 2013: *http://online.liebertpub.com/doi/abs/10.1089/big.2013.0037*

Kass, G. V. (1980). An exploratory technique for investigating large quantities of categorical data. *Applied Statistics*, *29*(2), 119–127.

Kaufman, S., Rosset, S., Perlich, C., & Stitelman, O. (2012). Leakage in data mining: Formulation, detection, and avoidance. *ACM Transactions on Knowledge Discovery from Data (TKDD)*, *6*(4), 15.

Kohavi, R., Brodley, C., Frasca, B., Mason, L., & Zheng, Z. (2000). KDD-cup 2000 organizers' report: Peeling the onion. *ACM SIGKDD Explorations*. *2*(2).

Kohavi, R., Deng, A., Frasca, B., Longbotham, R., Walker, T., & Xu, Y. (2012). Trustworthy online controlled experiments: Five puzzling outcomes explained. In *Pro-

ceedings of the 18th ACM SIGKDD International Conference on Knowledge Discovery and Data Mining, pp. 786–794. ACM.

Kohavi, R., & Longbotham, R. (2007). Online experiments: Lessons learned. *Computer, 40* (9), 103–105.

Kohavi, R., Longbotham, R., Sommerfield, D., & Henne, R. (2009). Controlled experiments on the web: Survey and practical guide. *Data Mining and Knowledge Discovery, 18*(1), 140-181.

Kohavi, R., & Parekh, R. (2003). Ten supplementary analyses to improve e-commerce web sites. In *Proceedings of the Fifth WEBKDD workshop.*

Kohavi, R., & Provost, F. (1998). Glossary of terms. *Machine Learning, 30*(2-3), 271-274.

Kolodner, J. (1993). *Case-Based Reasoning.* Morgan Kaufmann, San Mateo.

Koren, Y., Bell, R., & Volinsky, C. (2009). Matrix factorization techniques for recommender systems. *Computer, 42* (8), 30-37.

Kosinski, M., Stillwell, D., & Graepel, T. (2013). Private traits and attributes are predictable from digital records of human behavior. *Proceedings of the National Academy of Sciences*, doi: *10.1073/pnas.1218772110.*

Lapointe, F.-J., & Legendre, P. (1994). A classification of pure malt Scotch whiskies. *Applied Statistics, 43* (1), 237–257.

Leigh, D. (1995). Neural networks for credit scoring. In Goonatilake, S., & Treleaven, P. (Eds.), *Intelligent Systems for Finance and Business*, pp. 61–69. John Wiley and Sons Ltd., West Sussex, England.

Letunic, & Bork (2006). Interactive tree of life (iTOL): an online tool for phylogenetic tree display and annotation. *Bioinformatics, 23* (1).

Lin, J.-H., & Vitter, J. S. (1994). A theory for memory-based learning. *Machine Learning, 17*, 143–167.

Lloyd, S. P. (1982). Least square quantization in PCM. *IEEE Transactions on Information Theory, 28* (2), 129–137.

MacKay, D. (2003). *Information Theory, Inference and Learning Algorithms*, Chapter 20. An Example Inference Task: Clustering. Cambridge University Press.

MacQueen, J. B. (1967). Some methods for classification and analysis of multivariate observations. In *Proceedings of 5th Berkeley Symposium on Mathematical Statistics and Probability*, pp. 281–297. University of California Press.

Malin, B. & Sweeney, L. (2004). How (not) to protect genomic data privacy in a distributed network: Using trail re-identification to evaluate and design anonymity protection systems. *Journal of Biomedical Informatics*, 37(3), 179-192.

Martens, D., & Provost, F. (2011). Pseudo-social network targeting from consumer transaction data. Working paper CeDER-11-05, New York University – Stern School of Business.

McCallum, A. & Nigam, K. (1988). A comparison of event models for naive Bayes text classification. In *AAAI Workshop on Learning for Text Categorization*.

McDowell, G. (2008). *Cracking the Coding Interview: 150 Programming Questions and Solutions*. CareerCup LLC.

McNamee, M. (2001). Credit Card Revolutionary. *Stanford Business 69* (3).

McPherson, M., Smith-Lovin, L., & Cook, J. M. (2001). Birds of a feather: Homophily in social networks. *Annual Review of Sociology, 27*:415-444.

Mittermayer, M., & Knolmayer, G. (2006). Text mining systems for market response to news: A survey. Working Paper No.184, Institute of Information Systems, University of Bern.

Muoio, A. (1997). They have a better idea ... do you? *Fast Company, 10.*

Nissenbaum, H. (2010). *Privacy in context.* Stanford University Press.

Papadopoulos, A. N., & Manolopoulos, Y. (2005). *Nearest Neighbor Search: A Database Perspective.* Springer.

Pennisi, E. (2003). A tree of life. Available online only: *http://www.sciencemag.org/site/feature/data/tol/.*

Perlich, C., Provost, F., & Simonoff, J. (2003). Tree Induction vs. Logistic Regression: A Learning-Curve Analysis. *Journal of Machine Learning Research, 4,* 211-255.

Perlich, C., Dalessandro, B., Stitelman, O., Raeder, T., & Provost, F. (2013). Machine learning for targeted display advertising: Transfer learning in action. *Machine Learning* (in press; published online: 30 May 2013. DOI 10.1007/s10994-013-5375-2).

Poundstone, W. (2012). *Are You Smart Enough to Work at Google?: Trick Questions, Zen-like Riddles, Insanely Difficult Puzzles, and Other Devious Interviewing Techniques You Need to Know to Get a Job Anywhere in the New Economy.* Little, Brown and Company.

Provost, F., & Fawcett, T. (1997). Analysis and visualization of classifier performance: Comparison under imprecise class and cost distributions. In *Proceedings of the Third International Conference on Knowledge Discovery and Data Mining (KDD-97),* pp. 43–48 Menlo Park, CA. AAAI Press.

Provost, F., & Fawcett, T. (2001). Robust classification for imprecise environments. *Machine learning, 42*(3), 203–231.

Provost, F., Fawcett, T., & Kohavi, R. (1998). The case against accuracy estimation for comparing induction algorithms. In Shavlik, J. (Ed.), *Proceedings of ICML-98*, pp. 445–453 San Francisco, CA. Morgan Kaufmann.

Pyle, D. (1999). *Data Preparation for Data Mining*. Morgan Kaufmann.

Quine, W.V.O. (1951). Two dogmas of empiricism, *The Philosophical Review 60*: 20-43. Reprinted in his 1953 *From a Logical Point of View*. Harvard University Press.

Quinlan, J. R. (1993). *C4.5: Programs for machine learning*. Morgan Kaufmann.

Quinlan, J. (1986). Induction of decision trees. *Machine Learning, 1* (1), 81–106.

Raeder, T., Dalessandro, B., Stitelman, O., Perlich, C., & Provost, F. (2012). Design principles of massive, robust prediction systems. In *Proceedings of the 18th ACM SIGKDD International Conference on Knowledge Discovery and Data Mining*.

Rosset, S., & Zhu, J. (2007). Piecewise linear regularized solution paths. *The Annals of Statistics, 35*(3), 1012–1030.

Schumaker, R., & Chen, H. (2010). A Discrete Stock Price Prediction Engine Based on Financial News Keywords. *IEEE Computer, 43*(1), 51–56.

Sengupta, S. (2012). Facebook's prospects may rest on trove of data.

Shakhnarovich, G., Darrell, T., & Indyk, P.(Eds., 2005). *Nearest-Neighbor Methods in Learning and Vision*. Neural Information Processing Series. The MIT Press, Cambridge, Massachusetts, USA.

Shannon, C. E. (1948). A mathematical theory of communication. *Bell System Technical Journal, 27*, 379–423.

Shearer, C. (2000). The CRISP-DM model: The new blueprint for data mining. *Journal of Data Warehousing, 5*(4), 13–22.

Shmueli, G. (2010). To explain or to predict?. *Statistical Science, 25*(3), 289–310.

Silver, N. (2012). *The Signal and the Noise*. The Penguin Press HC.

Solove, D. (2006). A taxonomy of privacy. *University of Pennsylvania Law Review, 154*(3), 477-564.

Stein, R. M. (2005). The relationship between default prediction and lending profits: Integrating ROC analysis and loan pricing. *Journal of Banking and Finance, 29*, 1213–1236.

Sugden, A. M., Jasny, B. R., Culotta, E., & Pennisi, E. (2003). Charting the evolutionary history of life. *Science, 300*(5626).

Swets, J. (1988). Measuring the accuracy of diagnostic systems. *Science, 240*, 1285–1293.

Swets, J. A. (1996). *Signal Detection Theory and ROC Analysis in Psychology and Diagnostics: Collected Papers.* Lawrence Erlbaum Associates, Mahwah, NJ.

Swets, J. A., Dawes, R. M., & Monahan, J. (2000). Better decisions through science. *Scientific American, 283,* 82–87.

Tambe, P. (2013). Big Data Investment, Skills, and Firm Value. Working Paper, NYU Stern. Available: *http://papers.ssrn.com/sol3/papers.cfm?abstract_id=2294077.*

WEKA (2001). Weka machine learning software. Available: *http://www.cs.waikato.ac.nz/~ml/index.html.*

Wikipedia (2012). Determining the number of clusters in a data set. *Wikipedia, the free encyclopedia.* *http://en.wikipedia.org/wiki/Determining_the_number_of_clusters_in_a_data_set* [Online; accessed 14-February-2013].

Wilcoxon, F. (1945). Individual comparisons by ranking methods. *Biometrics Bulletin, 1*(6), 80–83. Available: *http://sci2s.ugr.es/keel/pdf/algorithm/articulo/wilcoxon1945.pdf.*

Winterberry Group (2010). Beyond the grey areas: Transparency, brand safety and the future of online advertising. White Paper, Winterberry Group LLC. *http://www.winterberrygroup.com/ourinsights/wp*

Wishart, D. (2006). *Whisky Classified: Choosing Single Malts by Flavour.* Pavilion.

Witten, I., & Frank, E. (2000). *Data mining: Practical machine learning tools and techniques with Java implementations.* Morgan Kaufmann, San Francisco. Software available from *http://www.cs.waikato.ac.nz/~ml/weka/.*

Zadrozny, B. (2004). Learning and evaluating classifiers under sample selection bias. In *Proceedings of the Twenty-first International Conference on Machine Learning,* pp. 903-910.

Zadrozny, B., & Elkan, C. (2001). Learning and making decisions when costs and probabilities are both unknown. In *Proceedings of the Seventh ACM SIGKDD International Conference on Knowledge Discovery and Data Mining,* pp. 204–213. ACM.

Index

Symbols

2-D Gaussian distributions, 301
"and" operator, 240

A

A Taxonomy of Privacy (Solove), 344
Aberfeldy single malt scotch, 179
Aberlour single malt whiskey, 146
absolute errors, 96
accuracy (term), 189
accuracy results, 128
ACM SIGKDD, 320, 344
ad impressions, 234
adding variables to functions, 123
advertising, 233
agency, 40
alarms, 188
algorithms
    clustering, 170
    data mining, 20
    k-means, 172
    modeling, 135
Amazon, 1, 7, 9, 11, 142
    Borders vs., 318
    cloud storage, 316
    data science services provided by, 316
    historical advantages of, 319

analysis
    counterfactual, 23
    learning curves and, 132
analytic engineering, 279–289
    churn example, 283–289
    expected value decomposition and, 286–289
    incentives, assessing influence of, 285–286
    providing structure for business problem/
        solutions with, 280–282
    selection bias, 282–283
    targeting best prospects with, 280–283
analytic skills, software skills vs., 35
analytic solutions, 14
analytic techniques, 35–41, 187–208
    applying to business questions, 40–41
    baseline performance and, 204–207
    classification accuracy, 189–194
    confusion matrix, 189–190
    data warehousing, 38
    database queries, 37–38
    expected values, 194–204
    generalization methods for, 193–194
    machine learning and, 39–40
    OLAP, 38
    regression analysis, 39
    statistics, 35–37
analytic technologies, 30
analytic tools, 113
Angry Birds, 247

We'd like to hear your suggestions for improving our indexes. Send email to index@oreilly.com.

managing data scientists effectively, 322–323

maturity of the data science, 329–331

thinking data-analytically for, 315–317

C

Caesars Entertainment, 11

call center example, 299–301

Capability Maturity Model, 330

Capital One, 11, 288

Case-Based Reasoning, 151

cases

creating, 32

ranking vs. classifying, 209–231

casual modeling, 23

causal analysis, 286

causal explanation, 311

causal radius, 269

causation, correlation vs., 178

cellular churn example

unbalanced classes in, 190

unequal costs and benefits in, 193

Census Bureau Economic Survey, 36

centroid locations, 173

centroid-based clustering, 175

centroids, 170–175, 175–178

characteristics, 41

characterizing customers, 41

churn, 4, 14, 191

and expected value, 198

finding variables, 15

performance analytics for modeling, 223–231

churn prediction, 317

Ciccarelli, Francesca, 168

class confusion, 189

class labels, 102–103

class membership, estimating likelihood of, 235

class priors, 201, 214, 219, 222

class probability, 2, 21, 97–107, 308

classes

exhaustive, 242

mutually exclusive, 242

probability of evidence given, 241

separating, 123

classification, 2, 20, 141

Bayes' Rule for, 239

building models for, 28

ensemble methods and, 308

neighbors and, 147

regression and, 21

supervised data mining and, 25

classification accuracy

confusion matrix, 189–190

evaluating, with expected values, 196–198

measurability of, 189

unbalanced classes, 190–193

unequal costs/benefit ratios, 193–193

classification function, 86

classification modeling, 193

classification tasks, 21

classification trees, 63

as sets of rules, 71–71

ensemble methods and, 311

in KDD Cup churn problem, 224–231

inducing, 67

logistic regression and, 129

predictive models and, 63

visualizing, 67–69

classifier accuracy, 189

classifiers

and ROC graphs, 216–217

baseline, 244

confusion matrix produced by, 210–211

conservative, 216

cumulative response curves of, 220–221

discrete (binary), 217

inability to obtain accurate probability estimates from, 210

lift of, 220

linear, 85

Naive Bayes, 242

operating conditions of, 219

performance de-coupled from conditions for, 218

permissive, 216

plus thresholds, 210

random, 213

scores given to instances by, 210

classifying cases, ranking vs., 209–211

climatology, 205

clipping dendrograms, 167

cloud labor, 346

clumps of instances, 119

cluster centers, 170

cluster distortion, 173

clustering, 21, 163–183, 251

algorithm, 170

business news stories example, 175–178

Glen Mhor single malt scotch, 179
Glen Spey single malt scotch, 179
Glenfiddich single malt scotch, 179
Glenglassaugh single malt whiskey, 169
Glengoyne single malt scotch, 181
Glenlossie single malt scotch, 181
Glentauchers single malt scotch, 179
Glenugie single malt scotch, 179
goals, 88
Goethe, Johann Wolfgang von, 1
Goodman, Benny, 261
Google, 252, 253, 323
    Prediction API, 316
    search advertising on, 233
Google Finance, 270
Google Scholar, 345
Graepel, Thore, 246–246
graphical user interface (GUI), 37
graphs
    entropy, 58
    fitting, 126, 140
Green Giant Consulting example, 353–355
GUI, 37

H

Haimowitz, Ira, 185
Harrahs casinos, 7, 11
hashing methods, 157
heterogeneous attributes, 156
Hewlett-Packard, 141, 175, 266
hierarchical clustering, 165–170
Hilton, Perez, 272
hinge loss, 94, 95
history, 39
hit rate, 216, 220
holdout data, 113
    creating, 113
    overfitting and, 113–115
holdout evaluations, of overfitting, 126
holdout testing, 126
homogenous regions, 83
homographs, 253
How I Met Your Mother (television show), 247
Howls Moving Castle, 247
human interaction and data science, 340–343
Hurricane Frances example, 3
hyperplanes, 69, 86
hypotheses, computing probability of, 238
hypothesis generation, 37

hypothesis tests, 133

I

IBM, 141, 179, 323, 324
IEEE International Conference on Data Mining, 344
immature data firms, 330
impurity, 50
in vivo evaluation, 32
in-sample accuracy, 114
Inception (film), 247
incorrect generalizations, 124
incremental learning, 243
independence
    and evidence lift, 246
    in probability, 236–237
    unconditional vs. conditional, 241
independent events, probability of, 236–237
independent variables, 47
indices, 174
induction, deduction vs., 47
inferring missing values, 30
influence, 23
information
    judging, 48
    measuring, 52
information gain (IG), 51, 78, 275
    applying, 56–62
    attribute selection with, 56–62
    defining, 52
    equation for, 53
    using, 57
Information Retrieval (IR), 253
information triage, 276
informative attributes, finding, 44, 62
informative meaning, 43
informative variables, selecting, 49
instance scoring, 188
instances, 46
    clumping, 119
    comparing, with evidence lift, 246
    for targeting online consumers, 234
intangible collateral assets, 320
intellectual property, 319
intelligence test score, 247–248
intelligent methods, 44
intelligibility, 181
Internet, 252

nearest-neighbor reasoning and, 151–153
parameter optimization and, 136–138
performance degradation and, 124–126
techniques for avoiding, 126

P

parabola, 107, 123
parameter learning, 81
parameterized models, 81
parameterized numeric functions, 301
parametric modeling, 81
    class probability estimation, 97–107
    linear classifiers, 83
    linear regression and, 95–97
    logistic regression, 97–107
    neural networks and, 107–110
    non-linear functions for, 107–110
    support vector machines and, 107–110
Parker, Charlie, 259, 261
Pasteur, Louis, 316
patents, as intellectual property, 319
patterns
    extract, 14
    finding, 25
penalties, 137
performance analytics, for modeling churn,
    223–231
performance degradation, 124–126
performance, of nearest-neighbor reasoning,
    157
phrase extraction, 266
pilot studies, 355
plunge (stock prices), 269
polynomial kernels, 108
positives, 188
posterior probability, 239–240
Precision metric, 204
prediction, 6, 45
Prediction API (Google), 316
predictive learning methods, 181
predictive modeling, 43–44, 81
    alternative methods, 81
    basic concepts, 78
    causal explanations and, 311
    classification trees and, 67–71
    customer churn, predicting with tree induc-
        tion, 73–78
    focus, 48
    induction and, 44–48

    link prediction, 303–304
    nearest-neighbor reasoning for, 147
    parametric modeling and, 81
    probability estimating and, 71–73
    social recommendations and, 303–304
    supervised segmentation, 48–79
predictors, 47
preparation, 30
principles, 4, 23
prior beliefs, probability based on, 240
prior churn, 14
prior probability, class, 239
privacy and data mining, 343–344
Privacy in Context (Nissenbaum), 344
privacy protection, 343
probabilistic evidence combination (PEC), 233–
    249
    Bayes' Rule and, 237–246
    probability theory for, 235–237
    targeted ad example, 233–235
Probabilistic Topic Models, 267
probability, 102–103
    and nearest-neighbor reasoning, 148
    basic rule of, 201
    building models for estimation of, 28
    conditional, 236
    joint, 236–237
    of errors, 198
    of evidence, 239
    of independent events, 236–237
    posterior, 239–240
    prior, 239
    unconditional, 238, 240
probability estimation trees, 64, 72
probability notation, 235–236
probability theory, 235–237
processes, 4
profiling, 22, 298–303
    consumer movie-viewing preferences exam-
        ple, 304
    when the distribution is not symmetric, 300
profit curves, 212–214, 229–230
profit, negative, 212
profitability, 40
profitable customers, average customers vs., 40
proposals, evaluating, 326–329, 353–355
proxy labels, 288
psychometric data, 295
publishing, 324

About the Authors

Foster Provost is Professor and NEC Faculty Fellow at the NYU Stern School of Business where he teaches in the Business Analytics, Data Science, and MBA programs. His award-winning research is read and cited broadly. Prior to joining NYU, he worked as a research data scientist for five years for what's now Verizon. Over the past decade, Professor Provost has co-founded several successful data-science-driven companies.

Tom Fawcett holds a Ph.D. in machine learning and has worked in industry R&D for more than two decades (GTE Laboratories, NYNEX/Verizon Labs, HP Labs, etc.). His published work has become standard reading in data science both on methodology (e.g., evaluating data mining results) and on applications (e.g., fraud detection and spam filtering).

Colophon

The cover font is Adobe ITC Garamond. The text font is Adobe Minion Pro and the heading font is Adobe Myriad Condensed.